THE
STUDENT
BIBLE
DICTIONARY

EXPANDED & UPDATED EDITION

THE STUDENT BIBLE DICTIONARY

EXPANDED & UPDATED EDITION

Johnnie Godwin
Phyllis Godwin
Karen Dockrey

BARBOUR BOOKS
An Imprint of Barbour Publishing, Inc.

Interior design by Greg Jackson, Thinkpen Design

Published by Barbour Books, an imprint of Barbour Publishing, Inc., P.O. Box 719, Uhrichsville, Ohio 44683, www.barbourbooks.com

Our mission is to publish and distribute inspirational products offering exceptional value and biblical encouragement to the masses.

 Member of the
Evangelical Christian
Publishers Association

Printed in the United States of America.

TABLE OF CONTENTS

PREFACE

The Student Bible Dictionary was written with your needs in mind. We know you basically want to look up a Bible word only once and in one place, find exactly the information you need to make the Bible passage clear, and then return to your Bible study. Because of this, we have defined words quickly and precisely in the first line or two and then added details in later sentences. Cross-references are rare. When we could, we added an illustration or map to help you know just what the item looked like or just where the place was. We've told you what people did what and who was related to whom, so you could understand some of the whys and wherefores of their actions and keep Bible families straight. We've added easy-to-read pronunciations for proper names so you'll know just how to say them.

Why a student Bible dictionary? Because you as a Bible student have special study needs. You have a curiosity that is ready for more specific information. You have an aptitude that lets you build on what you have learned during your childhood years.

You may be a youth, a young adult, or a more mature adult, but you still may be young in your Christian faith. This Bible dictionary is for you and for any Christian who wants clear, concise, need-meeting definitions. *The Student Bible Dictionary* puts Bible terms into language that will help the faith of the Bible become yours and will help you honor God in your life.

In *The Student Bible Dictionary,* you'll find words defined in the way they are used in the Bible rather than the way they might be used today in another context. For example, *conversation* in the King James Version of the Bible means "behavior, conduct, manner of life" rather than a talk between two people. You'll usually find primary meanings rather than remote or exhaustive ones. Though true to the original languages, the definitions use Hebrew and Greek references sparingly.

Each entry is organized so that the further you read the more detail you will find. If you want a simple definition of the word/person/place/idea, read the first word or sentence only. Many entries include only this basic information.

Special entries include features that will help you understand a word more thoroughly:

■ **REQUESTED WORD:** This symbol indicates a high-frequency word, requested by a group of over five hundred student leaders participating in leadership conferences. These leaders identified this word as one students need to understand and consider in living their Christian faith.

▲ **GREATER DETAIL:** This paragraph includes details that help you understand a specific usage of the word, aids you in completing a Bible study challenge, gives you information not available in other dictionaries, or provides fascinating facts.

● **CURRICULUM HOOKS:** This question or thought-provoker helps you think further about the word, discuss it in class, or apply it to daily life. Bible study teachers or curriculum writers may use this added thought for a curriculum hook in identifying, clarifying, or forming convictions and in guiding students to make applications to their lives.

Throughout *The Student Bible Dictionary* you'll find interesting lists and charts such as **NAMES OF GOD** (page 109), **TITLES FOR JESUS IN SCRIPTURE** (page 139), **TABLE OF WEIGHTS AND MEASURES** (pages 284–286), and **FEASTS AND FESTIVALS** through which believers celebrated (page 96). You'll also find summaries of all Bible books and definitions of theological words such as *millennium*. Though the dictionary is compatible with other Bible translations, the King James Version of the Bible is the base. The English language is steeped in the language of the King James Version; and since this most-used translation is more than four hundred years old, it requires the most definitions for readers of the Bible. Other versions are referenced as appropriate.

To save space, we refer to Bible translations by the following abbreviations:

KJV=King James Version
NASB=New American Standard Version
NIV=New International Version
NRSV=New Revised Standard Version
HCSB=Holman Christian Standard Version
GNB=Good News Bible, also called The Bible in Today's English

You'll find evangelistic inroads when defining such key words as "believe," "repent," "confess,"
and "salvation." These key words help you understand your salvation as well as guide you to lead your friends to Jesus Christ.

This Bible dictionary is unapologetically student-oriented and conservative in nature. Words selected for definition are those the authors and their research showed were most needed for students. The factors determining the length and details of definitions are accuracy, clarity, and developmental needs. The authors have attempted to create a unique and user-friendly student Bible dictionary both for students and leaders. Because it is directed toward lay students of the Bible rather than scholars, it does not focus on critical problems or peripheral matters that dictionaries intended for scholars might include. It focuses on central meanings of Bible words and helps students— which we all should remain for all our lives— apply those meanings in their daily experience.

You'll find approximately twenty-five hundred entries in *The Student Bible Dictionary,* chosen because of their appeal to or importance for students. We've aimed for strong, quick definitions that are accurate and clear. We hope you'll find this Bible dictionary different from the usual dictionary. We intend for this to be an inviting and usable tool that meets your needs and interests, spiritually, intellectually, and developmentally.

A NOTE ON THE EXPANDED AND UPDATED EDITION OF 2014

This edition of the *Student Bible Dictionary* keeps the best of the original while expanding upon and updating the original text. In the years since the first edition released, new Bible translations have come into being, and this volume takes advantage of many updates in language. Other advances in knowledge—such as Dead Sea Scrolls word studies—have helped bring further updates to this new edition. This volume includes both more terms and additional definitions to further explain many words from the original *Student Bible Dictionary,* an increase of approximately 20 percent of the overall text.

TIMELINES

FOR THE BIBLICAL HISTORY OF THE WORLD

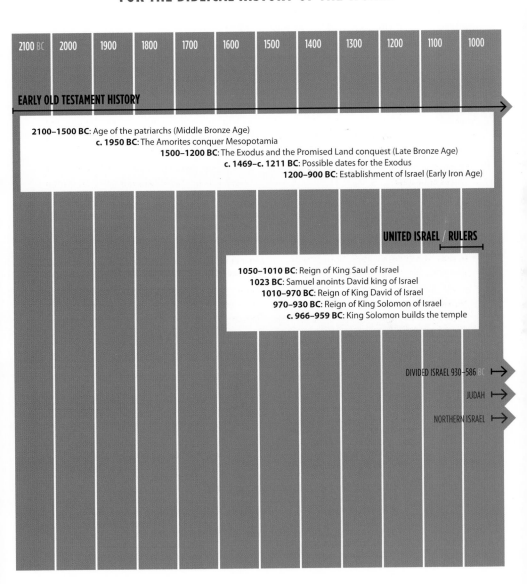

2100 BC	2000	1900	1800	1700	1600	1500	1400	1300	1200	1100	1000

EARLY OLD TESTAMENT HISTORY

2100–1500 BC: Age of the patriarchs (Middle Bronze Age)
c. 1950 BC: The Amorites conquer Mesopotamia
1500–1200 BC: The Exodus and the Promised Land conquest (Late Bronze Age)
c. 1469–c. 1211 BC: Possible dates for the Exodus
1200–900 BC: Establishment of Israel (Early Iron Age)

UNITED ISRAEL / RULERS

1050–1010 BC: Reign of King Saul of Israel
1023 BC: Samuel anoints David king of Israel
1010–970 BC: Reign of King David of Israel
970–930 BC: Reign of King Solomon of Israel
c. 966–959 BC: King Solomon builds the temple

DIVIDED ISRAEL 930–586 BC ⟼

JUDAH ⟼

NORTHERN ISRAEL ⟼

900 BC | 800 | 700

ASSYRIAN EMPIRE 1100–609 BC

EARLY OLD TESTAMENT HISTORY

NEO-BABYLONIAN (CHALDEAN) EMPIRE

859–824 BC: Reign of King Shalmaneser III
855–625 BC: Assyrian influence on Palestine
783–773 BC: Reign of King Shalmaneser IV
744–727 BC: Reign of King Tiglath-pileser III
c. 732–612 BC: Israel and Judah subject to Assyria
727–722 BC: Fall of Israel to Assyria; Samaria destroyed
722 BC: Reign of King Shalmaneser V
705–681 BC: Reign of King Sennacherib
612 BC: Fall of Nineveh to Neo-Babylonian (Chaldean) Empire
609 BC: Chaldeans defeat Assyria

PROPHETS & LEADERS

770–750 BC: Ministry of the prophet Jonah in Assyria
763–750 BC: Ministry of the prophet Amos in Israel
750–722 BC: Ministry of the prophet Hosea in Israel
742–687 BC: Ministry of the prophet Micah in Judah
740–700 BC: Ministry of the prophet Isaiah in Judah
640–621 BC: Ministry of the prophet Zephaniah in Judah
627–586 BC: Ministry of the prophet Jeremiah in Judah

DIVIDED ISRAEL ■ NORTHERN ISRAEL ■ JUDAH

NORTHERN ISRAEL

JUDAH

930–913 BC: Reign of King Rehoboam
930–909 BC: Reign of King Jeroboam I
913–910 BC: Reign of King Abijam
910–872 BC: Reign of King Asa
909–908 BC: Reign of King Nadab
908–886 BC: Reign of King Baasha
886–885 BC: Reign of King Elah
885–874 BC: Reign of King Omri
874–853 BC: Reign of King Ahab
872–853 BC: Reign of King Jehoshaphat
853–852 BC: Reign of King Ahaziah
853–841 BC: Reign of King Jehoram
852–841 BC: Reign of King Joram (Jehoram)
841 BC: Reign of King Ahaziah
841–835 BC: Reign of Queen Athaliah
841–814 BC: Reign of King Jehu
835–796 BC: Reign of King Joash
814–798 BC: Reign of King Jehoahaz

798–793 BC: Reign of King Jehoash
796–792 BC: Reign of King Amaziah
793–753 BC: Reign of King Jeroboam II
792–750 BC: Reign of King Azariah (Uzziah)
753–752 BC: Reign of King Zechariah
752 BC: Reign of King Shallum
752–742 BC: Reign of King Menahem
750–735 BC: Reign of King Jotham
742–740 BC: Reign of King Pekahiah
740–732 BC: Reign of King Pekah
735–715 BC: Reign of King Ahaz
732–722 BC: Reign of King Hoshea
715–697 BC: Reign of King Hezekiah
697–642 BC: Reign of King Manasseh
642–640 BC: Reign of King Amon
640–609 BC: Reign of King Josiah
609 BC: Reign of King Jehoahaz

600 BC   500   400

PERSIAN EMPIRE 538–331 BC

NEO-BABYLONIAN (CHALDEAN) EMPIRE 605–538 BC

538 BC: Cyrus conquers Babylon (Chaldea) and establishes Persian Empire
522–485 BC: Reign of King Darius I
486–465 BC: Reign of King Ahasuerus (Xerxes) of Persia
c. 479 BC: Esther made queen of Persia
465–423 BC: Reign of King Artaxerxes I of Persia
333 BC: End of Persian control of Palestine
331 BC: End of Persian Empire

c. 626 BC: Start of Neo-Babylonian (Chaldean) Empire
587 BC: Fall of Jerusalem to the Chaldeans; temple destroyed
539 BC: Fall of Neo-Babylonian Empire

MACEDONIAN EMPIRE 336–168 BC

336–323 BC: Rule of Alexander the Great
333 BC: Alexander the Great gains control of Palestine
331 BC: Alexander the Great conquers Persian Empire

PROPHETS & LEADERS

612–588 BC: Ministry of the prophet Habakkuk in Judah
c. 605–536 BC: Ministry of the prophet Daniel in Babylon
593–571 BC: Ministry of the prophet Ezekiel in Babylon
c. 586 BC: Book of Obadiah written to Judah
520 BC: Book of Haggai written to Judah
520–518 BC: Ministry of the prophet Zechariah in Judah
440–430 BC: Ministry of the prophet Malachi in Judah
586 BC: Babylonian Empire conquers Judah and destroys Jerusalem and Solomon's temple
538 BC: The first exiles return to Jerusalem
c. 516 BC: Second temple completed
457 BC: Ezra returns to Judah with more exiles
c. 445 BC: Nehemiah leads Jews back to Jerusalem
432 BC: Nehemiah's second visit to Jerusalem

DIVIDED ISRAEL 930–586 BC

JUDAH

609–598 BC: Reign of King Jehoiakim
598–597 BC: Reign of King Jehoiachin
597–586 BC: Reign of King Zedekiah

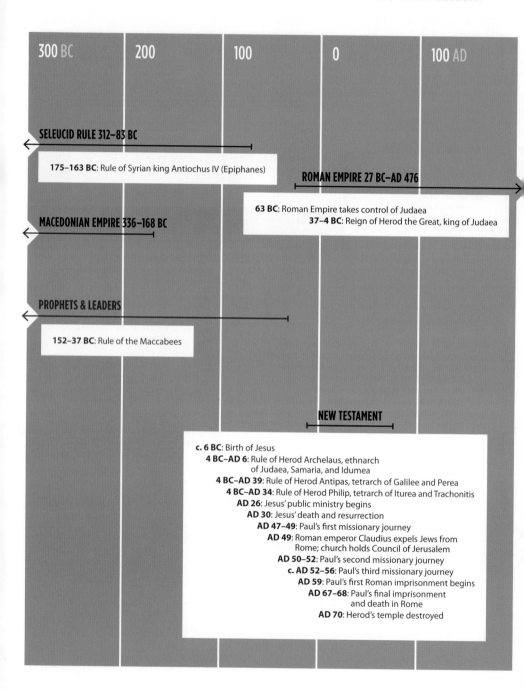

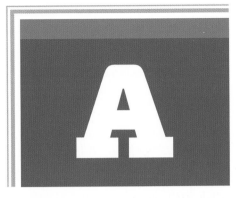

AB. Fifth Hebrew month. Matches part of our July and August (Numbers 33:38). See **CALENDAR CHART** on pages 265–266.

ABASE. To humble oneself or be humbled, to get the right view of oneself by choice or by force (Daniel 4:37; 2 Corinthians 11:7; Philippians 4:12).

ABATE. Decrease or withdraw (Genesis 8:8; Leviticus 27:18).

ABBA. "Father" in Aramaic, much like our word *daddy*. All three New Testament references are to God (Mark 14:36; Romans 8:15; Galatians 4:6). Shows that God is a loving, approachable Father.

AARON (AIR un). Older brother and early spokesman for Moses (Exodus 4:14–16). Became Israel's first high priest. The Aaronic priesthood (priests of the tribe of Levi) was named for him. (Exodus 28:1; 29; Leviticus 8; Numbers 18).

▲ *Early spokesman for Moses who helped him in battle (Exodus 17:9–12). But also made an idol (Exodus 32) and criticized Moses for his choice of a wife (Numbers 12:1–2). Parents were Amram and Jochebed; sister was Miriam (Numbers 26:59). Aaron lived until age 123 and died without entering the promised land because of his lack of faith in God (Numbers 20:12).*

AARON'S ROD. Walking stick used by Aaron to carry out God's commands. The rod was used in several miracles while persuading Pharaoh to let the Jewish slaves go: It became a serpent that swallowed the serpents from the rods of the Egyptian magicians (Exodus 7:8–13). It was used to bring about the first three plagues (Exodus 7:19–21; 8:5–7; 8:16–19).

Later in Aaron's life the rod sprouted, budded, and blossomed to signal Aaron as God's choice for the head of a priesthood (Numbers 17:1–11). It was displayed before (and later in) the Ark of the Covenant as a warning to those who rebelled against the Lord (Hebrews 9:4; Numbers 17:10).

ABEDNEGO (uh BED nih go). New name given to Azariah, friend of Daniel (Daniel 1:6). Abednego survived the fiery furnace along with Shadrach and Meshach (Daniel 3:16–29).

Aaron's rod—a walking stick that God miraculously turns into a snake—eats the snakes that Pharaoh's magicians had "created" from their own rods. As always, God's power is proven supreme.

Abel offers God a better sacrifice than his brother Cain. The painting is from the 1870s.

ABEL (AY bel). Second son of Adam and Eve. A shepherd who pleased God with his worship. After his brother Cain's sacrifice did not please God, Cain murdered Abel (Genesis 4:2–8; Hebrews 11:4; 1 John 3:12).

ABHOR. Hate, repel, reject. Shrink from in horror (Deuteronomy 7:26; Romans 12:9).

ABIATHAR (uh BIGH uh thar). A high priest during David's time. Followed his father, Ahimelech, but was later thrown out of the priestly office by Solomon because Abiathar favored Adonijah over Solomon (see 1 Samuel 22:20–22; 23:6, 9; 1 Kings 1:24–25; 2:26–27).

ABIDE. Remain, live, continue, persist (1 Samuel 1:22; John 15:4; Philippians 1:25). Forbear (Jeremiah 10:10).

ABIGAIL (AB ih gayl). Beautiful, wise, and poised wife of David, who married him after her first husband, Nabal, died (1 Samuel 25). Another Abigail was a sister of David who married Jether and became the mother of Amasa (1 Chronicles 2:16–17).

ABIHU (uh BIGH hyoo). The second son of Aaron and a priest (Exodus 6:23; 28:1). Went with Moses, Aaron, and others toward Mount Sinai to worship God (Exodus 24:1, 9). Later he died a fiery death with his brother Nadab after they had displeased God (Leviticus 10:1–2; Numbers 3:4).

ABIMILECH (uh BIM eh lek). A son of Jerub-baal (Gideon) who became king after killing his brothers (except Jotham who escaped). Abimelech ruled Israel for three years until he attacked Thebez where his skull was crushed by a stone in battle (Judges 8:29–9:57). Also a line of kings (Genesis 20–21; 26:1).

ABLUTIONS. Ceremonial washings (baptisms) for the expression of religious purity (Hebrews 6:2; 9:10 NRSV).

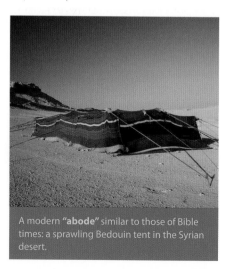

A modern **"abode"** similar to those of Bible times: a sprawling Bedouin tent in the Syrian desert.

Abihu, with his brother Nadab, offers "strange" (improper) fire before the Lord. They will soon pay for the mistake with their lives.

ABNER (AB nur). Saul's cousin and commander of Saul's army. Later served under Saul's son Ishbosheth and favored David. David's commander, Joab, was suspicious of Abner and murdered him (1 Samuel 14:50–2 Samuel 3:30).

ABODE. Home, room, place to stay (Numbers 9:17; John 14:23).

ABOLISH. Put to an end (2 Timothy 1:10), remove (Hebrews 10:9).

ABOMINABLE, ABOMINATION. A horrible, foul thing to God or man. Describes something hateful, loathsome, putrid, sickening, awful, disgusting, evil (Matthew 24:15; Genesis 43:32). Abominations are connected with idolatry (Revelation 17:4–5; 21:27), disrespect for God (Ezekiel 7:3–4), ceremonial uncleanness (Leviticus 7:21), and sexual sins (Revelation 17:4–5).

ABOMINATION OF DESOLATION. An indescribably evil, horrible, detestable thing to occur in the last days (see Daniel 9:27; 11:31; 12:11; Matthew 24:15; Mark 13:14). Scholars differ on whether the term refers to a person or persons called the Antichrist (literally means "against Christ"; see 1 John 2:18–22) or a profane symbol, event, or act.

▲ *The evil represented by this abomination always wants to make a desert of one's spiritual life. To keep this from happening, recognize the danger of evil and run or resist in the power of God (Matthew 24:15–16; 1 Corinthians 10:13).*

ABOUND. Overflow, increase, grow, have abundance (Proverbs 28:20; 1 Thessalonians 3:12).

ABRAHAM (AY bruh ham), **ABRAM** (AY bram). The first Hebrew (Genesis 14:13). God promised the childless Abraham that He would make him the father of a great nation. God was faithful to His promise (Genesis 12:1–2) and gave the almost one-hundred-year-old Abraham and his ninety-year-old wife a baby named Isaac (Genesis 17:1–8). But during the many years between the promise and the baby of promise, Abraham and Sarah got tired of waiting on God. So Abraham fathered Ishmael by the handmaid Hagar and gave birth to another nation. Despite Abraham's weakness, God's promise unfolded like a drama. Read Genesis 11:26–25:11 for the full story of Abraham and his faith in God.

The name *Abraham* (father of a multitude) is the longer form of *Abram* (exalted father) (Genesis 17:1–8). He lived in Ur, Haran, Egypt, and Canaan. He died at age 175 and was buried in a cave at Hebron (Genesis 25:7–10).

▲ *Abraham's experience teaches us that God's calling is worth responding to, and His promises are worth working toward and patiently waiting.*

LIFE OF ABRAHAM

EVENT	OT PASSAGE	NT REFERENCE
Birth of Abram	Gen. 11:26	
God's call of Abram	Gen. 12:1–3	Heb. 11:8
Entry into Canaan	Gen. 12:4–9	
Abram in Egypt	Gen. 12:10–20	
Lot separates from Abram	Gen. 13:1–18	
Abram rescues Lot	Gen. 14:1–17	
Abram pays tithes to Melchizedek	Gen. 14:18–24	Heb. 7:1–10
God's covenant with Abram	Gen. 15:1–21	Rom. 4:1–25; Gal. 3:6–25; Heb. 6:13–20
Birth of Ishmael	Gen. 16:1–16	
Abraham promised a son by Sarah	Gen. 17:1–27	Rom. 4:18–25; Heb. 11:11–12
Abraham intercedes for Sodom	Gen. 18:16–33	
Lot saved and Sodom destroyed	Gen. 19:1–38	
Birth of Isaac	Gen. 21:1–7	
Hagar and Ishmael sent away	Gen. 21:8–21	Gal. 4:21–31
Abraham challenged to offer Isaac as sacrifice	Gen. 22:1–19	Heb. 11:17–19; Jas. 2:20–24
Death of Sarah	Gen. 23:1–20	
Death of Abraham	Gen. 25:1–11	

ABRAHAM'S BOSOM. Term used for closeness, affection, place of honor, blessedness (Luke 16:22–23).

ABSALOM (AB suh luhm). Third son of David (2 Samuel 3:2–5). Absalom means "father in peace," but his name did not fit his personality. He arranged his half brother Amnon's murder (2 Samuel 13), and he rebelled against his father, King David, to make himself king (2 Samuel 15). Absalom was murdered against his father's wishes and much to his father's sadness (2 Samuel 18:6–17, 3l–33).

ABSTAIN. Avoid or keep away from. Examples of acts to abstain from include idols, sex outside marriage, and evil in general (Acts 15:20; 1 Thessalonians 5:22).

An 1850 painting entitled *Abraham's Journey from Ur to Canaan*. The youngsters would be from servants and extended family, since **Abraham** and his wife, Sarah, were childless at the time.

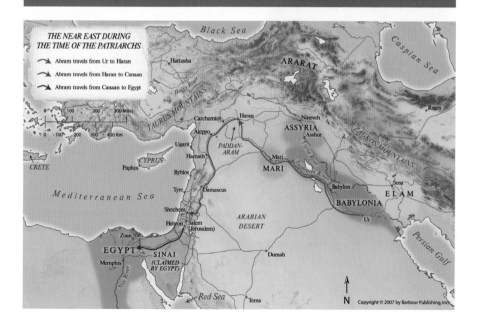

THE NEAR EAST DURING
THE TIME OF THE PATRIARCHS

Abram travels from Ur to Haran

Abram travels from Haran to Canaan

Abram travels from Canaan to Egypt

Copyright © 2007 by Barbour Publishing, Inc.

ABUNDANCE. A multitude, plenty, fullness, more than enough (Deuteronomy 28:47; Romans 5:17). The true abundant life is not made up of money or possessions but of such riches as commitment to God, love, joy, peace, and friendship (John 10:10; Luke 12:15).

ABUSE. Mistreat, misuse, damage physically or emotionally (1 Chronicles 10:4; Proverbs 22:10; Hebrews 10:33; 1 Corinthians 9:18).
● *Could it be that what we say to or about each other is the most frequent abuse that occurs? How might we abuse blessings by misusing them?*

ABYSS. Literally, the deep or bottomless pit (Revelation 9:1–2, 11; 11:7; 17:8; 20:1). Place of torment for demons (Luke 8:31), place of the dead (Romans 10:7).

An **acacia** tree in Israel's Negev region.

ACACIA (uh KAY shuh). Large tree whose hard wood was excellent for making furniture. Used to make the ark of the covenant and other wooden objects for the tabernacle (Deuteronomy 10:3; Exodus 25–27; 30; 37–38). Same as shittim wood from the shittah tree (KJV).

ACCEPTABLE. Pleasing, receivable, welcome, adequate (Psalm 51:17; Isaiah 61:2; Ephesians 5:8–11; Hebrews 11:4).

ACCESS. Ability to come into the presence. Qualified to approach. Most often used of the Christian's access to God. Accepting Jesus Christ who died for us is the sole requirement for access to God. Jesus' death has removed all barriers between God and people. Jesus enables believers to draw near to God with confidence (Romans 5:2; Ephesians 2:18, 3:12).
● *Ponder people you feel comfortable approaching and people you do not. What makes the difference? What about God makes it easy/hard to approach Him?*

ACHAIA (uh KAY yuh). A Roman province in the southern portion of Greece. Corinth was its capital (2 Corinthians 1:1; Acts 19:21; Romans 15:26).

ACHAN (AY kuhn), **ACHOR**. Israelite who stole items dedicated to God from the city of Jericho after its destruction. He hid what he stole and his sin threatened the security of the entire Israelite community. The Israelites put him to death after his sin was discovered (Joshua 7:1–26).

ACCOMPLISH. Fulfill, complete, succeed in doing, express (Isaiah 55:11; Jeremiah 44:25; Ezra 20:8; Luke 2:22; John 19:28).

ACCORD. Like-mindedness, harmony, unity, singleness of purpose, agreement. Can be with good or evil (Acts 2:46, 7:57; 15:25).

ACCOUNT. Reckon, calculate, consider. Let your mind dwell on. Give reasons for, accept responsibility for (Matthew 12:36; Luke 16:2; Romans 14:12). When something is accounted, it is credited to or recognized as belonging to someone (Galatians 3:6; Luke 22:24). Also, an account is a detailed record, count, or credit (Deuteronomy 2:11; Psalm 144:3).

● *God knows all about every person and holds us accountable. How should this affect your thoughts and actions?*

ACCURSED. Under a curse, set aside for condemnation or destruction (Romans 9:3; Galatians 1:8–9; 1 Corinthians 12:3; Joshua 6:17).

ACCUSE. Charge, credit with undesirable action (Proverbs 30:10; Acts 25:11; Luke 11:54). Accusation can be true or false (John 8:6; Luke 3:14). Satan is sometimes called the accuser (Revelation 12:10).

ACKNOWLEDGE. Admit, recognize, give attention to, agree with, accept, respond to. Opposite of ignore. When a person acknowledges transgressions or wrongs, that confession opens the door to repentance and change. To acknowledge God is to agree with Him in attitude and respond to Him in action (Jeremiah 24:5; Deuteronomy 21:17; Psalm 51:3; 1 Corinthians 14:37).
● *Can you identify one wrong in your life? How would acknowledging it free you from its burden?*

ACTS, BOOK OF. New Testament Bible book written by Luke and a continuation of the Gospel of Luke. Some scholars refer to this book as "The Acts of the Holy Spirit." Acts traces the birth and growth of the Christian church. Acts shows how the early church carried out Jesus Christ's command to make disciples of all nations (Matthew 28:18–20). Peter, a disciple, and Paul, a powerful convert to Christianity, serve as significant leaders in the growth of the Christian church. Acts tells about the unique coming of the Holy Spirit upon Christians and His work in the growth of the church. The first half of Acts focuses on the Jerusalem church, and the last half tells about Paul's and others' efforts to spread Christianity to surrounding areas such as Samaria, Damascus, Antioch,

God's angel drives **Adam** and his wife, Eve, from the Garden of Eden after their disobedience—also called "the fall of man."

Cyprus, Asia Minor, Europe, and Rome. The book of Acts ends with an unhindered sharing of the gospel (Acts 28:31). Acts is the first book of church history and colorfully depicts both the joys and growing pains of the first-century church.
▲ *Acts' teachings for today include examples of (1) how to present the Gospel (Acts 2:14–21), (2) demonstrations of refusal to let physical, economic, or social barriers prevent us from sharing the message of Christ (Acts 10–11), and (3) encouragement to keep on obeying God even in the worst of persecution (Acts 5:27–32).*

AD. *Anno domini* means "in the year of our Lord." Popularly, "after death"—the time since Jesus Christ's death. In recent years, many scholars have begun using the initials CE for "Common Era." See **BC**.

ADAM (AD duhm). First man. God created Adam in His image, as well as Eve (Genesis 1:27; 5:2). Adam (and Eve) chose to mar God's image by disobeying Him. This sin plunged the human race into sin (Genesis 3; Romans 5:12–21). Jesus Christ, the second Adam, came to deliver us from sin and transform us into His perfect image (1 Corinthians 15:45, 49; Romans 8:29). See **EVE**.

▲ *Self-image improves as one moves toward the God-image of creation. What kind of an image do you have of yourself? See Romans 12:3. We are accountable for our own sin, not for Adam's.*

The common **adder** (Vipera berus) is found from western Europe to east Asia.

ADAR (AD ahr). Twelfth Hebrew month. Corresponds to our mid-February to mid-March (Esth. 3:7). See **CALENDAR CHART** on pages 265–266.

ADDER. Snake (Genesis 49:17; Proverbs 23:32). See **SERPENT**.

ADHERE. Attach. Stick. Be loyal (2 Kings 17:34).

ADJURE. Plead, beg, command. Appeal in the most persuasive manner, cause to take an oath. Its goal is to make sure the information given is correct (1 Kings 22:16; Matthew 26:63; Mark 5:7; Acts 19:13).

ADMONISH. Recommend, suggest, show, encourage to do right. Warn, advise, counsel. Correct or praise to motivate obedience to God. Those who admonish are usually more mature believers. Those who admonish are always to be motivated and guided by Jesus Christ (Romans 15:14; Colossians 3:16; 1 Thessalonians 5:12; 2 Thessalonians 3:15).

● *Who or what has admonished you to obey God? With what words might you admonish a fellow believer?*

ADONIJAH (ad oh NIGH juh). Name meaning "My Lord is Yahweh." 1. Fourth son of David who tried without success to take over his throne. When Solomon inherited the throne after his father David's death, he had Adonijah killed (2 Samuel 3:4; 1 Kings 1:5–2:25). 2. A Levite whom Jehoshaphat sent to teach about God in the cities of Judah (2 Chronicles 17:8–9). 3. One of Nehemiah's chiefs who sealed the covenant (Nehemiah 10:16; Ezra 2:13).

ADOPT. 1. Choose to become a parent of a child you did not bear. Legally make a child of other parents your child (Esther 2:15). Every person who trusts God becomes a child of God by adoption and inherits His resources. (Romans 8:15, 23; Galatians 4:5; Ephesians 1:5). 2. Choose an action or item as your own (Job 15:5; Psalm 106:36).

● *How does God's adoption of you demonstrate His love for you?*

■ **ADULTERY**. Voluntary sexual intercourse of a married person with someone besides his mate (Hebrews 13:4). Spiritual adultery is when believers turn their love from God to someone or something else (Jeremiah 3:9; Ezekiel 23:37). Both sexual and spiritual adultery are forbidden in the Ten Commandments (Exodus 20:3, 14).

Jesus explained that looking lustfully at someone is an act of adultery (Matthew 5:27–30).

Adultery also is the generic term for many sexual sins including incest (sex with close relatives) and fornication (sex outside marriage).

▲ *Adultery continues as one of the more enticing sins. Many feel that saving sex for marriage is out of date, obsolete. But the Bible explains that sex outside of marriage is wrong. Why? It misunderstands and distorts God's design for marriage and sexual happiness. God designed sex to be best when it is an expression of unique love between husband and wife in marriage.*

ADVENT. Translates a Latin word for "coming." Usually refers to Christ's coming to earth as a baby, but now more broadly to the season of preparation to celebrate Christmas. Jesus' coming to earth began the Christ story as we know it, including His birthday, life and ministry, ascent, and promised second coming—or "second advent" (see Philippians 2:5–11).

ADVERSARY. 1. Enemy. One who is against a person or thing. May be a personal enemy, a national enemy, or a spiritual enemy (Numbers 22:22; Matthew 5:25; Esther 7:6; 1 Samuel 1:6; 1 Kings 5:4; 1 Peter 5:8; 1 Timothy 5:14). 2. Satan. A literal translation of the Hebrew "Satan" (1 Peter 5:8). See **SATAN**.

▲ *God is His people's adversary against their adversaries (Exodus 23:22; Luke 18:3).*

ADVERSITY. Trouble. Hard times. (2 Samuel 4:9; Proverbs 17:17; Proverbs 24:10).

● *Name a way God has or could help you through adversity.*

ADVOCATE. One called alongside to help (1 John 2:1 KJV). Helper, comforter, intercessor—one who takes our side, speaks on our behalf, pleads our case. In the New Testament both Jesus Christ and the Holy Spirit are our advocates (1 John 2:1; John 14:16, 26; 15:26; 16:7). In the Gospel of John, *comforter* translates the same Greek word that *advocate* translates in 1 John 2:1.

● *How does it feel to have someone on your side? What thoughts and feelings do you have about knowing Jesus is on your side?*

AFFECTION. Feeling, passion, or thought. The King James Version setting determines whether it is good or bad (Romans 12:10; Romans 1:26). Colossians 3:2 focuses on thought.

AFFLICTION. Our English word means a state or cause of pain, distress, grief, or misery. Generally, these definitions can serve for the Bible use of *affliction* also. But the Old Testament Hebrew and the New Testament Greek shades of meaning are worth noting: 1. The Old Testament Hebrew usually means oppressed or humbled—a sense of helplessness or defenselessness. If the affliction comes from God, it is a punishment for sin that comes to bless people by leading them to turn back to God (2 Kings 15:5; Psalm 119:71). However, Isaiah also used the word to refer to the forthcoming affliction of Christ for our sins (Isaiah 53:4, 7). 2. The New Testament Greek literally means pressure but also carries the thought of oppression or tribulation. The idea is most often that the distress comes upon a person from someone else because he follows Christ and not because of personal sin (Colossians 1:24).

● *Where does most of your misery come from? From within as you choose your will instead of God's? or from without as others pressure you because of your choice to follow Christ as Lord and Savior? In either case, the way to deal with affliction is to turn to God for relief or strength to endure for His glory.*

AGABUS (AG uh buhs). New Testament prophet from Jerusalem who foretold a great famine and the imprisonment of Paul (Acts 11:28; 21:10–11).

AGAPE. A Greek word for self-giving love. See **LOVE**.

AGE. Period of time. Can be past or future and is often unlimited. *Ages* often means "eternity" or unmeasurable time. God is the King of all ages (Colossians 1:26; Romans 16:25; Joel 2:2; Revelation 15:13; Isaiah 45:17; 1 Timothy 1:17).

AGRIPPA (uh GRIP uh). 1. Herod Agrippa I was known in the New Testament as Herod (Acts 12:2–4). 2. Herod Agrippa II (In New Testament, just Agrippa). Jewish king who listened to Paul's legal defense and found him innocent. Agrippa said Paul almost persuaded him to become a Christian (Acts 25:13–26:32). Paul was on trial because jealous Jews had him arrested for preaching what they considered heresy (Acts 21–23).

AHAB (AY hab). 1. Powerful but evil king who reigned over Israel for 22 years. Heavily influenced by his Baal-worshipping wife, Jezebel. Failed to stand up for justice and true worship even though God's prophets warned him (1 Kings 16:28–22:40). See **JEZEBEL**. 2. A false prophet (Jeremiah 29:20–21). See **KING CHART** on pages 152–155.

AHASUERUS (uh haz you EE russ). A king of Persia. Mentioned in three Old Testament books (Ezra 4:6; Daniel 9:1; Esther 1:1, 10:3). In the book of Esther, he chose Esther as his new queen. In the book of Daniel, he was the father of Darius the Mede.

AHAZ (AY haz). Twelfth king of Judah. He was very wicked and promoted idolatry (2 Kings 16; 2 Chronicles 28). See **KING CHART** on pages 152–155.

AHAZIAH (ay huh ZIGH uh). 1. Eighth king of Israel. Son and successor of Ahab. Like his mother, Jezebel, he trusted pagan gods rather

The prophet Elijah confronts **King Ahab** in an old woodcut image. The king seemed to fear Elijah—but Ahab feared his evil wife, Jezebel, even more.

than the true God (1 Kings 22:51–53; 2 Kings 1:2–3). 2. Sixth king of Judah who practiced idolatry (2 Kings 8:24). See **KING CHART** on pages 152–155.

AI (AY igh). Small city east of Bethel that was conquered by Joshua after he and his men conquered Jericho. After an initial setback due to Achan's sin, God said He had given Ai, its people, and its king over to Joshua. The destruction of Ai demonstrated God's power. (Joshua 7:2–5, 8:1–29, 10:1–2).

ALABASTER. Smooth cream-colored stone used to make containers for perfume and ointment. The alabaster box in the Bible was a flask with a long thin neck that was broken to release the contents (Matthew 26:7; Mark 14:3; Luke 7:37).

ALAS. "Oh no!" "Pay attention!" An expression of sorrow, fear, complaint, grief, or warning. (Joshua 7:7; Judges 6:22; 1 Kings 13:30; Jeremiah 30:7; Revelation 18:10).

ALEXANDER (al eg ZAN dur). 1. Member of high priestly family (Acts 4:6). 2. Jewish speaker (Acts 19:33). 3. False teacher (1 Timothy 1:20). 4.

Enemy of Paul (2 Timothy 4:14). 5. Alexander the Great is probably the king described in Daniel 8.

ALEXANDRIA. Capital city of Egypt from 330 BC. Second city only to Rome in that day. Alexander the Great founded Alexandria in 322 BC as he conquered his known world and brought Greek culture with him. For that reason, Greek became the universal or international language. It was the language used in writing the original New Testament letters. The Bible refers to Alexandria in Acts 6:9; 18:24; 27:6; and 28:11. Jewish rabbis gathered in Alexandria later to translate the Hebrew and Aramaic of the Old Testament into Greek. This translation is known as the Septuagint and often identified by the roman letters LXX.

ALIEN. Stranger. Traveler. Person away from home. Someone unknown to the area. Someone or something foreign (Ephesians 2:12). God cares for aliens and He encourages His people to do the same (Exodus 18:3; Genesis 21:23; Job 19:15; Deuteronomy 10:8).

ALLELUIA. "Praise God!" Same as *hallelujah*. Invitation to praise God. A part of many Psalms and an element of worship in Revelation (Psalm 104:35; 105:45; Revelation 19:1, 3–4, 6).

ALLOTMENT. Portion, part of land, assigned amount (Deuteronomy 14:27; Deuteronomy 18:1; Ezra 48:13).

Alabaster vases in an Egyptian shop.

ALMIGHTY. All powerful. Completely powerful. In control. Name for God. A reason to praise and worship God (Genesis 17:1; 2 Corinthians 6:18; Revelation 11:17). See NAMES OF GOD CHART on page 109.
● *The almighty God wants a close relationship with every person. How does His "almighti- ness" affect the way you relate to Him?*

ALMS. 1. Offering. Portion of one's possessions given to the poor (Leviticus 19:9; Acts 3:2 and following). 2. Kind act. Act of compassion moti- vated by wanting to please God (Acts 9:36). Guidelines for almsgiving include give privately, give so only God can see, and give from what you have (Matthew 6:1–4; Luke 11:41).

Alpha and omega.

ALPHA AND OMEGA (AL fuh) (oh MAY guh). First and last letters of the Greek alphabet. A name for Christ. Means beginning and end or first and last—our A to Z. Jesus is both first and last in time and in importance. Used by Christ of Himself in the book of Revelation (1:8; 1:11; 21:6; 22:13).

ALPHAEUS (al FEE uhs). 1. Father of James the apostle (Matthew 10:3: Acts 1:13). 2. Father of Levi the tax collector (Mark 2:14).

ALTAR. Place of worship. Place where animal sacrifices were slaughtered and presented to God (Genesis 8:20; Exodus 29:10–14). Also a place to burn incense for God (Exodus 30:1).

Altars in the Bible ranged from piles of stones to intricately constructed structures (Joshua 8:30–31; Exodus 27:1–8).

Old Testament blood sacrifices pictured repentance and forgiveness—but did not provide salvation, which eternally comes only in Christ Jesus. After the death and resurrection of Jesus, animal sacrifices were no longer needed. God welcomes a different type of offering at the altar: praise, confession, and good actions (Hebrews 13:15–16). See **SACRIFICE**.

AMALEK (AM uh lek). Descendant of Esau (twin of Jacob). His descendants, called Amalekites, tried to keep the Israelites from entering the promised land. Following this, the Amalekites and the Israelites remained enemies (Genesis 36:12; Exodus 17:8–16; Deuteronomy 25:17; 1 Samuel 15:2–3).

AMBASSADOR. Agent. Messenger. Interpreter. Representative. Christians are ambassadors for Christ: They help others to understand Him and encourage their reconciliation with Him (Joshua 9:4; Proverbs 13:17; 2 Corinthians 5:20; Ephesians 6:19–20).

▲ *In the Old Testament ambassadors were sent to other nations for such purposes as congratulations, to ask favors, to make alliances, or to protest wrongs (1 Kings 5:1; Numbers 20:14; Joshua 9:4; Judges 11:12).*

● *Name a situation in which an ambassador for Christ might serve as a messenger or interpreter for Him today.*

AMEN. Well said. I agree! Let it be as said. In the Bible it demonstrated excitement and conviction about God's promises. Used at the beginning and/or end of solemn statements or praises (Revelation 7:12). Repeated for emphasis (John l:51). Jesus' *amen* (*verily*, KJV) meant "truly" or "these words are God's words"

A reproduction of the incense **altar** from Timna, Israel.

or "may it happen" (Matthew 5:18, 26; 6:2). Jesus was called "the Amen" (2 Corinthians 1:20; Revelation 3:14) as the person in whom we find God's promises.

● *To what truth about God would you most like to say amen?*

AMOS (AY muhs). 1. A shepherd from Tekoa of Judah God called to be a prophet. He was from the Southern Kingdom but preached to the Northern Kingdom. He was poor but preached to the rich. Amos's name means "burden bearer." Read his message in the Bible book of Amos. 2. Ancestor of Joseph, husband of Mary (Luke 3:25).

AMOS, BOOK OF. This Old Testament Bible book is written by Amos, a shepherd whom God called to be a prophet in the eighth century BC. His main message was that God loves mercy more than formal sacrifices. He taught that greatness did not come through power but through justice and judgment (Amos 5:21–24). Amos reprimanded the wealthy for gaining their wealth at the expense of the poor, for their dishonesty and bribery, and for seeing God as a convenience. The book of Amos encourages readers to repent and let God be Lord and Master.

AMRAM. Father of Moses, Aaron, and Miriam (Exodus 6:20; 1 Chronicles 6:3).

ANANIAS (an uh NIGH uhs). 1. Believer who lied to Peter about the amount of money he had received for a possession and then died as an act of God's judgment (Acts 5:1–5). See **SAPPHIRA**. 2. A disciple at Damascus God used in the restoring of Paul's sight, baptism, and acceptance as a fellow disciple (Acts 9:10–18; 22:12). 3. A high priest who wanted Paul silenced (Acts 23:2; 24:1).

ANATHEMA. Accursed (1 Corinthians 16:22). This Greek word appears only the one time in the King James Version of the Bible. It is as if Paul had said, "If a person does not love the Lord, let the person be turned over to the Lord for His judgment." "Our Lord is coming" (see *Maranatha*—a Hebrew word—1 Corinthians 16:22).
▲ *The Hebrew and Greek words related to anathema basically mean to declare a thing or person turned over to God: as an act of devotion for a good thing, or for God's judgment if it is a bad thing.*

ANCIENT OF DAYS. Name for God used by Daniel. Pictures a white-haired God on a throne of judgment. Similar to "Most High" (Daniel 7:9, 13, 22). See NAMES OF GOD CHART, page 109.
● *The Bible uses many other names for God. Why do you think this image seems one of the most popular?*

ANDREW (AN droo). Disciple of Jesus. One of the twelve apostles. He asked Jesus many questions and he noticed the boy with the five loaves and two fishes (Matthew 4:18–19; Mark 13:3; John 6:8–9). Andrew is always seen bringing someone to Jesus (John 6:8–9).
▲ *He was a follower of John the Baptist before he met Jesus (John 1:35, 37, 40).*

■ **ANGEL**. Messenger. Heavenly beings created by God. They often serve as messengers for Him (Matthew 2:13–15; Genesis 18:2–10, 19:1 and following; Luke 1:26–38; Matthew 1:20–21; Luke 2:8–15). Angels serve in heaven (Revelation 8–9) and on earth (Luke 2:8–14); take care of and protect us (Matthew 18:10; Psalm 91:11–12); rejoice when someone becomes a Christian (Luke 15:10); will help execute judgment (Matthew 13:41–43, 49–50). They sometimes appear as humans (Genesis 18:2–10); other times they don't (Luke 2:13–14). Angels are not to be worshiped (Colossians 2:18). Angels are not humans who have died and gone to heaven (Hebrews 2:7).
▲ *Satan has evil angels who chose to disobey God and follow him (Jude 6, 9; 2 Peter 2:4; Revelation 12:9). We call these demons or evil spirits.*
● *How does God send His messages to you?*

ANGER. Fury (Exodus 32:19; Matthew 5:22). Sadness turned outward. Feeling of hostility toward a person or event that has wronged or injured you. Ranges from simple frustration to lasting resentment or catastrophic violence. Events closely related to anger include jealousy, cursing, revenge, violence, rebellion.

Several Hebrew and Greek words depict types of anger. In summary the words for angers carry these meanings: 1. Kindling or burning anger. 2. Rage or fury that overflows. 3. Stormy anger. 4. Passionate anger. 5. Anger about a moral wrong.

Anger appears in both man and God. In the Bible, human anger is presented as an emotion that has to be dealt with in a Christlike way (Ephesians 4:26; Proverbs 14:17; Psalm 37:8). Divine anger is different from human anger in that its goal is righteousness and justice (James 1:20; Romans 12:19). It is always provoked by sin, and God's reaction is consistent. When the Bible commands us to be angry and sin not, we are able to accomplish that only when our motivation for anger is like God's (Ephesians 4:26). Often God's anger is distinguished from human anger by using two or more anger words in succession (Isaiah 13:9).

● *What steps could you take to deal with your anger without sinning? (See Ephesians 4:26.) When could anger lead to good?*

ANNA (AN uh). Prophetess who recognized the infant Jesus as the awaited Messiah (Luke 2:36–38).

ANNAS (AN uhs). A high priest who took part in Jesus' trial before crucifixion (Luke 3:2; John 18:13, 24; Acts 4:6).

ANNIHILATE. Utterly destroy. Wipe out. Slaughter. Extinguish. Abolish (NIV: Deuteronomy 9:3; Esther 3:13).

ANNUNCIATION. The announcement to Mary that she would become the mother of Jesus. Read about it in Luke 1:26–38.

▲ *The angel's message explained that Jesus would be both human (Luke 1:32) and divine (1:34), the eternal ruler (1:33).*

ANOINT. To pour oil on. Usually a ceremony that indicates a person's appointment to a special task. Done for kings and priests (Exodus 28:41; 1 Samuel 15:1,17). Jesus was God's Anointed, the Messiah (Luke 4:18; Acts 10:38). Sometimes part of a healing process (Mark 6:13) or as a daily task (Ruth 3:3; Matthew 6:17).

▲ *A recipe for anointing oil is found in Exodus 30:22–25.*

ANTICHRIST. Opponent of Christ. 1. The evil figure to come during the last days who will oppose everything of God (1 John 2:18). 2. Anyone who denies through words or actions that Jesus is the Christ (1 John 2:19, 22; 1 John 4:3; 2 John 7).

▲ *Many Christians understand 2 Thessalonians 2:1–12 as describing the antichrist.*

ANTIOCH (AN tih ahk). 1. *Antioch in Pisidia* was a Galatian city where Paul preached, started a church, and was persecuted. To this and nearby churches, he wrote the letter of Galatians (Acts 13; 2 Timothy 3:11). 2. *Antioch in Syria* was a major city and early center of Christianity. Jesus' followers were first called Christians there, and from there were sent the first foreign missionaries (Acts 11:26; 13:1–4).

ANXIETY. Worries, cares, intense thoughts (1 Peter 5:7). To be anxious is to be afraid, worried, troubled, or distressed (Philippians 4:6; Daniel 7:15). The opposite of anxiety is trusting God and enjoying the peace He gives (Matthew 6:25–34).

● *What worries you? How can God help you with this anxiety?*

APOCALYPSE. Literally, an uncovering or unveiling. Often used as a synonym for the book of Revelation. However, the book of Daniel and a few others also use symbolic or pictorial language to refer to prophecy of forthcoming divine plans or interventions.

APOCRYPHA AND PSEUDEPIGRAPHA. Religious writings not commonly accepted as part of the Bible. Non-canonical writings. Roman Catholics accept the Apocrypha as a part of their Bible. *Pseudepigrapha* means false writings, and these are not a part of the Apocrypha. See CHART on pages 27–28.

THE APOCRYPHA

TITLES (LISTED ALPHABETICALLY)	APPROXIMATE DATES	LITERARY TYPES	THEMES	IN SEPTUAGINT?	IN ROMAN CATHOLIC CANON?
Baruch	150 BC	Wisdom; narrative (composite)	Praise of wisdom; law; promise of hope; opposition to idolatry	Yes	Yes
Bel and the Dragon	100 BC	Detective narrative at end of Daniel	Opposition to idolatry	Yes	Yes
Ecclesiasticus (Wisdom of Jesus Sirach)	180 BC in Hebrew; 132 BC Greek translation	Wisdom; patriotism; temple worship; retribution; free will	Obedience to law; praise of patriarchs; value of wisdom	Yes	Yes
1 Esdras	150 BC	History (621–458)	Proper worship; power of truth	Yes	No
2 Esdras	AD 100	Apocalypse with Christian preface and epilogue	Pre-existent, dying Messiah; punishment for sin; salvation in future; inspiration; divine justice; evil	No	No
Additions to Esther (103 verses)	114 BC	Religious amplification	Prayer; worship; revelation; God's activity; providence	Yes	Yes
Letter of Jeremiah	317 BC	Homily added to Baruch based on Jer. 29	Condemns idolatry	Yes	Yes
Judith	200 BC	Historical novel	Obedience to law; prayer; fasting; true worship; patriotism	Yes	Yes
1 Maccabees	90 BC	History (180–161 BC)	God works in normal human events; legitimates Hasmonean kings	Yes	Yes
2 Maccabees	90 BC	History (180–161 BC)	Resurrection; creation from nothing; miracles; punishment for sin; martyrdom; temple angels	Yes	Yes
3 Maccabees	75 BC	Festival legend	Deliverance of faithful; angels	Some manuscripts	No
4 Maccabees	10 BC	Philosophical treatise based on 2 Macc. 6–7	Power of reason over emotions; faithfulness to law; martyrdom	Some manuscripts	No
Prayer of Azariah and Song of Three Young Men	100 BC	Liturgy; hum and additions to Dan. 3:23	Praise; God's response to prayer	Yes	Yes

THE APOCRYPHA (CONTINUED)					
TITLES (LISTED ALPHABETICALLY)	APPROXIMATE DATES	LITERARY TYPES	THEMES	IN SEPTU-AGINT?	IN ROMAN CATHOLIC CANON?
Prayer of Manasseh	120 BC	Prayer of penitence based on 2 Kings 21:10–17; 2 Chr. 33:11–19	Prayer of repentance	Yes	No
Psalm 151	?	Victory hymn	Praise to God who uses young and inexperienced	Yes	No
Susanna	100 BC	Detective story at end of Daniel	Daniel's wisdom; God's vindication of faithfulness	Yes	Yes
Tobit	200 BC	Folk tale	Temple attendance; tithing; charity; prayer; obedience to Jewish law; guardian angel; divine justice and retribution; personal devotion	Yes	Yes
Wisdom of Solomon	10 BC in Egypt	Wisdom personified; Jewish apologetic	Value of wisdom and faithfulness; immortality	Yes	Yes

APOLLOS (uh PAHL uhs). Teacher with deep scriptural knowledge whose public teaching won many people to Jesus Christ (Acts 18:24–28; 1 Corinthians 3:6). He took coaching by Priscilla and Aquila that helped him better understand the Word of God (Acts 18:26).
● *How do you take coaching (better known as constructive criticism)?*

■**APOSTLE**. One sent on a mission. An apostle has a message and is authorized to act on behalf of the sender. Jesus' disciples were first learners and then became apostles, taking the message of salvation (Luke 6:13; 9:10). Jesus, himself an Apostle sent by God (Hebrews 3:1), chose twelve disciples to send out as apostles. Barnabas, Paul, and a few others were also called apostles (Acts 1:26, 4:36; 1 Corinthians 1:1; Acts 13:3). See **DISCIPLE**.
● *What does being a disciple (learner) have to do with being an apostle (one sent on a mission)?*

APPALLED. Repelled, morally offended, shocked, dismayed, turned off, strongly disappointed (1 Kings 9:8; Job 17:8; Isaiah 52:14, 59:16; Daniel 8:27).

APPAREL. Clothing, robe, dress. Apparel can show royalty, mourning, wealth, that one is God's messenger, and more (Esther 6:8; 2 Samuel 14:2; Ezekiel 27:24; Acts 1:10; 1 Timothy 2:9).
● *What does your apparel say about you and your lifestyle?*

APPEARING. Refers to the return of Jesus Christ (1 Timothy 6:14; Titus 2:13; 1 Peter 1:7).

APT. Prepared. Ready, capable, inclined toward, leaning toward, likely (2 Kings 24:16; Proverbs 15:23; 1 Timothy 3:2).

AQUILA (uh KWIL uh). Husband of Priscilla. Together with Paul they worked on tents and ministered (Acts 18:2–3, 18; Romans 16:3). They also helped a believer named Apollos understand the way of God more perfectly, and they had a church in their house (Acts 18:26; 1 Corinthians 16:19). See **PRISCILLA**.

ARCHANGEL. Chief messenger, head angel named Michael (1 Thessalonians 4:16; Jude 9). See **ANGEL**.

ARAMAIC. Though Greek had become the universal or international language of the day, Jesus and others usually spoke in Aramaic. Aramaic was closely related to Hebrew, and a few passages in the Bible remained in Aramaic instead of the Old Testament Hebrew or the New Testament Greek. For example, in Jesus' prayer of agony before His crucifixion, He said, "Abba, Father" (Mark 14:36). "Abba" is intimate Aramaic, much like our use of "Daddy" with our earthly fathers. "Father" translates the Greek word; some special terms don't translate well into other languages.

AREOPAGUS (er ih AHP uh guhs). 1. A rocky hill in Athens called Mars' Hill (Acts 17:22). 2. The name of a council that met on Mars' Hill and primarily dealt with morals and education (Acts 17:19). Paul explained who the Unknown God was to that council on that hill (Acts 17:23).

ARIMATHEA, JOSEPH OF (ahr ih muh THEE uh). A Pharisee who became a disciple of Jesus. With Nicodemus, he prepared Jesus' body for burial and buried Him in his own tomb (Matthew 27:57–60; Mark 15:43).

ARK. 1. Large boat built by Noah according to God's specifications. Only the people and animals on the ark survived the flood (Genesis 7:1–9:1). 2. The basket in which baby Moses was placed (Exodus 2:1–5). 3. See **ARK OF THE COVENANT** for a beautiful chest that held varied items and also symbolized the presence of God to the Israelites (Deuteronomy 31:26).

An artist's conception of the **ark of the covenant**, a wooden box covered in gold according to very specific plans given by God to Moses.

ARK OF THE COVENANT. A beautiful chest that held the Ten Commandments. It later also held the book of Law, manna bread, and Aaron's rod (Deuteronomy 31:26; Exodus 16:33; Numbers 17:10). For Israel, the ark was a symbol of God's promise. It was part of their tabernacle, a movable reminder of their exodus and of God's leadership (also called "ark of the covenant of the Lord," Deuteronomy 10:8). Some scholars think the ark was lost in the 587 BC destruction of Jerusalem.

ARMAGEDDON (ahr muh GED uhn). The final battleground between good and evil. Mentioned by name only in Revelation 16:16. Comes from Hebrew for *Valley of Megiddo*.

ART. Old English for *are* (Matthew 6:9).

■ **ASCENSION**. Going up. Refers to the return of the resurrected Jesus to the Father. Jesus reappeared to His followers on earth before He ascended (Luke 24:51; Acts 1:8–11; Mark 16:19; 1 Corinthians 15:6).

▲ *Jesus ascended to (1) prepare a place for His disciples (John 14:2–3), (2) sit at the right hand of the Father and intercede for His own (Romans 8:34; Hebrews 7:25), and (3) wait for His return to earth (1 Corinthians 15:24–26).*

The **archangel** Michael humbles Satan in a seventeenth-century painting by Guido Reni. In scripture, angels often generate fear when they appear among humans.

ASHER (ASH ur). 1. Eighth son of Jacob (Genesis 35:26). 2. The tribe composed of Asher's descendants (Numbers 1:41).

ASHERAH (ASH uh ruh). Canaanite goddess who was worshiped in obscene ways (Judges 3:7). Wooden images of her were used for worship and were called a grove (Judges 6:25–32 KJV) or Asherah poles (Exodus 34:13 NIV).

ASHTAROTH, **ASHTORETH** (ASH tuh rahth) Pagan goddess who was the female counterpart to Baal. Worship of her was obscene (Judges 2:13; 1 Kings 11:5).

ASLEEP. 1. Gentle word Christians used for *dead*. See John 11:11–13 for Jesus' reference to Lazarus's death; see also Acts 7:60; 1 Corinthians 15:6; and 1 Thessalonians 4:13. 2. Physical sleep (Jonah 1:5; Matthew 8:24).

ASP. Snake, serpent (Isaiah 11:8).

ASS. Donkey (Matthew 21:2; Numbers 21:21).

ASSAY. Begin (1 Sam 17:39) or try (Job 4:2; Acts 16:7).

ASSEMBLY. People who have come together for a common purpose (Joel 1:14). Used in New Testament for church or gathering of believers (Acts 19:39; James 2:2). See **CHURCH, CONGREGATION**.

ASSURANCE. Confidence, trust, full conviction, certainty, firmness of mind. The basis of our assurance is Jesus Christ Himself (Isaiah 32:17; Acts 17:31; Colossians 2:2; Hebrews 10:22; 1 Thessalonians 1:5).

ASSYRIA. Powerful kingdom of the ancient Middle East (2 Kings 15:29). Its armies conquered Israel (the Northern Kingdom) and other nations. It was a cruel nation that alternated between success and defeat until its capital, Nineveh, was conquered in 612 BC by the Medes and Babylonians. It then came to an end (2 Kings 17:6; 18:9–12).

ASTRAY. Off course (Exodus 23:4). Against God's ways. On a path to unhappiness and destruction (Psalm 58:3; Isaiah 53:6; Proverbs 28:10; Matthew 18:13).
● *What people or events lead you astray? What have you done or said that might have led someone astray? How do you get back on course?*

ASTROLOGERS. Persons who seek answers in the stars and try to predict the future by them (Isaiah 47:13). Astrologers feel the position and movement of stars and planets influence people and events. Though astrologers were sometimes called wise, the Bible cautioned against them (Isaiah 47:13). God's wisdom was demonstrated as ten times better than the astrologers' wisdom (Daniel 1:20, 2:2, 10, 27–28).

ASUNDER. Apart (2 Kings 2:11). Divided, separated. Something put asunder usually involves pain (Acts 15:39). Asunder is used in the Bible to describe the divided Red Sea, broken emotions, split nations, the division of divorce, and divided friendships (Leviticus 1:17; Psalm 136:13; Job 16:12; Habakkuk 3:6; Matthew 19:6).

ATHENS. Capital city of Attica, an ancient district of east-central Greece, centered around a commanding view called the Acropolis (or "high city"). The apostle Paul preached to the Athenians who worshiped many gods. They did not, however, know the one true God (Acts 17). The response to Paul's preaching of the gospel was mixed, as some mocked and others said they would listen further.

ATONEMENT, TO MAKE. To cover, to cancel one's sins (Exodus 30:16). Making two into one (Romans 5:11). Atonement is motivated by the love of God. It occurs through the shedding of blood. The Old Testament shedding of animal blood pictured repentance, turning to God, and God's forgiveness. It had to be repeated annually.

In the New Testament Jesus shed His blood on the cross, and no other blood sacrifice would ever be needed. Jesus made atonement so persons might become one with God. Its meaning can be remembered by "At-one-ment with God" (Exodus 29:36; Leviticus 17:11; Nehemiah 10:33; Romans 5:11).

ATONEMENT, DAY OF. A Jewish holy day with sacrifices and ceremonies related to God's forgiveness of sin (Leviticus 16). At a certain point the high priest entered the Holy of Holies—the most holy place of the tabernacle (later the Temple) to confess the sin of the nation and ask forgiveness. Jews now observe the day of atonement in early October and call it Yom Kippur (Exodus 29:36; Leviticus 16:30; 23:27–28; 25:9). See **AZAZEL**, **SCAPEGOAT**. See **CALENDAR CHART** on pages 265–266 and **FEAST CHART** on page 96.

AUGUSTUS (aw GUHS tuhs). 1. Caesar Augustus, Roman emperor when Jesus was born (Luke 2:1). 2. Title for several Roman emperors (Acts 25:21, 25).

AUTHORITIES. 1. Unseen powers in the heavenly realm (Ephesians 3:10; 6:12; Colossians 1:16). 2. People in positions of authority (Luke 12:11).

AUTHORITY. Power, right to exercise power over someone else (Matthew 21:23). When used rightly, authority brings happiness (Proverbs 29:2). Jesus is the ultimate authority in any Christian's life (Matthew 7:29; 21:23; Jude 25).
● *Name someone in authority over you who makes your life more enjoyable.*

AVENGE. To pay someone back for wrong done. Do full justice. Vengeance is to be directed by God or reserved for Him (Numbers 31:23; Jeremiah 46:10; Romans 12:19). When tempted to avenge, substitute love and forgiveness (Leviticus 19:18; Matthew 6:12–15; Romans 12:19).

AWAKE. 1. Come to life after death (Isaiah 26:19; Daniel 12:2). 2. Give attention to (Psalm 35:23; 1 Corinthians 15:34). 3. Wake up physically (Mark 4:38).

AWE. Amazement. Worship. Respect. Admiration of God in response to something He has done (Psalm 4:4, 33:8; Habakkuk 3:2; Luke 5:26).

AZARIAH (as uh RIGH uh). Friend of Daniel who was renamed Abednego. Ate healthy food with and entered fiery furnace with Daniel (Daniel 1:5–6, 15; 3:16–29).

AZAZEL (AZ uh zel). A Hebrew word with uncertain meaning (Leviticus 16:8, 10 NRSV). Could mean "removal." Translated *scapegoat* in King James Version. *Azazel* is left untranslated in some other versions, for example the *Holman Christians Standard Bible* and *The Message*. Probably represented symbolic removal of sins from the people. In Leviticus 16, one goat was killed as a sacrifice; the sins were symbolically transferred to a goat that was sent into the wilderness—the world of evil (Leviticus 16). All of this was part of the day of atonement ceremony. See **SCAPEGOAT**.

BAAL (BAY uhl). A false god (Numbers 22:41). *Baalim* is the plural (Judges 2:11). Means "master," and was the male god worshiped by the people of Canaan, Phoenicia, and sometimes by Israelites. This nature god was supposed to cause people and things to be fertile. The worship involved self-torture, child sacrifice, and sinful sexual practices outside of marriage.

BABEL (BAY buhl). "Gate to God." Once all people spoke the same language. In pride and self-trust they tried to build a great city and brick tower—a gate to God—on the Plain of Shinar (Genesis 10:10; 11:1–9). In judgment, the

A 3,000-year-old figurine of **Baal**, on display in Paris's Louvre Museum.

Nobody knows what the tower of **Babel** looked like. . .but here is an idea from sixteenth-century Flemish painter Pieter Bruegel.

Lord jumbled their languages and confused their communication, humbling and scattering the people. So the "Tower of Babel" has come to stand for the "Tower of Confusion." Humans, in and of themselves, could not reach God or ever match Him.

BABYLON (BAB ih lahn), **BABYLONIA** (bab ih LOH nih uh). Capital city and its kingdom (Ezra 2:1; Genesis 10:10; 2 Kings 17:24). *Babel* is also the Greek spelling of Babylon. The kingdom location was also known as Shinar and Chaldea.

The Babylonians captured Assyria in 612 BC and ruled Judah (the southern kingdom).

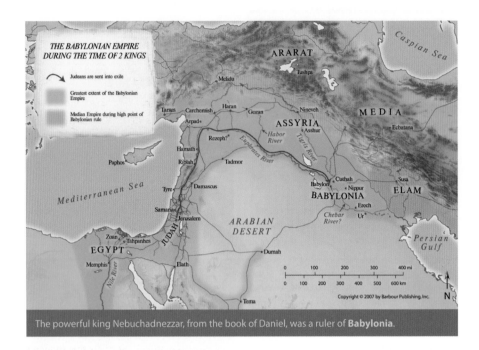

THE BABYLONIAN EMPIRE
DURING THE TIME OF 2 KINGS

Judeans are sent into exile

Greatest extent of the Babylonian Empire

Median Empire during high point of Babylonian rule

ARARAT

Caspian Sea

Tushpa

Melidu

Tarsus · Carchemish · Haran · Gozan · Nineveh

Arpad ·

MEDIA

Ecbatana

ASSYRIA · Asshur

Habor River

Rezeph? ·

Hamath ·

Paphos

Riblah ·

Tadmor

Mediterranean Sea

Tyre · Damascus

Babylon · Cuthah · Nippur

Susa

BABYLONIA · Erech

ELAM

Samaria ·

Jerusalem

ARABIAN DESERT

Chebar River? · Ur

Persian Gulf

Zoan · Tahpanhes

JUDAH

EGYPT

Dumah

Memphis

Elath

Tema

0   100   200   300   400 mi
0   100   200   300   400   500   600 km

Copyright © 2007 by Barbour Publishing, Inc.

N

The powerful king Nebuchadnezzar, from the book of Daniel, was a ruler of **Babylonia**.

They destroyed Jerusalem in 587 BC, but were defeated by Cyrus of Persia in 538 BC.

Babylon was so wicked it came to stand for evil and opposition to God. The similar condition of Rome in New Testament times seemingly caused it to be referred to as Babylon in 1 Peter 5:13 and Revelation 17:5.

BACKBITE. Slander (Psalm 15:3; Proverbs 25:23; Romans 1:30; 2 Corinthians 12:20). To say something bad about someone behind their back is the basic idea.

● *How can you avoid backbiting? When others backbite, what can you do? What would Christ want you to do?*

BACKSLIDE. To slide back from God or turn in unfaithfulness away from God (Jeremiah 2:19). Selfishness and stubbornness are at the heart of backsliding (Proverbs 14:14; Hosea 4:16). The

answer to backsliding is to return to God (Jeremiah 3:14, 22).

● *When anyone has decided to follow Jesus but turns back, he backslides. Which direction are you going in your commitment to Jesus?*

Balaam's is one of the funnier stories in the Bible—God caused Balaam's donkey to speak to him, and **Balaam** was so angry with the animal that he talked back! (See Numbers 22:21–35.)

BALAAM (BAY luhm). An evil prophet for hire. But he found himself blessing instead of cursing Israel because God controlled his tongue (Numbers 22–24). The Israelites he tried to lead away from God killed him (Numbers 31). In the New Testament Balaam is cited as a bad example (2 Peter 2:15; Jude 11; Revelation 2:14).
● *What does Balaam's life say to you about choosing a vocation? What are the results of trying to serve God without being committed to Him?*

BALANCES. Pair of scales (Revelation 6:5). The word used here is the same one translated "yoke" in Matthew 11:28–30, referring to Jesus' yoke. On spiritual scales, humans are always weighed and found wanting unless we are yoked to God in Christ and saved by His grace.

BALM. Soothing ointment or medicine from a plant found in Gilead and elsewhere (Jeremiah 8:22; 51:8).

BAPTISM. Immersion, submersion. (Romans 6:1–4.) Water baptism for new Christians calls for special attention (Matthew 28:18–20). Baptism doesn't save a person, but is a picture of his salvation and a sign of his obedience to Christ.

Going under the water is like a dead person being buried under the ground; it pictures that a person has died to his old way of life. Rising up from the water is like a dead person coming up from his grave in the earth; it pictures new life that is eternal and also pictures future resurrection from the grave (Romans 6:1–6).

This picture is not salvation any more than a picture of you is the real you, but the picture indicates what happened when a person accepted Christ as Lord and Savior. Baptism is never the salvation event but a picture of it.

Baptism is not a requirement of salvation, but it is a requirement of obedience. Baptism is the first step of discipleship.

Baptism can occur inside a church, in an outdoor river or lake, or in other settings—as with this US Navy mechanic being immersed in a front-end loader bucket in Iraq.

Scriptural baptism occurs only once and it is a matter between God and the individual when that once occurs. Wise and mature Christians may give helpful counsel to those who know Christ as Lord and Savior but are uncertain about whether their baptism was scriptural.

Baptism sometimes refers to the suffering and death of Christ (Mark 10:38–39; Luke 12:50). Christian baptism is in a sense a sharing of this death and resurrection and all that brought Christ to those events (Romans 6:1–7; Colossians 2:12). The baptism also gives witness to the death and resurrection of Christ and identifies with Him (Romans 6:3–6; Galatians 3:27).

▲ *Before Christian baptism, other uses of baptism existed. The Old Testament Mosaic laws in included a baptism of washing (Exodus 30:17–21; Leviticus 11:35). Naaman baptized himself in the Jordan River as an act of obedience related to his healing (2 Kings 5:4). When non-Jews became Jewish they immersed themselves.*

John the Baptist's baptism was like death to their old way of living and birth to a new kind of living (John 1:6, 11). It had the same elements of later Christian baptism: repentance, confession, evidence of changed lives, coming judgment, and a focus on Jesus.

Water baptism is for believers (Acts 2:38; Ephesians 4:5). That rules out the need for infant baptism. Many parents wisely dedicate their children to God, but water is not needed.

BAPTISM OF JESUS. John baptized Jesus, who never sinned (John 1:13–16). So Jesus' baptism was not one of repentance. Jesus said that His baptism was to fulfill all righteousness, which may simply mean that it was the right thing for him to do (Matthew 3:13–17). In this way, He identified with people and was a model for us to follow; Jesus affirmed John and his message. Perhaps Jesus also implied He would bear the sin of the whole world in carrying out the commission of God (see Matthew 10:38–40).

BAPTISM WITH THE HOLY SPIRIT. When Jesus comes into a life, the person is "baptized with the Spirit." That means he is filled with the presence and power of the Holy Spirit. The usual sequence of events is this: The Spirit comes into a person's life at conversion, and then the believer is baptized in water (John 1:33; John 14:16–17; Acts 11:15–16). So all Christians have been baptized with the Holy Spirit at conversion.

A thorough study of the Holy Spirit is helpful to understand what "baptism with the Holy Spirit" means (Acts 8:12–17). The unfolding drama of God's revelation through Pentecost and its sequence of events makes the relationship between water baptism and the Holy Spirit clearer. The Holy Spirit is the gift who comes with salvation (Acts 2:38) and as its seal (Ephesians 4:30).

BAPTIST (BAP tist). Biblical references identify John as the baptizer because he preached and practiced baptizing (Mark 1:4–5). Today *Baptist* refers to a number of Christian denominations who baptize believers by immersion.

The criminal **Barabbas** is portrayed as laughing at his good fortune—being released from prison while the innocent Jesus is falsely moved toward execution.

BARABBAS (buh RAB uhs). A treasonous murderer (Mark 15:7) and a robber (John 18:40) the crowd got Pilate to release instead of the innocent Jesus (Mark 15:6–15).

● *Every Christian is like Barabbas in at least one way: guilty of sin but freed from punishment by Christ. We don't know whether Barabbas ever accepted Christ as Lord and Savior. If not, it is sad that he accepted only the freedom of physical life and not the spiritual life Jesus came to bring.*

BARBARIAN. In the Bible, *barbarian* refers to anyone who did not speak Greek (Romans 1:14) or anyone who was not a part of the Greek-Roman culture (Colossians 3:11).

▲ *The idea of being a foreigner and being unable to understand each other's speech seems to apply to the word* barbarian *in 1 Corinthians 14:10–11. See* **GENTILE** *for another kind of religious, racial, and cultural prejudice.*

BAR-JESUS (bahr-JEE zuhs). A Jewish sorcerer and false prophet who was also known as Elymas (Acts 13:6–11). Not to be confused in any way with Jesus Christ. *Bar* means son, and *Jesus* was one of the spellings for Joshua, a popular Hebrew name.

BARNABAS (BAHR nuh buhs). Nickname that meant "Son of Encouragement" and was given to Joseph (or Joses), the son of Levi by the apostles (Acts 4:36 NRSV). The Greek word for *encouragement* implies the comforting, interceding, helping ministry that comes from the Holy Spirit (see John 14:16, 26; 15:26; 16:7). Barnabas was a generous person who gave others a second chance (Acts 9:27; 15:37–39).

● *Although Barnabas wasn't perfect (Galatians 2:13), his life was a model of someone who didn't mind being in second place as long as Christ was in first place (read Acts 11:15). Even if you have a nickname, why not try to earn another one: Son (or Daughter) of Encouragement?*

BARREN. Not bearing fruit (2 Kings 2:19), unable to bear children (Luke 1:7).

BARTHOLOMEW (bar THAHL uh myoo). An apostle (Matthew 10:3; Mark 3:18; Luke 6:14; Acts 1:13). We don't know anything else about him unless his complete name was Nathanael Bartholomew (see John 1:43–51; 21:2). John doesn't mention Bartholomew, and the other Gospels don't mention Nathanael. In each list of the apostles, Bartholomew and Philip are listed together. It was Philip who brought Nathanael to Jesus (John 1:45–49). For these reasons, some scholars believe Bartholomew and Nathanael refer to the same person.

BASE. As an adjective in the King James Version, *base* means humble or lowly (Daniel 4:17; Ezekiel 29:15; 2 Corinthians 10:1). The noun means a pedestal or thing to set something on (Ezra 3:3).

BASHAN. Area east and northeast of the Sea of Galilee (Deuteronomy 32:14). Fertile land famous for oaks and cattle (Amos 4:1).

BATH. A liquid measure of about 5.5 gallons (1 Kings 7:38).

BATHSHEBA (bath SHEE buh). The married woman David committed adultery with after he saw her bathing (2 Samuel 11). Bathsheba became pregnant by David while her husband Uriah was away at war. Then David caused Uriah to be thrust into the heat of battle to be killed, and David took Bathsheba to be his wife. After the death of their first son, Bathsheba bore David four more sons, including Solomon (2 Samuel 5:14; 1 Kings 1:11—2:19; 1 Chronicles 3:5).

BC. Before Christ. Note: Some prefer to use BCE and CE: "Before the Common Era" and "Common Era." See **AD**.

BEATITUDES. These statements tell who's happy (or blessed) and why. The term *beatitude* is not found in the English Bible but means a state of blessedness or happiness. It is used widely by Christians to refer to Jesus' sayings in Matthew 5:3–12.

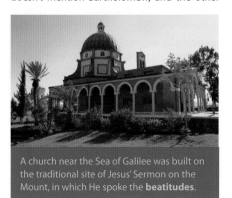

A church near the Sea of Galilee was built on the traditional site of Jesus' Sermon on the Mount, in which He spoke the **beatitudes**.

BEELZEBUB (bee EL zee buhb). Chief demon. A name for Satan, the prince of the demons (Matthew 12:24). Also spelled Beelzebul or Beelzeboul. Literally means "lord of flies" and was originally a Philistine god. All biblical uses of *Beelzebub* are in the New Testament.

BEERSHEBA (BEE ehr SHE buh). A historic site at the southern end of Canaan (Genesis 21:31–32; Judges 20:1).

BEFALL. Something that happens to a person—usually with the idea that the something is bad (Deuteronomy 31:17, 21).

■ **BEGET**. Father or bring forth. Used to list Jesus' ancestry (Matthew 1:2–16). Usually refers to physical fatherhood, but can refer to one who influences another and becomes a spiritual father (1 Corinthians 4:15). May be used of a woman to mean bearing children (see "gendereth," Galatians 4:24). *Begat* is the past tense and the form most often used.

BEGOTTEN. Past perfect form of *beget*. King James Version translation of Greek word meaning "unique," one and only (John 3:16, 18 NIV). One of a kind. John's writings use the word to refer only to Jesus (John 1:14, 18; 3:16, 18; 1 John 4:9). Some scholars translate the word with "only-begotten" or "begotten of the Only One."

BEHOLD. "Look!" (John 1:29). Consider (Luke 21:29). Often used for an introductory word as we use *now* or *then* (Matthew 1:20; Mark 1:2).

BELIAL (BEE lih uhl). A wicked or worthless person (1 Samuel 25:12). A synonym for Satan (2 Corinthians 6:15).

■ **BELIEVE**. Trust, have confidence in, have faith in, make a commitment to. May mean

Beryl.

simply "a head belief" (James 2:19), but in the Bible *believe* usually means a "heart belief" that trusts God with commitment, obedience, and faith (John 14:1; Romans 10:9–11; James 2:18–20). One who believes is willing to obey God, to put one's life into His hands. This belief is essential for eternal life and Christian living (John 20:31). *Believe* and *faith* are the verb and noun forms of the same root word. See **FAITH**.

BELTESHAZZAR (bel teh SHAZ ur). Name given to Daniel in Babylon (Daniel 1:7; 5:12). Means "may he protect his life." Bel was a Babylonian God (Daniel 1:7; 4:8). Daniel's life was protected, but by God, not Bel (Daniel 3:19–28; 6:22).

BENJAMIN (BEN juh min). Means "son of the right hand" (Genesis 35:18). 1. Youngest of Jacob's twelve sons. 2. Smallest of Israel's twelve tribes (Numbers 1:37). King Saul and the apostle Paul were Benjamites (1 Samuel 9:1–2; Philippians 3:5).

BEREA (also BEROEA) (buh **REE** uh). A city of Southern Macedonia (Acts 17:10–14).

▲ *The Bereans set a good example: They willingly listened to preaching, but they checked the preaching against the scriptures (Acts 17:11).*

BERYL. A hard stone that was usually green or bluish-green but sometimes yellow, pink, or white (Exodus 28:20; Revelation 21:20). Used in Ezekiel's description of the wheels in his vision (Ezekiel 1:16, 10:9; "crysolite" in NIV).

BESEECH. Appeal to, ask, beg (Luke 9:38; Romans 12:1). *Besought* is the past tense (Luke 8:38). Literally, the word translated "beseech" means to call alongside of (as in Ephesians 4:1).
▲ *Beseech also carries other varied shades of meaning (especially in Old Testament usage) such as to seek, to smooth feelings, to be gracious, to be in want, and to question or ask about something.*

BESET. Surround, encircle, attack from all sides (Psalm 22:12; Hebrews 12:1).
▲ *The rope of sin that surrounds us will tighten, trip us up, and drag us down as we try to race toward God (Hebrews 12:1). So we are to lay sin aside.*

BESIEGE. Surround a city with armed forces to starve it into surrender (Deuteronomy 20:19; 28:52). Press or hem in (1 Samuel 20:15).

BESTOW. Put, place, or stow; to give (Luke 12:17–18).

BETHANY (BETH uh nih). Means "house of figs." A village about two miles southeast of Jerusalem, near the Mount of Olives. Home of Mary, Martha, and Lazarus (John 11:1).

BETHEL (BETH uhl). Means "house of God." A town twelve miles north of Jerusalem (Genesis 28:19; 35:15). In the Old Testament only Jerusalem is mentioned more often. It was a sacred place to the Israelites.
▲ *Jacob had a life-changing, name-changing experience as God dealt with him at Bethel (Genesis 28:10–19; 35:1–15). Jacob experi-*

enced God there, and he came back there to another experience with God.
● *Have you had a Bethel experience in your life when you met God and received the new name Christian? If so, recall that experience and consider your present spiritual needs. If you are not a Christian, why not meet God in Christ now for His gift of eternal life and a new name? (See John 3; Acts 11:26.)*

BETHLEHEM (BETH lih hem). Means "House of Bread." A town six miles southwest of Jerusalem. David and Jesus were born there. (See Micah 5:2 and Luke 2:1–7 for the prophecy and fulfillment of Jesus' birth in Bethlehem.) David was anointed there, and it was known as the City of David (1 Samuel 16:13; Luke 2:4, 11).
▲ *Another Bethlehem lay seven miles northwest of Nazareth (Joshua 19:15). Jesus' birthplace was known as Bethlehem Judah, which distinguished it from the other Bethlehem.*

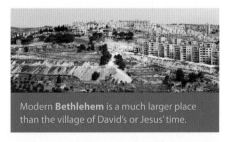
Modern **Bethlehem** is a much larger place than the village of David's or Jesus' time.

BETHSAIDA (beth SAY ih duh). City on the north shore of the Sea of Galilee—near the Jordan River. Home of Peter, Andrew, Philip (John 1:44; 12:21). Means "House of Fishing."

BETROTH. Engage to marry (Matthew 1:18; Deuteronomy 20:7). "Espouse" in King James Version. Much more binding than today's engagement. To end a betrothal required a divorce. Betrothal usually included exchange of gifts and a public announcement. Loyalty was required and the couple sometimes called each other husband and wife. Sex was postponed until marriage (Genesis 29:20–23).

BEWRAY. Reveal or disclose (Matthew 26:73). Much like *betray* except that it didn't carry the idea of disloyalty usually involved in betrayal.

BIBLE. The Bible is the inspired Word of God. The sixty-six books that make up Holy Scripture (thirty-nine Old Testament and twenty-seven New Testament books). *Biblia* is the Greek word for books; it is plural. But the books came to be known as one book: the Bible. The Old Testament was written in Hebrew (except for a little Aramaic in Ezra, Jeremiah, and Daniel). The New Testament was written in Greek. So most of the people in the world have to read a translation of the Bible from these original languages. The writing of the Old Testament was completed by about 300 BC, and the writing of the New Testament was completed between AD 90 and AD 100. Note: *Testament* also means "covenant." See **CANON**.

BIBLE TRANSLATIONS, ENGLISH. The Bible was first written in Hebrew and Greek, so translations are necessary for most of us. There are different kinds of translations: Word-for-word translations try to match the original Hebrew and Greek as

An Old Dutch **Bible**. God's Word has been translated into literally hundreds of languages around the world.

closely as possible in English (such as the King James Version and the New American Standard Bible). Other translations focus on thought-for-thought translation more than word-for-word translation (such as the New International Version). Then there are paraphrases: Paraphrases are efforts to get the Bible into very readable English, but they necessarily take a lot of liberty with the original Hebrew and Greek languages (such as The Living Bible or The Message).

● *Why not ask your pastor to list his favorite (1) word-for-word translation, (2) thought-for-thought translation, and (3) paraphrased edition? Then compare several chapters (such as John 5:39–40; Ephesians 4:11–12; 1 John 3:6–9). "The Word of God" is unchanging but dynamic!*

THE BIBLE IN ENGLISH

(DUE TO SPACE CONSTRAINTS, NOT EVERY TRANSLATION IS MENTIONED)
OLD ENGLISH TRANSLATION (AD 300–1100)
AD 300s—First Christians arrive in Britain
AD 400s—Angles, Saxons, and Jutes arrive in Britain
AD 500–700—Evangelization of Angles, Saxons, and Jutes
AD 700–1100—Only parts of the Bible translated into "Old English"

MIDDLE ENGLISH TRANSLATION (1100–1500)

1066—Norman invasion brings French influence into language development and creates "Middle English"

IMPORTANT PERSONS:

John Wycliffe—died 1384. Wanted to take gospel to commoners. Began translating from Latin into English in 1380. Was assisted by:

Nicholas of Hereford—whose translation followed the Latin Vulgate very closely, and

John Purvey—whose revision of Nicholas's translation used more idiomatic expressions

William Tyndale—c. 1494–1536. Bible translator whose completed English translation of the New Testament was much of the basis of the 1611 **KJV**. Sought to put the Greek and **LXX** into the vernacular so the common people could read scripture.

IMPORTANT EVENTS AT THE END OF THIS PERIOD:

The Renaissance—a revival of learning that prompted renewed interest in the original Hebrew and Greek. A new challenge to authority also emerged.

Invention of the printing press (1453)—made printed material accessible to the masses rather than to a few.

Protestant Reformation (beginning in 1517)—Martin Luther and those who followed had a tremendous desire to get the Bible into the hands of the common people.

MODERN ENGLISH TRANSLATION (1500–1900)

1525–26	William Tyndale translated New Testament into English from Greek. Was translating Old Testament at the time of his death as a martyr in 1536.
1535	Miles Coverdale completed and published first complete Bible in English from Tyndale's work, Greek and Hebrew, and other sources.
1537	**Matthew's Bible**. A complete English Bible from Tyndale's and Coverdale's work by John Rogers. Received royal sanction of King Henry **VIII**.
1539	**Great Bible.** A revision by Coverdale of Matthew's Bible. Was placed in every church in England at the order of King Henry.
1560	**Geneva Bible.** Produced by Protestant scholars in Geneva from the original languages and Tyndale's work. (Sometimes called the "Breeches Bible," because in Gen. 3:7 Adam and Eve make "breeches" for themselves from fig leaves.)
1568	**Bishop's Bible.** A revision of the Great Bible. Authorized by the Church of England as its official translation.
1582 and 1609–10	**Rheims/Douai Translation.** Roman Catholic translation from the Latin Vulgate of the Old and New Testaments so named because of where they were translated; the Old Testament at Douai in 1609–10 preceded by the New Testament at Rheims in 1582.
1611	**King James Version (or Authorized Version).** Commissioned by King James I of England and translated by a number of Bible scholars. A revision of the 1602 edition of the Bishop's Bible with the aid of the Hebrew and Greek texts and a dependence upon the work of William Tyndale.
1885	**Revised Version.** A revision of the Authorized Version incorporating more recently discovered manuscripts and more modern language usage. By a group of British and some American scholars.

TWENTIETH-CENTURY ENGLISH TRANSLATIONS

1901	**American Standard Version.** A revision of the 1885–1891 UK revision of the **KJV**.
1903	**New Testament in Modern Speech.** R. T. Weymouth's attempt to render Greek grammatical constructions carefully.
1924	**A New Translation of the Bible.** An idiomatic, colloquial, and sometimes Scottish translation by James Moffatt.
1927	**Centenary Translation of the New Testament.** Helen B. Montgomery's missionary heart produced a translation in the language of everyday life.
1937	**Williams New Testament.** By Charles B. Williams. A Baptist professor's attempt to translate into English the nuances of Greek verbs.
1938	**The Bible: An American Translation.** E. J. Goodspeed and J. M. Powis Smith produced the first modern American translation with the Apocrypha.
1952	**Revised Standard Version.** Revision of the American Standard Version and the King James Version by an international translation committee seeking to maintain literary awesomeness for worship.
1955	**Holy Bible.** Translated by Ronald Knox, a Roman Catholic, from the Latin Vulgate.
1958	**New Testament in Modern English.** A free translation by J. B. Phillips originally done for his youth club.
1965	**Amplified Bible.** A version by the Lockman Foundation suggesting various wordings throughout the text.
1966	**Jerusalem Bible.** Originally translated into French by Roman Catholic scholars from the original languages.
1969	**New Berkeley (Modern Language) Bible.** A Revision of the Berkeley Version of 1959 by Gerrit Verkuyl, with attached notes.
1970	**New English Bible.** A translation with literary quality but some idiosyncratic language. Translated by representatives of Britain's major churches and Bible societies and based on the most recent textual evidence.
1970	**New American Bible.** A new translation by Roman Catholic scholars (the Bishop's Committee of the Confraternity of Christian Doctrine) from the original languages.
1971	**New American Standard Bible.** A revision by the Lockman Foundation of the American Standard Version of 1901 with the goal of maintaining literal translation.
1971	**The Living Bible.** A conservative American paraphrase by Kenneth N. Taylor, begun in 1962 for his children.
1976	**Good News Bible (Today's English Version).** A translation by the American Bible Society into "vernacular" English.
1979	**New International Version.** A readable translation by evangelical scholars incorporating the most recent textual evidence.
1982	**New King James Version.** A modernization of the King James Version of 1611. Based on the original language texts available to the King James Version translators.
1987	**New Century Version.** A translation committee's update of the International Children's Bible.
1989	**New Revised Standard Version.** A translation committee's update of the Revised Standard Version.
1989	**Revised English Bible.** A British committee's update of the New English Bible maintaining literary quality but avoiding idiosyncratic language.
1991	**Contemporary English Version (New Testament).** A simplified text originally conceived for children and produced by the American Bible Society.
1996	**New Living Translation.** Revision plans for *The Living Bible* paraphrase grew into a new and enriched translation from the Hebrew and Greek texts. The original ease of reading continues to be a strong factor.
1996	**New International Reader's Version.** Translated by the International Bible Society, following the pattern of the New International Version, but with simpler English for ease of reading.

OTHER POPULAR ENGLISH TRANSLATIONS SINCE 2000

2001	**English Standard Version.** Adapted from the Revised Standard Version of 1952.
2002	**The Message.** A translation into "contemporary idiom," that keeps the Bible message fresh and understandable but includes strong language skills behind the paraphrase.
2004	**Holman Christian Standard Bible.** Begun in 1984 and completed twenty years later by an international, interdenominational team of 90 scholars, the **HCSB** was intended to be an accurate yet readable Bible in contemporary English.
2005	**Today's New International Version.** A new translation by the Committee on Bible Translation, which created the New International Version. A 2011 update of the **NIV** replaced the **TNIV**.

THE BOOKS OF THE BIBLE

39 OLD TESTAMENT BOOKS

LAW	HISTORY	POETRY/WISDOM	MINOR PROPHETS
Genesis	Joshua	Job	Hosea
Exodus	Judges	Psalms	Joel
Leviticus	Ruth	Proverbs	Amos
Numbers	1 Samuel	Ecclesiastes	Obadiah
Deuteronomy	2 Samuel	Song of Solomon	Jonah
	1 Kings	**MAJOR PROPHETS**	Micah
	2 Kings	Isaiah	Nahum
	1 Chronicles	Jeremiah	Habakkuk
	2 Chronicles	Lamentations	Zephaniah
	Ezra	Ezekiel	Haggai
	Nehemiah	Daniel	Zechariah
	Esther		Malachi

27 NEW TESTAMENT BOOKS

GOSPELS	LETTERS OF PAUL		
Matthew	Romans	1 Timothy	2 Peter
Mark	1 Corinthians	2 Timothy	1 John
Luke	2 Corinthians	Titus	2 John
John	Galatians	Philemon	3 John
HISTORY	Ephesians	**GENERAL LETTERS**	Jude
Acts	Philippians	Hebrews	**PROPHECY**
	Colossians	James	Revelation
	1 Thessalonians	1 Peter	
	2 Thessalonians		

BILDAD (BIL dad). Known as one of Job's comforters even though he brought no comfort (Job 8; 18; 25).

▲ *Though people speak of "the patience of Job," his kind of patience was more endurance and faith than merely listening to supposed comforters.*

BIRTHRIGHT. Special rights based on order of birth and inheritance. For example, the first-born Hebrew son received a double portion of the inheritance (Deuteronomy 21:15–17).

BISHOP. Overseer or leader of a church (Acts 20:17, 28; 1 Peter 5:2). Used interchangeably with elder and presbyter (see Titus 1:5, 7; 1 Timothy 3:1; 4:14).

BISHOPRICK. Supervision, leadership (Acts 1:20). The office or responsibility of a bishop.

BITTER HERBS. Herbs eaten with a lamb during the Passover feast that symbolize the bitter experiences of the Hebrews in Egypt before the Exodus (Exodus 12:8). The exact herb is unknown but horseradish is used today.

BLASPHEME, BLASPHEMY. Slander, insult the honor of, injure the reputation of, attack, say untruths about. Usually refers to cursing God or using abusive and cutting language about Him, His name, or His Word (Leviticus 24:16; Romans 2:24; Titus 2:5). Because the Pharisees did not believe Jesus was God's Son, they thought He was blaspheming God by admitting to be the Christ (Matthew 26:63–65).

BLESS. To give good, wish good, be thankful, praise God. When God blesses, He helps, favors, makes happy (Genesis 1:28; 12:2–3; 14:19–20 Acts 3:26; Matthew 5:3–12). When persons bless God, they praise, worship, and thank Him (Psalm 103). Persons can bless other persons

(Genesis 27:4). To bless food is to be prayerfully grateful for it (Matthew 14:19). Peace, not material prosperity, is the main goal of blessings.

■ **BLESSED**. Made happy by God, fortunate. (Matthew 5:2–12; Psalm 1:1). Used in Old Testament to praise God (Psalm 18:46).

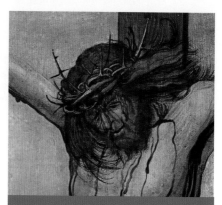

Many images of Jesus' final hours try to portray a bloodless crucifixion. . .but this sixteenth-century painting by Albrecht Altdorfer shows Jesus bleeding. New Testament writers were adamant that Jesus' shed **blood** was the atonement for sin.

BLOOD. A synonym for life (Genesis 9:4). Most of the references in the Old Testament use *blood* to refer to death or violence (Genesis 4:10; 9:6; Proverbs 1:16). Blood was a key element in the Old Testament sacrificial system (Leviticus 1:5; 3:2; 4:18). In the New Testament the shedding of Christ's blood or His death provided our way to salvation (Romans 5:9–10; Hebrews 9:12–14).

▲ *No one ever got saved by animal sacrifices: the animals' blood was symbolic of repentance and God's atoning grace that saves and is seen fulfilled in Jesus Christ for all ages (see Leviticus 16; Hebrews 10). It has been said that the sheep died for the shepherd in the Old Testament, but in the New Testament, the Shepherd died for the sheep. Only Jesus' blood saves as the unfolding Old and New Testaments reveal fully.*

BLOODGUILTINESS. Guilt resulting from killing someone (Psalm 51:14).

BLOT. To rub off or wipe away (Exodus 32:32–33). The Old Testament speaks of blotting out the enemy (Deuteronomy 9:14). Both the Old Testament and New Testament record requests asking God to blot out sin (Psalm 51:9; Acts 3:19).
- *Think of an action or attitude in your life that the Bible says is wrong. Have you asked Jesus to blot out that sin? Why or why not? The Bible reveals repentance as essential for receiving the atoning salvation of Jesus Christ. No work of any kind can blot out sin.*

BOAST. In a good sense, used to praise or speak about God, someone, or something (Psalm 44:8). In a bad sense, boasting over wrong actions or taking pride in oneself (Psalm 52:1; Ephesians 2:9).
- *How have you used boasting in a good way? How have you used it in a bad way?*

BOAZ. Ruth's husband (Ruth 4:13). A wealthy relative of Naomi (Ruth's mother-in-law) who allowed Ruth to gather grain in his fields to support her and her mother-in-law. Boaz later married Ruth and became an ancestor of David (Ruth 1–4).

Boaz speaks with Ruth in a seventeenth-century Dutch painting. He quickly noticed the new woman gleaning his fields near Bethlehem.

BODY. Often used as a symbol of the church or Christians (Romans 12:4–5; 1 Corinthians 12:12–14; Ephesians 4:12; Colossians 1:18).

BONDAGE. Slavery (Exodus 13:3; Romans 8:15). Also refers to life before knowledge of Christ (Galatians 4:7–9).
- *What unchristian habit enslaves you or puts you in bondage? How can Christ help you to be free? See Philippians 4:13 for assurance that Christ empowers us to do all things in Him.*

BONDS. Something that binds or restrains. The apostle Paul spoke of his imprisonment as bonds (Philippians 1:16; Colossians 4:3).

BONES. In the book of Ezekiel the valley of dry bones was a symbol of the people of Israel in their hopeless condition (Ezekiel 37:11). God promised the bones would rise, which offered hope to Israel.

BOOK. In Bible times books were rolled up parchments or skins called *scrolls* (Jeremiah 36:2).

BOOK OF LIFE. A book (or scroll) with the names of those who will have eternal life instead of judgment and punishment (Exodus 32:32–33; Luke 10:20; Hebrews 12:23; Revelation 13:8; 17:8; 20:12, 15).

BOOTHS, FEAST OF. Also referred to as Feast of Tabernacles. Popular and joyful fall feast lasting for seven days and ending with a solemn assembly on the eighth day (Leviticus 23:34–36). The feast celebrated the final harvest of olives and fruits and also the start of the civil new year. It was one of the three great feasts celebrated by the Hebrew people and would be similar to our Thanksgiving. See **FEAST CHART** on page 96.

BOOTY. Property or people captured in war (Jeremiah 49:32). Sometimes the conqueror kept the booty for his own use, and sometimes he destroyed it. Booty is also referred to as prey or spoil (Numbers 31:32).

BORN AGAIN. A second birth that is spiritual (John 3:3). In the Christian realm, to receive Christ as Lord and Savior and to commit your life to Him (1 Peter 1:23). Jesus told Nicodemus it was necessary to be born again to have a right relationship with God (John 3:5–18). Ephesians 2:1–10 identifies the factors of grace, faith, and salvation as a gift.
●List actions people do to try to have a right relationship with God. What does John 3:16 say about the matter?

BORNE. Carried, as a load (Matthew 23:4).

BOSOM. Chest or breast, center of emotions, heart (Exodus 4:6; Ecclesiastes 7:9; Luke 16:23).

BOTTLE. Container in the Old Testament. In the New Testament, the word *bottle* translates the word "skin" in Jesus' teaching about putting new wine into new bottles. The old skins (bottles) would break as the wine fermented (Luke 5:37–38 KJV).

BOUGHS. Branches of a tree (Daniel 4:12).

BOUNTY. Blessing or benevolence (2 Corinthians 9:5).

BOW. Rainbow (Genesis 9:13). Also, an important weapon in Old Testament times (1 Chronicles 5:18). The bow was usually made of seasoned wood with the string made from ox-gut. The metal-tipped arrows were made of reed or light wood.

BOWELS. The inner part of the body (Job 30:27) or deep feelings (1 John 3:17).

BRANCH. Sometimes refers to the Messiah and the kingdom that would come out of this Branch (Isaiah 11:1; Jeremiah 23:5). Tree branches were used to make booths in the Feast of Tabernacles (also called the Feast of Booths; see Leviticus 23:40). People paved Jesus' path with branches when He made His triumphal entry into Jerusalem (Mark 11:8).

BREACH. An opening or broken place (2 Kings 22:5).

BREAD. Usually made from barley or wheat, extremely important in biblical life (Genesis 3:19). Not only was bread a part of the diet, but the grain to make bread was used for trade and commerce. Unleavened bread (made without yeast) played a key role in the Exodus from Egypt and in the Passover Feast (Exodus 12:15–17).
    Satan tempted Jesus to turn a stone into bread (Matthew 4:3). Jesus claimed to be the bread of life (John 6:48) and used bread as a symbol for His broken body (Luke 24:30).

BREASTPLATE. A religious decorative garment worn by the high priest (Exodus 28:15–30). Also a protective garment of metal or leather worn by soldiers on the upper part of the body to protect the vital organs (Ephesians 6:14).

BREECHES. Undergarments worn by men (Exodus 28:42).

BRETHREN. Brothers. Used of family members (Genesis 47:1), people of the same nationality (Exodus 2:11), and of those who have a spiritual kinship (Acts 20:32).

BRIDE. Besides its usual sense, bride can also mean the church (Revelation 21:9). In John's vision he referred to the church as the bride of Christ (Revelation 21:9). Along with the Spirit, the bride invites all to partake of salvation (Revelation 22:17).

BRIDEGROOM. Christ used this term to refer to Himself (Mark 2:19–20).

BRIMSTONE. The English word means a burning stone. Sometimes referred to as *sulfur* (Luke 17:29 NRSV). Used in connection with God's judgment (Psalm 11:6; Revelation 19:20).

BROOD. Literally "nest." Used to refer to young birds cared for by their mother (Luke 13:34).

BUCKLER. Round or oblong shield used for defense and protection (1 Chronicles 5:18). Also used to refer to God's protective care (Psalm 18:2).

BULL. Animal used as a sacrifice (Hebrews 10:4). See **BULLOCK**.

BULLOCK. Steer, young neutered bull. Used extensively in the Jewish sacrificial system (Exodus 29:11).

Yoked **bulls** work together to plow a field in Italy, illustrating the New Testament command to "bear ye one another's burdens" (Galatians 6:2).

BULRUSH. A plant that grows by water, reed, papyrus (Exodus 2:3).

▲ *Papyrus was often used to make scrolls on which scripture was written.*

BULWARK. Fortress (Ecclesiastes 9:14).

BURDEN. A heavy load (2 Kings 5:17; Luke 11:46). Used with a prophecy of doom (Isaiah 15:1). *Burden* appears in Galatians 6:2 and 6:5, but separate Greek words are translated—the distinction being that we are to help each other bear life's heavy loads, but each person is to bear his own pack or carry his own weight.

● *What kind of heavy burdens are you carrying in life? What help can you find in Matthew 11:28–30?*

BURIED. Put in a grave or tomb (Numbers 20:1). In biblical times people were buried in an open grave and covered with stones or in a hillside cave or in a burial chamber. Paul compared baptism to death and burial followed by resurrection (Romans 6:1–6).

BURN. To consume or be consumed by fire (Exodus 3:2; Luke 3:17). Sometimes used to speak of emotions (Psalm 79:5; Luke 24:32; 1 Corinthians 7:9). The burning of offerings was part of the Jewish sacrificial system (Exodus 29:25).

BURNING BUSH. Probably a thorny bush found in the Sinai area (Exodus 3:2). God caused this plant to burn so He could catch Moses' attention.

● *What are some ways God uses to get people's attention today? your attention?*

BYWORD. A proverb, a term of scorn or derision (1 Kings 9:7; Job 30:9). Usually used in connection with God's judgment on Israel.

48

CAESAR (SEE zur). Name of a Roman family. Title of all Roman emperors after Julius Caesar (Matthew 22:17).

CAESAREA (sess uh REE uh). City that Herod the Great built and named in honor of Caesar Augustus. Located twenty-three miles south of Mount Carmel (on the coast of the Mediterranean Sea). Paul was imprisoned there for two years (Acts 23:33). Roman capital of Palestine.

This aqueduct, begun by Herod the Great, is still a prominent feature of **Caesarea** today.

CAESAREA PHILIPPI (FILL ih pigh). Different from Caesarea, located about twenty-five miles north of the Sea of Galilee in the mountains of Lebanon. Philip, son of Herod the Great, enlarged the city and named it in honor of the Roman emperor. Peter made his confession that Jesus is the Christ the Son of the living God there (Matthew 16:13–17).

CAIAPHAS. (KIGH uh fuhs) High priest who prophesied Jesus' death, plotted against Him, tried Him, and condemned Him (John 11:47–53; Matthew 26:3–68). Later took part in a trial of Peter and John (Acts 4:6–7).

▲ *Jewish priests did not have the power to put someone to death, so they came up with a charge that would anger the Roman authorities: The priests accused Jesus of claiming to be king of the Jews. The Romans saw this as a threat to Caesar's position.*

The high priest, **Caiaphas**, condemns Jesus in a stained glass window from a French chapel.

CAIN. (KAYN) First son of Adam and Eve (Genesis 4:1). Cain and his offering were unacceptable to God. Cain murdered his brother Abel, who—along with his offering—was acceptable to God. This murder was an example of the progression of sin: failing to please God led to jealousy, which led to anger, which led to murder, which led to lying to God, which led to abandoning God (Genesis 4:1–24; Hebrews 11:4; 1 John 3:12; Jude 11).

▲ *From Cain came the expression "raising Cain," which means to make trouble.*

● *What makes a person and his worship acceptable to God? For help in answering this question,* see **CONVICT OF SIN, REPENT, BELIEVE, CONFESS.**

EARLY CAESARS OF ROME

CAESAR	DATES	BIBLICAL REFERENCE
Julius Caesar	49–44 BC	
Second Triumvirate	44–31 BC	
Augustus (Octavian)	31 BC–AD 14	Luke 2:1
Tiberius	AD 14–37	Luke 3:1
Caligula (Gaius)	AD 37–41	
Claudius	AD 41–54	Acts 11:28; 17:7; 18:2
Nero	AD 54–68	Acts 25:11; Phil. 4:22
Galba, Otho, and Vitellius	AD 68–69	
Vespasian	AD 69–79	
Titus	AD 79–81	
Domitian	AD 81–96	
Nerva	AD 96–98	
Trajan	AD 98–117	
Hadrian	AD 117–138	

CALDRON. Large cooking pot (1 Samuel 2:14).

CALEB. (KAY luhb) 1. Son of Jephunneh who was appointed one of twelve spies sent to scout the land of Canaan (Numbers 13–14; 1 Chronicles 4:15). Of the spies only Caleb and Joshua believed the Israelites could conquer the Canaanites. The rest of the spies protested that the Canaanites were too big and strong for the Israelites to fight. Their doubts spread to the rest of the Israelites. Caleb and Joshua were rewarded by being the only adults of their generation to enter the promised land. See **CANAAN.** 2. A less well known Caleb, also of the tribe (family) of Judah, was the son of Hezron (1 Chronicles 2:18–19, 42).

▲ *The promised land was not empty but had people living there. Ten of the spies thought of themselves as grasshoppers against giants in Canaan (Numbers 13:33). Israel had to decide whether to obey God in faith and take the land or give in to their fear and poor self-image and disobey God.*

● *What do you think gave Caleb (and Joshua) courage to stand against the majority? How might these same factors help you?*

CALENDAR. See **FEAST CHART** on page 96 and **CALENDAR CHART** on pages 265–266.

CALL, CALLING. Noun: A summons or appointment from God to serve Him in specific ways for specific purposes (1 Samuel 3:4; Isaiah 49:1; Ephesians 4:1–3). May refer to a vocation, or to God's calling to say yes to Him for all of life. God's calling invites all people to become Christians, followers of God in Christ (Matthew 9:13; Philippians 3:14). Verb: To depend on God, invite His attention in prayer (Genesis 4:26; Jeremiah 33:3). To name, describe; often involves the beginning of a relationship with a person or thing (Genesis 1:5, 2:19; Matthew 1:21; Mark 10:18).

▲All Christians are called to ministry (2 Corinthians 5:18–20); many Christians are called to vocational ministry as pastors, teachers, evangelists, or other special roles. Whatever a person's vocation, their Christian calling is just as strong as a call to vocational ministry. Note that anyone can take away a person's job, but no one can take away God's calling (1 Corinthians 7:20–24; Ephesians 4:1–3).

●God's calling always continues, but His unfolding will occasionally requires a changed way of life. What is God calling you to do now? What are you willing to become?

Some believe the meaning of **Calvary**—"the skull"—indicated a skull-like appearance in the hillside where Jesus died.

CALVARY. Literally, "the skull." Place near Jerusalem where Jesus was crucified (Luke 23:33 KJV). Greek/Latin equivalent for the Hebrew *Golgotha* (Matthew 27:33; Mark 15:22; John 19:17).

▲Scholars are uncertain about the exact site of Calvary.

CANA. (KAY nuh) Village in Galilee north of Nazareth where Jesus attended a wedding and turned water into wine (John 2:1, 11). He also healed a nobleman's son there (John 4:46–50). Nathanael's home (John 21:2).

● How could miracles (or signs) encourage people to believe in Jesus (John 2:11)?

CANAAN. (KAY nuhn) 1. The promised land God gave to the Israelites (Genesis 17:8). A land between the Jordan River and the Mediterranean Sea and north of Philistia. Old name for Palestine. 2. Son of Ham, a son of Noah. Noah put a curse on Canaan because of Ham's improper behavior (Genesis 9:18; 10:22–25).

CANAANITES. A Semitic tribe that lived in Canaan before the Israelites conquered it (Exodus 13:5). They worshiped false gods—such as Baal—in wild and evil ways. The Canaanites were the descendants of Ham, the son of Noah (Genesis 9:18–19).

▲ Some Canaanites stayed and were a bad influence on the Israelites. This was even after God warned the Israelites to have nothing to do with them (Genesis 28:6). The Canaanites were huge people. Ten of the twelve spies said they felt like grasshoppers in comparison (Numbers 13:32–33).

CANON. Means "rule" or "standard." The canon is the list of books believers accept as the Bible. The English word *canon* is not in the Bible, but the concept is translated as "rule," or "standard" in Galatians 6:16. If a book is in the canon it is recognized as inspired by God and is called *canonical*. These books are the rule for the Christian's faith and life.

▲ Both Jewish and Christian believers decided with God's help which books were the Word of God. They thought the books showed themselves to be God's Word by their nature, content, usage, and authorship.

Jesus and His disciples had only the Old Testament. The Old Testament had come out

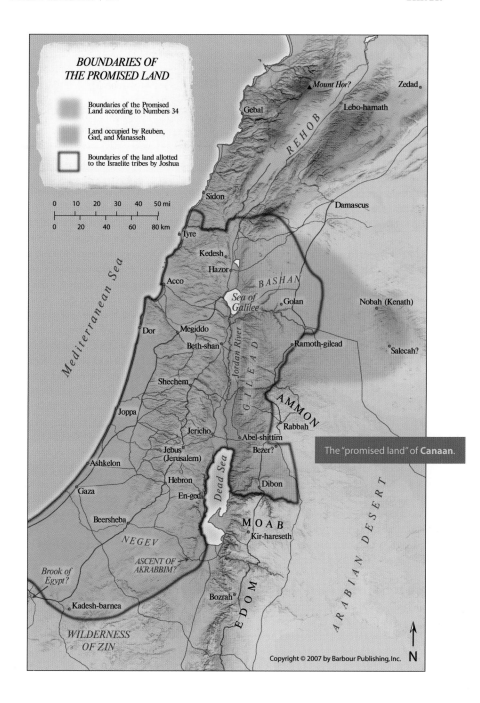

**BOUNDARIES OF
THE PROMISED LAND**

Boundaries of the Promised
Land according to Numbers 34

Land occupied by Reuben,
Gad, and Manasseh

Boundaries of the land allotted
to the Israelite tribes by Joshua

0   10   20   30   40   50 mi

0   20   40   60   80 km

Mediterranean Sea

Mount Hor?   Zedad

Gebal   Lebo-hamath

REHOB

Sidon   Damascus

Tyre

Kedesh

Hazor

Acco   BASHAN

Sea of
Galilee   Golan   Nobah (Kenath)

Dor   Megiddo

Beth-shan   Jordan River   GILEAD   Ramoth-gilead   Salecah?

Shechem

AMMON

Joppa

Jericho   Rabbah

Jebus
(Jerusalem)   Abel-shittim

Bezer?   The "promised land" of **Canaan**.

Ashkelon

Hebron   Dibon

Gaza   En-gedi   Dead Sea

Beersheba   MOAB

NEGEV   Kir-hareseth

ASCENT OF
AKRABBIM?   ARABIAN DESERT

Brook of
Egypt?

Kadesh-barnea   Bozrah

EDOM

WILDERNESS
OF ZIN

Copyright © 2007 by Barbour Publishing, Inc.

N

of God's revelation of Himself to the Hebrew nation. God further inspired the New Testament through Jesus' teachings, the apostles' writings, and some other Christians' writings. Most Christians agree that the Bible was complete by about AD 100. All scripture is to be tested against the life and teachings of Christ. See **BIBLE, BIBLE TRANSLATIONS.**

● *Why do you think some groups claim to have new or different writings from God other than the sixty-six books of the Bible? How can we tell these other books are false or not God's inspired Word?*

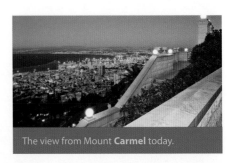
The view from Mount **Carmel** today.

CANOPY (NIV). 1. Used literally for a cover made of cloth, wood, or other material (2 Kings 16:18). The heavens are like a canopy to God (Isaiah 40:22). 2. Used figuratively to signify God's protection (Isaiah 4:5–6; 2 Samuel 22:12). 3. Nebuchadnezzar spread a royal canopy as a sign of God's sovereignty (Jeremiah 43:10).

CAPERNAUM (kuh PURR nay uhm). City on northwest shore of the Sea of Galilee. Jesus moved to Capernaum at the beginning of His ministry and Capernaum became His home base (Matthew 4:13–15; 9:1). Though Jesus did much teaching and many miracles there, few people from Capernaum followed Jesus. So Jesus grieved over Capernaum for its lack of faith (Matthew 11:20–24). Miracles occurring in Capernaum included healing a centurion's servant, a paralyzed man, and a nobleman's son (Matthew 8:5–13; Mark 2:1–12; John 4:47–53).
● *Literally means "Village of Nahum."*

CAPTIVE, **CAPTIVITY**. Being held as prisoner or an exile (Amos 1:15; Lamentations 1:5). Usually refers to the time in which the Hebrews were removed from their homeland. Ten tribes of Israel, the Northern Kingdom, were held captive by Assyria (2 Kings 17:6; 18:11). The

captivity began in stages from about 740 BC to 722–721 BC (when Samaria fell).

The tribes of Judah and Benjamin made up the Southern Kingdom. These tribes were held captive in Babylon from about 587–586 BC to 537 BC. Like the Northern Kingdom captivity, the Southern Kingdom's captivity occurred in stages, with portions of the Israelites taken captive over a period of several years. This captivity is known as the Babylonian Captivity.

The Southern Kingdom's captivity began under Nebuchadnezzar and ended under Cyrus of Persia. In 538 BC, the remnant of Hebrews returned to their home under the decree of Cyrus, king of Persia, who had conquered Babylon the year before. It's uncertain what happened to the Northern Kingdom exiles. See **BABYLON, EXILE.**
▲ *Read about the invasions of the Northern Kingdom and the Captivity in 2 Kings 15:29; 1 Chronicles 5:26; 2 Kings 17:3,5; 17:6–7; Ezra 4:2,10. Read about the Southern Kingdom's similar fate in 2 Chronicles 36:2–7; Jeremiah 45:1; Daniel 1:1–3; 2 Kings 24:14–16; 25:2–21; Ezra 1:1–4; 2:64–65; Nehemiah 1:11; Jeremiah 29:1, 5–7; Ezekiel 1:1; Daniel 2:48; 9:2; Zechariah 6:10.*

CARE, CAREFUL. Full of care, worried, anxious, afraid (Jeremiah 17:8; Daniel 3:16; Luke 10:41; Philippians 4:6; 1 Peter 5:7). Also used as we use *careful* today: caring, concerned, cautious, attentive to detail (2 Kings 4:13; Philippians 4:10; Titus 3:8).

CARMEL. (KAHR m'l) 1. Village in the country of Judah, south of Bethlehem and west of the Dead Sea where Nabal sheared sheep (1 Samuel 25). 2. Mount Carmel is a mountain at the head of a range of mountains with the same name. It extends into the Mediterranean Sea. At Mount Carmel Elijah challenged the prophets of Baal; and from Mount Carmel Elisha came to heal the Shunamite woman's son (1 Kings 18:20–40; 2 Kings 4:25).

▲ *Literally means "garden-land" or "fruitful land." Beautiful and plentiful plants covered Mount Carmel.*

CARNAL. Flesh, fleshly (Romans 8:7; 1 Corinthians 3:3). Controlled by human nature rather than by God. A carnal act is anything opposed to or in contrast to God and His purposes. Carnal attitudes and actions cannot please God (Romans 8:5–9). Occasionally *carnal* means simply material (Romans 15:27).

CENSER. Shovel-like holder used for carrying hot coals and for burning incense (Leviticus 16:12; 2 Chronicles 26:19; Hebrews 9:4; Revelation 8:3, 5). The coals and incense were used during worship and purification ceremonies, though not always together. Often incense was placed on top of the hot coals to burn (Numbers 16:46). Incense often represented prayers going up to God (Psalm 141:2; Revelation 5:8). See **INCENSE**.

▲ *Censers used in the temple were made of gold. Sometimes they were called firepans.*

CENTURION. Roman army officer over one hundred soldiers (Matthew 8:5–10; Acts 10). The highest rank an ordinary soldier could reach. Mentioned frequently in the New Testament.

CEPHAS (SEE fuhs). Aramaic term literally meaning "rock" (*Petros* in Greek). A name given to Simon Peter by Jesus (John 1:42). Used in New Testament to refer to Simon Peter (1 Corinthians 1:12; 3:22; 9:5; 15:5; Galatians 2:9). The name *Cephas* (rock) may signify Peter's strength as a leader in the early church.

CEREAL OFFERING. (NRSV; meat offering, KJV; grain offering, NASB and NIV) 1. An offering presented to God in response to His command (Leviticus 2). Consisted of flour, baked cakes, or raw grain combined with oil and frankincense. Can accompany burnt offerings and peace offerings (Numbers 15:1–9). 2. Also used without the frankincense as a substitute for an animal sacrifice by those who could not afford an animal (Leviticus 5:11–13). Giving one's best grain during worship was part of a ceremony that represented removal of past sins.

CHAFF. The bits of husk and other inedible parts of wheat plants that are blown away during threshing (Job 1:18). The edible grain falls to the ground or into a container and is

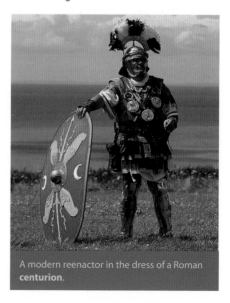

A modern reenactor in the dress of a Roman **centurion**.

kept. Chaff is also used as a figure of speech in the Bible to describe ungodly people (Psalm 1:4; Matthew 3:12). See **WINNOW**.

▲ *To picture what chaff is like, shell some peanuts to separate the good, edible nuts from the useless outer husk. Separating useless chaff from wheat is like that.*

CHARITY. "Love" in the KJV (1 Corinthians 13; Colossians 3:14). God-inspired, self-giving love for others. For some reason the KJV used *charity* to translate the Greek word *agape* twenty-six times—though the KJV uses *love* elsewhere to translate *agape*. In the Bible, the word *charity* does not specifically refer to giving to the poor but to any expression of love.

▲ *Every use of charity in the King James Version translates the Greek word* agape, *but usually the KJV translates* agape *with the English word* love. *William Tyndale translated all uses of* agape *with* love. *Charity had a Latin root that Tyndale said didn't match the English need for* agape.

CHASTE. Virtuous, morally pure, like God in thought and act (1 Peter 3:2).

CHASTEN. Punish to make better (1 Corinthians 11:32). Convict of sin, instruct, discipline (Deuteronomy 8:5; Revelation 3:19).

CHASTISE. Instruct, discipline, punish to make better (Psalm 94:10; 1 Kings 12:11–14; Luke 23:16; Hebrews 12:8).

▲ *Ideally, chastising or disciplining is positive and formative rather than corrective; but, at times, correction is required.*

CHEBAR (KEE bahr). River or canal in Babylonia where the Jewish exiles settled and Ezekiel had visions (Ezekiel 1:1, 3; 3:15, 23; 10:15, 20, 22; 43:3).

The prophet Ezekiel described **cherubim** as having four faces—of a man, a lion, an ox, and an eagle (Ezekiel 1:10).

CHERUB, CHERUBIM, CHERUBIMS. 1. Type of angel or creature with both human-like and animal-like characteristics. Some have human faces and others have animal faces. They have two or four wings. Cherubim were assigned to guard the tree of life in the garden of Eden (Genesis 3:24). Models of cherubim perched on the mercy seat, adorned other articles of Old Testament worship, and decorated Solomon's temple (Exodus 25:18–22, 26:31; 1 Kings 6:23–28). (Note: Both *cherubim* and *cherubims* are plural forms.) Cherubim were closely associated with God. At times He is pictured as dwelling between them or riding on them (Isaiah 37:16; 2 Samuel 6:2) 2. A place in Babylon from which some Israelites returned (Ezra 2:59).

CHINNERETH or **CHINNEROTH**. (KIN ih reth; KIN ih rahth). Old Testament names for the Sea of Galilee, which was also known as the Sea of Tiberias (Joshua 12:3; 13:27 and Numbers 34:11). Also a city (Deuteronomy 3:17; Joshua 19:35).

CHOOSE, CHOSEN. Appoint, select, call out (1 Samuel 17:8; Matthew 20:16). God's choice to establish a unique and exclusive relationship by calling a people to be His own (Deuteronomy 7:6–11).

CHOSEN PEOPLE. The Israelites, also called Hebrews or Jews (see Genesis 17:7, Psalm 89:3). God chose to reveal Himself to and establish a covenant with His chosen people. He wanted them to share with everyone their knowledge of God and how to trust in Him.

The eternal Christ came to earth as the baby Jesus. He was born a Jew but came to seek and save all the lost (Luke 19:10): Jesus began a new "chosen people" made up of everyone, Jew or non-Jew, who decides to follow Jesus (1 Peter 2:9–10). So Jesus fulfilled God the Father's original plan for the gospel of salvation to be for all the world (John 3:16).

▲ *The Hebrew or Jewish race began with Abraham (Genesis 12:2; Romans 4:16).*

■ **CHRIST.** Anointed one, one specially chosen for an important purpose. The title *Christ* identifies Jesus as the anointed Son of God, the true Messiah, the Savior of the world (Matthew 16:16; Mark 14:61–62; Acts 10:38). *Christ* was Jesus' title but also became a personal name for Jesus (John 17:3). "Jesus" was used most often as His earthly name and "Christ" as His eternal name. *Christ* is the Greek word for the Hebrew word *Messiah*. See **ANOINT** and the **NAMES FOR JESUS CHRIST CHART** on page 139.

From the Jews' reading of the Old Testament, they expected the Christ, the Messiah. But because their expectations did not match the person, methods, interpretations, and fulfill-

ment of Jesus Christ, they rejected Him as the true Messiah.

● *Christians believe Jesus Christ is the one anointed by God to give salvation. How do Christians know this to be true in their own lives? Why is this truth essential for others?*

■ **CHRISTIAN.** Follower of Jesus Christ (Acts 11:26; 26:28; 1 Peter 4:16). One who belongs to Christ. Christians commit themselves to Christ and ideally become increasingly like Him. They trust Jesus Christ to guide their decisions, actions, and attitudes. The name apparently was first used by pagans to ridicule Jesus' followers, but it became a label Christians wore proudly.

● *When others look at your life, do they see you as a follower of Christ? How? If not, why not?*

CHRONICLES, 1, 2, BOOKS OF. These Old Testament Bible books are a record of Israel's family history. The books retell, from a different perspective, events recorded in the books of Samuel and Kings. The books of Chronicles emphasize the faithfulness and greatness of God as He uses events of history to work out His purpose. They also emphasize the importance of demonstrating one's identity as a person belonging to God. Further, the books of Chronicles show that God still keeps promises to His people in spite of disasters. They show the origin of the worship of God in the temple at Jerusalem. Overall, the books emphasize man's chief purpose—to glorify God and give Him the right place in heart, home, and nation. Originally the two books were one.

In accomplishing their divinely inspired purposes, the books of Chronicles present evidence of God working: in events such as the achievements of David and Solomon, the reforms of Jehoshaphat, Hezekiah, and Josiah, and the actions of faithful people. To explain the worship, the book overviews the organization of the priests and Levites, David's dream of the temple, and Solomon's building of the temple.

▲ *First and 2 Chronicles are included in the books called Writings. The word Chronicles means the affairs of the days.*

● *First Chronicles begins by tracing Israel's genealogy back to Adam. Why is this useful?*

Chrysolite.

CHRYSOLITE. A golden yellow stone used in the description of the new heaven and new earth (Revelation 21:20).

■ **CHURCH.** Summoned assembly. Congregation. Believers who join together in a certain location (Matthew 18:17; 1 Corinthians 4:17). May also mean all Christians everywhere, of all ages, of all times (1 Corinthians 10:32; Ephesians 1:22–23). In the Bible, church is not a building but the Christians who inhabit a building or place (Romans 16:5). In fact, when Christians are gathered together, no building is required for the church to exist.

New Testament pictures of the church include (1) the bride of Christ (Ephesians 5:25–27), (2) the people of God (1 Peter 2:9–10), (3) the body of Jesus Christ (Romans 12:5; 1 Corinthians 12:12; Ephesians 4:16).

▲ *In the New Testament, church members accepted Jesus Christ as Lord and Savior, pictured this commitment in baptism, agreed to believe and behave like Christ, and committed to share Christ and a ministry like His with others (Matthew 28:19–20; Acts 1:8).*

A large **cistern** at Masada, the fortress Herod the Great built in the Judean desert.

● *How does a person become a church member today? What do you think should be the requirements of church membership? How does a church best serve its members?*

■ **CIRCUMCISION.** Literally, "cutting around." Physically, cutting around and off a small piece of excess skin that covers the tip of the penis. It was usually performed on the eighth day of life (Genesis 17:10–14; Romans 4:11–12).

Spiritually, circumcision was a physical reminder of the covenant between God and His people. A pure heart and a right relationship show one to be circumcised in a spiritual sense that is more important than the physical surgery (Jeremiah 4:4; Romans 2:25–29).

The Christian church refused to force non-Jewish Christians to be circumcised since it is not required for salvation (Acts 15:5–11; Galatians 5:2). The apostle Paul in particular insisted that salvation—as the gift of grace through faith—remain pure, not tainted by any requirement of work.

▲ *Today, circumcision is a relatively painless operation that usually occurs shortly after birth if the parents so choose. Doctors suggest that circumcision may help guard against irritation and infection of the penis while also noting that cleanliness in the uncircumcised may accomplish the same purposes. Circumcision may occur as a medical consideration, a religious one, or both—or not at all.*

CISTERN. Well, pit, artificial reservoir dug in rock or earth for collecting and storing water (Proverbs 5:15 KJV). Cisterns were necessary for Palestine's long and rainless summers.
▲ *Empty cisterns were sometimes used as prisons (Genesis 37:22 NIV).*

CITY OF DAVID. 1. In New Testament the reference is to Bethlehem as David's home (Luke 2:4, 11). 2. In Old Testament the reference is to Jerusalem, especially the part David built on Mount Zion (2 Samuel 5:7, 9).

CITY OF REFUGE. City where a person who had accidentally killed another person was safe from the vengeance of the dead person's loved ones (Exodus 21:13; Numbers 35:9–34). There were six cities of refuge, three on each side of the Jordan River (Numbers 35:14; Joshua 20).

CLEAVE. 1. To divide or split, as in splitting wood (Psalm 141.7). 2. To adhere, be joined together, hold fast to. Become inseparable with one's mate (Genesis 2:24–25; Matthew 19:5) and with God (Deuteronomy 11:22).

CLOVEN. Split, divided, especially referring to the hooves of an animal (Deuteronomy 14:7; Leviticus 11:3, 7, 26). When the Holy Spirit came at Pentecost, the believers saw cloven tongues that separated and rested on each one (Acts 2:3).

COLOSSE (koh LAHS ee). City in Asia (now southwest Turkey) where a Christian church was founded and to which Paul wrote a letter called Colossians (Colossians 1:2).

COLOSSIANS, BOOK OF (kuh LAHS uhns). Letter of the apostle Paul to believers at Colosse. Paul wrote to counter false teachings in Colosse. He explained the true Christian message: that unity with Jesus Christ brings salvation and all the false teachings detract from Jesus. In the closing chapters, Paul gave examples of how to live in unity in Christ. He urged action based on Christ's love, not on legalism. Paul probably wrote the letter while under arrest in Rome.

COMELINESS. Attractiveness, pleasing appearance, beauty (Isaiah 53:2).

COMFORTER. Name for the Holy Spirit in John 14:16, 26; 15:26; 16:7 (KJV). The English word translates the Greek word *parakletos*. Other Bible translations use terms such as Helper, Counselor, Advocate, Encourager, Intercessor, Strengthener, and Standby. The literal thought of the word is "one called alongside" to help.
▲ *The same Greek word for Comforter is translated Advocate in 1 John 2:1 (KJV): "If any man sin, we have an advocate with the Father, Jesus Christ the righteous."*

This close-up of young pigs shows their **"cloven"** (or divided) hooves. Deuteronomy 14 indicates the ancient Israelites could eat any animal with a cloven hoof that also chewed cud. Pigs, which do not chew cud, were disallowed as food.

A classic image of Moses carrying the Ten **Commandments** on tablets of stone. The seventeenth-century painting is by the Dutch master Rembrandt.

COMMANDMENT. Law, ordinance, charge (Deuteronomy 4:13). The most famous list of God's commandments is recorded in Exodus 20:3–17 and Deuteronomy 5:7–21. These Ten Commandments (or "ten words") were given to Moses on Mount Sinai and were intended to guide people in obeying and worshiping God and getting along with each other. True Christian love—toward God and others—is the highest commandment and fulfills all the commandments of God (Matthew 22:36–40; see Leviticus 19:18).

COMMEND. 1. Praise (Luke 16:8). 2. Demonstrate (Romans 5:8). 3. Entrust (Luke 23:46).

■ **COMMISSION**. Authorization, command, charge (Ezra 8:36; Acts 26:12). Matthew 28:18–20 is called "The Great Commission" because it is a command to share the good news of Christ with all the world, making disciples and baptizing them.

■ **COMMIT**. Entrust to (Psalm 31:5; 2 Timothy 1:12; Titus 1:3), or merely act or do (Leviticus 5:17). To commit to Christ is to let Him take charge of life as Lord. To be committed to Him is discipleship expressed in Christlikeness.

■ **COMMITMENT**. Sense of devotion, obligation, and faithfulness to someone or something. A promise to do something in the future. Those who have made a commitment to Christ try to obey Him in everyday living and decision making. This commitment is the kind Paul wrote of in Philippians 3:12–15 and 2 Timothy 1:12.

COMMUNE. Communicate, discuss, think about, confer (Genesis 18:33; Psalm 4:4; Zechariah 1:14). In scripture, the purpose and motive of "communing" affect whether the discussion is positive or negative (see Luke 6:11 and 22:4

for religious leaders communing in a negative context).

COMMUNION. Sharing, participation with, fellowship, communication, having something in common (2 Corinthians 6:14; 13:14). Includes both someone and something. Used as a one-word description for the Lord's Supper because partakers commune with Jesus Christ and one another (1 Corinthians 10:16).

▲ *You may have heard the word* koinonia *used to describe fellowship and belonging. Koinonia is the Greek word translated "communion." The term appears in unabridged English dictionaries.*

Though different churches have widely differing styles of celebrating **communion**, they all honor the "Lord's Supper" Jesus instituted the night He was betrayed.

COMPASSION. To bear with, to suffer with, to love, to have mercy (Lamentations 3:22; Matthew 9:36). Sympathetic consciousness of others' distress with a desire to lessen or ease it.

A human quality as well as a divine one. Anyone who has experienced God's compassion is responsible for having compassion on others. These others include fellow believers and outsiders, orphans and widows (Deuteronomy 10:18; 16:11; 24:19; Micah 6:8; 1 John 3:17). Jesus often is said to have had compassion as He looked upon those in need.

■ **CONCUBINE.** In the Old Testament, legal but secondary wife acquired by purchase, gift, or war victory. Often servants of wives. Bore children for the husband, especially when a wife could not conceive (Genesis 30:3; 1 Chronicles 1:32).

Concubines were popular in the Old Testament when believers failed to recognize God's ideal of creation: one wife for one husband. Those who had concubines included Abraham (Genesis 25:6), Gideon (Judges 8:30–32), David (2 Samuel 5:13), Solomon (1 Kings 11:3).

■ **CONDEMN, CONDEMNATION.** Declare guilty or wrong (Exodus 22:9). Refers to God's final judgment at the end of time but also to other judgments of His. Condemnation by man in a court is sometimes necessary (Deuteronomy 25:1), but man's judgment may be uncalled for (Matthew 7:1) or wrong (Matthew 12:7; Psalm 94:21). God's condemnation comes because of sin and is always accurate (Romans 2:1–2). Because of Christ's redemption, believers who walk in the Spirit can be confident that God will not condemn them (Romans 8:1; Psalm 34:22). God will take their side against all adversaries (Isaiah 50:8). See **JUDGMENT.**

CONFESS. Openly admit personal wrongdoing (Leviticus 5:5; Matthew 3:6). Confess to God (1 John 1:9) and to each other (James 5:16). Declare or acknowledge Jesus as Lord (Philippians 2:11). Generally, to acknowledge, admit to, agree to.

▲ *You can share any wrongdoing with God and know that He understands and still loves you.*

● *What good is confession without repentance?*

CONFOUND. Confuse or put to shame (Genesis 11:7, 9; 1 Corinthians 1:27). God's ways confound the world's ways; God's ways are not unreasonable but are beyond reason. Christians can find clarity and effectiveness in Jesus and no longer be ashamed or confused (1 Corinthians 1:27).

CONGREGATION. Group of people gathered for a common purpose, especially a religious purpose (Exodus 12:3; Acts 13:43). In the Old Testament *congregation* often referred to the entire Hebrew people, also called the people of Israel. Just as we have local congregations of believers today, *congregation* sometimes meant a specific group of believers in a specific place (Exodus 12:47; Numbers 16:3; 1 Kings 8:65). See **ASSEMBLY.**

▲ Congregation *came to mean both the meeting place (synagogue) and the gathering.* Assembly *and* church *are other terms used for a congregation.*

These ancient ruins, from Jesus' headquarters village of Capernaum, once housed a **congregation** of Jews just as modern churches are home to Christian congregations.

CONSCIENCE. Self-knowledge that leads us to feel an obligation to do right or be good (John 8:9; Romans 2:14–15; 1 Corinthians 8:10). Awareness or sense that an action or attitude is right or wrong.

● *What happens when your conscience dies? What can you do to bring it back to life? What would make your conscience dull? When would it be possible to do wrong and not sense it? What determines the quality of a person's conscience? (See 1 Timothy 1:19 for discussion.)*

■ **CONSECRATE**. Devote. Separate. Set aside for worship or service to God. A person or thing can be consecrated (2 Chronicles 29:31–33; Exodus 13:2).

In the Old Testament *consecrate* may also refer to the installation of a priest and to offerings (Leviticus 7:37; 8:22). In both the Old Testament and New Testament the concept is most often translated "sanctify" or "make holy" (John 17:17). Consecrate may also carry the idea of (1) make perfect (Hebrews 7:28) or (2) make new (Hebrews 10:20).

● *How does your life demonstrate that you are consecrated to God? What areas of your life need renewing?*

CONTRITE. Sorry for sin, humble (Psalm 34:18; 51:17; Isaiah 57:15; 66:2).

CONVERSATION. Behavior, conduct, manner of life. In the KJV, *conversation* never meant merely talk; it meant way of life or lifestyle (see Psalm 50:23; Galatians 1:13; Hebrews 13:5; James 3:13).

■ **CONVERSION, CONVERT**. Turn, turn about. Turn from sin to God (Psalm 51:13). Includes turning from wrong actions and attitudes to right ones (James 5:19–20). Converted persons trust and learn from God like a little child (Matthew 18:3). Closely associated with repentance (Acts 3:19). *Conversion* has come to mean the experience of turning to God, with a change of mind and heart, to receive the gift of salvation (Acts 9:1–22).

● *Each person chooses whether to turn to or from God. What have you decided? How has your life changed since you became a Christian? Or how would it change if you became one?*

■ **CONVICTION OF SIN, CONVINCE**. Becoming convinced of one's sin. Firm feeling that God wants one to choose or stop an action (John 8:9, 46; Acts 18:28; Jude 15). When a person becomes convinced that he is guilty of sin, the person is in a position to turn from sin and return to God (see Psalm 51). The Holy Spirit convinces us of our sin (John 16:8–11).

CORBAN. A Hebrew word that stood for money or possessions set aside for God or religious use (Mark 7:11). During Jesus' earthly ministry *corban* seemingly was understood to be the dedication of something as a trust (like an inheritance) to be used later. People could will money or possessions to God or the temple but keep usage while they lived. The Pharisees abused this practice by telling their needy parents they could not give them their "corban money." In this way, they avoided taking care of their parents. Read Jesus' evaluation of this in Mark 7:9–13.

● *What possible excuses might we be giving for not doing what the Bible teaches and what God wills for us to do? Consider, for example, tithing, use of the Sabbath, use of time, or use of our entire lives.*

CORINTHIANS, 1, 2, BOOKS OF. These New Testament books are letters from Paul to a spiritually struggling church. The city of Corinth was famous for its wickedness, including such sins such as greed, drunkenness, prostitution, pride, and a variety of false religions. The church had let some of these sins creep into their lifestyles and cause problems in their church. Paul wrote 1 and 2 Corinthians to correct these problems and give advice on how to live the Christian life. The problems prompted powerful teachings. These include the Holy Spirit (1 Corinthians 12), spiritual gifts (1 Corinthians 12–14), love (1 Corinthians 13), the resurrection (1 Corinthians 15), and close relationships (2 Corinthians 6:14–18).

▲ *Corinth was the capital of the Roman province of Achaia and was known for its prosperous commerce, multiple religions, and extensive immorality. The city was full of people like gamblers, prostitutes, and drug dealers. What sort of problems would a church established in a place like this have?*

● *Read the classic description of true love in 1 Corinthians 13 and the triumph over troubles that God will give in 2 Corinthians 4:8–9.*

CORRUPTIBLE. Perishable (Romans 1:23).

COUNCIL. 1. Gathering of people for deliberation or decision making (Psalm 68:27; Matthew 12:14; 13:9; Acts 25:12). 2. In the New Testament, usually the Jewish leaders called Sanhedrin (Matthew 26:59; Acts 24:20).

COUNSEL. Noun: Advice (Daniel 4:27; Luke 7:30). Verb: Advise, give advice (Luke 23:50; John 18:14). Examples of counselors include prophets, members of the Jewish Sanhedrin, or God (2 Samuel 17:11; Mark 15:43; Revelation 3:18).

COUNTENANCE. Noun: Facial expression (Psalm 10:4; Proverbs 15:13), appearance (1 Samuel 16:7). Verb: Honor (Exodus 23:3).

■ **COVENANT**. Mutual agreement between two persons or parties. The covenant between God and people is unique because God alone sets the conditions. In a covenant between two persons, the two negotiate the terms and promise with words or a written contract to keep the covenant (Genesis 31:49–53), or a powerful ruler dictates the terms to a compliant subject. In a covenant between God and humans, God sets the requirements and each person decides whether or not to agree to them and enter the covenant.

The covenant God offers requires obedience and loyalty to Him alone. For those who agree to this, God gives protective care, assurance, guidance, and His presence. Even when humans break their covenant with God, His loving grace continues. He always loves us. He is always open to truly repentant hearts, offering forgiveness freely.

God has made covenants with people from Adam and Eve to the present. One of the most far-reaching covenants God initiated was with Abraham (Genesis 15). The covenant offered Abraham included the Hebrew nation as God's instrument to reach the world. The covenant was based on grace, law, and obedience. Sometimes this covenant is called the Old Covenant. God sent a new covenant of grace through His Son, Jesus Christ (Jeremiah 30:22; Hebrews 7:22, 8:6; 2 Corinthians 3:6). The New Covenant is often called the New Testament. See **TESTAMENT**.

● *As a Christian you have a covenant with God. What does He expect from you? What do you expect from Him? If you're not a Christian, you can become one by entering the wonderful covenant God provides in Jesus Christ (see John 3:16; Romans 10:9–10).*

COVERING OF THE HEAD. An example used in 1 Corinthians 11:5, 15 to teach that ignoring social customs could hurt one's Christian

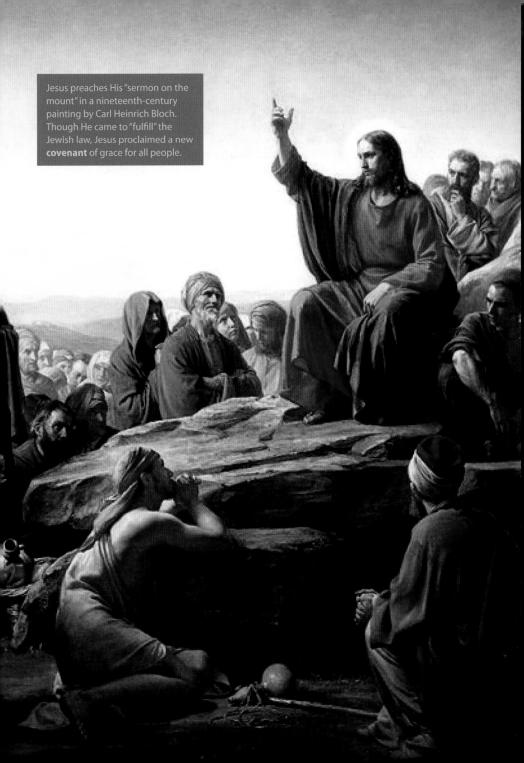

Jesus preaches His "sermon on the mount" in a nineteenth-century painting by Carl Heinrich Bloch. Though He came to "fulfill" the Jewish law, Jesus proclaimed a new **covenant** of grace for all people.

testimony. In Bible times it was customary for women to cover their heads. Because immoral women appeared in public with their heads uncovered, observers might draw the wrong conclusions about Christian women who did not cover their heads. The Corinthians especially needed a pure and undefiled witness in their corrupt society.

● *What social customs do you tend to ignore that may hurt your Christian testimony? What will happen if you take notice of the custom and change your habits? Read Romans 14 for help.*

COVET. Greedily want what belongs to someone else (Exodus 20:17; Romans 7:7). A person can covet things, money, people, or relationships (Acts 20:33; 1 Timothy 6:10; Romans 7:7).

CREATE, CREATION. Make, produce, form, fashion, bring into being (Genesis 1:1; Psalm 51:10; Colossians 1:16). God created the heavens and the earth; He created everything out of nothing. The Bible clearly teaches that all matter—everything in the universe—had a beginning that God Himself initiated. The Bible does not explain how much time occurred between "the earth was without form and void" and the creation of earth's structure, plants, and inhabitants. The critical belief is that God created everything—even time itself as an island in eternity.

Though many scientists disagree with the Bible's account—and often with each other's theories—scripture tells us that God created everything (Genesis 1–2). Some Christians— who are also scientists—have noted that the "scientific" order of our world's development reflects the outline of creation as stated in the Bible ("without form," "light," plants, creatures from water, birds, creeping creatures, beasts, humans). Properly understood, the Bible and science are not at odds with each other; science is only one realm within all God's created universe.

God is the true creator in that only He can create from nothing. All others take materials already at hand and alter them to be used in new ways.

● *Read Genesis 1 and make a chart of the order in which everything was created to help you see the orderliness and sequence of God's creation.*
● *If all people are created by God—and in His image—how should that affect the way you treat all other people? (See Malachi 2:10.)*

CRIMSON. Bright red (Isaiah 1:18). Crimson was used in the temple (2 Chronicles 2:7, 14), in royal clothes (Jeremiah 4:30), and to symbolize the seriousness of sin (Isaiah 1:18).

CROSS. Structure made by crossing two beams of wood (John 19:17). Some condemned persons were nailed or tied to an upright cross for crucifixion. Some crosses looked like Xs, others like a capital T, others like the Christian symbol for a cross—like a little t.

Jesus' cross is sometimes called a tree; being hung on a tree was an Old Testament symbol of humiliation (Deuteronomy 21:22–23; 1 Peter 2:24).

The cross is used figuratively as a symbol for the gospel, the good news of Jesus Christ (Galatians 6:14). "Taking up one's cross daily" means to be willing to obey Jesus Christ unconditionally— in life or even if it means death (Luke 9:23).

CRUCIFY. To put someone to death by fastening him to a cross (Matthew 27:31). Crucifixion comes from the Latin *Cruci figo*, which means "I fasten to a cross." Christians refer specifically to Jesus' death on the cross when they say "the crucifixion."

Roman crucifixion was a most shameful, painful, and lingering way to die. It was usually reserved for slaves and foreigners—not Roman citizens—and was carried on outside the city. Before crucifixion, most victims were beaten with a leather whip lined with bits of metal or bone tied to it (Matthew 20:19). The victim's hands and feet were then nailed or tied to a large wooden cross, and the cross was displayed upright. Death could come about from suffocation because each breath took extreme effort: the crucified one had to push up with his feet to fill his lungs with air. Exposure and starvation may have also contributed to death because most crucified persons hung on the cross for a number of days before death came.

Pharisees of Jesus' day were careful to tithe the **cummin** seeds they grew. . .but neglected more important matters of God's law.

Christians are said to be "crucified with Christ," which means they've died to their old self so that Jesus can live in them (Romans 6:6; Galatians 2:20).

● *If you are a Christian, how does your life show you are crucified with Christ?*

CUBIT. Linear unit of measure—from the elbow to the tip of the middle finger. Depending on the size of the person, a cubit was eighteen to twenty-one inches or about forty-six to fifty-two centimeters (Genesis 6:15).

CUMMIN. Plant whose seeds were used for seasoning foods (Isaiah 28:25, 27). Its name means "sharp smell." Cummin looks and tastes similar to caraway, and was believed to have medicinal properties. The scribes and Pharisees scrupulously paid tithes of their Cummin. While Jesus commended tithing, He chided the Pharisees for neglecting weightier matters (Matthew 23:23).

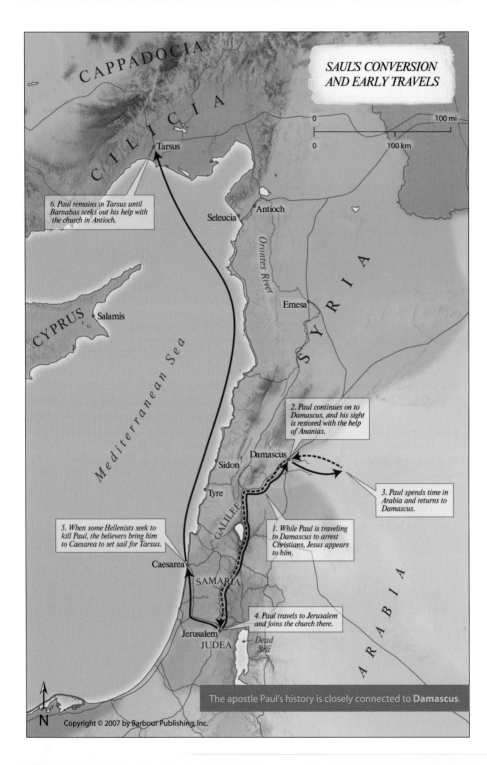

SAUL'S CONVERSION
AND EARLY TRAVELS

CAPPADOCIA

CILICIA

Tarsus

6. Paul remains in Tarsus until
Barnabas seeks out his help with
the church in Antioch.

Seleucia

Antioch

Orontes River

SYRIA

Emesa

CYPRUS

Salamis

Mediterranean Sea

Sidon

Tyre

GALILEE

Damascus

2. Paul continues on to
Damascus, and his sight
is restored with the help
of Ananias.

3. Paul spends time in
Arabia and returns to
Damascus.

5. When some Hellenists seek to
kill Paul, the believers bring him
to Caesarea to set sail for Tarsus.

1. While Paul is traveling
to Damascus to arrest
Christians, Jesus appears
to him.

Caesarea

SAMARIA

ARABIA

4. Paul travels to Jerusalem
and joins the church there.

Jerusalem
JUDEA

Dead
Sea

0   100 mi
0   100 km

N

The apostle Paul's history is closely connected to **Damascus**.

Copyright © 2007 by Barbour Publishing, Inc.

DAGON (DAY gahn). Pagan god worshiped by the Philistines. He is sometimes pictured with the body of a fish and the head and hands of a man. Dagon was probably a god of agriculture. Samson destroyed a temple of Dagon in Gaza (Judges 16:23–30). When the Philistines stole the ark of God and brought it to Dagon's temple, they encountered disastrous results (1 Samuel 5:2–7). The Philistines later put Saul's head in a temple of Dagon (1 Chronicles 10:10).

DAMASCUS (duh MASS cuss). Capital of Syria (Isaiah 7:8; Acts 9:2–3). Damascus, more than four thousand years old, is one of the oldest cities in the world. It served as a natural communication center, linking the Mediterranean coast and Egypt on the west, Assyria and Babylonia on the east, Arabia to the south, and Aleppo to the north.

Paul, a Jew, became a Christian while traveling on the Damascus Road (Acts 9:1–31).

DAMNATION. Judgment, condemnation. See 1 Corinthians 11:29 regarding self-condemnation in the taking of the Lord's Supper.

DAN. 1. Son of Jacob and Bilhah (Genesis 30:5–6). Dan was also considered Rachel's son because Bilhah was her maid. 2. The tribe that descended from Dan and the territory where they lived

A nineteenth-century illustration of **Dagon**. In 1 Samuel 5, a statue of Dagon fell to the ground and broke into pieces before the ark of the Lord.

(Numbers 1:38–39; Ezekiel 48:1). They originally lived between Judah and the Mediterranean Sea but because they failed to conquer the Philistines who lived there, the Danites moved north (Joshua 19:40–47; Judges 18:1–29). 3. The northernmost city of Israel (also called Canaan or Palestine; Judges 18:29). From Dan to Beersheba means the length of Israel from northernmost tip to southernmost tip (1 Kings 4:25).

DANIEL (DAN yuhl). 1. Governmental officer and prophet of God (Daniel 1:1–6; Matthew 24:15). As a young Jew he was taken captive and trained for service in the Babylonian royal court. He served in influential positions under four kings: Nebuchadnezzar, Belshazzar, Darius, and Cyrus. He firmly refused to do anything contrary to God, even when it meant risking his life (Daniel 1:8; 6:7–16). Daniel's gift of prophecy was evident early in life (Daniel 1:20; 2:16–19, 28; 5:5, 11–17; 7–13). He wrote the book of Daniel. The name Daniel means "God is my judge." Daniel was called Belteshazzar while in exile (Daniel 1:7). See **BELTESHAZZAR**. 2. The second son of David (1 Chronicles 3:1). 3. A descendant of Ithamar who grew up with Ezra and helped seal the covenant (Ezra 8:2; Nehemiah 10:6).

● Daniel was a refugee in a land far from home. Read Daniel 1–6 for ways he coped with this difficult situation. Which actions could help you get through your own rough situations?

DANIEL, BOOK OF. This Old Testament book depicts Daniel's loyalty to God in the face of imprisonment, pagan religion, and false teaching. It also includes Daniel's visions. Daniel and fellow Jews were captives in a foreign land during the Babylonian and Persian Empires.

Daniel was frequently pushed to compromise his faith, but he didn't do it. The book of Daniel records Daniel's faithful decisions and the results of them. Well-known choices include choosing to eat a healthy diet (Daniel 1), worshiping rather than avoiding the fiery furnace (Daniel 3), the writing on the wall

(Daniel 5), and praying rather than avoiding the lions' den (Daniel 6). The last portion of the book (chapters 7–12) records visions God gave to Daniel that depict Israel's future. This portion of Daniel is apocalyptic or picturesque literature that tells about the future with symbols and signs. These passages gave hope that the cruelty would end and God's triumph would become obvious.

Daniel is a "major prophet" (because of the length of the book) but placed by the Hebrews in a section called Writings. The term "minor prophet" refers to those with shorter books.

● Because Daniel showed his faith, Kings Nebuchadnezzar and Darius honored God. How might your convictions and actions influence someone powerful to honor God?

DARIUS (duh RIGH uhs). Common name for rulers of the Medes and Persians. Three examples are: 1. Darius the Mede ruled Babylon briefly (Daniel 5:31). 2. Darius Hystaspes, the fourth and greatest of the Persian rulers, reorganized the government into provinces, extended boundaries of the empire, renewed the edict of Cyrus, and helped rebuild the temple (Ezra 4:5, 6:1–12). 3. Darius the Persian, the last king of Persia, was defeated by Alexander the Great in 330 B.C. Many identify this Darius with Darius Nothus (Nehemiah 12:22).

DARKNESS. 1. Absence of light, obscurity, gloom (Genesis 1:2; Amos 4:13). 2. Symbol of all that is evil, wrong, or opposed to God (1 John 1:5–7; 2:11). 3. A characteristic of death, especially for the unsaved (Job 10:22; 2 Peter 2:4; Jude 6). See **LIGHT**.

DAUGHTER. 1. Female descendant (Genesis 26:34). 2. A woman (Mark 5:34). 3. A worshiper or group of worshipers of the true God (Zechariah 2:10; Matthew 21:5).

DAVID (DAY vid). Youngest son of Jesse, he became the second king of Israel and was an ancestor of Jesus Christ (1 Samuel 16:7–13; Acts 13:22–23). While a young shepherd boy, David was anointed by Samuel to succeed Saul as future king.

At first Saul had great affection for David, his music, and his bravery. David's harp music soothed Saul when he felt troubled. But later Saul became jealous of David's military popularity and tried to kill him. After Saul died, David was crowned king and became the best-loved king of Israel.

David is remembered for many adventures, such as killing the giant Philistine with a slingshot (a powerful weapon in that era, not just a toy), his faithful friendship with Jonathan, and for refusing to get revenge on King Saul (1 Samuel 17:32–54; 18:1, 26:9). He is also known for blatant disobedience against God such as having sex with Uriah's wife, Bathsheba, which resulted in her pregnancy (2 Samuel 11:5). Then David arranged Uriah's death in battle so David could marry Bathsheba (2 Samuel 11:2–27). David wrote many psalms about both his disobedient actions and his obedient ones in praying for cleansing (compare Psalm 51 with Psalm 101).

▲ *Read about David's life and adventures in 1 Samuel 16 through 1 Kings 2:11.*

● *David's sin hurt both him and his family. His sin created family problems for generations and David was not permitted to build God's temple, which David loved. Consider ways your disobedience has or may now be affecting your relationship with God and others. How does disobeying God hurt you? Hurt your family? How does it hurt God?*

DAY. May refer to a twenty-four-hour period, some other duration of time, or a time of God's judgment or Christ's return (Malachi 3:16–18; 4:5–6; 2 Thessalonians 2:1–2).

■ **DAY OF THE LORD**. Scholars see this reference from different perspectives: 1. when the Lord will return, 2. when the world as we know it will end, or 3. when God will rid the world of evil once and for all (Joel 2:28–32; Philippians 1:6, 10). The Day of the Lord will mean disaster and judgment for the enemies of the Lord but salvation and deliverance for believers (Amos 5:18–20; Zephaniah 1:14–18).

In the Old Testament the Day of the Lord was something for the unfaithful to dread and for the faithful to anticipate (Amos 5:18; Daniel 7:22, 27; 12:2). In the New Testament the Day of the Lord often refers to the day Jesus will return (Philippians 1:6, 10). He will bring judgment and will deliver believers to eternal joy (John 5:27; 6:40; Romans 2:5–11). The Day of the Lord will result in a new heaven and a new earth (2 Peter 3:10–13).

DEACON. Servant, minister, helper (Philippians 1:1; 1 Timothy 3:8–13). A church leader who ministers to others. Though *deacon* appears only five times in the King James Version, the Greek word translated "deacon" appears over thirty times. It is usually translated "servant" and many times describes how Christians meet material needs of fellow Christians (2 Corinthians 8:4). Jesus said He came to serve, not to be served—which translates the Greek verb for "deacon" in Matthew 20:28.

▲ *Phoebe is a woman in the New Testament referred to as a* diakonon, *translated servant (KJV) or deaconess (NIV, footnote; Romans 16:1).*

DEAD SEA. Salt lake with no outlet into which the Jordan River flows. Usually called the Salt Sea in the Bible (Genesis 14:3; Numbers 34:12). It is the lowest spot on earth with a surface about thirteen hundred feet below sea level and its deepest point thirteen hundred more feet below sea level. Because it has no outlet

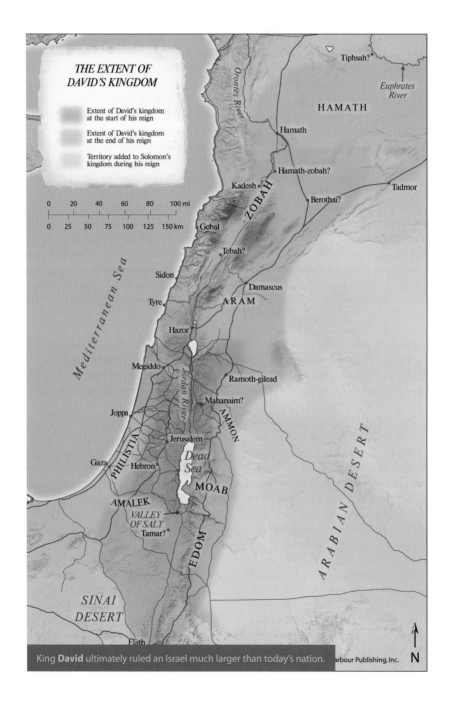

THE EXTENT OF DAVID'S KINGDOM

Extent of David's kingdom at the start of his reign

Extent of David's kingdom at the end of his reign

Territory added to Solomon's kingdom during his reign

| 0 | 20 | 40 | 60 | 80 | 100 mi |
| 0 | 25 | 50 | 75 | 100 | 125 | 150 km |

Tiphsah?

Euphrates River

HAMATH

Orontes River

Hamath

Hamath-zobah?

Kadesh

Tadmor

ZOBAH

Berothai?

Gebal

Tebah?

Sidon

Damascus

Tyre

ARAM

Hazor

Megiddo

Ramoth-gilead

Mediterranean Sea

Jordan River

Mahanaim?

Joppa

AMMON

PHILISTIA

Jerusalem

Gaza

Dead Sea

Hebron

MOAB

AMALEK

VALLEY OF SALT

Tamar?

EDOM

ARABIAN DESERT

SINAI DESERT

Elath

King **David** ultimately ruled an Israel much larger than today's nation.   arbour Publishing, Inc.

N

The **Dead Sea** coastline, showing salt deposits along the shore.

the Dead Sea is several times saltier than an ocean. No plant or animal can live in its extra-salty waters, so the name Dead Sea. The Dead Sea is located between Jordan and Israel with its northern half extending into Jordan.

DEAD SEA SCROLLS. Copies of Old Testament text written on scrolls found near the Dead Sea beginning in 1947. They are important because they assure us of the accuracy of the Hebrew texts we have today and help us better know the precise wording of the Old Testament. They also contain non-biblical texts that tell about the time just before, during, and after Jesus' earthly life. The Dead Sea Scrolls contain parts of every book of the Old Testament except Esther. Some entire books are included. The scrolls are dated as early as the second century B.C.

▲ *Arabic Bedouins (nomadic desert dwellers) discovered the first scrolls in 1947 in caves about a mile west of the northwest corner of the Dead Sea at a place called Qumran. Near the caves are the remains of a monastery where Jews called the Essenes lived. They per-haps hid the scrolls in the caves. These scrolls are also called manuscripts.*

■ **DEATH**. Used at least four ways in the Bible: 1. End of physical life. After physical death, persons enter a new realm of life: believers to eternal joy and non-believers to eternal torment (Matthew

25:46; Revelation 20:15; 21:3–5). Finally, Jesus removes the sting of physical death (1 Corinthians 15:55–57; Romans 6:9–10). 2. Lack of spiritual life. Spiritual death means separation from God (1 John 3:14). All who do not accept Jesus are spiritually dead. They become alive only in Christ (Ephesians 2:1–5). 3. End of an old way of life. Christians have died to their old life without Jesus and have been raised to new life with Jesus (Romans 6:4–8). 4. "Second death." A final and irreversible separation from God after judgment (Revelation 20:6).

● *How do you feel about death? How do you feel about eternal life? How does Jesus' promise of eternal life affect your feelings about death? See 1, 2, 3 John for signs of eternal life.*

■ **DEBAUCHERY**. Drunkenness, unbridled lust (Galatians 5:19; 1 Peter 4:3 NIV).

DEBORAH. 1. A prophetess and judge of Israel (Judges 4:4–5:15). Deborah's skilled leadership and presence gave courage to Barak and the people of Israel. She composed and sang a song of praise to God after He gave victory over Israel's enemies. 2. Rebekah's nurse (Genesis 35:8). Rebekah was Isaac's wife, the mother of Jacob and Esau.

One of the Qumran caves where the **Dead Sea Scrolls** were found.

DECAPOLIS (dih KAP oh liss). Ten cities spoken of as a region (Matthew 4:25; Mark 5:20; 7:31). The name is Greek for "Ten Cities." These ten towns cooperated to protect their interests. They had their own coins, courts, and armies. Most of the original ten towns lay east of the Jordan River. More towns were added later. Listings of the cities differ. One list of the original ten cities is: Damascus, Raphana, Kanatha, Hippos, Dion, Gadara, Scythopolis, Pella, Gerasa, and Philadelphia.

DECEIT. Subtle lie, fraud, making wrong look right or right look wrong, treachery (Proverbs 12:20; Amos 8:5; Romans 1:29). Deceit is not only destructive itself but leads to other destroyers such as using people, refusing to accept God's truth, and distancing friend from friend.

One of the devil's main tools is deceit. Temptation likely wouldn't be so appealing if it didn't look right, good, or fun. (See Revelation 20:10 for the fate of the deceiving devil.)

● *When have you been harmed by deceit? Recall a time you deceived someone or lied. What are some instances when you or others suffered from deceit? The preventive and the antidote for deceit is to align your life with Jesus, the Truth (John 14:6).*

DECLARE. Make known, tell good news, explain, tell fully (Acts 13:32).

DECREE. Official ruling, law, or order (Ezra 5:13; Esther 2:8; Daniel 2:13).

■ **DEDICATE**. Set apart or sanctify things or people for God's use (Ephesians 5:26). Devote. Make holy. Both things and people can be dedicated (Numbers 7:10; 2 Samuel 8:11; Exodus 19:14).

● *What evidence is there that your life is dedicated to God? What skills do you have to dedicate to God's service?*

A nine-branched candelabrum is lit to observe Hanakkuh, originally known as the **Feast of Dedication**.

DEDICATION, FEAST OF. An eight-day Jewish festival that commemorated the cleansing and rededication of the temple (John 10:22). Today known as Hanukkah (HA noo kah) or the "Feast of Lights." See **FEAST CHART** on page 96 and **DATE CHART** on pages 265–266.

DEED. Action, work (Jeremiah 25:14; Acts 7:22). Deeds can be good or evil (John 3:19–21).

DEEP, THE. 1. The ocean, the Red Sea, the deepest part of the sea, another deep body of water (Genesis 7:11; Exodus 15:5, 8; Nehemiah 9:11; Luke 8:31). 2. Very deep place or abyss. The abyss is a bottomless or unfathomably deep place understood as the underworld or place of the dead (Psalm 88:6; Romans 10:7).

DEFILE. Make unclean, especially in the religious or ethical sense (Daniel 1:8; Mark 7:15).

DEFRAUD. Cheat, oppress, deprive of, gyp (Leviticus 19:13). To misrepresent by claiming to have more than you have or less than you have, to take or keep away by willful deceit or trickery (Acts 5:1–11). The Bible strictly forbids defrauding (Mark 10:19; 1 Thessalonians 4:6).

● *How has someone cheated you? How did it make you feel? When are you most tempted to cheat in something or against another person?*

DEFY. Rebel against, deliberately disobey, openly resist, challenge someone or something considered impossible, invite to combat (Numbers 23:7–8; 2 Samuel 23:9–10).

■ **DEITY**. God or a god.

DELIVER. 1. Rescue, free, cause to escape from evil, give safety or salvation, redeem, transfer or allow another to take (2 Kings 18:30; Acts 7:25). Frequently used to describe God's deliverance of His people from the power of sin, death, and Satan through Jesus Christ. Deliverance goes hand in hand with salvation and redemption (Matthew 6:13; Luke 4:18). See **REDEEM**. 2. Simply give or bring to (2 Kings 18:23).

DELIVERER. God Himself or human deliverers sent by God (Exodus 3:7–8; 2 Samuel 22:2–3; Romans 11:26; Judges 3:9, 15). In the Old Testament, the next of kin (*go'el*) served as deliverer by rescuing his relatives from distress, slavery, suffering, oppression, and danger.

A Roman silver **denarius**, dated to the second century.

DEMAS (DEE muhs). A fellow disciple with Paul at Rome who later deserted Paul (Colossians 4:14; 2 Timothy 4:10; Philemon 24).

DEMETRIUS (dih MEE trih uhs). 1. A Christian commended for his witness (3 John 12). 2. A silversmith in Ephesus who stirred up a riot against Paul (Acts 19:24–41).

DEMONIAC (NRSV). Someone possessed by a demon or demons (Matthew 8:28–32; Mark 5:15–16).

DEMONS (NASB). Evil spirits who oppose God and work against people (Matthew 4:24, 8:16; Luke 10:17).
▲ *Demon and devil are represented by different words in the Greek language (demon, Luke 4:33; devil, 4:2—see NRSV). But the King James Version translates both words with the English word devil.*
● *Can you be demon possessed? Not if you live in the Spirit of Christ, because no demon was able to face Christ and stay (Mark 1:34). The Bible treats demons as real and not just some form of mental illness.*

DENARIUS (NIV, NRSV). Roman silver coin that amounted to one day's wage in Jesus' time (Matthew 20:1–16; Mark 12:15). Equivalent to a Greek drachma. In the KJV, translated *penny* (*pence* is the plural).

DENY. 1. Reject, pretend not to know, decide not to believe, disown (Matthew 10:33; Luke 20:27). 2. Decide to give other things priority (Matthew 16:24). 3. Lie, withhold, keep back (Genesis 18:15; 1 Kings 20:7).

DEPRAVITY (NIV). Moral pollution that biases a person toward evil action and away from God (Romans 1:29; 2 Peter 2:19). Depravity

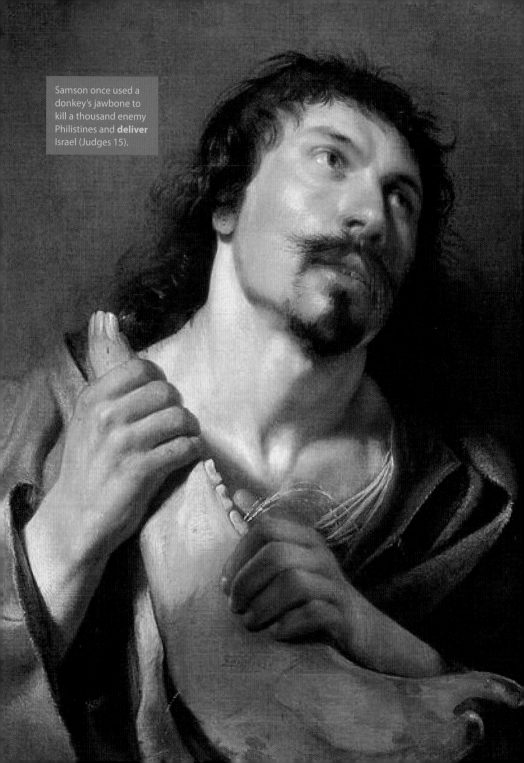

Samson once used a donkey's jawbone to kill a thousand enemy Philistines and **deliver** Israel (Judges 15).

is a condition that comes as a result of human choice to sin (Romans 3:23). The word is not found in the KJV, but see Romans 1:29 in the NIV.

DEPTH, DEPTHS. Deep places, lowest parts, depths of the sea, uttermost reaches (Psalm 130:1; Exodus 15:5; Romans 8:39).

DERBE (DUR bih). City in the province of Galatia where Paul preached while beginning churches in that area (Acts 14:6, 20; 16:1; 20:4). Galatia has been identified as modern Turkey.

DERIDE. Make fun of, ridicule, laugh at, turn up nose at (Habakkuk 1:10; Luke 16:14; 23:35).

DERISION. Scorn, ridicule, mocking, criticism (Psalm 79:4; Jeremiah 20:7).

DESCEND. Go down or come down (Genesis 28:12; Matthew 7:25; Luke 3:22).

DESCENDANT (NIV). One who comes from a parent or ancestor; child of, grandchild of, great grandchild of and so on (Leviticus 21:21; Luke 1:27; Romans 11:1). The King James Version often uses "seed of" or "house of" rather than "descendant of." Jesus was a descendant of David (Matthew 1:1 NEB).

DESIRE. Want, long for, request, delight in, urgently seek after (1 Peter 2:2; Psalm 37:4). Desire in itself is neutral, but both the motive and the object reveal whether desire is good or bad.

DESOLATE. Lonely, deserted, gloomy, separated from people, not occupied (Isaiah 49:21; Jeremiah 33:12).

DESPAIR. Loss of hope. Feel there is no possible way out (Ecclesiastes 2:20; 2 Corinthians 4:8).

DESPISE. Detest, loathe, reject, scorn, look down upon (Proverbs 1:7; Matthew 6:24; Hebrews 12:2; 1 Timothy 4:12).

● *Though Jesus despised or scorned the shame of the cross (Hebrews 12:2), the word despise seems to be used most often in the Bible by humans. Would God call us to despise anyone or anything? Perhaps we should identify the things God hated (Proverbs 6:16–19; 8:13). Consider hating only what God hates.*

DESTITUTE. In great need, naked, exposed, deprived of, lacking (Psalm 141:8; 1 Timothy 6:15).

DETESTABLE. Abominable, disgusting, arousing intense dislike (Deuteronomy 7:26; Ezekiel 5:11).

DEUTERONOMY, BOOK OF. Fifth book of the Old Testament; means "second law." Deuteronomy reviews and explains God's work with His people and encourages renewed commitment to God. This commitment is prompted by God's love and blessings. It is to be expressed through loyalty and obedience. Deuteronomy explains repeatedly that God's way is the way to true life (Deuteronomy 30:19–20).

Deuteronomy was written shortly before Moses died, and includes an account of his death in the last chapter. Moses commissioned Joshua as the next leader of God's people (Deuteronomy 34:5–12). Deuteronomy contains Moses' addresses to the people

The Judean desert, near the Dead Sea, provides a good picture of the biblical word *desolate*.

of Israel in Moab, on the edge of the Promised Land (Canaan). The book reviews the Ten Commandments, emphasizing the First Commandment. Deuteronomy was probably the "book of the law" found by Josiah and prompting widespread religious reform (2 Kings 22–23).

● *Many call Deuteronomy 6:4–9 the key words of Deuteronomy. For the Hebrews, those words became a confession of faith for all generations to hear (Hebrew* shema*) and obey. Evaluate your own life: How well do you obey these words of God?*

DEVICE. Thought, meditation (Proverbs 19:21; Acts 17:29).

DEVIL. Satan, slanderer, opponent to God (1 Corinthians 10:20). Supernatural being who tries to take away people's happiness by blocking God's purposes. He does this mainly through temptation and deception. He is also called "Beelzebub," the "evil one," and "Lucifer." The devil has superhuman power but can be resisted with God's help. His powers are limited to what God permits. See **SATAN**.

▲ *The devil was not created evil. Many believe that the devil is a rebellious angel (see Isaiah 14:12–20, Ezekiel 28:12–19, and Luke 10:18). Second Peter 2:4 indicates that other angels, now called demons, rebelled with him. The devil does not live only in hell but also on earth (Revelation 12:12). He will be cast in hell on judgment day (Revelation 20:12).*

● *Though the devil cannot possess a Christian, he can influence one. Do you see ways the devil might be tempting you or working in your life? If so, how? (See 1 John 1:7.)*

● *James 4:7 encourages you to resist the devil and submit to God. What does God promise you if you resist the devil?*

DIDYMUS (DID ih muhs). Means "twin." It is the Greek name for the apostle Thomas (John 11:16; 20:24; 21:2). *Thomas* is Aramaic for twin.

■ **DISCERN**. Be able to separate the things from God and the things not from God (Job 6:30; Ezekiel 44:23). Distinguish between good and evil (1 Kings 3:9; Hebrews 5:14). "Discerning of spirits" is the ability to tell whether one is speaking by the Holy Spirit or a false spirit (1 Corinthians 12:10).

■ **DISCIPLE**. Learner. Student. Follower. Apprentice. Implies acceptance of the teacher's teachings and imitation of his practices (Luke 6:40; Isaiah 8:16). Jesus' followers were called disciples (Luke 22:14, 38) as are all Christians (Luke 14:26–27; Acts 9:36). See **APOSTLE**.

▲ *The word* disciple *is used only in the four Gospels and Acts. After the disciples learned from Jesus, they were sent out as apostles (disciples sent on a mission).*

A stained glass window from Belgium shows Jesus surrounded by **disciples**. Though He had twelve specially chosen followers (later called "apostles"), many people—both male and female—followed Jesus.

DISCIPLES OF JESUS

MATTHEW 10:2–4	MARK 3:16–19	LUKE 6:13–16	ACTS 1:13–14
Simon Peter	Simon Peter	Simon Peter	Peter
Andrew	James son of Zebedee	Andrew	John
James son of Zebedee	John	James	James
John	Andrew	John	Andrew
Philip	Philip	Philip	Philip
Bartholomew	Bartholomew	Bartholomew	Thomas
Thomas	Matthew	Matthew	Bartholomew
Matthew the tax collector	Thomas	Thomas	Matthew
James son of Alphaeus	James son of Alphaeus	James son of Alphaeus	James son of Alphaeus
Thaddaeus	Thaddaeus	Simon who was called the Zealot	Simon the Zealot
Simon the Zealot	Simon the Zealot	Judas son of James (compare John 14:22)	Judas son of James
Judas Iscariot	Judas Iscariot	Judas Iscariot	(Judas Iscariot) Matthias (v. 26)

■**DISCIPLESHIP**. The commitment to live as a disciple of Jesus Christ. Discipleship is a process that includes learning Bible truth, applying that Bible truth to everyday life, becoming like Christ, sharing Christianity with others, serving the church, and fulfilling the goals God has personally designed for each person (Matthew 11:28–30; 28:18–20 NASB).

■ **DISCIPLINE**. God's teachings in the lives of His people: both formative and corrective (Job 36:10). In the King James Version, the word *discipline* occurs only in Job 36:10 but the concept weaves through many passages in words like *correction, instruction, chastisement, reproof,* and *nurture* (2 Timothy 2:25; Ephesians 6:4).

Discipline includes training and knowledge balanced with correction and punishment. Based in love and concern for our well-being, its purpose is our maturity and happiness in serving God (Psalm 94:12–13; Proverbs 3:11–12).

▲ *Discipline may be self-imposed to learn a skill or body of knowledge. Bible reading, prayer, and service are often called the Christian's daily disciplines.*

● *What discipline could you choose to serve God more effectively? How might God be disciplining you now? What does it mean to "disciple" someone? (Note: It is related to discipline.)*

DISPENSATION. Law or arrangement (Ephesians 1:10; 3:2). The New Testament uses the concept in two ways: 1. When referring to one in authority, it means a plan, specifically God's plan of salvation in Ephesians 1:10. 2. When referring to one under authority, it means

Lazarus begs outside the house of a rich man—traditionally called **Dives**—from a parable of Jesus.

managing as a stewardship for the one in authority (1 Corinthians 9:17; Ephesians 3:2; Colossians 1:25).

DISPERSE. Scatter, spread, burst forth (Proverbs 15:7; Ezekiel 12:15; 2 Corinthians 9:9).

DISPERSION. Scattering (Jeremiah 25:34; Acts 5:37). When capitalized, usually refers to the scattering of the Jews to many non-Jewish lands after their exile in Babylon and Assyria. The scattered Jewish people themselves were called "the diaspora."

DIVERS. Different kinds, diverse, various (Deuteronomy 22:9; Proverbs 20:23; Mark 1:34).

DIVES (DI vez). The name traditionally given to the rich man in Jesus' parable about Lazarus and the rich man (Luke 16:19–31). It is actually the Latin word for "rich" used in Luke 16:19 in the Latin Vulgate; in time, the term came to be used as the rich man's name.

DIVINATION. Practice of foreseeing or foretelling the future through such unreliable efforts and methods as astrology, reading omens, watching water, consulting with the dead, and casting lots (Deuteronomy 18:10; Ezekiel 21:21; Acts 16:16). Condemned except when God is the source of information about the future (Numbers 22:7; Micah 3:6–7; Ezekiel 13:6–7; Zechariah 10:2).

DIVINE. 1. Adjective: Godly, godlike (2 Peter 1:3–4; Hebrews 9:1). 2. Verb: To seek what to do from a religious or magic source other than God—obviously not a wise practice (Genesis 44:5, 15; 1 Samuel 28:8).

■ **DIVORCE**. End of marriage. Contrary to God's ideal (Mark 10:4–9) but seemingly permitted if one is sexually unfaithful (Matthew 5:31–32) or if one deserts the other (1 Corinthians 7:15). Jesus said Moses recognized that the hardness of people's hearts led to divorce; consequently, there are set requirements and limitations for divorce (Matthew 19:8; Deuteronomy 24:1–4). Jesus commanded married couples to work toward lifelong love and unity (Matthew 19:5–6).
● *God forgives repentant sinners, whatever the sin might be. Even if a divorce occurs for the wrong reasons, it is not unpardonable. God continues to work in and through us when we let Him, in all stages and circumstances of life (see Romans 8:28).*

■ **DOCTRINE**. Instruction. Teaching about God and how to live for Him (Proverbs 4:2). Doctrine affects words and actions (Titus 2:1; 1 Timothy 1:10). Jesus Himself was the best teacher of doctrine (Matthew 7:28; John 7:16–17).

DOMINION. Rule. Power to rule, own, or control (Genesis 1:26; 37:8). Exercise lordship over (Romans 6:9).

DOOM. (NIV) Calamity, judgment (Deuteronomy 32:35; Revelation 18:10).

DOOR. Entrance, opening (Genesis 6:16; Matthew 6:6). Often used in the New Testament as a name for Christ (John 10:1) or as an opportunity (Matthew 25:10; Acts 14:27; Colossians 4:3).

DOORKEEPER. One who stays at the door to guard it or wait for someone (Psalm 84:10; Mark 13:34). Doorkeepers served buildings, temples, and walled cities. Sometimes called a porter (2 Kings 7:10). This humble task would be a joy for a believer in the house of the Lord (Psalm 84:10).

DOORPOSTS. Lintels, pieces that support the structure around a door and that the door fits into (Ezekiel 41:6).

DORCAS (DAWR kuhs). Means "gazelle" and is the Greek translation of *Tabitha*. Dorcas was a female disciple who did many good works in Jesus' name. After she had died, Peter prayed for her, called her name, and she was restored to life (Acts 9:36–42).

DOUBLE-MINDED. Literally, "two-souled." Uncertain, wavering, divided (James 1:8; 4:8). The word implies instability, unsettledness, maybe deceitfulness.
● *How does being double-minded affect a person's convictions? How does it affect one's prayers and the answers of them? (See James 1 for additional thoughts.)*

An ancient doorway in Jordan. **Doorposts** factored prominently into the Israelites' escape from Egypt (see Exodus 12).

DOUBLE-TONGUED. Literally, "double-worded" (1 Timothy 3:8). The word suggests insincerity, hypocrisy, or lack of integrity.
▲ *The phrase "talking out of both sides of his mouth" captures the idea of being double-tongued.*

DOUBT. Lack of faith or belief (Matthew 14:31). Literally, to be without resource, to judge differently, or to stand divided (Acts 10:17, Mark 11:23; Matthew 28:17). In addition to doubting God, one may also doubt a person's actions or motives (Acts 25:20).
▲ *Doubt needs to be resolved. When Thomas doubted, he admitted it; Jesus gave evidence*

that answered his doubt (John 20:24–28). Faith is the evidence of things hoped for but not seen (Hebrews 11:1).

DOVE. Bird similar to a pigeon (Genesis 8:8; Matthew 10:16). At Jesus' baptism, God's Spirit descended like a dove (Matthew 3:16; Mark 1:10; Luke 3:22; John 1:32). In Song of Solomon, *dove* was a term of affection, possibly because doves are loyal to their mates and gentle (2:14; 4:1). Doves were sold as items for a sacrificial offering (John 2:14).

DOWRY. Marriage present; the property, money, or servant that came with a bride for her husband in marriage (Genesis 30:20). Sometimes a dowry was a price paid by the suitor to parents of the bride (1 Samuel 18:25).

DRACHMA. Silver coin equivalent to a day's pay (Luke 15:8–9). Equivalent to a Roman denarius. Translated "piece of silver" in the King James Version and "silver coin" in several other translations. Drachma is referenced in Bible footnotes but does not appear in the King James Version. See **DENARIUS**.

DREAD. 1. Verb: Fear, be afraid (1 Chronicles 22:13). 2. Noun: Reverence (Isaiah 8:13).

DREAM. Thought or experience while asleep (Genesis 20:3; Acts 2:17). God can communicate with His people through dreams (1 Kings 3:5; Ezekiel 2:1; Matthew 1:20), but not all dreams are from God (Deuteronomy 13:1–3). God gave some the ability to interpret dreams. Examples include Joseph (Genesis 40:5–23) and Daniel (4:19–27). Many dreams may come from overly busy minds, too much work, and the experiences of the day (Ecclesiastes 5:3 KJV; HCSB; NASB).

DRUNK, DRUNKENNESS. Stupor caused by consumption of an alcoholic beverage (Genesis 9:21). Drunkenness was a major vice of Bible times, especially among the wealthy. Drunkenness is condemned in the Bible (Leviticus 10:9; Ecclesiastes 10:17; Galatians 5:21). Being filled with the Spirit is advocated instead (Ephesians 5:18).

● *Why do people drink alcohol? How do people become alcoholics? How does God provide for cravings, emotional wants, or helping us avoid destructive social habits in a way that helps instead of harms? Without being judgmental toward those who drink wine or other beverages containing alcohol, what spiritual and social factors might lead a Christian to totally abstain from such beverages?*

DULCIMER. Musical instrument, perhaps like a bagpipe (Daniel 3:5, 10, 15).

DULL. Slow to understand, not paying attention, lazy, mentally sluggish (Hebrews 5:11).

DUMB. Silent, voiceless, mute, cannot talk (Mark 7:37). In the King James Version, *dumb* does not mean stupid or unable to learn.

Jacob **dreams** of a ladder to heaven, in a stained glass window from Chartres, France.

● *Those with speech impediments sometimes are mocked or made fun of. Besides never ridiculing or embarrassing those with impairments, how can you as a Christian incorporate into your group one who struggles to speak clearly?*

DUNG. Manure, excrement of humans and animals (Ezekiel 4:15). There were rules about sanitary disposal of dung (Deuteronomy 23:12–14). Dried dung was used for fuel, fertilizer, or sacrifice (Ezekiel 4:12, 15; Luke 13:8; Exodus 29:14; Leviticus 8:17). Also simply dirt or rubbish (Nehemiah 2:13; Philippians 3:8).

DUNGHILL. Place where manure was piled up to use as fertilizer (Isaiah 25:10).

DURST. Past tense of *dare* (Esther 7:5; Luke 20:40).

DUST. Clay, earth, small bits of matter (Isaiah 40:15; Mark 6:11). God formed people from dust, and their earthly bodies will return to dust or ashes (Genesis 2:7; 3:19).

▲ *The resurrection body Christians will receive is fit for all eternity (see 2 Corinthians 5:1–10). This truth applies regardless of how a person dies— even if the body is destroyed in some way.*

Dunghills aren't pretty—and neither was God's threat to make Moab like a dunghill (Isaiah 25:10).

DWELL. Live, stay, make your home, settle among (Psalm 4:8; 2 Peter 3:13). Christ dwells in Christians (Ephesians 3:17).

▲ *The New Testament Greek word often translated "dwell" in the KJV also means to settle down, remain, or abide in a house.*

● *How does Christ's dwelling in you affect your words? Your actions? Your attitudes?*

EAR. Physical organ of hearing, sometimes referred to at consecration of priests (Leviticus 8:24), and cleansing of lepers (Leviticus 14:14). If a bondservant chose not to go free after his six years of service, his master would pierce the servant's ear, which would then indicate permanent servitude (Exodus 21:6). Symbolically referred to in heeding, obeying, or paying attention to (2 Timothy 4:3–4; Revelation 2:7).

EARNEST. Down payment, pledge, guarantee (Ephesians 1:14).

EARTH, EARTHLY. Place people live, as opposed to heaven (John 3:12, 31). Can include the people who live on the earth and their characteristics (2 Corinthians 5:1). *Earthly* describes actions, attitudes, and ideas that are opposed to God or of this life only—such as revenge, jealousy, greed (James 3:15; Philippians 3:19); it includes but is not limited to physical things.

EAST, MEN OF. People of lands east of Palestine (Job 1:3). "East" was the place of the sunrise and a significant direction for the Hebrews (Numbers 3:38). The wise men who saw the child Jesus were from the east (Matthew 2:1–2).

EAST WIND. Refers to a hot, dry, dusty, destructive wind from the desert (Genesis 41:27; Isaiah 27:8).

EBEDMELECH (EE bed-MEE lek). Ethiopian eunuch who served King Zedekiah and who helped Jeremiah escape from prison and death (Jeremiah 38:7–13; 39:16–18).

EBENEZER (EB uhn-EE zur). 1. A stone set up by Samuel as a memorial of God's help in defeating the Philistines (1 Samuel 7:12). The word means "stone of help." 2. A town of Ephraim where the Israelites were defeated by Philistines (1 Samuel 5:1).

ECCLESIASTES, BOOK OF. Book in the Old Testament emphasizing that life not centered in God is meaningless. The book reflects on the shortness, contradictions, and mysteries of human life. Traditionally, the writer of Ecclesiastes is known as "The Preacher" or Solomon. He repeatedly concludes that life is vain or empty—referring to "vanity" thirty-nine times (see Ecclesiastes 1:2). However, he advises people to work hard, enjoy the gifts of God as much and as long as they can, and let nothing turn them away from faith in and obedience to God.

Though the book appears negative, it gives assurance that God is the source of hope and strength for times of crisis. Perhaps the most popular passage from Ecclesiastes is, "To every thing there is a season, and a time to every purpose under the heaven" (see 3:1–8).

EDEN (EE d'n). God-planted garden of delight, where God also placed man (see Genesis 2:7–8, 23 for Adam and Eve). *Eden* means "delight."

EDICT (NIV). Official order (Esther 1:20; Hebrews 11:23).

■ **EDIFY, EDIFICATION**. Build up, encourage, strengthen, unify in love (Ephesians 4:12–16, 29). Edification can come from other Christians, from the Holy Spirit, or from activities (Romans 14:19; Acts 9:31; 1 Corinthians 10:23). Its goal—especially

THE STUDENT BIBLE DICTIONARY | 83

God's Garden of **Eden** certainly appears delightful in this 1828 painting by Thomas Cole.

within the church—is wholeness and completion in Jesus and harmony with other Christians.

● *How do your words and actions edify those you see daily? The Holy Spirit enables spiritually gifted people to build up the church (Ephesians 4:11–12). Consider what God's Spirit wants you to do to help build up the church.*

EDOM (EE duhm), **EDOMITES** (EE duhm ights). Means "red" or "ruddy." Isaac's older son, who was earlier called Esau (Genesis 25:30). He was renamed *Edom* because of his complexion and because he sold his birthright to his twin brother Jacob for a pot of red porridge. His descendants, the Edomites (who lived in Edom), became enemies of Israel (Deuteronomy 23:7; 2 Kings 8:21–22; Isaiah 34:5–8). See **ESAU**.

EGYPT (EE jipt). Land of northeast Africa, watered by the 4,160-mile Nile, the longest river in the world (Genesis 12:10). One of the oldest nations. Jacob's sons came there to buy food when their land was barren—and found their brother Joseph, whom they had sold into slavery, in charge. Jacob's descendants later became slaves in Egypt, but God used Moses to lead them to freedom (Genesis 42:2; Exodus 3:9–10). Jesus' parents fled

Iconic images of **Egypt**: a sphinx and pyramids. Both were apparently in existence during much of Bible history.

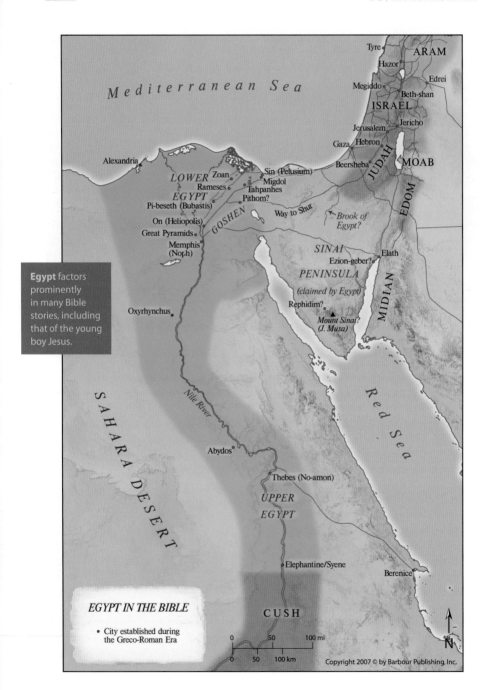

Egypt factors prominently in many Bible stories, including that of the young boy Jesus.

Mediterranean Sea

Tyre
ARAM
Hazor
Edrei
Megiddo
Beth-shan
ISRAEL
Jerusalem
Jericho
Gaza Hebron
Alexandria
JUDAH
MOAB
LOWER Zoan
Sin (Pelusium)
Beersheba
EGYPT
Rameses
Migdol
EDOM
Tahpanhes
Pi-beseth (Bubastis)
Pithom?
On (Heliopolis)
GOSHEN
Way to Shur
Brook of
Egypt?
Great Pyramids
SINAI
Elath
Memphis
(Noph)
Ezion-geber?
PENINSULA
(claimed by Egypt)
MIDIAN
Oxyrhynchus
Rephidim?
Mount Sinai?
(J. Musa)

SAHARA DESERT

Nile River

Red Sea

Abydos

Thebes (No-amon)

UPPER
EGYPT

Elephantine/Syene
Berenice

EGYPT IN THE BIBLE

- City established during
  the Greco-Roman Era

CUSH

0   50   100 mi
0   50   100 km

N

Copyright 2007 © by Barbour Publishing, Inc.

with Jesus to Egypt for safety (Matthew 2:13). Rome controlled Egypt in New Testament times.

ELAM (EE luhm). At least six Bible persons were named Elam. The most prominent was a son of Shem and grandson of Noah. This Elam gave his name to a land south of Assyria and east of Persia, which his descendants inhabited (Genesis 10:22). Also one of the earliest civilizations (Isaiah 11:11; Acts 2:9).

ELDER. Older member of a family, tribe, or religious group (Genesis 27:42). Elders were respected because of wisdom and experience (Exodus 3:16; 1 Timothy 5:17). Some elders led well (Acts 20:17, 32); others caused problems (Mark 7:3). Elders led New Testament churches.
▲ *Also used interchangeably with* pastor *and* bishop.
▲ *The Greek root word meaning "elder" comes into English as presbyter, from which we get Presbyterian. One who has presbyopia has "elder eyes" that often require reading glasses for magnification.*

ELEAZAR (EL ih AY zur). Aaron's third son, who became a high priest (Exodus 6:23; Numbers 3:32). The name means "God has helped." Others were also called by this name, such as Abinadab's son who kept the ark of the Lord (1 Samuel 7:1).

■ **ELECTION**. Choosing, selection. God's sovereign decision to choose people to be His own. It occurs in relationship to Christ (2 Peter 1:10; Ephesians 1:4–5, 11). Election does not remove each person's freedom and responsibility to choose God in Christ as Lord and Savior.

ELI. A judge and high priest for Israel. Eli taught young Samuel (1 Samuel 1–4). Samuel came to live with and serve with Eli at Shiloh following a vow Samuel's mother made. Eli failed to discipline his own sons, Hophni and Phinehas; both Eli and his sons bore the consequences (1 Samuel 4:10–18).

ELI, ELI, LAMA SABACHTHANI (EE ligh EE ligh Lah mah-sah bahk thah NEE). "My God, My God, why hast Thou forsaken Me?" This Aramaic expression is a quote from Psalm 22:1. Jesus spoke it as He died on the cross (Matthew 27:46). Same as "Eloi, eloi, lama sabachthani" (Mark 15:34). It's unclear whether the words stand as a prophetic fulfillment, reflect the fully human component of Jesus' divine being, or both. We do know these intense words came from the heart of Jesus' experience in atoning for the world's sins.

ELIEZER (el ih EE zur). Abraham's chief servant (Genesis 15:2; 24). Also, Moses' second son, whose name is a tribute of gratitude to God (Exodus 18:4). The name means "God is help." Several other persons bore this name (1 Chronicles 7:8; 15:24; 27:16; 2 Chronicles 20:37; Ezra 8:16; 10:18, 23, 31; Luke 3:29).

ELIJAH (ih LIGH juh). A well-loved prophet of Israel who took a stand for God against false religious leaders and kings (1 Kings 17:1; 18; 21:17–29). Elijah prophesied in the Northern Kingdom of Israel about 875–850 BC. He is best known for discrediting Baal and Baal's prophets on Mount Carmel and for hearing a still small voice (1 Kings 18; 19:12). Rather than dying, Elijah was taken up into heaven in a whirlwind (2 Kings 2:11). John the Baptist was referred to as Elijah. Elijah appeared to Jesus on the Mount of Transfiguration (Matthew 11:14; 17:3). The name *Elijah* means "Yahweh is God." Elijah was succeeded by Elisha, who took up Elijah's mantle and a double portion of his blessing (1 Kings 19:16–21; 2 Kings 2:9–15).

ELISABETH (ih LIZ uh beth). Wife of Zacharias and mother of John the Baptist. She came from a priestly family and was a relative of Mary, the mother of Jesus (Luke 1:5–57). Her name means "God is my oath."

Elisha brings a widow's dead son back to life, in a children's illustration from the early twentieth century. The story, recorded in 2 Kings 4, includes the Bible's only mention of sneezing, as the boy sneezed seven times before opening his eyes.

ELISHA (ih LIGH shuh). Shaphat's son who became a disciple of and successor to Elijah (1 Kings 19:16–21; 2 Kings 2:9–16). Elisha ministered to Elijah when he was worn out after confronting the prophets of Baal. Elisha performed miracles and ministered during the reigns of the Israelite kings Jehoram, Jehu, Jehoahaz, and Joash—over forty years (2 Kings 2:12–13:20). The name *Elisha* means "God is salvation."

EMMANUEL (ih MAN yoo el). Name for Jesus that means "God with us" (Isaiah 7:14; Matthew 1:23). Also spelled **IMMANUEL** (see Isaiah 7:14).

EMMAUS (eh MAY uhs). Village about seven miles from Jerusalem. Shortly after Jesus' resurrection, He joined two followers walking from Jerusalem to Emmaus. Before Jesus disappeared from the two, He taught them from Moses, opened their eyes to Him as the risen Lord, and left them amazed with burning hearts (Luke 24:13–25). Then the two returned to join the eleven disciples and share in the proclamation, "The Lord Jesus is risen indeed" (Luke 24:33–34).

ENCHANTMENT. Use of any form of magic or charm; strictly forbidden in the Bible (Leviticus 19:26). Whisper or secret (Ecclesiastes 10:11).

ENDURE. Stay, remain, lodge, be firm, bear up under (Psalm 30:5; 2 Timothy 2:3).

ENGEDI (en GED ih). Town on the west shore of the Dead Sea (1 Samuel 23:29).

ENMITY. Opposition, hatred (Genesis 3:15; Romans 8:7; Ephesians 2:15).

ENOCH (EE nuk). Eldest son of Cain. Enoch walked devoutly with God and pleased Him. God took Enoch to be with Him without Enoch experiencing physical death (Genesis 4:17; 5:18–24; Hebrews 11:5).

ENSAMPLE. Example, pattern, model (Philippians 3:17).

ENTICE. To bait, allure, persuade (James 1:14).

ENTREAT, INTREAT. Ask, request, desire (Ruth 1:16; Philippians 4:3). Treat (Jeremiah 15:11; Luke 20:11).

ENVY. Jealousy (Job 5:2; 1 Timothy 6:4).
● *You can't always stop jealousy from beginning, but you can stop it from continuing. How does*

God help you do this? (Consider: Jesus washed His disciples' feet after they argued over being the greatest.)

EPHAH. Unit of dry measure equaling about fifteen cups or 3/5 bushel or twenty-two liters (Judges 6:19).

EPHESIANS, BOOK OF (ih FEE zhuhns). This New Testament Bible book is a letter from the apostle Paul to Christians in the city of Ephesus. Many scholars think it may have been a circular letter to Christians in other cities also, because the earliest manuscripts seemingly had a space to write in other church names, as well. (The expression "at Ephesus" is not in the oldest manuscripts of Ephesians, but it is in many of the best ones.) Paul was probably in prison in Rome when he wrote Ephesians, and the time may have been about AD 61–62.

Ephesians gives readers mountaintop views of Christ, His church, the Holy Spirit, salvation, and how to live the Christian life. No wonder the book has been called "the Alps of the New Testament." Ephesians explains that the church is composed of individual Christians, drawn from different backgrounds and nationalities, each redeemed by Jesus Christ. Jesus is the Head of this church and each member has a specific purpose.

▲ Ephesians uses beautiful images of the church such as the body of Christ, the temple of God, and the bride of Christ.

EPHESUS (EF uh suhs). Famous seaport city in Ionia. Ephesus was located at about the middle of the western coast of Asia Minor (Acts 18:19). Paul founded a church in Ephesus and preached there overall for about three years. Paul wrote the Bible book of Ephesians to the church at Ephesus (and probably to other churches in Asia Minor also).

▲ The temple to the goddess Diana (also called Artemis) was in Ephesus. When people began converting to Christianity, those who profited from worship of the goddess became worried about Christianity's effects and started a riot (Acts 19:23–25).

EPHOD. Short smock worn by priests and later by others (Leviticus 8:7; 1 Samuel 2:18).

The high priest's clothing included the **ephod**, a short smock shown here underneath the golden, twelve-stoned breastplate.

EPHRAIM (EE frah ihm). 1. Name of Joseph's second son (Genesis 42:50–52). 2. A tribe of Israel (Genesis 48; Joshua 16:5). 3. A name for Israel when its territory was almost all that was left of the northern kingdom (Hosea 5:3). 4. A forest (2 Samuel 18:6). 5. A gate of Jerusalem (2 Kings 14:13). 6. A town north of Jerusalem (John 11:54).

EPICUREAN (ep ih kyu REE uhn). Usually thought of as believing "Eat, drink, and be merry, for tomorrow you may die" (see Acts 17:16–33). The name came from the Greek philosopher Epicurus (who lived 341–270 BC).

● *What is appealing about this philosophy? Besides giving in to indulgence, what else is wrong with this kind of thinking?*

EPISTLE. Letter (2 Peter 3:1). Bible books called *epistles* are letters that God inspired disciples to write to give instruction and encouragement to other Christians. For example, Romans is one of Paul's epistles to the church at Rome. First, 2, 3 John are John's epistles written to believing groups and individuals.

● *Read all of Colossians 3 from Paul's letter to the Christians at Colosse. Which instructions best fit your own needs?*

EQUAL. Having the same value as (Psalm 55:13; John 5:18; Philippians 2:6); upright or right (Psalm 17:2). To be "not equal" is to be thin or weak (Proverbs 26:7).

ER (UR). 1. Eldest son of Judah (Genesis 38:3). 2. A grandson of Judah (1 Chronicles 4:21). 3. An ancestor of Jesus through Joseph (Luke 3:28).

ESAU (EE saw). Eldest son of Isaac and Rebekah (Genesis 25:25–28). Isaac favored Esau and

In a seventeenth-century painting by Matthias Stom, red-haired **Esau** agrees to sell his birthright to his younger twin, Jacob, for a bowl of stew.

Rebekah favored Jacob, Esau's twin brother. Jacob took advantage of Esau's hunger to talk Esau into selling his birthright for a pot of stew (Genesis 25:29–34). Rebekah later encouraged and helped Jacob to trick his father into giving Esau's blessing to Jacob (Genesis 27). Esau sought to kill Jacob for tricking him out of Isaac's blessing but was later reconciled to Jacob (Genesis 27; 32). Esau's descendants lived in the land of Edom (Genesis 36:8). See **EDOM**.

ESCHATOLOGY. The study of last things or the end time, particularly referring to the return of Christ (see Matthew 25; Mark 13; Revelation 22).

ESPOUSE. Engage to be married (Matthew 1:18). Much more binding than today's engagement. To end it required a divorce. To be espoused required faithfulness. Espoused couples sometimes called each other husband and wife. In keeping with God's good plan, sex was postponed until marriage (Genesis 29:20–23). See **BETROTHED**.

ESCHEW. Turn away from, shun (Job 1:1; 1 Peter 3:11).

ESTABLISH. Strengthen, harden, confirm, make stable or strong, cause to dwell, make firm (Proverbs 8:28; Psalm 78:69; Job 36:7; Hebrews 13:9).

ESTEEM. Consider, value, judge, think of, regard (Isaiah 53:3–4; Philippians 2:3; Hebrews 11:26).

ESTHER (ESS tur). Jewish cousin of Mordecai (Esther 2:7). Esther became queen of Persia, and God used her great courage—with Mordecai's help—to save the Jewish people from destruction.

ESTHER, BOOK OF. A Bible book about God's use of Queen Esther to save the Hebrew people.

It explains the background and meaning of the Jewish festival of Purim, a feast that celebrates deliverance from a cruel and subtle anti-Jewish plot. The book of Esther does not mention God directly, but is obviously about Him because of the people committed to Him. See **PURIM, FEAST OF.**

ESTRANGE, ESTRANGED. Make unknown, alienate, become strange (Jeremiah 19:4; Ezekiel 14:5).

■ **ETERNAL LIFE.** Life that begins the instant a person turns from his sin in commitment and trusts Jesus Christ as Lord and Savior (John 3:15–16). It refers to supreme quality of life as well as unending life. Heaven is the ultimate home for Christians to enjoy eternal life in fellowship with God (Philippians 3:20).
● *How does eternal life affect your present decisions and actions? To know you have received eternal life gives assurance that your life is not temporary. The alternative to eternal life is eternal punishment—like a second or unending death.*

ETHIOPIAN (ee thih OH pih uhn). A descendant of Cush, a son of Ham (Jeremiah 13:23). The people who occupied Ethiopia, a land in eastern Africa. Ebedmelech and the man Philip told about Jesus were Ethiopians (Jeremiah 38:7; Acts 8:27).

■ **EUNUCH.** A male who is impotent—unable to produce children—because he lacks functioning sexual organs that enable procreation. It refers to a male who is castrated or from birth lacks the ability to have reproductive sexual relations (2 Kings 9:32; Acts 8:27).

EUPHRATES (yoo FRAY teez). Great river whose name means "bursting" or "sweet." Located in western Asia, it stretches from Armenia to the Persian Gulf. It is sometimes called the great river or simply, the river (Deuteronomy 1:7; Isaiah 7:20). Today called the Firat (in Turkey).

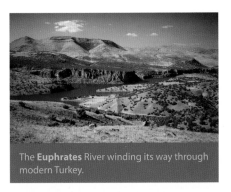

The **Euphrates** River winding its way through modern Turkey.

EUTYCHUS (YOO tih kuhs). Name that means "fortunate" (Acts 20:9). During one of Paul's long sermons, Eutychus fell asleep, fell off his window seat to the ground below, and died. Paul interrupted his preaching just long enough to revive Eutychus miraculously (Acts 20:7–12).
● *If you were Eutychus, would you have gone back to church? Why or why not? How long do you think sermons should be? Why?*

■ **EVANGELIST, EVANGELIZE.** A "good-newser." An evangelist announces the good news about Jesus Christ (2 Timothy 4:5). The verb form is usually translated as "preach the gospel" (Luke 1:19; Romans 15:20–21; Galatians 3:8; Acts 21:8; 2 Timothy 4:5; Luke 9:6). Christians can evangelize in any place (Acts 8:4). Though all Christians can evangelize, the Holy Spirit especially endows some with the spiritual gift of evangelism (Ephesians 4:11).
● *How and where do you share the good news about Jesus Christ? How does your lifestyle affect your evangelism (or your witness)?*

EVE. First woman (Genesis 3:20). Made by God from Adam's rib. In Genesis 5:2, the name *Adam*—for mankind—included Eve. See **ADAM.**

EVERLASTING LIFE. Never-ending life (Daniel 12:2; John 4:14). Life that lasts forever, continues, perpetuates. The opposite of dying. Also speaks of quality of life. See **ETERNAL LIFE.**

● *Everlasting also describes the covenant between people and God, the arms of God, God Himself, the kingdom of God, joy, and more (Genesis 9:16; Deuteronomy 33:27; Psalm 41:13; 145:13; 51:11; Jeremiah 31:3).*

EVIL. Bad, wrong, worthless, vain (Psalm 23:4; Romans 12:21). Any force, action, or attitude that works in opposition to God; anything not in harmony with God. God did not create evil; man chose evil rather than God's will (see Genesis 1–3).

● *First Timothy 6:10 explains that the love of money is "a root" of all kinds of evil. Name several specific evils that grow from love of money.*

EVIL ONE (NIV). Satan, the devil (John 17:15; 1 John 3:12).

EWE. Female sheep (Leviticus 14:10).

EXALT. Lift up, make high, raise high (Exodus 15:2; Matthew 23:12; Acts 5:31; 1 Peter 5:6). To exalt God is to worship or praise Him.

● *Why is God worthy of exaltation? Note the exaltation of Jesus in Philippians.*

EXAMPLE. Sample, type, model, someone or something to be copied or learned from (1 Timothy 4:12). Can be positive or negative (1 Peter 2:21; Jude 7). Jesus is our supreme positive example.

EXCEEDING. Beyond measure, abundant, more than usual, extreme, very strong (Genesis 13:13; Ephesians 1:19).

EXECRATION. Oath, curse (Jeremiah 42:18; 44:12).

■ **EXHORT, EXHORTATION.** Encourage, comfort, or appeal to (Acts 27:22). Speak seriously to in order to prevent a dangerous action or bring one to an end (1 Thessalonians 5:14). Bring the truth to light. Motivate to live God's way (Acts 14:22). Can be translated "admonish." Remind of past knowledge or give new knowledge (Colossians 3:16). Warn, exert influence on the will and decision making with the goal of guiding a believer toward obeying God (Colossians 1:28).

EXILE. The period when the Hebrews (Jews) were overcome, and a large number of the people were taken from their homes and placed in captivity in foreign lands. "The Exile" may include the Assyrian captivity of Israel, the Northern Kingdom (740 and 721 BC). Often, however, it refers only to the Babylonian captivity of the Southern Kingdom of Judah. See **CAPTIVE, CAPTIVITY.**

Occasionally in the New Testament, *exile* is used figuratively to mean life on earth (Hebrews 11:13).

EXODUS, BOOK OF. Second book of the Bible. Literally, *Exodus* means "a going out" or "way out." Tells about Moses' leading of the Israelites out of Egyptian captivity and to the Promised Land—but not into it—over some forty years. The Exodus began after the final plague of death on Egypt's firstborn and the Passover sparing of Israelites (Exodus 12). Exodus contains the Ten Commandments (chapter 20), Israel's sin and Moses' intercession for them (chapters 32–33), and the building of the tabernacle (chapters 35–40).

EXORCIST. One who drives out demons or evil spirits (Acts 19:13). Jesus has true authority over demons (Matthew 12:27–28; Mark 9:38; Acts 19:13–16).

EXPEDIENT. Beneficial, helpful, in one's interest, profitable. Literally, "to bear together" (John 11:50; 1 Corinthians 6:12).

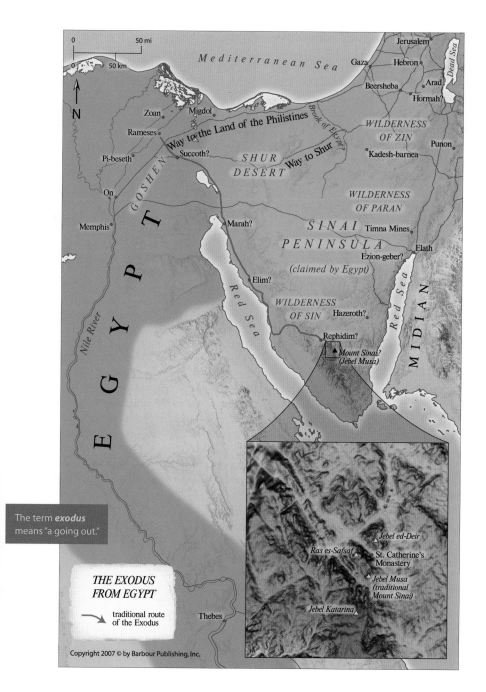

The term *exodus* means "a going out."

THE EXODUS FROM EGYPT

traditional route of the Exodus

Copyright 2007 © by Barbour Publishing, Inc.

EXTOL. Exalt, raise up, praise highly (Psalm 68:4).

EYESERVICE. Doing right to please those who are watching (Ephesians 6:6; Colossians 3:22). Service performed to attract attention, not service for its own sake nor to please God or conscience.

EZEKIEL (ih ZEE kih uhl). Ezekiel was a priest who prophesied to the exiles as a fellow captive in Babylonia (Ezekiel 1:3). He prophesied before the fall of Jerusalem that Jerusalem would be punished for its sin. After Jerusalem was destroyed in 587 BC, Ezekiel spoke of hope and encouragement for the future restoration of Israel, and more importantly hope for the coming Kingdom of God.

EZEKIEL, BOOK OF. Old Testament Bible book in the major prophets section that records divinely inspired visions and insights of the prophet Ezekiel. The book of Ezekiel often refers to God's Spirit. It emphasizes the inner renewal of heart and spirit, personal responsibility for sins, renewal of the nation, and personal holiness. Ezekiel uniquely gives a glimpse into the past of the diabolic adversary (Ezekiel 28:11–19).The book helps people see God's steady presence and involvement in daily events. Many find the book of Ezekiel fascinating because of its vivid symbolism.

EZRA (EZ ruh). Jewish priest and scribe who came back from Babylonia to Jerusalem probably in 458 BC. He helped restart the pure worship of God and taught God's laws (Ezra 7–10). He worked with Nehemiah to bring about religious reform (Nehemiah 8–10).

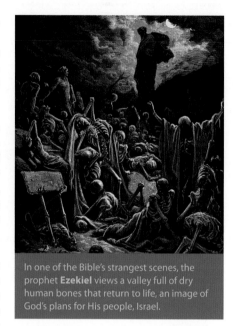

In one of the Bible's strangest scenes, the prophet **Ezekiel** views a valley full of dry human bones that return to life, an image of God's plans for His people, Israel.

EZRA, BOOK OF. An Old Testament Bible book that describes the return of Jewish exiles from Babylon, where they had been held captive. Ezra documents the rebuilding of life and worship in Jerusalem. A first group of exiles, who returned under Cyrus the Persian emperor, rebuilt and dedicated the temple in Jerusalem. Other groups returned later, including a group under Artaxerxes II led by Ezra. Ezra helped them reorganize their religious and social life in a way that expressed their spiritual heritage. Ezra is a sequel to 1–2 Chronicles.

FACE. The front of a person, presence (Psalm 13:1). Often used in connection with emotions; falling on one's face was a sign of reverence, respect, humility, or submission (Genesis 17:3; Revelation 7:11). "Setting" one's face was a sign of determination (Luke 9:53). Hiding one's face meant to reject (Psalm 27:9). Our face (or countenance) often gives away our feelings: When God rejected Cain's offering, literally Cain's face fell (Genesis 4:6).

It is interesting to note that in the KJV, "respect of persons" (judging the outer appearance) translates the Greek word for "face-receiver" (Romans 2:11; James 2:1). God does not judge by the face or outer appearance, and neither should we.

FAINT. Adjective: Weary, weak (Isaiah 40:30). Verb: Give up (2 Corinthians 4:16).

■ **FAITH**. Belief, trust (Habakkuk 2:4; Mark 11:22). Faith in Jesus Christ is essential for salvation (Ephesians 2:8–10). Faith is always active; it is a trusting into someone or something. Faith is a commitment of both mind and heart. Acts 16:5 and Jude 3 use the noun "faith" to refer to all that we as Christians believe.

● *List some ways faith in Jesus Christ helps you meet the pressures of every day.*

FAITHFUL. True (Proverbs 20:6). Steady (Acts 16:15).

FAITHLESS. Unbelieving or not faithful (Matthew 17:17).

FALL, **FALLEN**. Stumble (Isaiah 31:3; Romans 11:11). The coming of sin into the world is sometimes referred to as the "fall of humanity." Those who commit sin are sometimes called "the fallen."

In the KJV, Romans 3:23 says that we "come short of the glory of God." Other translations read that we "fall short of the glory of God." Even though we are saved, we continue to fall short of God's glory—but remain saved by His grace through faith (Ephesians 2:8–10).

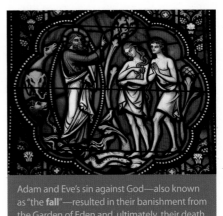

Adam and Eve's sin against God—also known as "the **fall**"—resulted in their banishment from the Garden of Eden and, ultimately, their death.

FALLOW. Type of deer (Deuteronomy 14:5). Unplowed ground (Jeremiah 4:3).

FALSE, FALSEHOOD. Lie, untruth (Deuteronomy 5:20; Micah 2:11); emptiness (Lamentations 2:14).

FAMILY. Household. In biblical times included parents and children and often in-laws and servants (Exodus 12:21). *Family* also referred to tribes or a nation (Jeremiah 2:4).

FAMINE. Lack of food brought on by drought, insects, war (Ruth 1:1; Luke 15:14). God sometimes

The baby Jesus touches the beard of His earthly parent, Joseph. Though conceived by God's Holy Spirit, Jesus grew up with a human **father** figure.

used famine as a discipline for His unbelieving and disobedient people (Jeremiah 29:17). In Amos 8:11 lack of the Word of God—or of hearing the Word of God—is called a famine.

FARE. Noun: Peace, prosperity, completeness (1 Samuel 17:18). The Hebrew word used here is the greeting *Shalom*. Verb: to make merry (Luke 16:19).

FAST. To go without food or drink for a period of time (Jeremiah 36:9; Matthew 6:16). Groups or individuals fasted on occasions. Sometimes people fasted for spiritual purposes in connection with a religious observance (Joel 1:14) or to have a better relationship with God (Ezra 8:23). The Day of Atonement was the only fast period required by Mosaic law (Leviticus 16:29; 23:31). Fasting was often a natural expression of grief (2 Samuel 1:12). Jesus fasted for forty days and nights at the beginning of His earthly ministry (Matthew 4:2).

▲ *Fasting and prayer often seemed to go together (Luke 2:37; Acts 14:23; 2 Corinthians 6:5). The New Testament commends fasting but does not command it. When Jesus cast out a demon His disciples had been unable to cast out, they wondered why. Jesus explained such an exorcism required faith, prayer, and—except in earliest New Testament manuscripts—fasting (Matthew 17:21; Mark 9:29). Religious leaders often fasted in a way that drew attention to themselves. Jesus taught that the right spiritual motives needed to be part of any fasting.*

FATHER. Male parent (Genesis 2:24). Could refer to ancestors (Genesis 48:15). Founder (Genesis 17:4). God is our spiritual Father (Philippians 1:2).

FATHOM. Length of outstretched arms, about six feet; used to measure the depth of water (Acts 27:28).

FATLING. An animal fattened for a special occasion such as an offering to God or a banquet (Psalm 66:15; Matthew 22:4).

FAULT. Error, sin, failure (Daniel 6:4; Galatians 6:1).

FAVOR. Grace, approval, kindness, goodwill (Esther 2:15; Luke 1:30; 2:52).

FEAR. In the usual sense, being afraid, but also reverence, respect, realization of holiness (Job 25:2; Luke 5:26; Acts 2:43). Not terror but honor and recognition of position. True religion includes fear of God and reverence for God (Proverbs 1:7). See **AWE**.

FEAST. Festival, banquet, religious celebration (Daniel 5:1; John 12:20). The Hebrews established several feasts to celebrate God's intervention in history or His daily care. The Feast of Unleavened Bread or the Passover Feast celebrated God's deliverance from slavery in Egypt (Exodus 23:15). See **PASSOVER**. The Feast of Weeks was later called Pentecost (Deuteronomy 16:16). See **WEEKS, FEAST OF**. The Feast of Tabernacles or Booths lasted seven days (Deuteronomy 31:10). See **BOOTHS, FEAST OF**.

The Day of Blowing Trumpets was a memorial feast and a time of sacrificial offerings and rest from work (Numbers 29:1). The Day of Atonement occurred once a year for the chief priest to make sacrifices for the sins of the nation (Leviticus 16). See **ATONEMENT**; **ATONEMENT, DAY OF**. The sabbath was a time of solemn assembly, rest from work, and joy (Hosea 2:11). See **SABBATH**. The Feast of Purim was started during the time of Esther to celebrate deliverance of the Jews from their enemy (Esther 9). See **PURIM**.

JEWISH FEASTS AND FESTIVALS

NAME	MONTH: DATE	REFERENCE	SIGNIFICANCE
Passover	Nisan (Mar/Apr): 14–21	Exodus 12:2 –20; Lev. 23:5	Commemorates God's deliverance of Israel out of Egypt.
Feast of Unleavened Bread	Nisan (Mar/Apr): 15–21	Lev. 23:6–8	Commemorates God's deliverance of Israel out of Egypt. Includes a Day of Firstfruits for the barley harvest.
Feast of Weeks, or Harvest (Pentecost)	Sivan (May/Jun): 6 (seven weeks after Passover)	Exodus 23:16; 34:22; Lev. 23:15–21	Commemorates the giving of the law at Mount Sinai. Includes a Day of Firstfruits for the wheat harvest.
Feast of Trumpets (Rosh Hashanah)	Tishri (Sep/Oct): 1	Lev. 23:23–25; Num. 29:1–6	Day of the blowing of the trumpets to signal the beginning of the civil new year.
Day of Atonement (Yom Kippur)	Tishri (Sep/Oct): 10	Lev. 23:26–33; Exodus 30:10	On this day the high priest makes atonement for the nation's sin. Also a day of fasting.
Feast of Booths, or Tabernacles (Sukkot)	Tishri (Sep/Oct):15–21	Lev. 23:33–43; Num. 29:12–39; Deut. 16:13	Commemorates the forty years of wilderness wandering.
Feast of Dedication, or Festival of Lights (Hanukkah)	Kislev (Nov/Dec): 25–30; and Tebeth (Dec/Jan): 1–2	John 10:22	Commemorates the purification of the temple by Judas Maccabaeus in 164 BC.
Feast of Purim, or Esther	Adar (Feb/Mar): 14	Esther 9	Commemorates the deliverance of the Jewish people in the days of Esther.

FELIX. (FEE liks) A cruel Roman governor of Judea who presided over Paul's first trial in Caesarea and kept Paul in prison (Acts 23:24 and following). Felix kept Paul in jail to please the Jews (Acts 24:27).

■ **FELLOWSHIP**. The family feeling and partnership between Christians (Galatians 2:9). Translates the Greek word *koinonia* (koy-know-KNEE-ah). Association, close relationship, participation with, sharing. You experience fellowship when you share life events, commitment, trust, and understanding with other Christians.

Fellowship expresses like-mindedness (Philippians 2:1), communicates acceptance (Galatians 2:9), helps believers grow (Acts 2:42), encourages the sharing of the work of the church (2 Corinthians 8:4), and includes bad times as well as good (Philippians 3:10). The Bible points out the dangers of fellowshipping with wrongdoers (Psalm 94:20; Ephesians 5:11), with unbelievers (2 Corinthians 6:14), and with demons (1 Corinthians 10:20). The person who lives in sin does not live in fellowship with God (1 John 1:6).

● *What do you like best about being with other Christians?*

FESTUS. (FESS tuhs) Governor of Judea following Felix. He presided over Paul's second trial, when Paul made his defense before Herod Agrippa II. After Paul appealed to Caesar, Festus sent him to Rome (Acts 24:27–26:32).

FETTERS. Chains for the feet of prisoners (Psalm 149:8; Mark 5:4).

FIERY. Burning, blazing (Daniel 3:6; Ephesians 6:16). Shadrach, Meshach, and Abednego survived Nebuchadnezzar's fiery furnace with God's protection (Daniel 3).

Unripe **figs** on a tree branch.

FIG, FIG TREE. A fruit tree native to Asia Minor and Syria (Genesis 3:7). A fig looks like a small pear but is brownish when ripe. Adam and Eve sewed fig leaves together to make clothing.
▲ *Jesus placed a curse on a fig tree that took up space and nourishment but bore no fruit (Mark 11:13).*
● *What lesson does the cursing of the fig tree imply for us?*

FILLETS. Fastenings, used for the hanging of curtains in the tabernacle (Exodus 27:10).

FILTH. Dirt, excrement (Isaiah 4:4; 1 Peter 3:21).

FIRM. Steadfast, sure (Hebrews 3:6).

FIRMAMENT. Sky, expanse (Genesis 1:6).

FIRSTBORN. First child (Genesis 27:19; Matthew 1:25). In the Hebrew culture the firstborn son ranked in authority after the father. His inheritance was double that of any other sons, and he received his father's special blessing.

FIRSTFRUITS. The first part of the harvest; used as a sacrifice offering to God (Nehemiah 10:35). Also used in the New Testament as a figure of speech to speak of Christ's resurrection as the first resurrection with other Christians to follow in resurrection (1 Corinthians 15:22–23). See **FEAST CHART** on page 96 and **CALENDAR CHART** on pages 265–266.

FIRSTLING. Firstborn of an animal, used in the sacrificial system (Leviticus 27:26).

FISH GATE. A gate on the east side of Jerusalem where Tyrians held a fish market (2 Chronicles 33:14).

FIT. Ready (Leviticus 16:21; Luke 9:62).

FLAGON. Large wine pitcher (Isaiah 22:24); in some verses should be translated "a cake of raisins" (2 Samuel 6:19).

A Roman **flagon** on display in a Paris museum.

FLATTER. Compliment with a view to advantage or gain (Proverbs 28:23). Make false statements to hide selfish aims (1 Thessalonians 2:5).
● *Do you ever use flattery to try get your way with others? Since this kind of flattery tries to manipulate people, identify a better way of expressing wants or convictions.*

FLEE. Escape, run away (Genesis 16:8; Matthew 2:13).

FLESH, FLESHLY. Besides the usual meaning of body tissue, the Bible often uses *flesh* to refer to anything worldly in contrast to anything spiritual or godly (Romans 8:9). Also used to describe the sinful condition of man (Romans 8:3).

FLINT. Hard rock used for making tools and weapons (Deuteronomy 8:15).

FLOCK. Herd or group of animals, usually sheep or goats (1 Samuel 30:20; Luke 2:8). Jesus used this term to describe His followers (Luke 12:32).

FLOOD. A deluge of water (Isaiah 28:2; Matthew 7:25). God sent a great flood to destroy those who would not turn from sin. God spared the righteous Noah and his family who obeyed Him (Genesis 6–9).

FOE. Enemy (Psalm 27:2; Matthew 10:36).

FOLD. Fenced or hedged place for animals (Numbers 32:16). Flock (John 10:16).

FOLLOW. To come after (Joshua 14:8; Mark 2:14). To be actively committed to a leader regardless of the cost (Luke 9:23).
● *Each person has the responsibility to choose the person or way of living he or she will follow:* the ways of the world or the will of God. List actions you carried out during your social activities this past week. How did these actions reflect the choice of your followship?

FOLLY. Foolishness, senselessness (Proverbs 5:23; 2 Timothy 3:9).

FOOL. A person who is self-confident or thinks too highly of himself, lacking in judgment, careless (Romans 1:22; Proverbs 12:23; Luke 12:20).
● *Ultimately, God is the judge of who is a fool. See the caution of Matthew 5:22 about the mixture of anger and calling other persons "fool" (senseless).*

FORBEAR. To quit, neglect, or refrain (Deuteronomy 23:22; Numbers 9:13). To endure or put up with (Ephesians 4:2).
▲ *Notice the almost opposite meaning of these words in the Old and New Testaments.*

FORBEARANCE. A holding back, delaying, pausing (Romans 3:25).

A sheep **fold**.

FORBID. Restrain, hinder, prevent (Numbers 11:28; Matthew 19:14).

FORD. A shallow area in a stream where people and animals could cross to the other side (Genesis 32:22).

FOREFATHER(S). Ancestors (Jeremiah 11:10; 2 Timothy 1:3).

FOREIGNERS. Strangers, those from other nations (Deuteronomy 15:3). The Israelites were warned not to marry those of other nations because those people worshiped other gods and would lead the Israelites away from God (Deuteronomy 7:1–6). One who lives in a place that is not his home (Ephesians 2:9).

FOREKNOW, FOREKNOWLEDGE. To know first or beforehand (Romans 8:29). Also used to indicate that God knows everything: past, present, and future (1 Peter 1:2).

FORESKIN. A fold of skin that covers the end of the penis (Genesis 17:11). See **CIRCUMCISION**.

■ **FORGIVE, FORGIVENESS**. Pardon or excuse a wrong (Matthew 6:12, 14–15). Cancel a debt. Give up claim for revenge or resentment. Reestablish a broken relationship. To forgive is to trust others as if the wrong is forgotten. It includes a new start in attitudes and actions (John 8:11).
● *How easy or difficult is it for you to forgive? To be forgiven? Forgiving others opens a bridge we, too, must cross over to receive forgiveness from God. Jesus forgave sins (Mark 2:5) and encourages us to forgive each other the same way (Colossians 3:13; Matthew 18:22–35). What place does repentance have in forgiveness? (See Acts 2:38–39.)*

FORM. Verb: To bring forth, to give shape to (Genesis 2:7; Psalm 90:2). Noun: Appearance (2 Timothy 3:5).

■ **FORNICATION**. Sexual intercourse between two people who are not married to each other (1 Thessalonians 4:3–5). Sometimes translated *immorality,* the word can refer to sexual or sensual sins in general. Fornication is not a new sin. The Old Testament records that many sinned this way, including King David (2 Samuel 11). Old Testament prostitutes practiced fornication in religious ceremonies. (Obviously this was condemned by God—Leviticus 19:29.) In the New Testament fornication is included in several lists of sins (Romans 1:29; Acts 15:29; Colossians 3:5). Fornication hurts people (1 Corinthians 6:18; 1 Thessalonians 4:6). The word is also used to picture unfaithfulness to God (Isaiah 23:17; Jude 7; John 8:41).
▲ *Sex itself is God's invention and, therefore, "very good" in the context of God's overall creation (Genesis 1:31). The sexual expression of love within marriage is God's good plan. The Bible points to marriage as the divine design for producing children and sharing the joy of His gift of sexuality. But we are to avoid fornication, adultery, or any form of sexual immorality (Proverbs 5:19; 1 Corinthians 7:2).*
● *Why did God design the fulfillment of sexual expression only within marriage? Why is sex outside of marriage so attractive? Sexual discipline within God's will brings blessings; otherwise, sex outside God's will is sinful and leads to pain and trouble.*

FORSAKE. Give up, leave, let go, abandon (Deuteronomy 31:6; Matthew 19:27).

FORTH. Forward, outside, out, into view (Genesis 39:13; John 11:43).

Though it was built some twelve hundred years after Christ's earthly ministry, the Nimrod **fortress** on the Golan Heights is a good illustration of a biblical stronghold.

FORTRESS. Fenced place, stronghold (Isaiah 25:12). The psalmist spoke of God as his fortress (Psalm 18:2).

FOUL. Adjective: Unclean (Mark 9:25). Verb: To trample (Ezekiel 34:18).

FOUNDATION. Base or support, anything laid down as a beginning point on which to build (2 Chronicles 23:5; Acts 16:26). In the New Testament, often used in a spiritual sense (1 Corinthians 3:11). Christ is the cornerstone of the foundation of the church (Ephesians 2:20).

FOWL. Any type of bird or birds (Genesis 1:21; Matthew 6:26).

FRAME. Verb: Establish, form (Jeremiah 18:11; Hebrews 11:3). Noun: A form (Psalm 103:14).

FRANKINCENSE. Substance made from tree resin. Used in Old Testament religious ceremonies and presented as a gift from the wise men to Christ (Exodus 30:34; Matthew 2:11).

FREE. At liberty, not enslaved; freed from sin (Exodus 21:2; John 8:34–36; Romans 6:18).

FREEWILL OFFERING. Voluntary offering (Leviticus 22:18).

FRO. Back. Used with *to and* to mean back and forth (Genesis 8:7).

FRONTLET. Small box made of animal skin that contained scripture passages (Deuteronomy 6:8). Men strapped it to their foreheads during morning prayer except during sabbaths and festivals.
▲ *Scriptures contained were Exodus 13:1–16; Deuteronomy 6:4–9; 11:13–21. See* **PHYLACTERIES**.

A young Jewish man wears a **frontlet**—also called *teffilin*—for prayer time.

FROWARD. Turned the wrong way, wicked, corrupt, perverse (Psalm 101:4; Proverbs 2:15; 1 Peter 2:18).
▲ *In the King James Version, seventeen of the twenty-four uses of froward and frowardness are in Proverbs. As a preposition, froward is the opposite of toward.*

FRUIT. Besides the usual reference to food, *fruit* is often used in a symbolic sense. It may refer to children as the fruit of the womb (Genesis 1:11; Exodus 21:22); or fruit may refer to good characteristics as fruit of the Spirit (Galatians 5:22).

FRUSTRATE. Cancel, put aside (Ezra 4:5; Galatians 2:21).

FUGITIVE. One who runs away (Genesis 4:14).

FULFIL. Complete the measure of, fill up, make full, make happen (1 Kings 2:27; Matthew 3:15).

FULNESS OF TIME. The time when everything was just right (Galatians 4:4). Christ's birth occurred at the exact time God planned—when the time was "brim full." Rome ruled the world, and there was peace; Roman-built roads allowed travel to all places where civilized society existed. Greek was the universal language and became the language of the New Testament. Mankind—every individual person—desperately needed the Messiah (or, the Christ) who came as the Savior in the birth of Jesus. Two key Bible references show this eternal need and truth for today and all time: Romans 3:23 and Romans 6:23. Romans 9–10 answer this need.

This image of an industrial **furnace** indicates the danger that Shadrach, Meshach, and Abednego faced after incurring King Nebuchadnezzar's wrath.

FURNACE. Different types of ovens used for baking bricks, pottery, bread, or smelting metals (Daniel 3:6). Sometimes used in connection with God's judgment (Matthew 13:42).

▲ *Daniel's three friends were thrown into a fiery furnace because they would not bow down to a pagan god. But the one true God spared them from the flames (Daniel 3).*

FURY. Rage, violent anger (Nahum 1:6).

FUTURE. What lies ahead unseen. An opportunity to trust what God has done in the past to give us faith and hope in what He will do in the future (Jeremiah 31:17 NRSV; Hebrews 11:1).

church at Galatia. He wrote the letter to combat the heresy of the Judaizers, which essentially was to add works to God's grace as a requirement for salvation. The Judaizers believed that Gentiles had to be circumcised in addition to their commitment to Christ to be saved. (See Acts 15 for more on the problem of Judaizers and heresy.)

▲*Galatians is often called "Little Romans" because Romans is a fuller development of the themes of Galatians.*

GABRIEL (GAY brih uhl). Name meaning "man of God." God's angel who delivered four messages in scripture (Daniel 8:15–27; 9:20–27; Luke 1:11–38). Gabriel helped interpret Daniel's visions; announced the birth of John the Baptist to Zacharias; and foretold the birth of Jesus to Mary.

GAD (GAD). Seventh son of Jacob whose mother was Zilpah (Genesis 30:10–11). His descendants became the tribe of Gad, one of the twelve tribes of Israel. Also the name of a prophet during the time of King David (1 Samuel 22:5).

GADARA, GADARENES, (GAD uh ruh; GAD uh reenz). One of the ten cities of the Decapolis, where Jesus healed a demon-possessed man (Mark 5:1).

▲*Most modern translations use the alternate reading of "Gerasenes."*

GALATIA (guh LAY shuh). An ancient kingdom of Asia Minor that later became a Roman province (Acts 16:6). Paul established churches in the cities of this region on his first missionary journey. He later wrote a letter to the church, which is the New Testament book Galatians.

GALATIANS, BOOK OF (guh LAY shuhns). This New Testament Bible book is Paul's letter to the

GALILEE (GAL ih lee). Small region in northern Palestine (Israel). In Galilee Jesus grew up, chose His disciples, and did much of His ministry (Matthew 3:13; 4:15, 18, 23, 25; 21:11). Nazareth, Jesus' hometown, was part of Galilee. Galilee was rich agriculturally; its sea provided plentiful fish; and it was crossed by several major routes through the Roman empire. Though Galilee was mainly a Jewish region, Gentiles (non-Jews) and early Christians also lived there.

▲*In the Old Testament, Galilee was part of the land allocated to the twelve tribes of Israel and prophesied to be the home of the Messiah (Isaiah 9:1–4; Matthew 5:14–15).*

GALILEE, SEA OF. Heart-shaped, freshwater body about sixty miles north of Jerusalem.

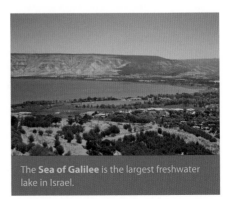

The **Sea of Galilee** is the largest freshwater lake in Israel.

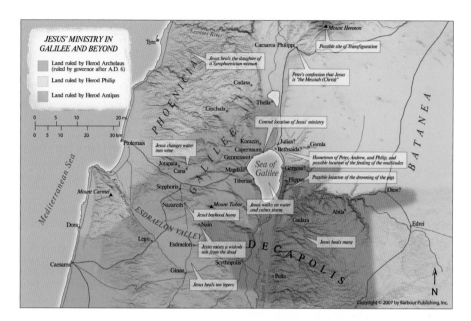

JESUS' MINISTRY IN GALILEE AND BEYOND

Land ruled by Herod Archelaus (ruled by governor after A.D. 6)

Land ruled by Herod Philip

Land ruled by Herod Antipas

Leontes River

Tyre

Caesarea Philippi

Mount Hermon

Possible site of Transfiguration

Jesus heals the daughter of a Syrophoenician woman

Cadasa

Peter's confession that Jesus is "the Messiah (Christ)"

PHOENICIA

Gischala

Thella

0   5   10   20 mi

0   5   10   20   30 km

Central location of Jesus' ministry

Ptolemais

Jesus changes water into wine

Korazin

Capernaum

Julias?

Bethsaida?

Gamla

BATANEA

Gennesaret

Hometown of Peter, Andrew, and Philip, and possible location of the feeding of the multitudes

Mediterranean Sea

Jotapata

Cana

Magdala

Sea of Galilee

Gergesa?

Hippus

Possible location of the drowning of the pigs

Mount Carmel

Sepphoris

Tiberias

Dion?

GALILEE

Nazareth

Mount Tabor

Jesus walks on water and calms storm

Kishon River

Jesus boyhood home

Dora

Nain

Gadara

Abila

Edrei

Legio

ESDRAELON VALLEY

Esdraelon

Jesus raises a widow's son from the dead

DECAPOLIS

Jesus heals many

Caesarea

Ginae

Scythopolis

Pella

Jesus heals ten lepers

Jordan River

N

Copyright © 2007 by Barbour Publishing, Inc.

It was some thirteen miles long and eight miles wide at the widest point—and about seven hundred feet below sea level. Many of Jesus' ministries and miracles took place on or around the Sea of Galilee (Matthew 8:23–27; Mark 3:7–12; 6:35–56). On its shores were the towns of Capernaum, Bethsaida, Magdala, and Tiberias. The sea is prone to sudden dangerous storms because of the way the wind whips down nearby mountains (Mark 4:37).

▲ *Also called Tiberius, Gennesaret, and Chinnereth (Chinneroth, Cinneroth).*

● *Contrast the Sea of Galilee as a freshwater body against the Dead Sea at about thirteen hundred feet below sea level. Water flowed through the Sea of Galilee but only into the Dead Sea. Consider the parallel effect in human lives when we only receive but do not give to others.*

GALL. A bitter thing (Job 20:14; Matthew 27:34). A bitter and poisonous plant. Bile, secretion of the gallbladder (Job 16:13).

GAMALIEL (guh MAY lih uhl). A leader in the Old Testament tribe of Manasseh (Numbers 7:54). Also, a New Testament Pharisee and teacher of the Law, who counseled reasonableness and a wait-and-see approach to whether the message of the apostles was from God or would come to nothing (Acts 5:34–40). He also taught Paul (Acts 22:3).

GARMENT. Piece of clothing (2 Kings 5:22; Matthew 9:16).

GARRISON. A military station or stronghold (1 Samuel 14:1).

GATE. Door, entrance to houses, buildings, or cities (Genesis 19:1; Acts 3:10).

GAZA (GAY zuh). One of the five main Philistine cities, located southwest of Jerusalem on the seacoast (2 Kings 18:8; Acts 8:26).

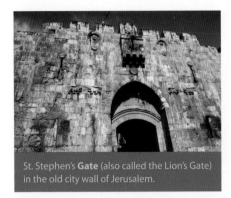

St. Stephen's **Gate** (also called the Lion's Gate) in the old city wall of Jerusalem.

GEHENNA. The root of this word from Aramaic and then Greek is translated in the KJV as "hell." In the Gospels, it refers to the place of punishment beyond this life (Matthew 5:22). See **HADES, HELL**.

GENEALOGY. List of names of descendants (2 Chronicles 31:16; Titus 3:9). Jesus' ancestors are listed in Matthew 1:1–17 and Luke 3:23–38.

GENERATION. Descendants; people living at the same time (Genesis 6:9; Mark 8:12).

GENESIS, BOOK OF. The first book in the Bible. Hebrew word meaning "beginning." Genesis tells about the beginning of creation and the beginning of human disobedience to God. It tells familiar accounts of the flood, Tower of Babel, and patriarchs. Genesis is the seedbed of doctrine for the New Testament and is invaluable for understanding much of the New Testament.
▲ *The book of Genesis gets its name from the first words of the book, "In the beginning. . ." (Genesis 1:1).*

GENNESARET, LAKE OF (geh NESS uh ret). New Testament name for the Sea of Galilee (Luke 5:1). In Old Testament same as Sea of Chinnereth. See **GALILEE, SEA OF**.

GENTILE (JEN tighl). Literally, "nation." The word refers to a person who is not a Jew (Romans 9:24). Jewish Christians at first had trouble accepting Gentiles and, in effect, felt they needed to become Jewish, also. However, the Jews learned that Gentiles become a part of God's family as anyone does: by accepting Jesus Christ as Lord and Savior (Galatians 3:14).
▲ *All salvation comes by the grace of God through faith (Ephesians 2:8–10). The atonement of Jesus Christ in grace provides for all believers for all the ages.*
● *In faith, are you a member of the family of God regardless of race? How do you become part of God's family?*

GERGESENES (GUR guh seens). Inhabitants of a district southeast of the Lake of Tiberias (Matthew 8:28; see also Mark 5:1). Translations vary in using Gerasa, Gergesa, and Gadara.

GETHSEMANE (geth SEM uh nih). A place about a mile from Jerusalem at the Mount of Olives (Mark 14:32). Jesus prayed His prayer of agony here shortly before Judas led Jesus' enemies to the spot to arrest Him.

GIANTS. Men who were strong, mighty, and of great stature (Deuteronomy 2:20).

GIDEON (GID ih uhn). Son of Joash, called by God to free the Israelites from Midian (Judges 6:13–14). God led him to accomplish this with only three hundred men. Gideon ruled the Israelites as a judge for forty years.

GIFT. Present, offering, favor (Daniel 2:6; 2 Corinthians 9:15). The gift of God is eternal life (Romans 6:23; Ephesians 2:8–10). The gift of the Holy Spirit comes with salvation (Acts 2:38).
▲ *Gifts are always free. Salvation is a gift from God that cannot be worked for; it comes only*

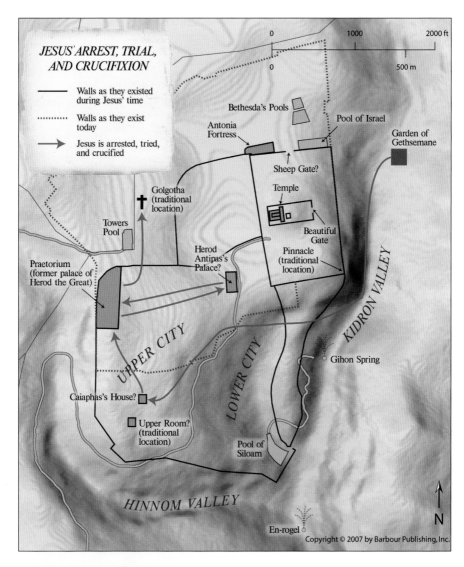

JESUS' ARREST, TRIAL, AND CRUCIFIXION

—— Walls as they existed during Jesus' time

········· Walls as they exist today

——→ Jesus is arrested, tried, and crucified

0 .... 1000 .... 2000 ft

0 .... 500 m

Bethesda's Pools

Antonia Fortress

Pool of Israel

Garden of Gethsemane

Sheep Gate?

Golgotha (traditional location)

Temple

Towers Pool

Beautiful Gate

Praetorium (former palace of Herod the Great)

Herod Antipas's Palace?

Pinnacle (traditional location)

KIDRON VALLEY

UPPER CITY

LOWER CITY

Gihon Spring

Caiaphas's House?

Upper Room? (traditional location)

Pool of Siloam

HINNOM VALLEY

En-rogel

N

Copyright © 2007 by Barbour Publishing, Inc.

by repenting of sin and trusting Jesus as Lord and Savior (Romans 10:9–10).

■ **GIFTS, SPIRITUAL.** Abilities or powers given to an individual by God through the Holy Spirit (1 Corinthians 7:7). Each person has at least one gift and the responsibility and accountability for the use of that gift (Matthew 25:14–30; 1 Peter 4:11).

▲ *For listings of some spiritual gifts, see 1 Corinthians 12–13 and Romans 12.*

The garden of **Gethsemane** today, with olive trees estimated at nearly a thousand years of age.

● *Identify at least one spiritual gift you feel God has given you. How are you trying to be a good steward in developing and using this gift?*

GILEAD (GILL ih uhd). Wooded and hilly area east of the Jordan River (Genesis 37:25). Known as a refuge for fugitives and for its association with medicinal balm.

GILGAL (GILL gal). City located west of the Jordan River, not far from Jericho (Joshua 4:19). First camp of the Israelites after they crossed the Jordan River to claim the Promised Land and became Joshua's headquarters.

GIRD. To put on an article of clothing such as a belt, or fasten with a belt (1 Samuel 17:39; Acts 12:8). To "gird up" means to get ready for responsibility and action in a determined way (Job 38:3; 40:7; 1 Peter 1:13).

GIRDLE. Belt made of cloth or leather (2 Kings 1:8; Mark 1:6). Often same as loincloth or waistcloth.

GLEAN. Gather (Ruth 2:2). A Hebrew law allowed the poor and strangers to gather grain or grapes left from a harvest (Leviticus 19:9–10).

■ **GLORIFICATION**. Process of becoming pure or holy, of becoming all God wants us to be. Completion of salvation—after we die and go to heaven—that reflects both the suffering and the lifting up of our Lord and Savior (Romans 8:17). Sanctification relates closely to glorification in that God's Spirit works within us to make us holy now but also in a time of completion.

■ **GLORIFY**. Praise, worship (Psalm 86:9). Admire, point out the good in, recognize as glorious. All Christians' greatest calling is to glorify God through their actions, words, and

A nineteenth-century painting entitled *The Gleaners* shows how biblical people also gathered leftovers from recently harvested fields.

character (Matthew 5:16; Ephesians 1:4–14). Christians glorify God by obeying Him and living His way. Specific examples include sexual purity (1 Corinthians 6:20), choosing the right words (1 Peter 4:11), showing our faith by good works (James 2:18), imitating Jesus (John 17:10–11), and having the mind of Christ (Philippians 2:5).

▲ *In the Old Testament people glorified God (Leviticus 10:3–4; Isaiah 44:23) and God glorified Himself (Ezekiel 28:22; Daniel 5:23). In the New Testament Jesus' actions caused observers to glorify God (Matthew 9:8; 15:31), and God glorified Jesus (Hebrews 5:5; Luke 4:15).*

● *With what actions and attitudes do you glorify God and praise Him in worship?*

■ **GLORY**. A divine quality (Acts 7:2; 1 Corinthians 2:8; James 2:1). The brightness, splendor, and radiance of God's presence. God's visible revelation of Himself. Our word *doxology* ultimately comes from *doxa*, the Greek word for "glory."

▲ *God has revealed Himself through His glory. God's glory was known by Ezekiel and others in the Old Testament, by the shepherds at the time of Jesus' birth in the New Testament, at the transfiguration, and will be seen by everyone when Jesus returns. Paul described God's glory as unapproachable light (1 Timothy 6:16). We will experience God's glory as part of our inheritance with Him (Ephesians 1:18) and as an unfading crown for present trials (1 Peter 1:7, 5:4).*

In the New Testament, Jesus—God the Son—demonstrated the personality, presence, and character of God. He made the glory of God forever visible (John 1:14; 2 Corinthians 4:6). Jesus' presence in Christians enables us to share in the reflection of God's glory (Colossians 1:27).

● *How do you experience God's glory? What makes you aware of His glory?*

GLUTTON. Excessive eater, hoggish person (Proverbs 23:21; Matthew 11:19).

GNASH. Grinding of teeth together that expresses great emotional upheaval such as rage or anguish (Lamentations 2:16; Matthew 8:12).

GNAT. Tiny insect (Matthew 23:24).

▲ *Jesus chided religious leaders for straining out gnats but swallowing camels.*

● *What does this say about your priorities and your values?*

GNOSTICISM. A know-it-all religion that taught salvation comes through a special or secret knowledge of God. Gnosticism taught that the body was either evil or did not matter. Gnostics expressed this belief in one of two ways: either by living a life of extreme self-denial or in contrast by self-indulgence. To the Gnostics, spirit was eternal and was what really mattered. Though the word *Gnosticism* is not in the Bible, the concept is there. Full-blown Gnosticism developed a hundred years later. Biblical writers argued against people holding ideas that later developed into Gnosticism. For example, the book of Colossians underlines the truths of God's supremacy and Christ's headship of the church. Colossians combats any heresy of worshiping angels or celestial objects, and other errors of doctrine.

■ **GOD**. The Eternal One, without beginning and without end (Exodus 3:14). The uncreated One who created everything and everyone (Genesis 1:1; John 1:1–3). He is One (Deuteronomy 6:4–9), yet He reveals Himself to us as three in One: God the Father, God the Son, and God the Holy Spirit (Matthew 3:16–17). He is characterized by His creative work, the grace of His loving mercy, His intolerance of sin, His forgiveness of people who turn from sin and trust Him, His guidance for quality living (Genesis 1:31; Ephesians 2:8–10; Romans 6:23; Romans 10:9–10; John 3:16; 10:10).

The way to come to know God the Father and God the Spirit is to come to know God the Son, who is Jesus Christ (John 14:15–20). God is all-powerful, all-knowing, all-present, and all-loving.

▲ *No definition of God is adequate, but His revelation and our experience with Him are sufficient for us to know Him and trust Him completely, for now and for all eternity. See also* **FATHER, HOLY SPIRIT, JESUS,** *and* **TRINITY.**

GOD, NAMES FOR. The Bible uses many names for God and each one describes something about His character, abilities, or the way He relates to us. These first six are Hebrew words that are translated into English in your Bible. How does each one make a difference in your life?

ELOHIM = God, Majesty, Mightiness, Unchanging Love (Genesis 1:1). The one who brought order out of chaos. This name describes the one True God. It stresses God's Almighty Mind and Creatorship. This name is used to describe God who wants a covenant relationship with His people. Elohim is a plural form of a Hebrew word with a singular meaning. It could also be used for idols and false gods.

YHWH = Often translated LORD; God's personal name (Exodus 3:14; Colossians 1:15) God is both loving and righteous and must therefore judge evil. *YHWH* expresses God's moral and spiritual attributes of love, holiness, righteousness. (Notice *YHWH* has no vowels. The correct pronunciation is probably *Yahweh* rather than *Jehovah*; and some English versions now retain *Yahweh* in its transliterated form as a title or personal name.)

EL SHADDAI = God Almighty who is able to carry out His own will and purpose (Genesis 17:1; 2 Corinthians 6:18). His strength is made perfect in our weakness. *El* is translated God and primarily means might or power. God gives or pours out Himself and His power for the sake of others.

EL ELYON = Most High God (Genesis 14:22; Romans 3:29). *El* means God as in El Shaddai. *Elyon* refers to the special and distinct nature of God, that He is the highest God ruling all other heavenly beings and superior to all beings claiming to have divine power. Though God made us human beings "in His image," He and only He has the power to rule, possess, and be exalted above all other beings, powers, and elements of creation. God alone is God; humans are always less than divine (Psalm 8).

ADONAI = Lord (Genesis 15:1ff; Psalm 8:9; Acts 9:6). This term is distinct from **YHWH** (see above) because it focuses on God's personal relationship to us: He as Creator and us as created. *Adonai* highlights the characteristics of both a master/slave (ownership) and a husband/wife (together forever) relationship. God takes care of our needs and He is sufficient for us.

EL OLAM = Everlasting God or God of the Age who reveals Himself to persons (Hebrews 1:1). He works in time to help us understand Him, how to serve Him, how to act as His people.

● *The above Hebrew names are translated into God, Lord, or other English words with the exception of "Yahweh" now retained in a transliterated form in some English translations. The following are English descriptions of God. What do you like about each?*

I AM (Exodus 3:14).

ABBA = Daddy (Mark 14:36; Romans 8:15).

LOVE (1 John 4:8).

THE LIVING GOD (Matthew 16:16).

FATHER, SON, and *HOLY GHOST* [or *HOLY SPIRIT*] (Matthew 28:19).

NAMES OF GOD

NAME	REFERENCE	MEANING	NIV EQUIVALENT
HEBREW NAMES			
Adonai	Ps. 2:4	Lord, Master	Lord
El-Berith	Judges 9:46	God of the Covenant	El-Berith
El Elyon	Gen. 14:18–20	Most High God/Exalted One	God Most High
El Olam	Gen. 21:33	The Eternal God	The Eternal God
El Shaddai	Gen. 17:1–2	All Powerful God	God Almighty
Qedosh Yisra'el	Isa. 1:4	The Holy One of Israel	The Holy One of Israel
Shapat	Gen. 18:25	Judge/Ruler	Judge
Yahweh-jereh	Gen. 22:14	Yahweh Provides	The Lord Will Provide
Yahweh-seba'ot	1 Samuel 1:3	Yahweh of Armies	Lord Almighty
Yahweh-shalom	Judges 6:24	Yahweh Is Peace	The Lord Is Peace
Yahweh-tsidkenu	Jer. 23:6	Yahweh Our Righteousness	The Lord Our Righteousness
ARAMAIC NAMES			
Attiq yomin	Dan. 7:9	Ancient of Days	Ancient of Days
Illaya	Dan. 7:25	Most High	Most High

GODS. Any persons or things that are objects of worship (Exodus 20:23; Acts 19:26). People have always struggled with the pull toward worship of false gods (idolatry). There is only one true God.

● *Name some gods that people have today. Instead of an object, could an activity be a god?*

■ **GOD'S WILL**. The divine design and the desire of God for all of His creation (Matthew 6:10; Mark 3:35).

▲*Scholars view God's will from different perspectives: (1) God has a will that will be done because He is God and controls eternity and creation. (2) God has a will that He allows to be frustrated—or chosen against—because He chooses to give freedom of choice to mankind. (3) When man chooses against God's will, God does not give up on man; He wills and works for man what is the best despite all circumstances and at every age and stage of life and history. God works together all things for His glory and to mold us back into His image (Romans 8:28–30). Note: The qualifiers for this context in Romans 8:28 are for those who love God and are called according to His purpose.*

GOLGOTHA (GAHL guh thuh). Hebrew word for "skull." The spot near Jerusalem where Jesus was crucified (Matthew 27:33; Mark 15:22; John 19:17). Same as Calvary (Luke 23:33).

Though its exact site is unknown, many artists throughout history have attempted to depict what happened at **Golgotha**—the death of Jesus Christ on the cross.

▲ *No one today knows the precise location of Golgotha, though supposed locations are marked or suggested by local guides.*

GOLIATH (guh LIGH uhth). A Philistine warrior over nine feet tall, killed by David with a slingshot and stone (1 Samuel 17).

▲ *Slings in Bible days were serious weapons, not toys.*

GOMORRAH (guh MAWR uh). One of the five cities of the plain in the vicinity of the Dead Sea. When God announced He was going to destroy the city because of the people's sin, Abraham begged God to change His mind about the destruction if a minimum number of righteous people could be found. God agreed. When that number could not be found, the unrepentant people were not spared. Only Lot's family—except for his wife, who "looked back"—escaped the destruction (Genesis 19).

▲ *Sodom and Gomorrah have become symbols for wickedness and destruction.*

GOOD. Pleasant, joyful, agreeable, admirable, worthy (Genesis 1:31; Matthew 7:11). God alone is morally perfect and is our example of goodness (Matthew 19:17). We please God when we try to follow His example of goodness within His Spirit's leadership (Romans 8:6–9; 1 Thessalonians 4:1).

▲ *Although living a good life and doing good works are pleasing to God, in His Spirit, this does not bring salvation. Only obedience to God through repentance and trust in Jesus Christ can accomplish this through God's grace.*

GOPHER WOOD. Wood, probably similar to cypress; used in the building of Noah's ark (Genesis 6:14).

GOSHEN (GO shuhn). An area in Egypt assigned to Joseph's family by Pharaoh (Genesis 47:6). The Hebrews lived there until the time of the Exodus.

GOSPEL. Literally, "good news" (Mark 1:14). Christian message about the life and sacrificial death of Jesus Christ that brings salvation to all who believe. The first four books of the New Testament that tell about Jesus are referred to as the Gospels.

GOVERNMENT. Rule, power (Isaiah 9:6; 2 Peter 2:10). The Old Testament world saw a variety of authority structures and figures: heads of families; theocracy (rule of God); kings. In New Testament times Rome ruled the known world.

GOVERNOR. A ruler of an area, who was under the authority of another ruler—such as a king (Genesis 42:6; Luke 2:2). Joseph served as governor under Pharaoh, and Pontius Pilate and Felix were governors in the New Testament.

■ **GRACE**. Favor (Genesis 6:8). God's free and undeserved love that never quits (Ephesians 2:8). Grace is the gift of God that comes as eternal life through Jesus Christ our Lord (Romans 6:23). Salvation comes only by receiving the grace of God in Jesus Christ; there is no other name, person, or way of salvation (Acts 4:10–12).

▲ *One writer said that grace is the richest word in the Bible because all of God's blessings grow out of this essential loving gift of God.*

Pontius Pilate—**governor** of Judea—presents Jesus to the angry crowd. Pilate will give in to the crowd's call for crucifixion.

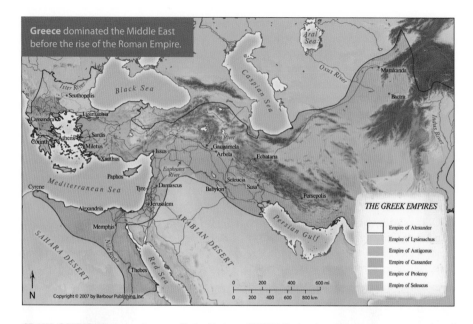

Greece dominated the Middle East before the rise of the Roman Empire.

THE GREEK EMPIRES

Empire of Alexander
Empire of Lysimachus
Empire of Antigonus
Empire of Cassander
Empire of Ptolemy
Empire of Seleucus

Copyright © 2007 by Barbour Publishing, Inc.

GRAIN OFFERING (in KJV, "meat offering"). 1. An offering presented to God in response to His command (Leviticus 2). Consisted of flour, baked cakes, or raw grain combined with oil and frankincense. Could accompany burnt offerings and peace offerings (Numbers 15:1–9). 2. Also used without the frankincense as a substitute for an animal sacrifice by those who could not afford an animal (Leviticus 5:11–13). Giving one's best grain during worship was part of a ceremony that represented removal of past sins.

GRANT. Noun: permission. Verb: give (Ezra 3:7; Psalm 85:7; Revelation 3:21).

GRAVE. Burial place (Genesis 50:5; John 12:17). Burial practices were similar in the Old and New Testaments. Often the deceased were buried in a family tomb. Graves were in the ground, natural caves, or cut-out caves. Sometimes graves were marked with stones or pillars.

GRECIAN. In the Old Testament, people of Greece (Joel 3:6). In the New Testament, could refer to Greeks but particularly to Greek-speaking Jews, especially those born or living outside Palestine (Acts 6:1). See **HELLENISTS**.

GREEK. Language spoken in Greece, which Alexander the Great made universal in a political and cultural sense. A choice language capable of expressing nuances of meaning and providentially the language for the writing of the New Testament. Language of philosophers such as Plato, Aristotle, and poets like Homer. Pilate had "Jesus of Nazareth the King of the Jews" inscribed on the cross in Hebrew, Greek, and Latin (John 19:19–20).

▲ *Though Rome ruled the known world of New Testament times, the conquering nation's language of Latin did not immediately overcome the previous Greek language and culture. This explains why one nation ruled, but the language of another culture was still universal.*

THE GREEK ALPHABET

A	α	alpha	N	ν	nu
B	β	beta	Ξ	ξ	xi
Γ	γ	gamma	O	ο	omicron
Δ	δ	delta	Π	π	pi
E	ε	epsilon	P	ρ	rho
Z	ζ	zeta	Σ	σ, ς	sigma
H	η	eta	T	τ	tau
Θ	θ	theta	Y	υ	upsilon
I	ι	iota	Φ	φ	phi
K	κ	kappa	X	χ	chi
Λ	λ	lambda	Ψ	ψ	psi
M	μ	mu	Ω	ω	omega

GROPE. To feel or search (Job 12:25).

GROW. Increase and mature—physically, mentally, and spiritually (Genesis 21:20; Luke 2:40). Christians are to grow in their spiritual lives (2 Peter 3:18).

GUILTY. Responsible for a crime, delinquency, or sin (Leviticus 6:4; 1 Corinthians 11:27).

▲ *Guilt may be a condition or a feeling. True guilt is when we disobey God's will—a real condition whether we feel guilty or not. False guilt is when we're okay with God but feel guilty—and shouldn't. Others may impose false guilt on us if we let them set our standards and values. We are best to avoid false guilt, answering to God for true guilt when we look to His Word and His Spirit to guide us.*

HABAKKUK (huh BAK uhk). Prophet of Judah about 600 BC, responsible for the book of Habakkuk. His name means "to embrace." Habakkuk lived and prophesied about the same time as Jeremiah. He spoke to people who had seen prosperous and free times become disastrous and oppressive—through national turmoil, fall, and captivity. Habakkuk had hard questions for God, but God had timeless answers, calling His people to live by faith in Him and His sovereignty (Habakkuk 2:4).

HABAKKUK, BOOK OF (huh BAK uhk). Old Testament book containing dialogues with God, prophecies, and poetry from the prophet. Habakkuk asked God why bad people seem to win and why good people suffer. God answered that evil eventually destroys people who do it but the just shall live by faith (2:4). The rest of the book celebrates God's faithfulness in every circumstance.

HABITATION. Place to live, stop, or rest; fixed place (Psalm 89:14; Ephesians 2:22).

HADES (HAY deez). Place or state of the dead. The word *hades* does not appear in the King James Version but in other translations (see Matthew 16:18 NIV).
▲ The Greek word hades *appears eleven times in the Greek New Testament and is translated ten*

times with the word "hell" in the KJV (Matthew 11:23; 16:18; Luke 10:15; 16:23; Acts 2:27, 31; Revelation 1:18; 6:8; 20:13–14). In 1 Corinthians 15:55, hades *is translated "grave" in the KJV. All other KJV usages of hell translate sheol in the Old Testament and Gehenna in the New Testament.*

HAGAR (HAY gahr). Sarah's maid who became the mother of Ishmael by Abraham (Genesis 16:1–16). Hagar's pregnancy was a source of animosity between Hagar and Sarah because Sarah hadn't been able to have children. Sarah later drove Hagar away, and God took care of Hagar and Ishmael (21:1–21).
▲ It was common practice in Old Testament times to have children by a wife's maid. Abraham had a child by Hagar instead of waiting for the one God had promised through Sarah. The division caused by Ishmael's birth continued for generations and illustrates one danger of not waiting for God to fulfill His promises His way. See **CONCUBINE**.

At Sarah's demand, Abraham sends **Hagar** and her son, Ishmael, into the wilderness. Abraham had fathered Ishmael with Hagar after the barren Sarah suggested it.

HAGGAI (HAG ay igh). Prophet in Jerusalem who encouraged returning Jewish exiles to rebuild God's temple. He prophesied about 520 BC and was a contemporary of Zachariah. His name means "festive."

HAGGAI, BOOK OF. An Old Testament book written by the prophet Haggai. Contains God's messages through Haggai for the Israelite people who had returned from exile. They had rebuilt their community but not the temple, so Haggai asked God's question: Why were the people living in well-built houses while the Lord's temple still lay in ruins? (see Haggai 1:1–4). After this prophetic admonition, the people were stirred up and rebuilt the temple (Haggai 1:12–15).

HAIL. 1. "Rejoice, be of good cheer" (Isaiah 32:19; Matthew 28:9). 2. Damaging balls of ice that fall like rain from the sky (Exodus 9:23–24).

HALF TRIBE. Term used in Old Testament referring to the tribe of Manasseh (Joshua 12:6). Manasseh's tribe was called a half tribe because after Moses defeated Sihon of Heshbon and Og of Bashan, half the tribe requested permission to settle east of the Jordan (Numbers 32). This group that settled east of the Jordan group is usually called the half tribe. It settled along with the children of Reuben and Gad. The other half of the tribe settled in on the west side of the Jordan.

The tribe of Ephraim is also called a half tribe. Ephraim and Manasseh, Joseph's sons, were adopted by Jacob (Genesis 48:5). Because the twelve sons of Jacob were fathers of tribes, Ephraim and Manasseh became fathers of tribes in Joseph's line. So each was the father of half a tribe.

HALLELUJAH. "Praise God!" (Revelation 19:1–6). While most translations use "Hallelujah," the KJV has "Alleluia": a Hebrew combination of divine name *Jah* (short for Yahweh) and *hallel*, meaning "to praise."
● *What causes you to say or shout, "Hallelujah" or "Praise God"?*

HALLOWED. Set apart, separated from ordinary things (Exodus 20:11). In Matthew 6:9, the Lord's Prayer calls for keeping God's name hallowed, or holy.
● *Christians hallow God's name when they call positive attention to Him through their attitudes, actions, words, and prayers. How do you hallow God's name?*

HAMAN (HAY muhn). Prime minister of King Ahasuerus (Xerxes). Haman plotted to destroy all the Jews in the Persian empire because Mordecai, a Jew, would not bow to him (Esther 3:2). Queen Esther, herself a Jew, foiled his plot. Haman was hanged on the gallows he had constructed for the Jews.

HANANIAH (han uh NIGH uh). Friend of Daniel. He was renamed Shadrach. He ate healthy food and entered the fiery furnace (Daniel 1:6, 15; 3:16–29).

HANDMAID. Female slave or servant (Genesis 29:24; Luke 1:38).

HANNAH (HAN uh). Name means "grace." Samuel's mother, who prayed for his conception and birth, then dedicated him to God's work (1 Samuel 1:2–11). She was the wife of Elkanah.
▲ *Some scholars suggest that Hannah may have written Psalm 2.*

HANUKKAH. English spelling of the Hebrew word for the eight-day religious festival that commemorates the cleansing and rededication of the temple following the victories of Judas

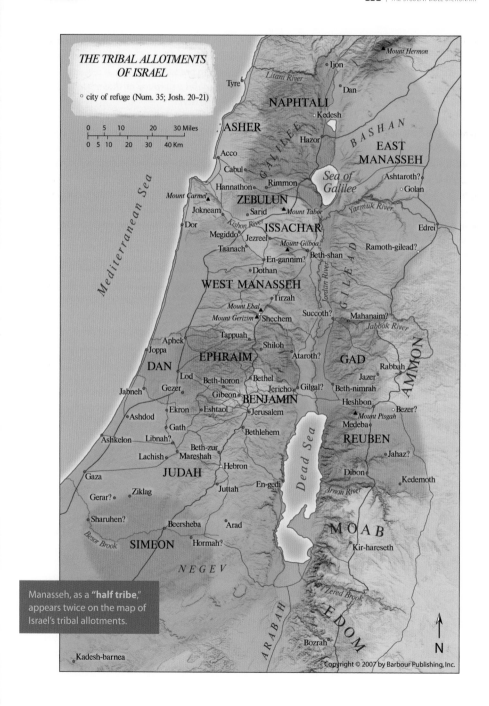

THE TRIBAL ALLOTMENTS
OF ISRAEL

° city of refuge (Num. 35; Josh. 20–21)

0   5   10   20   30 Miles
0   5   10   20   30   40 Km

Mount Hermon

Ijon

Litani River

Tyre

Dan

NAPHTALI

Kedesh

ASHER

Hazor

BASHAN

EAST
MANASSEH

Acco

GALILEE

Cabul

Hannathon

Rimmon

Sea of
Galilee

Ashtaroth?

Golan

Mount Carmel

ZEBULUN

Yarmuk River

Jokneam

Sarid

Mount Tabor

Dor

Kishon River

ISSACHAR

Edrei

Megiddo

Jezreel

Mount Gilboa

GILEAD

Ramoth-gilead?

Taanach

En-gannim?

Beth-shan

Dothan

Jordan River

WEST MANASSEH

Tirzah

Mount Ebal

Succoth?

Mahanaim?

Mount Gerizim

Shechem

Jabbok River

Tappuah

Shiloh

Aphek

Joppa

EPHRAIM

Ataroth?

GAD

Rabbah

DAN

Lod

Beth-horon

Bethel

Jazer

Gezer

Jericho

Gilgal?

Beth-nimrah

Jabneh

Gibeon

BENJAMIN

Heshbon

AMMON

Ekron

Eshtaol

Jerusalem

Bezer?

Ashdod

Mount Pisgah

Gath

Medeba

Ashkelon

Libnah?

Bethlehem

REUBEN

Beth-zur

Mareshah

Jahaz?

Lachish

Hebron

Dibon

Kedemoth

Gaza

JUDAH

Juttah

En-gedi

Gerar?

Ziklag

Dead Sea

Arnon River

Sharuhen?

Beersheba

Arad

MOAB

Bezor Brook

SIMEON

Hormah?

Kir-hareseth

NEGEV

Zered Brook

ARABAH

EDOM

Bozrah

N

Kadesh-barnea

Manasseh, as a **"half tribe,"** appears twice on the map of Israel's tribal allotments.

Maccabeus in 167–165 BC. Same as the Feast of Dedication or Feast of Lights. John 10:22 mentions this "feast of the dedication." See **FEAST CHART** on page 96.

HARAN (HAY ran). The most prominent Haran was the third son of Terah and youngest brother of Abram (Abraham). Haran was the father of Lot and had two daughters (Genesis 11:26–28). Haran is also the place to which Abram and his family moved from Ur of the Chaldees (Genesis 11:31). There were other persons and places by that name.

HARD BY. Close to (Leviticus 3:9).

HARDEN. Besides the usual meaning, to proudly turn away from God (1 Kings 17:14).

HARDHEARTED. To be hardhearted is to close oneself off from God (Ezekiel 3:7); also, to be stubborn and unyielding in heart (Mark 10:5).

HARLOT. Prostitute; one who has sexual relations for pay or possibly as a pagan religious duty (Judges 16:1). A fornicator or sexually immoral person. Also used figuratively to describe people unfaithful to God (Hosea 4:15). Both are strictly forbidden by God.
● Consider God's design for purity in sexuality and faithfulness in worship of God. Which kind of harlotry do you think is worse—unfaithfulness to a spouse or unfaithfulness to God? Both kinds of harlotry are sin, but faithfulness to God has priority over all else.

HAST. Old form of have, meaning "you [singular] have" (Job 33:32).

HASTE. Hurry, speed (Exodus 12:11; Luke 1:39).

HAUGHTY. Arrogant, proud (Ezekiel 16:50).

HEAL. Repair, make thoroughly sound or whole (Exodus 15:26; Matthew 4:23).
● What physical, emotional, or spiritual sickness or weakness do you most want God to heal in you?

HEAP. Pile upon, add, press together (Proverbs 25:22; 2 Timothy 4:3).

HEAR. Besides physical hearing, also means to listen, pay attention, heed, and respond obediently (Psalm 135:17; Isaiah 41:17; Matthew 13:43).

HEARKEN. Listen carefully, be attentive, give ear to, obey an authority (Isaiah 28:23; Acts 27:21).

HEART. In addition to the usual physical meaning, the Hebrews believed the heart was the place of thought, will, and decision (Genesis 6:5; Acts 1:24). Hebrews referred to the heart when we might say "mind" or "brain" (1 Kings 3:9; Romans 1:21). Without God, the heart is wicked and selfish (Jeremiah 17:9).
● How might God describe your heart? Or the essence of your whole being?

HEARTH. Stove, fire pan, burning (Jeremiah 36:22; Zechariah 12:6; Psalm 102:3).

HEATHEN. A person who is not a Jew (Nehemiah 5:17; Psalm 47:8; Galatians 2:9). Also a person who does not know or obey the true God (2 Kings 17:15; Matthew 6:7).

■ **HEAVEN**. 1. Place of perfect happiness. A Christian's home after death. Though heaven is indescribable in human terms, we know these facts about heaven: (1) Christians will be with God. (2) There will be no more tears, death, sorrow, or pain (Revelation 21:4). (3) We will have new bodies and new experiences (1 Corinthians15:35–57; 2 Corinthians 5:1–10). 2.

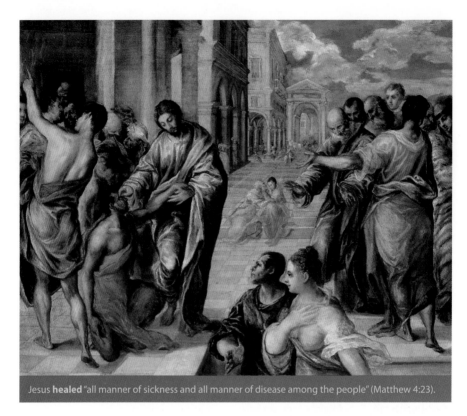

Jesus **healed** "all manner of sickness and all manner of disease among the people" (Matthew 4:23).

The physical heaven in which God placed the sun, stars, and moon (Genesis 1:1; 22:17).

▲ *God is not limited to heaven; He is present everywhere and exists on earth, too (Deuteronomy 4:39).*

● *What do you think heaven will be like? If "kingdom of heaven" and "kingdom of God" mean the same thing, what might that indicate to you about the nature of heaven?*

HEBREW (HEE broo). Abraham or a descendant of Abraham; same as an Israelite or Jew (Genesis 14:13). Also, the language in which the Old Testament is written (except for some Aramaic). The language is written from right to left. Hebrew is a colorful language dominated by verbs. Its alphabet has twenty-two letters, four of which have alternate styles. In Bible times, Hebrew writing indicated only consonants. Much later, small points were added to the letters to indicate vowels.

HEBREWS, BOOK OF. New Testament Bible book written to Hebrew believers in danger of abandoning the Christian faith (Hebrews 13:9). They were tempted to give in to persecution and return to the lure of old beliefs. The key word of the book is "better," and a recurring theme is, "Let us go on." These Christians had remained babes in Christ (Hebrews 5:13). The writer knew that the Christian life was far better than any alternatives and that Jesus was truly the only Messiah. We don't know who the divinely inspired writer was, but he showed Jesus as the true and final revelation of God: the eternal Son of God superior to all prophets and angels, an eternal priest superior to all priests, and the only provider of true salvation. Hebrews encourages readers to face opposition with God's power by confidently standing on His truth in faith. Hebrews emphasizes the uniqueness of Christianity.

HEBRON (HEE bruhn). 1. A city nineteen miles southwest of Jerusalem. Abraham lived there and was buried nearby (Genesis 13:18). It was David's first capital city (2 Samuel 2:11). 2. A son of Kohath (Exodus 6:18). 3. A town in Asher (Joshua 19:28). 4. A relative of Caleb (1 Chronicles 2:42).

HEED. Give careful attention, observe, watch, be warned against (Jeremiah 18:19; Matthew 16:6; 1 Timothy 1:4).

God specifically required a "red **heifer**" in a cleansing ceremony recorded in Numbers 19.

HEIFER. Young cow (Genesis 15:9; Hosea 10:11).

HEIR. One who inherits another's possessions or position (Genesis 15:3; Romans 8:17). Christians are heirs of the kingdom of God with its security

and blessings, both present and future. Christians are joint heirs with Jesus Christ (Romans 8:17).

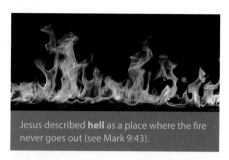
Jesus described **hell** as a place where the fire never goes out (see Mark 9:43).

■ **HELL**. Place and condition of eternal punishment for those who reject Jesus Christ as Lord and Savior (Deuteronomy 32:22; Matthew 5:22, 29–30; 10:28; 16:18). Words related to hell include *gehenna, hades,* and *Sheol.* The KJV translates the Hebrew word *Sheol* as "hell" thirty-one times, "grave" thirty-one times, and "pit" in the other three Old Testament instances. Contemporary translations vary in how they render the original terms for a place or state of existence beyond death; but in relationship to sin, *hell* refers to the eternal punishment avoidable only by receiving God's grace in Christ.

HELLENISTS (hehl lih NIHSTS) (NRSV). People who spoke Greek and came under Grecian culture—especially, in the New Testament, Jewish people who spoke Greek (Acts 6:1; 9:29). In Acts 6:1, the KJV refers to "Grecians" and "Hebrews." The NIV and HCSB refer to "Hellenistic Jews" in contrast with "Hebraic Jews."

HELMET. Head protection worn during battle (1 Samuel 17:5). Figurative term for salvation as part of the spiritual armor against satanic forces (Ephesians 6:10–17).

HEMORRHAGE (NASB, NRSV). Uncontrolled bleeding (Mark 5:25).

HENCE. From this place (Genesis 37:17; Matthew 17:20); after this time (Acts 1:5).

HENCEFORTH, HENCEFORWARD. From this time on (Numbers 15:23; John 15:15).

HERALD. One who shouts an important message (Daniel 3:4).

Grated horseradish, used today as the "bitter **herb**" in Passover celebrations.

HERB. Tender grass, grain, or green plant; not necessarily limited to the plants we call herbs today (Isaiah 66:14); also a cultivated garden plant (Luke 11:42).
▲ *Bitter herbs were eaten with a lamb during the Passover Feast to symbolize the bitter experiences of the Hebrews in Egypt before the Exodus (Exodus 12:8). The exact herb is unknown, but Jews use horseradish today. See* **PASSOVER**.

HEREAFTER. After this, from now on (Isaiah 41:23; Revelation 4:1). May refer to our life in heaven or simply the future (Mark 11:14).

HERITAGE. Inheritance, that which is received from parents or ancestors (Exodus 6:8; Psalm 16:5–6; 1 Peter 5:3). May be spiritual, material, or both.

HEROD (HAIR uhd). A line of Judean kings or rulers who were evil. 1. Herod the Great was king of Judea when Jesus was born and killed many baby boys in an attempt to locate and kill Jesus (Matthew 2:1–22). He lived from 47 BC to AD 2. 2. Herod Antipas had John the Baptist beheaded and led one of Jesus' trials (Mark 6:17–28). His two brothers ruled the other parts of the kingdom. 3. Herod Agrippa I had James killed and planned to execute Peter (Acts 12:1–3). He died in AD 44. 4. Paul appeared before Herod Agrippa II (Acts 26:28). See **KING CHART** on pages 152–155.

HERODIANS (hih ROH dih uhns). A political Jewish party that opposed Jesus and supported the Herods. They wanted to be ruled by the Herods rather than by Rome (Mark 3:6). Jesus' warning about the "leaven (yeast) of Herod" in Mark 8:15 may refer also to the Herodians.

HERODIAS (hih ROH dih uhs). Granddaughter of Herod the Great and daughter of Aristobulus. She married her uncle Herod Philip but left him for his brother Herod Antipas. When Herodias's daughter danced at a feast and Herod offered

Tourists view the Herodium, a hill on which **Herod** the Great built a palace in the two decades before Jesus' birth. The Herodium was destroyed by the Romans in AD 71.

her anything she wanted, Herodias told the girl to demand the head of John the Baptist, who had rightfully opposed Herodias's marriage to Herod (Mark 6:17–27).

HESHBON (HESH bahn). Levitical city twenty miles east of Jordan (Numbers 21:25; Joshua 21:39). Originally belonging to Moab, Israel conquered Heshbon and gave it to Reuben and then Gad. Heshbon means "stronghold."

HEW. Cut, dig, cut out, cut down (Deuteronomy 19:5; Mark 15:46).

HEZEKIAH (hez ih KIGH uh). Son and successor of Ahaz as the thirteenth king of Judah (2 Kings 16:20; 18–20). Hezekiah means "Jehovah has strengthened." Hezekiah was a great religious reformer and a good king (2 Chronicles 29–32; Isaiah 36–39). Hezekiah's prayer in the face of his prophesied death illustrates that God listens to and answers prayer. Isaiah had to revise his prophecy, and Hezekiah received fifteen more years of life (see Isaiah 38:1–21). See **KING CHART** on pages 152–155.

HIGH PLACES. Places of worship on high ground, which were often associated with immorality and human sacrifice (Numbers 33:52). God commanded the Israelites to destroy all the high places, but they did not. Later they used the high places to worship Baal. Occasionally God's people worshiped Him on high places (1 Kings 3:2). God's judgment of the kings of Israel and Judah was directly related to whether or not they had destroyed the high places.

HIGH PRIEST. The highest religious position among the Hebrews (2 Chronicles 24:11; Matthew 26:3). The high priest supervised other priests and performed special ceremonies such as going into the most holy place in the temple to make a sacrifice for the sins of the people. This happened once a year. Only the high priest could enter this holy place (Leviticus 16). Jesus is our true High Priest (Hebrews 2:17). See **HOLY OF HOLIES, TEMPLE, AARON.**

HILKIAH (hil KIGH uh). Several Hilkiahs are mentioned in the Bible. The two most notable are: 1. A high priest during Josiah's reign as king of Judah who found the book of the law and sent it to Josiah (2 Kings 22:4; 2 Chronicles 34:14). 2. A priest who stood by Ezra while Ezra read the book of the law to the people (Nehemiah 8:4).

HIN. Liquid unit of measure equaling about 3.66 liters or one gallon (Exodus 30:24). See **WEIGHTS AND MEASURES CHART** on pages 284–286.

HINDER. Adjective: Behind, last, rear (Zechariah 14:8). Verb: delay, keep back, withhold, injure, interrupt (Genesis 24:56; Nehemiah 4:8; 1 Thessalonians 2:18).

HINNOM (HIN ahm). A valley where human sacrifices were burned, located on land owned by the son of Hinnom (2 Chronicles 33:6). It was associated with the worship of Molech. After Josiah put an end to the sacrifices, the site was used to burn corpses and garbage and came to be used as a synonym for hell: *Gehenna*. The Hebrew *ge'hinnom* ("valley of Hinnom") was translated into Greek as *Gehenna*. See **HADES, HELL.** *Sheol* is the Old Testament word translated "hell."

HIRAM (HIGH ruhm). 1. King of Tyre who was friendly with both King David and King Solomon. He sent logs of cedar and cypress for Solomon's building projects (1 Kings 5:8). 2. Brass worker and architect from Tyre who

The Jewish **high priest.**

worked on Solomon's temple (1 Kings 7:13). See **KING CHART** on pages 152–155.

HIRE. Besides the usual sense, can mean "to bribe" (Ezek 16:33).

HISS. Scoff (1 Kings 9:8), to catch one's breath in amazement or derision.

HITHER. Here (Genesis 15:16; John 4:15).

HITHERTO. From then, from that time, until now (2 Samuel 15:34; John 16:24).

HITTITE (HIT tight). Descendant of Ham through Heth who was the second son of Canaan (Genesis 15:20). Hittites were a powerful people who inhabited the mountains of Judah. Some lived among the Israelites (2 Samuel 11:6). Original Hittites controlled an empire centered in Hattushah in Asia Minor from about 1780 until 1270 BC.

Statue of the **Hittite** god and king Ura-Tarzhunzas.

■ **HOLY**. Persons, places, or things set apart for use by God (Deuteronomy 7:6). All holiness originates with God, and all Christians are called to live a holy life—a life like God wants you to live (Leviticus 21:8; Acts 3:12; 1 Thessalonians 3:13–4:1; 1 Peter 2:9).

▲ *The Bible term* saints *means "holy ones" and refers to Christians—all who have received the Holy Spirit (see Acts 1:8).*

● *How are your life, your words, your personality "holy"? What remains for you to dedicate to God?*

HOLY GHOST. Frequent KJV translation of "Holy Spirit" (Matthew 1:18). In 1611, when the KJV was first published, "Holy Ghost" and "Holy Spirit" meant the same thing. To "give up the ghost" means to die or expire.

HOLY OF HOLIES. The innermost part of the tabernacle or temple (Exodus 26:34). Only the high priest could enter, and he could enter only once a year. There he made a sacrifice for the sins of the people. Inside the holy of holies was the ark of the covenant, which was a small wooden structure covered with gold; it contained the Ten Commandments, a pot of manna, and Aaron's rod (Exodus 25). See **MOST HOLY PLACE, ORACLE**.

■ **HOLY SPIRIT**. God's Spirit. Lives within all Christians to help them, communicate God's truth to them, convict them of sin, convince them that God's ways are right, and comfort them when they are sad (John 15:26; 16:7–8,13–15). The Holy Spirit was also referred to as the Holy Ghost, the Comforter, the Counselor, the Helper, and the Advocate. God sent the Holy Spirit to guide us after Jesus left earth (John 14:16–17). The Holy Spirit gives gifts and godly characteristics called fruit of the Spirit (Romans 12:4–13; 1 Corinthians 12–13; Galatians 5:22–23) to each Christian.

▲ God the Father, God the Son, and God the Holy Spirit complete God's expression of Himself (Matthew 28:19). See **GOD, TRINITY**.

● How is your life different because the Holy Spirit lives in you? As well as receiving the Spirit, people may resist the Spirit, quench the Spirit, or grieve the Spirit. How do you treat the Spirit?

HOMER. A dry measure equaling ten ephahs, about six bushels, or about 220 liters (Hosea 3:2). See **WEIGHTS AND MEASURES CHART** on pages 284–286.

HONOR. Noun: Respect, reverence, greatness, value, dignity given or received (1 Chronicles 16:27). God is most worthy of honor (1 Timothy 1:17). He has given honor to each person (Psalm 8:5). Persons lose their honor when they disobey God. Verb: Value, show respect for, esteem, cherish. We are to honor God and persons to whom it is due (Proverbs 3:9; Romans 12:10).

● God has commanded us to honor our father and mother (Exodus 20:12). What are ways to express honor to and for your parents? Note that we can honor our parents by thanking God (the perfect parent) for using them to give us physical life. If our parents are seemingly not honorable, wise children might help them spiritually and find new honor in them.

HOMOSEXUAL. One whose sexual preference is with the same sex (1 Corinthians 6:9 NIV). Homosexuality is against the will of God (see Romans 1–2).

● In a changing society that increasingly accepts homosexuality and "gay marriage," what responsibility do faithful Christians have under

the will of God? Manmade laws never change God's laws and will, but He always expects us to have the mind of Christ and His compassion toward others, whatever their lifestyle.

■ **HOPE**. Belief that God will accomplish what He has promised (Psalm 71:5; Ephesians 2:12; Hebrews 11:1). Christian hope is based on the fact that God has always been faithful to do what He said He would do. In the New Testament, Christian hope is never wishful thinking; it is a divine certainty. It points to resurrection (1 Corinthians 15).

HOREB (HOH reb). Hebrew name meaning "drought, desert"; alternate name for Sinai, "the mountain of God" (Exodus 3:1; 1 Kings 19:8).

The dramatic mountain peak known as **Horeb**, or Mount Sinai.

HOSANNA. "Help or save, I pray" (Psalm 118:25; Matthew 21:9–15). Chanted when Jesus entered Jerusalem (Matthew 21:9–15).

● Contrast the prayer of "Hosanna" with the fickle crowd's plea changed to "Crucify Him!" (Matthew 27:22–23). Can others negatively affect our own faithfulness and belief in God and His Word? If the answer is yes, how do we remain faithful and say no to the world?

Hosea embraces his unfaithful wife, Gomer, in an illustration from a fourteenth-century Bible.

HOSEA (hoh ZAY uh). Old Testament prophet about 750 BC. The name means "salvation." Hosea's preaching produced the book of Hosea. His personal experience with an unfaithful wife matched that of the nation of Israel in its unfaithfulness to God (Hosea 1–14). However, God used Hosea to prophesy of God's love and call for Israel to repent (Hosea 11–14).

HOSEA, BOOK OF. An Old Testament book of the prophet Hosea's sermons from about 750 BC. The sermons reflect the unfaithfulness of Israel to God and of Hosea's wife to the prophet himself. The book offers hope of restoration after repentance. Hosea's personal life was a prophetic parable of symbolism that showed God's relentless love for His people, but also a warning of judgment for sins.

HOST. Army (Joshua 5:14; 1 Samuel 17:45); huge number (Genesis 2:1; Jeremiah 33:22); one who shows hospitality (Luke 10:35). The "host of heaven" in 1 Kings 22:19 is a group of heavenly beings who work with and for God.

They are not to be worshiped (Deuteronomy 4:19).

HOUSE. Family, family line, household (Joshua 24:15; Jeremiah 21:12; John 4:53); place to live (Ezra 1:2; Mark 1:29). People lived in caves, tents, houses made of limestone, clay, straw, and other materials. Sometimes animals lived downstairs and the people upstairs. The more wealthy built houses with open courtyards or other elaborate features.

HUMANS. Mankind. See **MAN**.

■ **HUMILITY**. Freedom from pride (Proverbs 18:12; Matthew 11:29). A humble person has the right view of God, self, and others (2 Chronicles 7:14; Luke 18:14; James 4:6). Humility is not weakness but a strong quality, praised in the Bible and commanded for all Christians (Proverbs 15:33; James 4:10). Humility shows trust in God (James 4:10; 1 Peter 5:6).

● *How does humility strengthen relationships? What fears do you have about being humble? How do you go about having the right self-image—not thinking too highly or too lowly of yourself? (See Romans 12:3.)*

HYPOCRITE. Pretender, a play actor (Matthew 6:2, 5, 16). One whose walk doesn't match his talk. A person who doesn't possess what he professes, or do what he says. Jesus warned that hypocrites who reject God and His will are under judgment (Matthew 24:51).

● *What's the difference between a hypocrite and a Christian who sins? Compare and contrast 1 John 1:8–10 with 1 John 3:6–9. In the original Greek, the implication is that a Christian may fall or lapse into sin, but he will not return to sin as his lifestyle or nature. True Christians repent of sin and persevere.*

HYSSOP. A small bushy plant used in religious ceremonies and in relieving pain (Exodus 12:22; John 19:29).

Hyssop branches

I AM. Name that God used to refer to Himself in replying to Moses, "I AM THAT I AM" (Exodus 3:13–14).

● *Compare Jesus' expressions in the Gospel of John (8:24, 28, 58; 18:5). The KJV translates, "I am he" with "he" in italics to show it was understood but not specifically stated in the Greek text. In these Gospel verses, the Greek text has emphatic words only for "I am." The Amplified Bible cites Exodus 3:14 in these verses. The point is that God the Father and God the Son are one eternally—as is God the Spirit.*

ICONIUM (igh KOH nih uhm). City in Galatia, Asia Minor, present-day Turkey. Paul preached in Iconium on his missionary journeys and was stoned there (Acts 13:51; 14:1–5; 2 Timothy 3:11).

IDLE. Lazy, unprofitable (Exodus 5:17; Matthew 20:3).

IDOL. Image of a god (Exodus 20:3–4).
● *We often think of idols as statues. But anything that we put in the place of God can become an idol or form of idolatry. What or whom do people idolize today?*

IDOLATRY. Putting anything in the place of God or putting anything ahead of God (Exodus 20:4–6). Idols are usually things, but they can be people (Exodus 32:1–8; 1 Corinthians 10:14). Wanting another's possessions is a form of idolatry (Colossians 3:5).
● *Who or what has first place in your life? Could an obsession—over a person, thing, or practice—be idolatrous?*

IMAGE. Likeness (Genesis 1:26; 2 Corinthians 3:18). God created us to be like Him in our ability to think, feel, and decide. When Adam and Eve sinned, God's image in humanity was marred but not destroyed. Though the Bible records the "fall of man" in the Garden of Eden, no one can blame his own sin on Adam—each person chooses to sin (Isaiah 53:6; Romans 3:23). The sinless Christ is the perfect "image of God" (2 Corinthians 4:4), and God is molding those who trust Christ as Lord and Savior back into that perfect image (Romans 8:28–30).

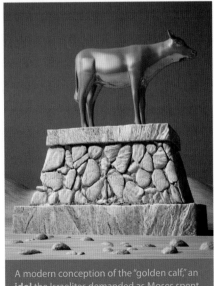

A modern conception of the "golden calf," an **idol** the Israelites demanded as Moses spent forty days on Mount Sinai with God (see Exodus 32).

IMMANUEL (ih MAN yoo el). "God is with us" (Isaiah 7:10–14; Matthew 1:23). In the Old Testament this name was announced to Ahaz as God's deliverer from the enemies. In the New Testament it is the name applied to the coming Messiah, Jesus. Also spelled **EMMANUEL.**

IMMORTALITY. Living forever, life beyond physical death (1 Corinthians 15:53–54; 2 Corinthians 4:14–5:10; 2 Timothy 1:10). A Christian is promised eternal life as a gift through personal faith commitment to Jesus Christ (Romans 6:23). Eternal life is not simply existence but a quality relationship with God and other Christians. Human bodies are not immortal. We all die physically. But God raises the dead in Christ to eternal, immortal, imperishable life. Christians do not experience a "second death" (Revelation 2:11).

▲ *Apart from Christ, the New Testament refers to unbelievers as being dead—but made alive in Christ upon becoming believers (see Ephesians 2:1–10).*

IMPART. To give a share or portion to (Job 39:17; Romans 1:11).

IMPORTUNITY. Persistence, relentless asking, shameless pleading (Luke 11:8).

▲ *God honors faith-filled persistence in prayer, but gladly answers prayer rather than being nagged into action. One person referred to biblical persistence in prayer as "the soul of prayer." Such praying has to mean something to us if it is to mean anything to God. It lays hold on God's highest blessing but follows Jesus' model by ending with, "Not My will but Thine be done."*

IMPUTE. Count, assign to the account of another (Psalm 32:2; Romans 4:8).

■ **INCARNATION.** Literally, "in flesh." Technical theological term used to describe God the Son

From His birth until His crucifixion some thirty years later, Jesus was "**incarnate**"—in human flesh.

taking on human flesh and living as a person on earth. The eternal Christ became fully human in taking upon Himself an earthly body, but He still kept the perfectness of His divine and sinless nature (John 1:14; Philippians 2:5–8; see also Isaiah 9:6).

INCENSE. Perfume (Exodus 30:1; Luke 1:9). Sweet-smelling spices burned as an offering in worship. Used as symbols to acknowledge God's presence or prayers going up to God (Psalm 141:2). See **CENSER.**

▲ *The recipe for incense was specified in Exodus 30:34–37.*

INCLINE. Stretch out, turn toward (Psalm 119:36).

INCREASE. Noun: Fruit, produce (Leviticus 26:4). Verb: To grow, progress, advance, multiply (Proverbs 1:5; Acts 6:7).

129 | STUDENT BIBLE DICTIONARY

▲ The Bible says that Jesus increased in wisdom and stature (Luke 2:52). All of His early earthly life was preparation for obedience to the Father's call—as our lives should be.

INDIGNATION. Anger, wrath, fury (Psalm 69:24; Revelation 14:10).

INERRANT. Free from error or mistake. A confession used to describe the Bible as the work of the perfect God. God inspired His word into man's language for God's own purposes (2 Timothy 3:14–17). The NIV says, "All Scripture is God-breathed" (2 Timothy 3:16) to equip us for every good work.

▲ Why are there so many different Bible translations? Besides the languages of the world, we find the Bible in multiple English translations partly because our language keeps changing. As one translator explained, "Every generation needs to put the faith of its fathers into the language of its children." Though God's inspired Word itself does not change, we find it easier to understand that God-given revelation in updated English rather than that of earliest Bible translators. Standard Bible translations tend to stick closer to original wording of Hebrew and Greek. Paraphrases or other versions may be less word-for-word, but try to clarify meanings.

A Bedouin tent housing **inhabitants** of the modern Sahara desert.

INFIRMITY. Sickness, disease, weakness (Proverbs 18:14; John 5:5).

INHABITANT. Someone who dwells or lives in a place (Genesis 19:25; Revelation 17:2).

INHERIT, INHERITANCE. To possess (Genesis 15:7; Luke 10:25). To receive something from an ancestor (Deuteronomy 21:16).

INIQUITY. Sin, unrighteousness, wrong, corruption, lawlessness, wickedness, the opposite of what is right (Psalm 25:11; Luke 13:27; 2 Thessalonians 2:7).

● Since none of us is perfect, we do well to carefully evaluate our lives in light of what pleases or displeases God—what is right or wrong. As we read God's Word, the Holy Spirit helps us evaluate our lives according to God's will. Consider at least one way that you might ask God to mold you more into His righteous image (see Romans 12:1–3).

INJUSTICE. A wrong, an injury (Job 16:17).

INNOCENT. Guiltless (Matthew 27:4).

INSPIRATION. Breath (Job 32:8), God-breathed (2 Timothy 3:16 NIV). God inspired men to write the scriptures.

▲ God breathed His Word into the writers of the Bible over hundreds of years in what became our sixty-six books of the Bible. So inspiration may refer to a general insight, but it uniquely refers to the God-breathed Bible itself (2 Timothy 3:14–17).

INSTRUCT. Discipline, train, teach, nurture (Deuteronomy 4:36; 2 Timothy 2:25).

▲ The word discipline may be used more often to describe correction than the positive meaning of learning. Ideally, discipline is positive and formative; though correction is necessary, too.

INSURRECTION. Rebellion, uprising (Ezra 4:19; Mark 15:7).

INTEGRITY. A state of completeness; innocence, blamelessness, consistency, dependability (Psalm 26:1; Titus 2:7 HCSB).

▲ *Biblically, the opposite of having integrity is to be double-minded, wavering, or hesitant (see James 1:8; 4:8 for this concept). Integrity is strength of personhood matching our inner being with what others see and experience of us outwardly.*

■ **INTERCESSION**. Praying or pleading on someone else's behalf (Isaiah 53:12; Hebrews 7:25). An intercessor serves as a go-between. Jesus Christ and the Holy Spirit intercede for Christians (Romans 8:26–27, 34; 1 John 2:1). Christians are to intercede for one another (1 Timothy 2:1).

● *How could your prayers help someone else? What do you think about Jesus interceding for you? When Christ came to earth, He took upon Himself flesh and humanity along with the trials, tribulations, and temptations we all face. How might these truths affect His intercession for us?*

INTEREST. In the KJV, the word "usury" translates a Greek word that modern translators usually render "interest" (Matthew 25:27; Luke 19:23). Hebrews under the Old Testament law were not to charge each other usury or interest, but could charge outsiders (Deuteronomy 23:19–20). See **USURY**.

ISAAC. (I ZIK) Son of Abraham and Sarah (Genesis 17:15–20). God's promised covenant would come through a son named Isaac instead of Ishmael. Abraham laughed at God's promise that he and his aged wife, Sarah, would have a child through whom God would channel His everlasting covenant. But Isaac was indeed born. In the boy's youth, Abraham obeyed God to the anguishing point of preparing to offer Isaac as a sacrifice. But it was Abraham's loyalty rather than Isaac's life that God wanted, so the Lord provided a substitute, a ram for sacrificing. After Isaac married Rebekah, they had twin sons: Jacob and Esau (Genesis 25:19–26).

ISAIAH (i ZAY uh). Old Testament prophet of Judah whose personal name meant "Yahweh saves." He prophesied during the reign of four kings, beginning his ministry the year King Uzziah died, about 740 BC (Isaiah 6:1). Isaiah continued until 701 BC or slightly longer. Isaiah had two sons (Isaiah 7:3; 8:3). "Esaias" is the Greek form of Isaiah (Matthew 3:3). See **KING CHART** on pages 152–155.

The prophet **Isaiah** holds a pen while listening for God's voice, in a statue from Rome's Piazza de Spagna.

ISAIAH, BOOK OF. God's messages about Judah and Jerusalem as revealed to Isaiah are recorded in this Old Testament book, first of the "major prophets." This designation refers to the length of these prophetic books, and Isaiah stands tall in all prophecy. His messages were later divided into sixty-six chapters, the same figure as the total number of books in the biblical canon. Isaiah answered "yes" to God's prophetic visions that called him to be a prophet and speak God's Word. He prophesied about the coming Messiah and the holiness of God. The book emphasizes sincere religion that shows itself in action, not lip service. The book of Isaiah reveals God's warning against sin and the coming destruction and captivity of Judah—but also hope and the confidence that a remnant of the people would repent and return. This majestic prophecy focuses on the eternal God and His Messianic promises of covenant fulfillment. Isaiah emphasized the importance of righteousness, justice toward others, sabbath observance, and prayer.

The first thirty-nine chapters of Isaiah emphasize the importance of obeying God, no matter what other people choose to do. In chapters 40–55, many people of Judah were held captive in Babylon. Isaiah gave the people hope that God would work in history to set them free and give them a mission. These chapters include beloved descriptions of Jesus, the "Servant of the Lord" (see Isaiah 53). In chapters 56–66, the people of Judah returned home but needed assurance that God would fulfill His promises.

▲ *Jesus quoted from Isaiah 61:1–2 to express His own calling.*

ISHMAEL (ISH may el). Son of Abraham by Hagar, who was Sarah's handmaid (Genesis 16:11–15). Sarah jealously insisted that Abraham cast Ishmael and Hagar from their home because Sarah wanted her son, Isaac, to receive the inheritance (Genesis 21). *Ishmael* means "God hears," and God did hear as He cared for Hagar and Ishmael as well as Abraham and Sarah's family (see Genesis 17:18–20; 21:20). Ishmael became the father of the nation of Ishmaelites.

ISRAEL (IZ ray el). Personal name meaning "God rules." God gave the name to Jacob after Jacob, a grandson of Abraham, had struggled with a divine messenger (Genesis 32:28; 35:10). Israel had twelve sons, whose descendants became the twelve tribes of Israel. The tribes were collectively known as the nation of Israel. Israel later became the name of the Northern Kingdom.

Israel also had referred to Judah after the Northern Kingdom fell in 722 BC and again in the New Testament in referring to a new covenant with Israel and Judah—which essentially was the combined Hebrew nation of Israel. Also in the New Testament, *Israel* was a term used to refer to the true and obedient people of God, whatever their descent (Ephesians 2:12; Hebrews 8:8–13).

ISRAELITE. A Hebrew, a descendant of Abraham; same as a Jew (Romans 11:1).

THE HOLY LAND TODAY

0 5 10   20 30 Miles
0 5 10 20 30   40 Km

LEBANON

Dimashq (Damascus)

Sour (Tyre)

Kiriath Shemonah

Al Qunaytira

GOLAN HEIGHTS (occupied by Israel)

SYRIA

Akko

Haifa

Nazareth

Teverya

Sea of Galilee

Dara

Afula

Irbid

Mediterranean Sea

Hadera

Jenin

Beth-shean

Netanya

Nablus

Jordan River

WEST BANK

As Salt

Az Zarqa

Tel Aviv-Yafo

Karama

Amman (Rabbah)

Ramallah

Ariha (Jericho)

Ashdod

Jerusalem

Madaba

Ashqelon

Bayt Lahm (Bethlehem)

Qiryat Gat

Dead Sea

GAZA STRIP

Ghazzah (Gaza)

Al Khalil (Hebron)

Beersheba

Arad

ISRAEL

Kerak (Kir-hareseth)

JORDAN

Dimona

El-Gi

Maan

The nation we know as "**Israel**" gets its name from a new name God gave Jacob.

EGYPT

SAUDI ARABIA

Elat

N

Copyright © 2007 by Barbour Publishing, Inc.

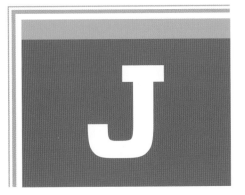

J

JACOB (JAY kuhb). Name means "one who schemes to take the place of another"—a grasping trickster (Genesis 25:26). Jacob later became *Israel*—meaning "ruling with God" (Genesis 32:28; see **ISRAEL**). Jacob's name change to Israel also included a change in his relationship to God.

Jacob and his elder twin brother, Esau, were born to Isaac and Rebekah. Jacob exchanged a bowl of soup with his hungry brother to get Esau's birthright. Later, Jacob tricked Esau out of his father's blessing that rightly went to the eldest son. After this deceit, Jacob ran away to escape Esau's anger but was later reconciled to him. Jacob married two sisters, Leah and Rachel, and, with them and two maidservants, fathered twelve sons, the ancestors of Israel's twelve tribes.

▲ *Jacob's life was a watershed period in the nation of Israel's history because it factored so largely into God's covenant for His chosen people. Essential names in this covenant context include Abraham, the father of the Hebrews (Genesis 14:13); Isaac, Abraham's son of promise; Jacob/Israel, as both a person and nation; Judah/Jew, as a person, tribe, nation, and sometimes name for all Israel; and Jesus, the Messiah or Christ.*

● *Are there any parallels between Jacob's and your family situations? What can you learn from Jacob's life?*

JAIRUS (JIGH ruhs). A synagogue ruler who had only one daughter. When she became sick unto death, Jairus pled with Jesus to come to his home and heal her. Jesus agreed and brought the girl back to life (Mark 5:22–43; Luke 8:41–56).

JAMES (JAYMZ). Name of several men in the New Testament. 1. Son of Zebedee and brother of John (Matthew 4:21; Luke 5:10). James

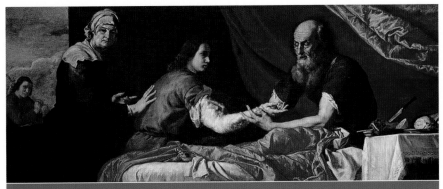

Smooth-skinned **Jacob** wears a goat skin to trick his elderly, nearly blind father into bestowing the blessing due to his hairy older brother, Esau. See the whole story in Genesis 27.

and his brother were fishermen in partnership with Simon Peter, and all were called to follow Jesus as disciples (later called apostles). 2. Son of Alphaeus and one of the twelve apostles (Matthew 10:3). 3. Half brother of Jesus, considered by many to be author of the book of James (Matthew 13:55). This James rejected Jesus' earthly ministry but later believed and became a leader in the church at Jerusalem. 4. James the Less (also translated as "James the Younger"), was perhaps the son of Alphaeus (Mark 15:40). 5. Brother (KJV) or father (modern translations) of the apostle Judas, also known as Judas—not Iscariot (Luke 6:16; the Greek text simply says "Judas of James").

JAMES, BOOK OF. New Testament book, probably written by the half brother of Jesus between AD 48 and AD 66 when James was martyred. James was pastor of the church at Jerusalem. As an inspired author, James penned this book to Christians who needed to focus on matching beliefs with actions, showing faith by godly works and maintaining integrity to God's will.

● *How might Christians today be different if we lived by James 1:22–26?*

JAPHETH (JAY feth). One of the sons of Noah (Genesis 5:32). He and his wife were among the eight survivors of the Great Flood (1 Peter 3:20).

JAVELIN. Spear (1 Samuel 18:10; 19:10).

JEALOUS. Intolerant of rivalry or unfaithfulness (Exodus 20:5); zealous or ardent. God declared Himself to be a jealous God demanding the faithfulness of His people. In human terms, jealousy may include envy, coveting, and suspicious rivalry.

● *How is God's jealousy different from human jealousy?*

JEBUSITE (JEB yoo sight). A member of a tribe of Canaanite people who lived in and around Jerusalem and fought against Joshua. The Jebusites ultimately held out till the time of David (Joshua 10; Judges 1:21).

JEHOIACHIN (jih HOY uh kin). Son of evil King Jehoiakim (2 Kings 24:6). At his father's death, eighteen-year-old Jehoiachin became king of Judah. His evil reign lasted only three months. See the **KING CHART** on pages 152–155.

JEHOIADA (jih HOY uh duh). The name of at least six Old Testament persons. 1. Most notably, the high priest at the temple in Jerusalem, who was active in political affairs (2 Kings 11:4). He and his wife rescued the child Joash from being murdered and hid him six years (2 Kings 11:2). When Joash was finally placed on the throne, Jehoiada helped him rule until Joash became older (see 2 Chronicles 22–24). 2. The father of one of David's officers (2 Samuel 8:18). 3. Mentioned as a priest deposed in Jeremiah 29:25–26.

JEHOIAKIM (jih HOY uh kim). Son of Josiah and king of Judah 609–598 BC (2 Kings 24:36). His

In an ancient relief, one Assyrian warrior drives a chariot, one wields a bow and arrow, and two carry **javelins** into battle.

evil reign of eleven years was marked by heavy taxation, religious decay and murder. See **KING CHART** on pages 152–155.

JEHORAM (jih HOH ruhm). 1. Son of Jehoshaphat and king of Judah 850–843 BC (1 Kings 22:50). He was a wicked king who had his six brothers put to death and practiced idolatry. 2. Son of Ahab who ruled the Northern Kingdom, Israel, 851–842 BC (2 Kings 3:1). Same as Joram. See **KING CHART** on pages 152–155.

JEHOSAPHAT (jih HAHSH uh fat). King of Judah, the Southern Kingdom (1 Kings 15:24; 2 Chronicles 17–20). He reigned twenty-five years (873–848 BC) and was a good king who tried to do away with places of idol worship and see that the people were taught the Law. See **KING CHART** on pages 152–155. Other royal officials were also named Jehoshaphat (2 Samuel 8:16; 1 Kings 4:17; 2 Kings 9:2, 14)

JEHU (JEE hyoo). Tenth king of Israel, the Northern Kingdom of ten tribes (1 Kings 19:16). He killed his predecessor's family and the king of the Southern Kingdom of two tribes. He killed many followers of Baal but was not a true follower of God. See **KING CHART** on pages

Many consider **Jericho** one of the oldest cities in the world. It continues today as a Palestinian community in the West Bank.

152–155. Others named Jehu include a prophet (1 Kings 16), a soldier (1 Chronicles 12:3), and a tribal leader (1 Chronicles 4:35).

JEREMIAH (jer ih MIGH uh; sometimes JEREMY [JER uh mih] and JEREMIAS [jer ih MIGH uhs]). One of the greatest Old Testament prophets (Jeremiah 1:1). 1. Born into a priestly family near Jerusalem, he prophesied to Judah, the Southern Kingdom, under the reign of the last five kings. A lonely man (see Jeremiah 16:2), he preached judgment for the sins of the people, but his warnings were not heeded. Jeremiah cried out to God trying to understand why he had to be a prophet (11:18–12:6; 15:10–21; 17:14–18; 18:18–23; 20:7–18). He was a prophet with a broken heart, who saw his message from God rejected for more than forty years, from 627 BC onward. Jeremiah may have lived to be about seventy years old, roughly from 650–580 BC. He was ultimately taken as a captive to Egypt, where he likely died. 2. Several other Jeremiahs each have a single mention in scripture.

JEREMIAH, BOOK OF. Old Testament book the prophet Jeremiah dictated to his secretary Baruch. The book we read in the Bible is a second draft, after the first version was destroyed by King Jehoiakim. The book describes Jeremiah's life and work and his message to the people of Judah, the Southern Kingdom. Jeremiah showed loyalty to God above his nation, other prophets, and his own desires. Despite being "the weeping prophet," Jeremiah also pointed to a new covenant and new hope for a remnant of God's people.

JERICHO (JER ih koh). An ancient city located a few miles west of the Jordan River and a few miles north of the Dead Sea (Joshua 2:1; Matthew 20:29). Jericho is known for God's deliverance and destruction of the

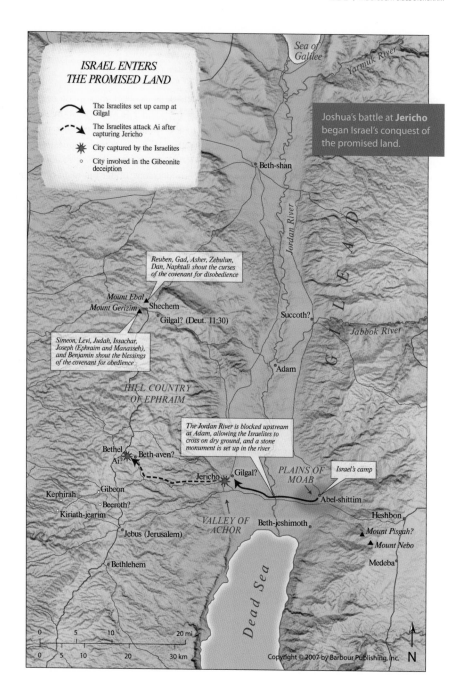

ISRAEL ENTERS
THE PROMISED LAND

The Israelites set up camp at Gilgal

The Israelites attack Ai after capturing Jericho

City captured by the Israelites

City involved in the Gibeonite deception

Joshua's battle at **Jericho** began Israel's conquest of the promised land.

Sea of Galilee

Yarmuk River

Beth-shan

Jordan River

G I L E A D

Reuben, Gad, Asher, Zebulun, Dan, Naphtali shout the curses of the covenant for disobedience

Mount Ebal
Mount Gerizim — Shechem

Gilgal? (Deut. 11:30)

Succoth?

Jabbok River

Simeon, Levi, Judah, Issachar, Joseph (Ephraim and Manasseh), and Benjamin shout the blessings of the covenant for obedience

Adam

HILL COUNTRY OF EPHRAIM

The Jordan River is blocked upstream at Adam, allowing the Israelites to cross on dry ground, and a stone monument is set up in the river

Bethel
Ai?   Beth-aven?

Jericho   Gilgal?   PLAINS OF MOAB   Israel's camp

Kephirah   Gibeon
Beeroth?

Kiriath-jearim   Abel-shittim

VALLEY OF ACHOR   Beth-jeshimoth   Heshbon

Jebus (Jerusalem)   Mount Pisgah?
Mount Nebo

Bethlehem   Medeba

Dead Sea

0   5   10   20 mi

0   5   10   20   30 km

Copyright © 2007 by Barbour Publishing, Inc.

N

walls of Jericho after Joshua followed God's commands (see Joshua 6). In the New Testament Jericho is cited as the home of Zacchaeus (Luke 19:1–2).

JEROBOAM (jer uh BOH uhm). 1. First king of the Northern Kingdom—about 931–910 BC (1 Kings 11:26). He built rival places of worship at Dan and Bethel and encouraged pagan idolatry. 2. Jeroboam II was the thirteenth king of Israel (2 Kings 13:13). Although successful by human standards, he was not true to God. See **KING CHART** on pages 152–155. (Note: The twelve tribes of King Solomon's Israel divided into a Northern Kingdom of ten tribes known as Israel and a Southern Kingdom of two tribes [Judah and Benjamin] called Judah. This division occurred about 950 BC, upon the death of Solomon and during the time of Jeroboam I [see 1 Kings 12]. The twelve tribes had been united as a single nation under a king from about 1020 BC. After the division occurred, the Northern Kingdom continued until its defeat in 722 BC; the Southern Kingdom lasted until its defeat in 587 BC. Some Jews remained in the land, but many were taken into captivity in other lands. A remnant of God's people always remained and later returned—to take up God's promises and covenant.)

JERUBBAAL (jer uh BAY uhl). Name given to Gideon by his father, Joash (Judges 6:32).

JERUSALEM (jih ROO suh lem). Ancient city, the name of which may mean "City of Peace." First mentioned in the Bible in Genesis 14:18 as Salem. "Salem" sounds like the Hebrew *shalom* (meaning "peace") and is referred to in Hebrews 7:2. It is ironic that the name indicates "peace" when the city has known so little peace throughout its history. Jerusalem was a capital city and center of worship for the

Prominent features of modern **Jerusalem** include two ancient structures—the Western Wall, remnant of Israel's second temple, and the golden-topped Muslim Dome of the Rock, built in the AD 600s.

United Kingdom of David and Solomon, then for the Southern Kingdom of Judah. David had captured the city from the Jebusites (2 Samuel 5:1–10), and Solomon ultimately built the temple there. Located in the hills of Judah between the Mediterranean Sea and the Dead Sea, Jerusalem was overtaken by Babylon in 598 BC, and destroyed in 587. It was rebuilt from 538 to 440. In Jesus' day, though ruled by the Romans, Jerusalem was the center of Jewish worship and life. Later, rebellion against the Romans led to the destruction of Jerusalem as Jesus had prophesied (Luke 19:41–44).

▲ *Jerusalem is located between two rocky hills at an altitude of 2500 feet, about 35 miles from the Mediterranean Sea. It is considered the holy city of Jews, Christians, and Muslims. Its history is long and rich and requires special study to fully understand its importance.*

JESSE (JES ih). Grandson of Boaz and the father of David (1 Samuel 16:1). The New Testament refers to Jesse in tracing Jesus' lineage or prophecy about Jesus lineage (Matthew 1:5–6; Luke 3:32; Acts 13:22; Romans 15:12).

childhood. However, Jesus' growth in wisdom and stature (Luke 2:52) is reflected in what became apparent to Him in His divine being as God in Christ, the Son of God, whose Spirit would come in fullness after Jesus' earthly life, ministry, death, and resurrection.

● *Jesus died for everyone. Do you know how a person receives eternal life? By believing that Jesus is God's Son and that He can save you from your sins. Repent by turning from your sins to Jesus. Trust Him to save you from your sins and to eternal life. Ask Him to do this. Confess to others that Jesus is Lord of your life. See* **CONFESS**, **REPENT** *to better understand the process. Then, having been saved, be baptized to picture the salvation experience (see Romans 6:1–4).*

A thoughtful **Jesus**, as envisioned by the classic Dutch painter Rembrandt.

■ **JESUS** (JEE zuhs). Savior. Name prophesied and given to Christ when He was born to Mary (Matthew 1:21; Luke 1:31). Jesus is the divine Son of God; He is God the Son (Matthew 3:17). He is eternal; that means He always was, is, and always will be. He existed and was active with God the Father in creation (Colossians 1:15–16). The New Testament often uses "Jesus Christ" as the full reference for Jesus as the Savior-Messiah. *Messiah* is the Hebrew term; *Christ* is the Greek.

His earthly ministry began when He was about thirty years old and lasted for three years (Luke 3:23). In obedience to God the Father, Jesus lived a sinless life, suffered an agonizing death, and provided salvation by grace through faith for mankind (Ephesians 1:4; Philippians 2:5–11). God raised Jesus from death to reign with Him forever.

▲ *Other than events surrounding Jesus' birth and the story of His temple experience at age twelve, we can only speculate about Jesus'*

JESUS, NAMES OF. Jesus Christ called Himself many names and was called by many names in the Bible. What do each of these names teach you about Him?

- The Word (John 1:1)
- The Way (John 14:6)
- The Truth (John 14:6)
- The Life (John 14:6)
- Good Shepherd (John 10:11)
- Chief Shepherd (1 Peter 5:4)
- Advocate (1 John 2:1)
- Holy One of God (Mark 1:24)
- The Light (John 1:7)
- Bread of Life (John 6:35)
- Immanuel (Isaiah 7:14)
- Savior (2 Peter 3:18)
- Wonderful Counselor (Isaiah 9:6)
- Mighty God (Isaiah 9:6)
- Everlasting Father (Isaiah 9:6)
- Prince of Peace (Isaiah 9:6)
- The Resurrection (John 11:21)
- Lord (Matthew 8:8)
- Son of Man (Mark 2:28)
- Son of God (1 John 4:15)
- God (John 20:28)

TITLES FOR JESUS IN SCRIPTURE

TITLE	SIGNIFICANCE	REFERENCE
Advocate	The "defense attorney" who represents Christians who sin; same word translated "Comforter" in John 14:16	1 John 2:1
Alpha and Omega	The beginning and ending of all things	Revelation 21:6
Bread of Life	The one essential food	John 6:35
Chief Cornerstone	A sure foundation of life	Ephesians 2:20
Chief Shepherd	Gives guidance and protection	1 Peter 5:4
Christ	The Anointed One of God foreseen by Old Testament prophets	Matthew 16:16
Firstborn from the Dead	Leads us into resurrection	Colossians 1:18
Good Shepherd	Gives guidance and protection	John 10:11
High Priest	The perfect mediator	Hebrews 3:1
Holy One of God	Perfect and sinless	Mark 1:24
Immanuel	God with us	Matthew 1:23
Jesus	His personal name, meaning "Yahweh saves"	Matthew 1:21
King of Kings, Lord of Lords	The sovereign almighty	Revelation 19:16
Lamb of God	Offered His life as a sacrifice for sins	John 1:29
Light of the World	One who brings hope and gives guidance	John 9:5
Lord	Sovereign creator and redeemer	Romans 10:9
Lord of Glory	The power of the living God	1 Corinthians 2:8
Mediator	Redeemer who brings forgiven sinners into the presence of God	1 Timothy 2:5
Prophet	One who speaks for God	Luke 13:33
Rabbi/Teacher	A title of respect for one who taught the scriptures	John 3:2
Savior	One who delivers from sin	John 4:42
Son of David	One who brings in the Kingdom	Matthew 9:27
Son of God	A title of deity signifying Jesus' unique and special intimacy with the Father	John 20:31
Son of Man	A divine title of suffering and exaltation	Matthew 20:28
Word	Eternal God who ultimately reveals God	John 1:1

JETHRO (JETH roh). Father-in-law of Moses and a priest of Midian (Exodus 3:1). Also called Reuel (Exodus 2:18).

JEW. The term first applied to an inhabitant of Judah (2 Kings 16:6). Later it came to refer to all descendants of Abraham, who were also called "Hebrews" or "Israelites." Colossians 3:11, Galatians 3:28, and other references in the New Testament show that God's salvation is for all people, regardless of race. The determining factor is the spiritual experience of knowing God in Christ and receiving His grace. We come into God's family by way of grace—rather than by race—and in that way are spiritual descendants of Abraham, true Israelites. All come into God's family by adoption (Romans 8:15, 23; 9:4; Galatians 4:5; Ephesians 1:5).

A familiar image of modern **Jewish** men, with full beards, wearing special hats, and praying at Jerusalem's Western (or Wailing) Wall.

JEZEBEL (JEZ uh bel). Wife of Ahab, king of Israel, the Northern Kingdom (1 Kings 16:31). She was a wicked woman who led the Israelites deeper into idolatry. Jezebel used treachery and murder to get her way. She opposed Elijah (1 Kings 19:2) and ultimately died a horrible death (2 Kings 9:36–37). She was so wicked her name was used to condemn a prophetess in Thyatira (Revelation 2:20). See **AHAB**.

The **Jezreel** Valley, where some speculate the end-time battle of Armageddon will occur.

JEZREEL (JEZ reel). Means "God sows." 1. City and fertile valley in the hill country of Judah (1 Samuel 29:1). 2. City between Megiddo and Bethshean protecting northeast entrance to valley of same name; a favorite place of King Ahab and his family (1 Kings 18:45). Ahab coveted Naboth's vineyard here, and Jezebel had Naboth killed to obtain it (1 Kings 21).

JOAB (JOH ab). Nephew of King David who became commander of David's army (1 Chronicles 11:4–9). Although a competent military man and loyal to the king, he was very cruel. He murdered David's rebellious son, Absalom, even though David had instructed that Absalom be spared (2 Samuel 18:14).

JOASH (JOH ash). Shorter form of *Jehoash*. 1. Son of Ahaziah and the ninth king of Judah, the Southern Kingdom (2 Kings 11:2). Spared of murder as an infant, he was hidden and placed on the throne at age seven by the high priest Jehoiada. He reigned forty years and directed the people back toward God. However, at Jehoiada's death, Joash let the nation fall back into idolatry. 2. Son of Jehoahaz and the twelfth king of Israel, the Northern Kingdom. He had a successful reign and was befriended by the prophet Elisha. 3. In Judges 6:11, Joash is identified as the father of Gideon. See **KING CHART** on pages 152–155. Six other minor Bible characters bore the name Joash.

JOB (JOHB). Old Testament personality whose story is told in the book of the same name (Job 1:1; James 5:11). Job lived in the land of Uz, apparently about the same time as Jacob, the patriarch. Although he is usually referred to as having great patience, Job questioned God and wanted answers. Job demonstrated that the kind of patience he had was persistent trust and steadfastness in God (Job 13:15).

▲ *Though we may be very familiar with sayings and clichés, we would do well to examine their truthfulness. People speak proverbially of the "patience of Job," but he had no patience with his supposed comforters who were more of an affliction to him. What Job did have was persistent faith in God. God blessed Job for that.*

JOB, BOOK OF. Old Testament book included in the poetry division. Job describes how God allowed Satan to test Job, taking his possessions, family, and health, though not his life. Job's many trials and sufferings and the responses of his wife and friends were all temptations from Satan to lead Job to renounce God. But Job persisted in faith. Throughout the ordeal, Job found God's presence to be more meaningful than the answer to Job's questions. By the end of Job's story, God had restored the lost possessions and given Job ten more children.

JOEL (JOH el). 1. Author of the Old Testament book listed with the minor prophets; son of Pethuel (Joel 1:1). We know nothing else about him. 2. Thirteen other Joels are mentioned in the Old Testament.

JOEL, BOOK OF. Old Testament Bible book of sermons of Joel, son of Pethuel. The book views destruction by a locust plague as the judgment of God upon sin. Joel prophesied that the further judgment of God would be much worse than the locusts. He also called for a genuine repentance

Job's wife pours water on her suffering husband. Though the Bible doesn't record her name, it does record her suggestion to Job: "Curse God, and die" (Job 2:9).

that the loving God would follow with blessing. And Joel looked ahead to the coming of God's Spirit (2:28–29; compare Acts 2:16–21).

JOHN, APOSTLE. Son of Zebedee and a fisherman by trade (Matthew 4:21). He was one of the twelve disciples and among the closest to Jesus. Most scholars credit him with writing the Gospel of John, 1, 2, and 3 John, and Revelation.

JOHN, 1, 2, 3, BOOKS OF. New Testament letters written by John, sometimes called the "Johannine Epistles." First John warns Christians of false teachers and urges them to show love to others. Second John also warns of false teachers. Third John is written to an individual, Gaius, to express appreciation for his Christian life and hospitality.

John wrote these letters to help Christians know they have eternal life and that their joy can be complete (1 John 1:4; 5:13). Some form of the word *know* appears approximately thirty times in the letters.

JOHN, BOOK OF. New Testament book focusing on Jesus as the Son of God, His miracles or signs, and His teachings to individuals and groups. The purpose of the Gospel is to lead people to accept Christ as Lord and Savior (John 20:30–31). The Gospel is both simple in readability and profound in theology and thought. Whatever else John knew about Jesus, he knew that Jesus is God the Son, who loves the world and is the light of the world. Most scholars believe John the apostle wrote this book around AD 90–95.

COMPARISON OF THE GOSPELS

EVENT OR POINT OF COMPARISON	IN SYNOPTIC GOSPELS?	IN GOSPEL OF JOHN?	SCRIPTURE REFERENCE
Wedding at Cana	No	Yes	John 2:1–11
Encounter with Nicodemus	No	Yes	John 3:1–14
Encounter with woman at the well	No	Yes	John 4:1–45
Washing of the disciples' feet	No	Yes	John 13:1–17
Last Supper	Yes	No	Luke 22:7–23
Jesus' final priestly prayer	No	Yes	John 17:1–26
Extensive prologue to the Gospel	No	Yes	John 1:1–18
Concluding epilogue to the Gospel	No	Yes	John 21:1–25
Birth narratives	Yes	No	Luke 2:1–20
Jesus' use of parables	Yes	No	Matthew 13:1–52
Casting out demons	Yes	No	Mark 1:21–28
Jesus with tax collectors	Yes	No	Luke 6:27–32
Jesus heals lepers	Yes	No	Luke 17:11–17
Jesus with children	Yes	No	Mark 10:13–16
Sermon on the Mount	Yes	No	Matthew 5:1–7:27
Discourses on the end times	Yes	No	Matthew 24:1–51
Emphasis on miracles	Yes	No	Matthew 8:1–9:8
Emphasis on interpretation of miracles/signs	No	Yes	John 5:1–47
Jesus' teaching on hell	Yes	No	Matthew 23:1–39
Temptations of Jesus	Yes	No	Matthew 4:1–11
"I Am" sayings	No	Yes	John 14:6

JOHN THE BAPTIST. Son of Elisabeth and Zacharias (also spelled Zachariah) and a cousin of Jesus (Luke 1:13). His birth was an answer to the prayers of his elderly parents. He grew up in the isolation of the desert. He came out of seclusion to preach a message of repentance and to prepare the way for Jesus. He is called the forerunner of Jesus. At Jesus' request, John baptized Jesus to "fulfil all righteousness" (see Matthew 3:13–17). Relatively early in Jesus' ministry, Herod Antipas imprisoned John for

The Holy Spirit, appearing as a dove, descends on Jesus after His baptism by **John**.

preaching against the sins of Herodias and Herod. Then Herod had John beheaded to please a request of his wife, Herodias, and her daughter (Mark 6:14–30)

JONAH (JOH nuh). Son of Amittai and a prophet of Israel (Jonah 1:1) about 750 BC. He lived in a town near Nazareth and gave good advice to King Jeroboam II of Israel (2 Kings 14:23–29). Because Jonah preached to the Ninevites, some see him as the first recorded missionary to a heathen or Gentile (non-Jewish) nation.

● *Jonah resisted God's command to preach to Nineveh (Jonah 1:3 and following). Why? Usually, God calls people to preach and answer His calling with a yes, but He may also "draft" people as He did Jonah and Paul. What calling do you have?*

JONAH, BOOK OF. This Old Testament book tells how Jonah reluctantly went to preach the message of God's judgment to the people of Nineveh. Jonah was disappointed when the judgment did not come about after the people repented. The book is listed in the division of minor prophets. The book is unusual among the prophets, having only one brief sermon (3:4). But the book of Jonah tells an extensive story about a prophet and about his downcast attitude over the people's complete repentance. The biblical account emphasizes God's great love for all people (4:10–11).

▲ *God is eternally unchanging. But the book of Jonah indicates that God may change His announced intent if people listen, repent, and turn to Him. Always remember that people can change.*

JONATHAN (JAHN uh thuhn). Son of King Saul and loyal friend to David (1 Samuel 14:1). Jonathan defended David to Saul and helped spare David's life. He died with his father in battle against the Philistines. Fourteen other Jonathans appear in the Bible.

JOPPA (JAHP uh). Town where Peter prayed and then raised Dorcas to life and received his vision to preach to the Gentile Cornelius (Acts 9:36–41). Seacoast city thirty-five miles northwest of Jerusalem. Cedar logs for King Solomon's temple were shipped here (2 Chronicles 2:16). Israel contested the Philistines and Phoenicians for control of Joppa.

JORAM (JOH ruhm). Wicked king of Judah (same as Jehoram). See **KING CHART** on pages 152–155.

JORDAN (JAWR d'n). River of Palestine that played an important role in biblical history (Joshua 1:2; Mark 1:9). The Jordan originates above the freshwater Sea of Galilee and ends in the Dead (Salt) Sea, which has no outlet. Although it is only

seventy miles from the Sea of Galilee to the Dead Sea, the Jordan meanders two hundred miles. It is three to ten feet deep and about a hundred feet wide. The Israelites crossed over the Jordan River to enter the Promised Land. John baptized Jesus in the Jordan. Note that the modern country named Jordan includes large areas east and south of the Jordan River.

JOSEPH (JOH zif). 1. Son of Rachel and Jacob and the favorite of his father's twelve sons (Genesis 37:3). Joseph's jealous brothers sold him into Egyptian slavery. After Joseph spent time in prison due to false charges, he was given the opportunity to interpret the Pharaoh's dreams. Then Joseph found favor in Pharaoh's eyes and became second in authority in Egypt— as one commentator has said, from prison in the morning to prime minister in the evening. Joseph rescued Egypt by planning for seven

The **Jordan** River appears very green in this photograph, but is often muddy. An Old Testament figure, the Syrian commander Naaman, resisted bathing in the Jordan to be cleansed of his leprosy, saying "Are not Abana and Pharpar, rivers of Damascus, better than all the waters of Israel?" (2 Kings 5:12).

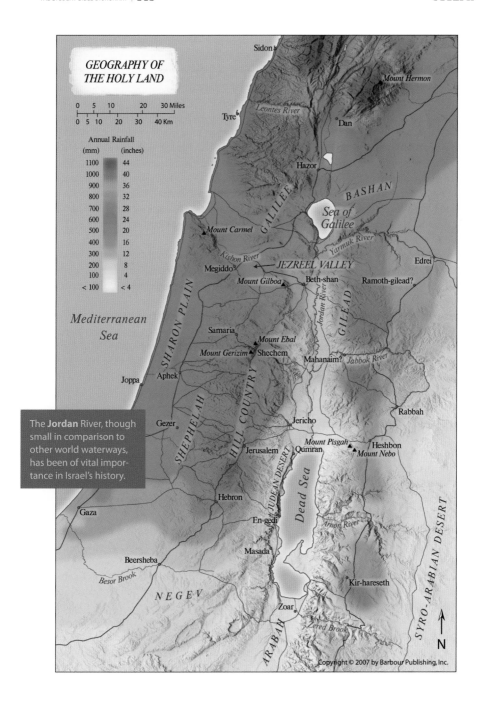

GEOGRAPHY OF
THE HOLY LAND

0	5	10		20		30 Miles
0	5	10	20	30	40 Km

Annual Rainfall

(mm)	(inches)
1100	44
1000	40
900	36
800	32
700	28
600	24
500	20
400	16
300	12
200	8
100	4
< 100	< 4

Sidon

Mount Hermon

Leontes River

Tyre

Dan

Hazor

BASHAN

GALILEE

Sea of
Galilee

Mount Carmel

Yarmuk River

Edrei

Kishon River

JEZREEL VALLEY

Megiddo

Mount Gilboa

Beth-shan

Ramoth-gilead?

Mediterranean
Sea

SHARON PLAIN

Samaria

Mount Ebal

Mount Gerizim Shechem

Jordan River

GILEAD

Mahanaim?

Jabbok River

Joppa

Aphek

HILL COUNTRY

Rabbah

Gezer

Jericho

SHEPHELAH

The **Jordan** River, though small in comparison to other world waterways, has been of vital importance in Israel's history.

Jerusalem

Qumran

Mount Pisgah

Heshbon

Mount Nebo

Hebron

JUDEAN DESERT

Gaza

En-gedi

Dead Sea

Arnon River

SYRO-ARABIAN DESERT

Masada

Beersheba

Besor Brook

Kir-hareseth

NEGEV

Zoar

ARABAH

Zered Brook

N

years of prophesied famine by storing up the abundant harvest of seven preceding years. He forgave his brothers for selling him into slavery and brought his family and father to live in Egypt after the brothers had come to buy grain during the famine. 2. A carpenter who became the husband of Jesus' mother, Mary (Matthew 1:18). Joseph was betrothed to Mary when she conceived Jesus by the Holy Spirit. Betrothal was like engagement, but stronger in that it required a writing of divorcement to break. An angel's testimony convinced Joseph that Mary had conceived by the Holy Spirit. So the kind and gentle Joseph took Mary as his wife to save her from public disgrace for being pregnant out of wedlock. Joseph and Mary then waited to have sexual relations until after Jesus' birth. 3. A Jew of Arimathea, member of the Sanhedrin, and secret disciple of Jesus. He came forward after the crucifixion to ask for Jesus' body to bury it in his own tomb. 4. The Old Testament mentions four other Josephs, and the New Testament, six.

● *The Josephs mentioned here were able to face difficult situations with God's help. Which situations are most like ones you have faced—or like ones you might face?*

JOSHUA (JAHSH yoo uh). Son of Nun, assistant and successor to Moses (Exodus 17:9). Joshua and Caleb differed from the other ten spies by being confident the Israelites could conquer the land of Canaan (Numbers 13–14). After forty years of wilderness wanderings and Moses' death, Joshua led the Israelites—including Caleb—into the promised land to obey God and overcome the inhabitants there.

JOSHUA, BOOK OF. This Old Testament book tells how Israel entered, conquered, and divided Canaan. In the closing chapter, Joshua testified and called the people to absolute faithfulness to God, and the renewal of the covenant with them

(Joshua 24:13–18). Though dates of events in the book of Joshua are uncertain, many scholars believe they occurred in the last half of the thirteenth century BC.

JOSIAH (joh SIGH uh). Sixteenth king of Judah; he began to rule at age eight and ruled from 640–609 BC. Though his father was the evil King Amon, Josiah was one of the best of the kings (2 Kings 22:1). He was known for his good reforms: repairing the temple, discovering and implementing the lost book of Law, and abolishing idolatry. See **KING CHART** on pages 152–155.

JOT. A reference to the smallest letter in the alphabets of Greek (*iota*) or Hebrew (*yod*). A "jot" refers to the least bit (Matthew 5:18). See **TITTLE**.

JOY. Gladness, rejoicing (Psalm 16:11; Matthew 2:10). An evidence of a Holy Spirit–filled life (Galatians 5:22). Joy is the keynote of the New Testament, and Jesus taught so that His joy might remain in His disciples and be full (John 15:11).

● *How is joy similar to or different from happiness? Happiness may come and go—but what about Jesus' kind of joy? See John 16:21–22.*

JUBILEE, YEAR OF. An Old Testament celebration held every fifty years (Leviticus 25:10 and following). During this time of thanksgiving the land was not to be planted in crops, Hebrews enslaved for debt were to be freed, and property was to be returned to its original owners.

JUDAH (JOO duh). Fourth son of Jacob and Leah (Genesis 29:35). Judah's descendants became the tribe of Judah, and the land they occupied was known as Judah. When the Hebrew kingdom divided, Judah was the name of the Southern Kingdom. To be a "Jew" was to be a descendant of Judah. See **JACOB**.

Judas Iscariot betrays Jesus with a kiss while Jewish religious leaders—in anachronistic, sixteenth-century outfits—move in to arrest the Lord.

JUDAS (JOO duhs). A common name in Jewish history; the name of seven men in the New Testament. They include: 1. A disciple of Jesus (John 6:71), called Judas Iscariot, who betrayed Jesus and later hanged himself (Matthew 27:3–10). 2. A brother of Jesus (Matthew 13:55), probably the same as the brother of James and author of the book of Jude. The New Testament mentions at least five other Judases.

▲ *Judas Iscariot tarnished the name Judas forever and appears last in each list of the disciples.*

JUDE, BOOK OF. New Testament book written by Jude, brother of James, to combat false teachings in the early Christian church. Scholars suggest a date perhaps around AD 80. Refers to contending for the faith that was once delivered to the saints (Jude 3). He committed the readers to the keeping of the Lord in a beautiful benediction (Jude 24–25). The author was probably also the brother of Jesus.

JUDEA (joo DEE uh). Land located between the Dead Sea and the Mediterranean Sea (Matthew 3:1). Earlier this area was called Judah after the Israelite tribe that claimed it, but after the return from Babylonian captivity it became Judea. Spelled Judaea in the King James Version.

▲ In New Testament times, Judea had decreased in size and lay west of the Jordan along with Galilee, divided by Samaria.

JUDGE. Noun: A public official who helps interpret the laws (Ezra 7:25; Matthew 5:25).

The judges from the time of Joshua to Samuel were also spiritual and military leaders. Verb: To discern or criticize (Genesis 15:14; Matthew 7:1). Spiritually, the Bible cautions us not to be judgmental toward others because only God is qualified to do so. God is the great and righteous judge (Revelation 20:13). We are responsible to Him for our beliefs and actions.

● How may human motives for judging be different from God's motives for judging? When is judgment destructive? Constructive? Consider that there is a difference in "being judgmental" and in evaluating teachings and behaviors according to scripture.

JUDGES OF THE OLD TESTAMENT

NAME	REFERENCE	IDENTIFICATION
Othniel	Judges 1:12–13; 3:7–11	Conquered a Canaanite city
Ehud	Judges 3:12–30	Killed Eglon, king of Moab, and defeated Moabites
Shamgar	Judges 3:31	Killed 600 Philistines with an oxgoad
Deborah	Judges 4–5	Convinced Barak to lead an army to victory against Sisera's troops
Gideon	Judges 6–8	Led 300 men to victory against 135,000 Midianites
Tola	Judges 10:1–2	Judged for 23 years
Jair	Judges 10:3–5	Judged for 22 years
Jephthah	Judges 11:1–12:7	Defeated the Ammonites after making a promise to the Lord
Ibzan	Judges 12:8–10	Judged for 7 years
Elon	Judges 12:11–12	Judged for 10 years
Abdon	Judges 12:13–15	Judged for 8 years
Samson	Judges 13–16	Killed 1,000 Philistines with a donkey's jawbone; was deceived by Delilah; destroyed a Philistine temple; judged 20 years
Samuel	1 and 2 Samuel	Was the last of the judges and the first of the prophets

JUDGES, BOOK OF. Old Testament book that deals with the history of the Israelites from the time of Joshua to the time of Samuel. The book is a sad repetition of sin, judgment, and rescue or salvation—only for the cycle to repeat again. Depending on who is included in the number of judges, there were fourteen or fifteen in the period referred to. The author is not known. Judges shows how lack of godly leadership destroys a nation.

▲ Humans are prone to sin even after coming to know God, but God continues to forgive the truly repentant and restore them to fellowship. Psalm 51:12 reads, "Restore unto me the joy of thy salvation." Although Romans and the epistles of John focus on the certainty of salvation, the Bible itself shows that sin brings grief and calls for renewing the joy of our salvation in repentance and the restoration of our fellowship with God and others.

■ **JUDGMENT**. Pronouncement of a decision (Joshua 20:6). Often used to refer to God's discipline of His people (Psalm 9:16; Romans 2:2). The Bible also speaks of a future and final judgment (Revelation 14:7).

JUST. Righteous, fair, right—especially in God's eyes (Genesis 6:9; Romans 1:17).

JUSTICE. Rightness, fairness (Isaiah 59:4).
● With what actions do you show justice? How might you improve in attitudes of fairness and being charitable?

■ **JUSTIFICATION**. God's act of declaring and making a repentant person right with Him (Romans 4:24–25; 5:17; 1 Corinthians 1:30). Remember the definition by recalling that justification essentially means "just-as-if-I-had-not-sinned." God makes provision for resolving the sins of repentant sinners, releasing them from sin's penalty, and declaring them righteous (see Romans 3:24–26; 4:5–8; Ephesians 2:1–10).

▲ Being made right with God frees us spiritually from sin's penalty—but the harm or results of sin may continue in wounded souls, spirits, and generations.

JUSTIFIED. Made right—as in being made right with God (Psalm 143:2; Galatians 2:16).

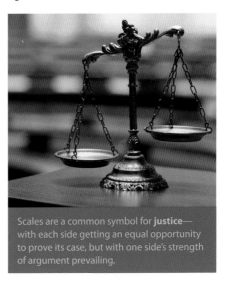

Scales are a common symbol for **justice**—with each side getting an equal opportunity to prove its case, but with one side's strength of argument prevailing.

than the act of preaching. An example occurs in 1 Corinthians 1:21, which speaks of God's pleasure, "by the foolishness of preaching to save them that believe" (KJV). The NIV refers to the message of the cross itself appearing to be "foolishness" (a stumbling block). On the contrary, the thing preached is not foolishness; rather, it is the gospel message preached that leads to salvation for those who believe it and trust Jesus Christ as Lord and Savior.

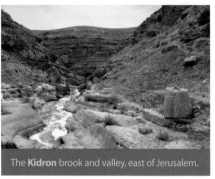

The **Kidron** brook and valley, east of Jerusalem.

KADESH (KAY desh), **KADESH-BARNEA** (KAY desh BAHR nee uh). Kadesh was a place in the wilderness area about seventy miles south of Hebron (Genesis 14:7; Numbers 13:26). It was south of Judah and near the border of Edom. The Israelites wandered in and near that area for most of their exodus experiences. Moses sent the twelve spies from here to scout out the promised land (Numbers 13:21–26).

KENOSIS (keh-NO-sis). A Greek word that means "emptying." Bible students and scholars often use the term to refer to Philippians 2:5–11, the experience of the divine Christ taking upon Himself the form and existence of man. In the eternal Christ's incarnation—becoming human and taking on flesh—He "emptied Himself" (Philippians 2:7 NASB), in some ways: limiting Himself to human restrictions while still remaining fully divine. For a time on earth, Jesus seemingly limited His all-powerful, all-knowing, all-present existence. Though scholars explain kenosis in varying terms, we might simply describe the term as the apostle Paul's inspired statement of the Christmas story in theological terms.

KERYGMA (KEH rig muh). Greek word for a proclamation. Scholars often use this word to refer to the *thing* preached—the content rather

KIDRON (KID ruhn), **CEDRON** (SEE druhn). A brook and valley along the east side of Jerusalem. During the time of the kings, idolatrous items were burned or destroyed here. Note that Kidron and Cedron are different spellings of the same place: In John 18:1 (KJV), "Cedron" appears; contemporary translators use "Kidron" instead.

KIN, KINSMAN, KINDRED. Family member, relative, of the same tribe or race (Genesis 12:1; Luke 14:12). The Hebrew culture provided many marriage guidelines and family responsibilities relating to relatives. Many of these guidelines came out of the Mosaic Law or Leviticus.

KINDLE. To light or cause to burn (Exodus 35:3; Acts 28:2). In Acts 28:2, the people of Malta (Melita,

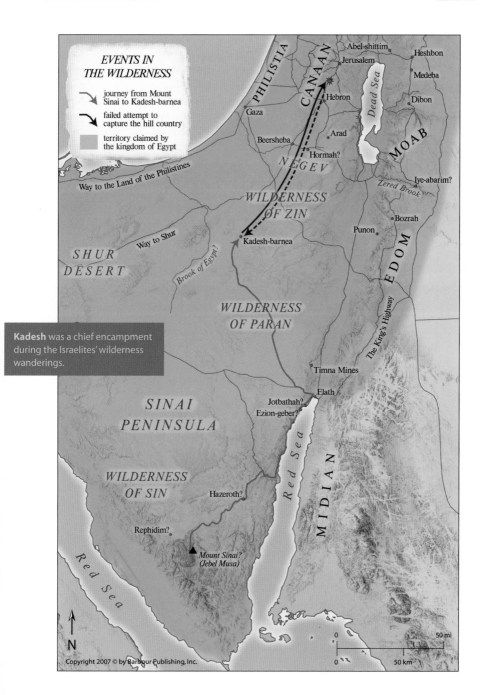

EVENTS IN THE WILDERNESS

journey from Mount Sinai to Kadesh-barnea

failed attempt to capture the hill country

territory claimed by the kingdom of Egypt

Abel-shittim
Heshbon
Jerusalem
Medeba
PHILISTIA
CANAAN
Hebron
Dibon
Gaza
Dead Sea
Arad
Beersheba
MOAB
Hormah?
NEGEV
Iye-abarim?
Way to the Land of the Philistines
Zered Brook
WILDERNESS OF ZIN
Bozrah
Punon
Way to Shur
Kadesh-barnea
SHUR DESERT
Brook of Egypt?
EDOM
WILDERNESS OF PARAN
The King's Highway

Kadesh was a chief encampment during the Israelites' wilderness wanderings.

Timna Mines
Elath
Jotbathah?
Ezion-geber?
SINAI PENINSULA
Red Sea
MIDIAN
WILDERNESS OF SIN
Hazeroth?
Rephidim?
Mount Sinai? (Jebel Musa)
Red Sea
N

0 — 50 mi
0 — 50 km

Copyright 2007 © by Barbour Publishing, Inc.

KJV) were kind to Paul and others who had been shipwrecked, and kindled a fire to warm them.

KINE. Cows (Amos 4:1). Amos used the phrase "kine (cows) of Bashan" to refer to women of Samaria who oppressed the poor and would suffer judgment for it.

KING. Ruler of a nation (Exodus 1:8; Matthew 2:1). During the time of Samuel, at the Israelites' insistence, God allowed the Israelites to have their first king, Saul. A king was mainly looked upon as a military leader, but most of Israel's kings also influenced the people spiritually, both good and bad. See **KING CHART** on pages 152–155.

RULERS OF ISRAEL AND JUDAH

RULERS OF THE UNITED KINGDOM

Saul (1 Samuel 9:1–31:13)
David (1 Samuel 16:1–1 Kings 2:11)
Solomon (1 Kings 1:1–11:43)

RULERS OF THE DIVIDED KINGDOM

RULERS OF ISRAEL	RULERS OF JUDAH
Jeroboam I (1 Kings 11:26–14:20)	Rehoboam (1 Kings 11:42–14:31)
	Abijah/Abijam (1 Kings 14:31–15:8)
Nadab (1 Kings 15:25–28)	Asa (1 Kings 15:8–24)
Baasha (1 Kings 15:27–16:7)	
Elah (1 Kings 16:6–14)	
Zimri (1 Kings 16:9–20)	
Omri (1 Kings 16:15–28)	
Ahab (1 Kings 16:28–22:40)	Jehoshaphat (1 Kings 22:41–50)
Ahaziah (1 Kings 22:40–2 Kings 1:18)	Jehoram (2 Kings 8:16–24)
Jehoram/Joram (2 Kings 1:17–9:26)	Ahaziah (2 Kings 8:24–9:29)
Jehu (2 Kings 9:1–10:36)	Athaliah (2 Kings 11:1–20)
Jehoahaz (2 Kings 13:1–9)	Joash (2 Kings 11:1–12:21)
Jehoash/Joash (2 Kings 13:10–14:16)	Amaziah (2 Kings 14:1–20)
Jeroboam II (2 Kings 14:23–29)	Azariah/Uzziah (2 Kings 14:21; 15:1–7)
Zechariah (2 Kings 14:29–15:12)	
Shallum (2 Kings 15:10–15)	Jotham (2 Kings 15:32–38)

Menahem (2 Kings 15:14–22)

Pekahiah (2 Kings 15:22–26)

Pekah (2 Kings 15:25–31)

Hoshea (2 Kings 15:30–17:6)

Ahaz/Jehoahaz (2 Kings 16:1–20)

Hezekiah (2 Kings 18:1–20:21)

Manasseh (2 Kings 21:1–18)

Amon (2 Kings 21:19–26)

Josiah (2 Kings 21:26–23:30)

Jehoahaz II/Shallum (2 Kings 23:30–33)

Jehoiakim/Eliakim (2 Kings 23:34–24:5)

Jehoiachin/Jeconiah (2 Kings 24:6–16;25:27–30)

Zedekiah/Mattaniah (2 Kings 24:17–25:7

RULERS OF OLD TESTAMENT PAGAN NATIONS *(LISTED ALPHABETICALLY)*

NAME	REFERENCE	NATIONALITY
Abimelech	(1) Genesis 20	Philistine
	(2) Genesis 26	Philistine
Achish	1 Samuel 21:10–14; 27–29	Philistine
Adoni-Zedek	Joshua 10:1–27	Canaanite
Agag	1 Samuel 15:8–33	Amalekite
Ahasuerus	*See* Xerxes I	
Ammon, king of (unnamed)	Judges 11:12–28	Ammonite
Artaxerxes	Ezra 4:7–23; 7; 8:1; Nehemiah 2:1–8	Persian/Mede
Ashurbanipal (also known as Osnapper)	Ezra 4:10	Assyrian
Baalis	Jeremiah 40:14	Ammonite
Balak	Numbers 22–24	Moabite
Belshazzar	Daniel 5; 7:1	Babylonian
Ben-Hadad I	1 Kings 20:1–34	Syrian
Ben-Hadad II	2 Kings 6:24	Syrian
Bera	Genesis 14:2–24	Canaanite

NAME	REFERENCE	NATIONALITY
Cyrus the Great	2 Chronicles 36:22 –23; Ezra 1; Isaiah 44:28; 45:1; Daniel 1:21; 10:1	Persian/Mede
Darius the Great	Ezra 4–6; Nehemiah 12:22; Hagai 1:1; Zechariah 1:1, 17	Persian/Mede
Darius the Mede	Daniel 11:1	Persian/Mede
Edom, king of (unnamed)	Numbers 20:14–21	Edomite
Eglon	Judges 3:12–30	Moabite
Egypt, pharaoh of (unnamed)	(1) Genesis 12:18–20	Egyptian
	(2) Genesis 41:38–55	Egyptian
	(3) Exodus 1:8	Egyptian
	(4) Exodus 2:15	Egyptian
	(5) Exodus 3:10; 5:1	Egyptian
	(6) 1 Kings 3:1	Egyptian
Esarhaddon	Ezra 4:2	Assyrian
Evil-Merodach	2 Kings 25:27–30; Jeremiah 52:31–34	Babylonian
Hanun	2 Samuel 10:1–4	Ammonite
Hazael	1 Kings 19:15; 2 Kings 8:7–15	Syrian
Hiram	1 Kings 5:1–18	Tyrian
Hophra	Jeremiah 44:30	Egyptian
Jabin	(1) Joshua 11:1–11	Canaanite
	(2) Judges 4:2	Canaanite
Jericho, king of (unnamed)	Joshua 2:2	Canaanite
Merodach-Baladan	2 Kings 20:12; Isaiah 39:1	Babylonian
Mesha	2 Kings 3:4–27	Moabite
Nahash	1 Samuel 11:12	Ammonite
Nebuchadnezzar	2 Kings 24–25; Daniel 1–4	Babylonian
Neco	2 Kings 23:39–30	Egyptian
Nergal-Sharezer	Jeremiah 39:3, 13	Babylonian
Osnapper	*See* Ashurbanipal	
Pul	*See* Tiglath-Pileser III	
Rezin	2 Kings 15:37; 16:5–9	Syrian
Sargon II	Isaiah 20	Assyrian
Sennacherib	2 Kings 18–19; Isaiah 36–37	Assyrian

NAME	REFERENCE	NATIONALITY
Shalmaneser V	2 Kings 17:1–6	Assyrian
Shishak	1 Kings 14:25–26; 2 Chronicles 12:2–9	Egyptian
Tiglath-Pileser III	2 Kings 15:19, 29; 16:7–10	Assyrian
Tyre, prince of (unnamed)	Ezekiel 28:1–10	Tyrian
Xerxes I (also known as Ahasuerus)	Ezra 4:6; Esther	Persian/Mede

■ **KINGDOM**. Refers to a king's authority or rule over a territory or over the hearts of people (as in the kingdom of God; 1 Samuel 10:16; Matthew 6:10).

KINGDOM OF GOD, **KINGDOM OF HEAVEN**. A kingdom is a territory ruled over by a king (Genesis 10:10), so the phrase "kingdom of God" (or "kingdom of heaven"—used interchangeably) refers to the place and time that God rules, both present and future (Mark 1:15; Matthew 6:10). Matthew tended to use the phrase "kingdom of heaven" while the other gospels refer more often to "kingdom of God"; they mean the same thing. This kingdom is also considered to be a place where God's reign is complete (Revelation 12:10). John 3:3–5 notes the requirement for entrance into the kingdom of God—a new birth. In Matthew 12:28, Jesus indicated that the kingdom of God was evident when He did the will of God—in this passage, by casting out demons.

▲ *Hebrew "parallelism" was a poetic way of saying the same thing in two different ways. For example, when Jesus prayed, "Thy kingdom come, Thy will be done," the context indicates the two phrases mean the same thing.*

● *What expressions of the kingdom of God do you see today? How do you show citizenship in it?*

KINGS, 1 AND 2, BOOKS OF. Old Testament accounts of history that were originally one book. They cover the last days of David; the reign of Solomon; the divided kingdoms of Israel and Judah through their fall (722 and 587 respectively); and a few other events. The books deal with God's judgment of His rebellious people during this time.

● *During the time covered in 1 and 2 Kings, kings and prophets led God's people. The kings were mostly bad; the prophets were mostly ignored in their messages from God. What conclusions might we draw from our contemporary political and religious leaders? What is our own responsibility to discern and obey God's Word?*

KISH. Father of Saul (1 Samuel 9:1–2). Four other Bible personalities were named Kish.

KISHON (KIGH shahn). A stream flowing from Mount Tabor westward toward the Mediterranean (Judges 4:7).

The **Kishon** River meets the Mediterranean sea at the Israeli port city of Haifa.

KISS. An expression of greeting and affection among both males and females. A kindly greeting among early believers, perhaps like our handshake or gentle hug (Romans 16:16; 1 Corinthians 16:20; 2 Corinthians 13:12). In the New Testament, believers were generally instructed to greet each other with a "holy kiss"; but 1 Peter 5:14 says, "Greet one another with a kiss of love" (NASB). Coupled with this *agape* kiss is a benediction of peace.

KNEEL. Bend the knee or bow in a sign of worship, reverence, or subjection (Psalm 95:6; Acts 9:40). The Bible's first instance of kneeling in prayer is recorded in 1 Kings 8:54; before that, standing was noted as a prayer posture (1 Samuel 1:26). But the heart, motive, and content of prayer are far more important than the physical position of the body.

KNIT. Joined together, bound (1 Chronicles 12:17; Acts 10:11; Colossians 2:2).

KNOW. A term that may refer to intellectual knowledge of facts or knowing by personal experience. Two different Greek words are used to express experiential knowledge versus a merely intellectual knowledge or belief. For example, Paul wrote from experience, "I *know* whom I have believed" (2 Timothy 1:12, emphasis added). James 2:19, however, refers to

an intellectual knowledge only: "the demons also believe, and tremble." The KJV sometimes uses the verb *know* (implying intimate knowledge) to describe sexual intercourse (Genesis 4:1, 25; Luke 1:34).

● *Knowing with the intellect or mind is good and necessary in life. Knowing by experience is critically important—and in becoming a Christian, eternally important. We can't just know in our minds that Jesus is the Son of God and came to save the world. Rather, we have to repent of our sins, trust Jesus Christ with our whole heart, and confess that truth with our mouths and lives (Romans 10:9–10).*

KNOWLEDGE. Understanding (Proverbs 1:7; Philippians 1:9).

KORAH (KOH ruh). Man who led a rebellion against Moses and Aaron (Numbers 16:19). Four other people and a town bear the name.

● *Note: Many other personal and place names that begin with the letter K in English are beyond the scope of this dictionary that focuses primarily on "turning-point" aspects of the Bible. Further study in a larger, more comprehensive Bible dictionary would be helpful for the reader regarding particular names not found here.*

LABAN (LAY buhn). Abraham's nephew, brother of Rebekah (Genesis 24:15, 29), and father of Leah and Rachel (Genesis 29:16 and following). Laban tricked Jacob into marrying Leah—instead of Rachel—at the end of seven years of labor. After a week of marriage to Leah, Jacob also got Rachel for his wife. However, Laban required Jacob to serve him another seven years for Rachel (see Genesis 29:28–30). Because of their deceitful natures, Jacob and Laban experienced further conflict, but the strife between them was eventually settled through a covenant (Genesis 31:44 and following).

Labor predated the fall of man, since God "took the man, and put him into the garden of Eden to dress it and to keep it" (Genesis 2:15), sometime before the serpent convinced Adam and Eve to disobey God (Genesis 3).

LABOR. Work (Genesis 31:42; 1 Corinthians 3:8). Note that labor is not the result of sin; rather, it reflects the image of God, who was at work from the beginning of recorded time. After working, God rested, later prescribing that pattern for humans (Exodus 20:8–11).

LAD. Young person, child, servant (Judges 16:26; John 6:9).

LAMB. A young sheep used as an offering in the Jewish sacrificial system (Exodus 29:38). Jesus is our sacrificial Lamb in the sense that He died as a sacrifice in our place (Revelation 7:14).

LAMB OF GOD. Title for Jesus, as stated by John the Baptist. It pointed to Jesus' sacrificial death (John 1:29, 36; see also Isaiah 53:7–12).

LAME. Limping, crippled (Deuteronomy 15:21; Matthew 11:5).

LAMECH (LAY mek). 1. Descendant of Cain (Genesis 4:18). 2. Son of Methuselah and father of Noah (Genesis 5:30).

LAMENT. Mourn or show deep sorrow (Jeremiah 4:8; John 16:20).

LAMENTATIONS, BOOK OF. Old Testament book in the division of major prophets. Jeremiah is traditionally recognized as author. The book mourns the complete Babylonian capture of Jerusalem in 587 BC, God's judgment on Judah's sin. Lamentations is written in a poetic style, with the first four chapters in an acrostic pattern, in this case, the letters of the Hebrew alphabet.

LAMP. A torch or light. The term appears in a parable Jesus told about the kingdom of heaven; the idea of keeping lamps filled with oil represented readiness for the visit of the bridegroom, or Jesus' return (Matthew 25:1–13). In Revelation 1–3, seven lampstands represented the churches the Lord evaluated, urging most to repent or have their lights removed.

LANGUISH. Become weak, fade (Hosea 4:3).

LAODICEA (lay ahd ih SEE uh). Chief commercial city of Asia Minor (Colossians 4:15), it was a banking center also known for its medicines and black woolen garments. The church at Laodicea received Jesus' condemnation for being lukewarm, rather than hot or cold (Revelation 3:14–16). This passage gives us the English word *Laodicean*, meaning lukewarm or indifferent in religion or politics.

■ **LASCIVIOUSNESS**. Shameless immorality, conduct shocking to public decency (Galatians 5:19; Ephesians 4:19).

LATIN. Language of the Romans (John 19:20). Note that while Romans ruled Israel in New Testament times, the earlier Greek language was still universal. Hebrew was the language of the Old Testament, except for a few Aramaic texts. Aramaic was the common language of the Jewish people in Israel.

LAVER. Large brass bowl containing water, used in the tabernacle and temple for ceremonial cleansing (Exodus 30:18; 1 Kings 7:38).

LAW. Teaching, commandment (Psalm 19:7). 1. God's rules or commandments (Exodus 20:1–17; Deuteronomy 5:1–20). 2. First five books of the Old Testament; division of Old Testament. 3. Part or all of the Old Testament. 4. Rules made by humans (Esther 1:19).

When a Pharisee once tested Jesus by asking which was the greatest Commandment (or Law), Jesus answered that it was to love God completely and love one's neighbor as oneself (Matthew 22:37–40). In other words, loving and living God's way fulfills the Law.

LAWFUL. Authorized, allowed, permitted by law (Ezekiel 18:19; Matthew 12:2). Determining what was "lawful"—allowed or disallowed by Mosaic Law—was a source of great conflict between Jesus and the religious leaders of His day.

LAWLESS. Unauthorized, unguided by the law, unruly, disorderly (1 Timothy 1:9).

LAYING HANDS ON. A symbolic act of dedication and consecration (Leviticus 4:4; Acts 6:6).

Occasionally, this phrase indicated something negative: Religious leaders and others "laid hands on" Jesus to wrongfully seize Him (Matthew 26:50; Mark 14:46). But when church leaders laid hands on Paul and Barnabas, it

A modern reconstruction of the bronze **laver**, part of a model of the entire tabernacle in Israel.

was much like an ordination recognizing their calling before sending them out with the gospel (Acts 13:1–3).

LAZARUS (LAZ uh ruhs). 1. Brother of Mary and Martha (John 11:1). Jesus raised this close friend from the dead. 2. Name of a beggar in a parable of Jesus. In this parable, Jesus described people's eternal blessing or separation based on their trust in God while on earth (Luke 16:20–31).
▲ *Lack of compassion is one indication that a person has not trusted and followed Jesus.*

LEAH (LEE uh). Laban's older daughter who became Jacob's first wife. The relationship was the result of Laban's trickery to marry off his older daughter before the younger daughter, Rachel (Genesis 29:16–28).

LEARN. Grow in knowledge and understanding (Deuteronomy 5:1; Matthew 11:29). Learning involves knowledge, but may also include wisdom. Jesus grew in "wisdom and stature, and in favor with God and man" (Luke 2:52). It is possible, though, to learn facts and grow

Ruins of ancient **Laodicea**, home of one of the seven churches of Revelation—the sole church to receive only condemnation from Jesus.

in knowledge without a matching increase in wisdom. The book of James says that if we ask God for wisdom, He will give it to us (James 1:5).

LEAVEN. Literally, a substance (such as yeast or baking soda) that makes bread dough rise. The Bible uses the term both literally (Exodus 12:15–17) and symbolically (Luke 13:20–21; Galatians 5:9). As a symbol, *leaven* could refer to anything that influences something far larger than itself, either for good or bad (Matthew 13:33; Luke 12:1). "Unleavened bread" was often used in Old Testament worship and was a part of the Passover meal. See **PASSOVER.**

Yeast, or **leaven,** awaiting mixture into bread dough. People of Bible times used yeast like we do, but the substance often has a negative connotation in scripture.

LEBANON (LEB uh nuhn). Name meaning "white"—perhaps from the snow-covered mountain range that extends approximately a hundred miles through the nation of the same name. Lebanon was at the northern border of Canaan and along the Mediterranean Sea (Deuteronomy 1:7). It was heavily wooded in Bible times and known especially for its magnificent cedar trees (Psalm 104:16).
▲ *Lebanon has been significant both in biblical references and in modern times. Jeremiah 18 contrasts God's faithfulness against*

Israel's unfaithfulness, making reference to the snow-covered white mountains of Lebanon.

LEES. Sediment from wine (Isaiah 25:6).

LEFT SIDE. Along with the right-hand side, a position of honor next to a king (Matthew 20:21–27; Mark 10:35–40). But in other cases, being on the left hand was considered a lesser thing (Genesis 48:13–19). In the Bible, references to the right side and right hand are usually favorable and preferred over the left.

LEGION. A Roman army division of forty-five hundred to six thousand men that sometimes included a cavalry unit. "Legion" was the name the Gadarene demoniac gave for himself—or the demons possessing him gave for themselves (Mark 5:9).

LENTILS. Pea-like seeds used in stew or soup (2 Samuel 17:28).

Three kinds of **lentils**. In Genesis 25:27–34 (NIV), Esau traded his birthright to his younger brother, Jacob, for a bowl of red lentil stew.

LEPER, LEPROSY. Term applied for several kinds of skin diseases including the devastating condition referred to today as Hansen's disease (see Leviticus 13; Luke 17:11–13). Besides physical suffering, leprosy made its sufferers outcasts who were forced to live apart from family and society in general. Though lepers could be a health threat to others, Jesus never hesitated to touch and heal them (Luke 5:12–13). Lepers were considered ceremonially unclean, as well, so after Jesus had cleansed lepers, He told them to show themselves to the priest to be pronounced ceremonially cleansed.

LEST. For fear that, unless, except (Genesis 4:15; Matthew 7:6).

LET. Usually, permit or allow (Exodus 3:19; Matthew 8:22), but can mean hinder, forbid, prevent, or restrain (Isaiah 43:13; Romans 1:13; 2 Thessalonians 2:6–7). In the KJV, the context determines whether the meaning is permission or prohibition.

LETTER. Same as *epistle* (Ezra 4:7; Acts 15:30; Galatians 6:11); compare KJV and NRSV. About half the New Testament books were letters or epistles.
▲ *In John 7:15, the Jews wondered how Jesus knew "letters" without a formal education. A Greek word similar to "grammar" is used here to refer to writing or education.*

LEVI (LEE vigh). Jacob's third son by Leah (Genesis 29:34). The tribe of Levites descended from Levi (Number 18:2).
▲ *Priests were Levites who belonged to Aaron's family, but not all Levites were priests. Aaron had become high priest at Sinai, and his sons inherited the priestly role (Exodus 28:1; Leviticus 8–10).*

LEVIATHAN (lih VIGH uh thuhn). A large water creature spoken of negatively in various biblical passages. Its exact description is unknown, but scriptural hints are found in Isaiah 27:1; Psalm 74:14; Job 3:8, 41:1–9; and Psalm 104:24–30. Whatever it was, Leviathan was part of God's creation and subject to Him (see Psalm 104:24–30).

LEVITE (LEE vight), **LEVITICAL** (leh VIT ih kuhl) **PRIESTHOOD**. Descendants of Levi—one of the twelve tribes (Numbers 3:6). The Levites did not receive a territory assignment but were allowed to live in forty-eight cities (Joshua 21). They performed duties in the tabernacle, and later, the temple. They received support from the tithes and offerings. The Levitical priesthood consisted of Aaron and his descendants.

LEVITICUS, BOOK OF. Third book of the Old Testament. It outlines the duties of the Levitical priesthood and guidelines for the sacrificial system, purification, and feasts.

● *Read about the Day of Atonement in Leviticus 16. Understand that no animal sacrifice actually paid for sins or provided salvation; rather, the sacrifice was symbolic of God's forgiveness and humans' restored relationship with Him. Most importantly, the Day of Atonement pointed to the coming of Christ and His actual payment and provision for the sins of all those who repent and trust in Him.*

LEVY. Refers to men forced into slave labor (1 Kings 5:13; 9:15). May also refer to what is gotten in war (livestock, slaves, and other things) and turned over to tabernacle service (1 Kings 9:15–23; Numbers 31:26f).

LEWD. Wicked (Acts 17:5), lustful (Ezekiel 16:27; 23:44); sexually unchaste; evil in thought or action.

LIBERAL. 1. Noble, free, willing (Isaiah 32:8). 2. Single-minded, sincerity (2 Corinthians 9:13).

LIBERTY. Physical, mental, and spiritual freedom (Isaiah 61:1; Galatians 5:1). Liberty brings responsibility (Galatians 5:13).

LIBYA (LIB ih uh). A region west of Egypt (Ezekiel 30:5; Acts 2:10). Ancient Greek name for North Africa.

LICENTIOUS. Immoral (2 Peter 2:18 NRSV).

LIFE. Existence, in all its forms and activities, that in one way or another reflects God's creation of everything that thinks, breathes, moves, or acts. Only the eternal God has absolute life that

THE LANDS OF
THE BIBLE TODAY

Copyright © 2007 by Barbour Publishing, Inc.

N

The biblical name of **Libya** continues with a modern-day nation in northern Africa.

is before, during, and after time (Genesis 1–2). Humanly speaking, life is breath and thought; the end of those activities speaks of physical death (Genesis 6:17; Exodus 21:14). The counterpart of life is death; though death is humanity's assigned lot (to be followed by judgment), no one who has eternal life suffers what the Bible refers to as the "second death"—eternal punishment in hell for rejecting Christ as Lord and Savior (see Romans 3, 6; Matthew 25:14–30).

God has provided eternal life for all who choose to receive Him in faith and obedience and respond to the saving grace He provided in the eternal Christ—who came to earth in the form of flesh as Jesus, the Savior (Luke 2; John 1, 3; Romans 8:6; Colossians 3:4). Eternal life is the gift of God, by grace through faith, that comes the instant one receives Christ as Lord and Savior. By definition, it can never cease (see

Ephesians 2). Eternal life restores humans' relationship of oneness with God that existed in the beginning. God moves and molds the saved on earth back toward that perfect image of God (see Romans 8:29–30). Eternal life's fulfillment occurs when we die or God in Christ returns at the end of time to receive His own to be with Him eternally.

LIFE, BOOK OF. God's all-knowing record of those who belong to Him (Revelation 3:5; see also Psalm 139:16; Luke 10:20; Revelation 13:8).

LIGHT. Opposite of darkness (Genesis 1:3–4); radiance (Matthew 17:2); spiritual awareness and right living (1 John 1:7); a characteristic of God (Psalm 27:1; John 8:12). See **DARKNESS**.

The sun and the Son both provide **light**. . . though the Son created the sun (see John 1).

▲ God created light (Genesis 1). In the New Testament, John refers to Jesus as the creative Word who was "in the beginning" to bring spiritual light and life to all who would receive Him (John 1:1–12). John 12:35–41 indicates there is a deadline for receiving Jesus as "Light of the world" and His eternal life.

● Jesus is sometimes called the Light (John 1:9), and He called His own followers "the light of the world" (Matthew 5:14–16). How can we have the same title or role as Jesus? Think of how the sun gives light and the moon reflects the sun's light. That's our calling!

LIKENESS. The image of, made like another (Genesis 1:26; Romans 8:3). Spiritually speaking, "likeness" and "image" may be synonyms. In choosing sin, humans marred the image of God in which they were created. This did not, however, totally destroy the image of God. Becoming a Christian turns us back toward God's image as a new creation (Ephesians 4:24; 2 Corinthians 4:4).

● How would you describe your own self-image? How do you see yourself? Read Genesis 1:26–28; Psalm 8; Romans 8:28–29; 12:1–3, and see if your view of yourself changes or needs to change.

LO. Look, see, behold (see Daniel 7:6; Matthew 2:9).

LOATHE, **LOATHSOME**. Verb: Despise (Job 7:16). Adjective: Rejected (Proverbs 13:5).

LOCUST. Insect with an enormous appetite in all stages of maturity (Joel 2:25). One of the ten plagues God sent upon the Egyptians (Exodus 10:14). John the Baptist ate locusts and wild honey (Matthew 3:4).

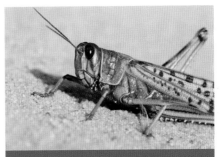

The desert **locust** is found throughout North Africa, the Middle East, and the Indian subcontinent.

LODGE. Rest, spend the night (Ruth 1:16; Luke 13:19).

LOFTY. Describes the unique highness of the holy and exalted God (Isaiah 57:15). When used of man, often indicates self-centeredness and pride (Isaiah 2:12).

LOINS. Area of the body between the waist and the knees, clothed for modesty's sake (2 Kings 1:8; Mark 1:6). Sometimes used for the reproductive organs (Genesis 35:11).

LOINCLOTH. (Job 12:18 NIV). Piece of clothing worn by men next to the skin and around their waist; made of leather or animal skin and used to "gird up the loins," that is, tie the long-flowing robe up around the waist for easy travel. For comfort could be loosened at night or when resting. Priests were to have their hips and thighs covered so as not to be exposed when in service to Yahweh.

▲ *The command to "gird up thy loins" might be the equivalent of "brace yourself" or "man up" for commitment and action (see Job 38:3; 40:7; Jeremiah 1:17).*

LONGING. Desire (Psalm 119:20).

■ **LORD**. Master, sir; a title of respect (Ruth 2:13; Luke 12:46). The title is used for both God the Father and God the Son (Exodus 15:2; Luke 2:11). Accepting Jesus as our "Lord" is essential for salvation and represents the first Christian confession of faith (Romans 10:9–10; 1 Corinthians 12:3).

▲ *The word* Lord *appears hundreds of times in the Old and New Testaments. Interestingly, the word* Savior *appears only twenty-four times in the New Testament. To claim Jesus as Lord and declare ourselves His servants is to follow the New Testament pattern; that was the apostle Paul's usual description of his own relationship with Jesus Christ. We belong to Jesus as Lord, and our calling is to obey Him completely.*

● *Is Jesus your Lord in the walk of your life as well as in your words? How do you know? How can others know He is your Lord?*

LORD'S PRAYER. A prayer Jesus gave His disciples as an example of how to pray (Matthew 6:9–13; Luke 11:2–4). Also called the "model prayer."

● *Can you pray this prayer from memory? What does each sentence of it teach you about how to pray?*

▲ *Jesus' pattern is an invaluable guide to praying in private or public settings as long as*

it remains a genuine prayer and not empty repetition. Interestingly, the verses following the "Lord's prayer" in Luke (11:5–13) emphasize our persisting in prayer. Though God may gladly answer our prayers immediately, He also expects us to persist in prayer. Such persistence shows that our prayers mean something to us and, therefore, to God.

LORD'S SUPPER. A memorial observance Jesus instituted with His disciples to point toward His sacrificial death (Matthew 26:26–29; Luke 22). Today, Christians participate in this observance (1) to recall Christ's atoning death, (2) to focus on the salvation He brings, and (3) to anticipate His return. Christians should examine their lives before God, then participate in a worthy manner (1 Corinthians 11:27–32).

▲ *In the Old Testament, when the Exodus was about to occur, the Hebrews were to eat unleavened bread (bread that hadn't had time to rise from yeast or another substance) because they were in a hurry to leave Egypt. When Jesus and His disciples enjoyed the food, drink, and fellowship of the Lord's Supper, there was no hurry. Contrasting the speed of the Passover against the reverent but unhurried partaking of the Lord's Supper should speak to us.*

● *Have you taken the Lord's Supper? What does the experience mean to you? Do you examine yourself and your relationship to God in repentance as well as memorial, thanksgiving, and anticipation of Jesus' return? In your church, is there enough time and silence to meditate on what it means to partake symbolically of the body and blood of Christ?*

LOST. Used to describe people without God (Jeremiah 50:6; Luke 19:10).

● *Are you lost or saved? Scripture can help you know (see John 3; Romans 10:9–13; Ephesians*

Many artists have depicted the scene of the **Lord's Supper**. This Austrian church mosaic is based on a painting by Leonardo da Vinci.

2:1–10). Do you know someone who is spiritually lost—one who has never trusted Christ as Lord and Savior? In following Jesus then, what are the implications of Luke 19:10 for you?

LOT. Nephew of Abraham (Genesis 12:4). Lot lived with his uncle in Canaan. When Abraham's servants and Lot's servants had a dispute over land, Lot chose the best land near Sodom—since Abraham had given Lot first choice of the land. Lot's decision reflected negatively upon his character and had disastrous consequences (Genesis 19).

LOTS. Objects that could be cast and interpreted to reach a decision. Their exact description is unknown. The Bible records a number of instances when the casting of lots was used to reach a decision and sometimes to try to arrive at God's will (for example, see Joshua 19:51). In Acts 1:20–26, the disciples chose two godly men as possible replacements for Judas Iscariot, then prayed and cast lots to select Matthias. Jesus' garments were divided by lots at His crucifixion (Psalm 22:18; Matthew 27:35).

■ LOVE. Deep, enduring concern for others' welfare; affection, friendship (Genesis 37:3; Matthew 5:47). An essential characteristic of God that comes only as a gift (John 3:16). Two different Greek words for *love* are used as synonyms in John 16:27; 15:9; 21:15–17. A general definition of love from a biblical perspective is "an earnest and anxious desire for and an active and beneficent interest in the well-being of the one loved" (from *the International Standard Bible Encyclopaedia*). However, "love" expressed in the biblical languages has various shades and meanings; the context often determines the exact meaning more than the word itself.

Lot reluctantly leaves the doomed city of Sodom in a seventeenth-century painting by Peter Paul Rubens. The story is found in Genesis 19.

LOVINGKINDNESS. Merciful and steadfast love; God's kind of love (Psalm 17:7). It is covenant love that calls for commitment and mutual faithfulness. God expects His people to follow His loving nature of mercy, goodness, and kindness in their treatment of others.

LOW, LOWLY. Humble (Isaiah 2:12; Luke 1:52). See **HUMILITY**.

LUCIFER (LYOO sih fur). The KJV followed the Latin translation of the Hebrew word for "shining one" or "day star." In Isaiah 14:12, the term is used as a title for the king of Babylon, who had elevated himself to be a god. Early Christian commentators interpreted this name as a reference to the archangel hurled from heaven for his wickedness. Modern translations read "Morning Star" or its equivalent.

LUKE (LYOOK). Physician, coworker and companion of Paul. Author of Luke and Acts. Luke seemingly was the only Gentile (non-Jewish) writer of the New Testament. His sources were other written accounts, eyewitnesses, and his own personal experiences (Luke 1:1–4). Luke accompanied Paul on some of his journeys and was with Paul shortly before his martyrdom (2 Timothy 4:11).

LUKE, BOOK OF. New Testament book written by Luke, a Gentile physician and companion of Paul (see Colossians 4:14; 2 Timothy 4:11; Philemon 24). Luke points to Jesus Christ as the Son of God and Redeemer of all people who

Luke is often portrayed in art alongside an ox or bull, a symbol of the sacrifice of Jesus recorded in Luke's Gospel.

accept Christ as Lord and Savior. Luke's writings focus on healing, prayer, parables, the status of women, and especially the Gentiles (non-Jews) in God's plan of salvation.

LURK. To hide, watch secretly (Proverbs 1:11).

■ **LUST**. Desire that turns bad when it wants something besides what God wills or wants (Galatians 5:16–21). Self-seeking craving for a person, thing, or experience (Romans 1:27; 7:7). Lust never satisfies (James 4:2). Lust is a sin of attitude that becomes more serious if it leads to action (James 1:14–15). Lust never satisfies (James 4:2).

● *What are some problems lust creates? How can and does the Holy Spirit help us recognize lust and deal with it? (See James 1:14–15; 1 John 2:16; Colossians 3:2.) We can't always keep lustful thoughts from coming, but we can get rid of them once they arrive. Walking in the Holy Spirit's power (Galatians 5:16–21) and finding joy and sexual expression within marriage are ways to do this (1 Corinthians 7:9).*

LUZ (LUHZ). 1. City of the Canaanites later called Bethel (Genesis 28:19). 2. City of unknown location (Judges 1:26).

LYDIA (LID ih uh). 1. A woman of Thyatira. She became Paul's first European convert to Christianity in Philippi. Lydia was the head of her household and a businesswoman dealing in a famous purple dye. She opened her home to Paul and his companions (Acts 16:14–15). 2. Country in Asia Minor with Sardis as capital (Ezekiel 30:5).

LYRE. A small harp.

LYSTRA (LISS truh). City in Lycaonia in Asia Minor (Acts 14:6). Timothy joined Paul on one of his missionary journeys here. Jewish enemies of the gospel arrived in Lystra and almost stoned Paul to death (Acts 14:19).

MACCABEES. [MACK-uh-bees]. Celebrated Jewish family who defended Jewish rights and customs in the second century BC—during the intertestamental period (the years between the Old and New Testaments). Though some think the name means "hammer," others believe the name means "extinguisher of persecution."

MACEDONIA (mass uh DOH nih uh). Country north of Greece. In New Testament times it was a Roman province. Paul responded to a vision of a man pleading for him to come to Macedonia (Acts 16:9–15). Paul and those with him took the vision as a sign from God to go preach the gospel in Macedonia, so they went to the province and stopped in Philippi.

When the Sabbath came, Paul and the others went to the riverside where they had learned people gathered to pray. The first ones to hear Paul's message were women praying by the water. Lydia, a businesswoman who sold purple, became the first convert. She believed and was baptized with her family, and the church began in Europe.

MAD, MADNESS. Insane, raving mad, foolish (1 Samuel 21:13; Ecclesiastes 1:17; John 10:20). These words are used to describe various degrees of mental derangement or unhealthy behavior that might be permanent or tempo-

rary. The perfect-minded Jesus was called mad (John 10:20).

MAGDALENE (MAG duh leen). Resident of the city of Magdala, as in Mary Magdalene (Matthew 27:56). Mary was one of the women who came to the tomb to anoint Jesus and discovered He had risen. See **MARY**.

MAGISTRATE. Judge, ruler (Ezra 7:25; Luke 12:11).

MAGNIFY. To praise highly, exalt, increase (Psalm 68:31; Luke 1:46).
● *How do you magnify the Lord? How might sharing your testimony magnify the Lord?*

MAGOG (MAY gahg). Second son of Japheth (Genesis 10:2); land and residents of this land (Ezekiel 38:2; Revelation 20:8).

A beggar in Nepal raises a **maimed** limb. In Bible times, as well, the maimed often had to resort to begging.

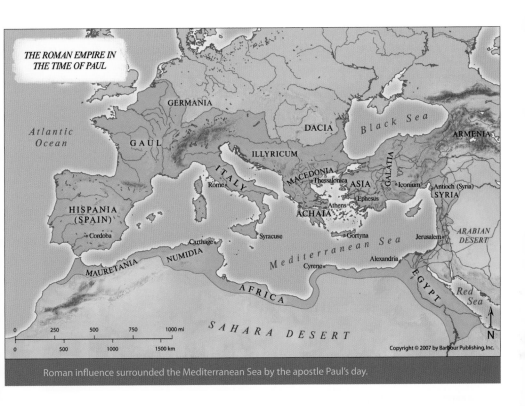

THE ROMAN EMPIRE IN THE TIME OF PAUL

Roman influence surrounded the Mediterranean Sea by the apostle Paul's day.

MAHANAIM (may huh NAY im). A town east of Jordan, where angels met Jacob (Genesis 32:2).

MAIMED. Deprived of a limb, crooked, distorted; crippled (Mark 10:43; Luke 14:13–14).

MAKER. One who forms; creator (Habakkuk 2:18). Often refers to God as Creator (Job 35:10).
▲ As Creator, the eternal God made everything out of nothing; all other "makers" start with something to make something else.

MALACHI (MAL uh kigh). Name meaning "my angel" or "my messenger." Old Testament prophet whose sermons produced the book of Malachi. He preached about 450 BC.

MALACHI, BOOK OF. Old Testament book of the minor prophets; the final book of the Old Testament. In dialogue fashion, Malachi records eight sarcastic questions the people asked God, then gave prophetic answers from God. Malachi's messages contained love, rebuke, and hope. The themes of the book are Israel's sin and God's judgment. Malachi denounced the priests and the people for unfaithfulness and practices dishonoring God and His worship. Sadly, the keynote of the book is the robbery of God.
▲ In the New Testament, tithing is commended but not commanded. Malachi's focus, however, is on "robbing God," described as a failure to tithe and give offerings. There is no argument that God expects no less under the grace of the New Testament than the required tithe of the Old—though

He would want the offerings from a rightly moti-vated, pure heart (see Matthew 5:38–48).

MALCHUS (MAL kuhs). Servant of the high priest (John 18:10). At Jesus' arrest, Peter drew a sword and cut off Malchus's right ear. But Jesus told Peter to put away his sword, then healed Malchus's ear.

▲ *Some have suggested that Peter meant to cut off Malchus's head, not just his ear. Inter-estingly, one of Malchus's relatives later rec-ognized the ear-cutting disciple of Jesus and accused Peter of being with Jesus. Upon Peter's denial of this third accusation, a cock crowed, just as Jesus had said it would (John 18:26–27).*

MALEFACTOR. Evildoer, criminal (Luke 23:33).

MALICE, MALICIOUSNESS. Evil (1 Corinthians 5:8; Romans 1:29).

MAMMON. Wealth, riches, possessions (Mat-thew 6:24).

MAMRE (MAM rih). A place located two miles north of Hebron, where Abraham settled after he had given his nephew Lot first choice of the land before them (Genesis 13:18).

MAN. Human being created in God's image (Genesis 1:26), including male and female (Genesis 5:2). To be created in God's image in-cludes freedom of choice and responsibility over self and the rest of creation. All humans choose to sin (Genesis 3) and, therefore, have to receive salvation for eternal life (Genesis 3; Isaiah 53:6; John 3: Romans 3:23; 6:23). See **IMAGE**.

MANASSEH (muh NASS uh). 1. Older son of Joseph, born to his Egyptian wife but adopted into the lineage of Jacob (Genesis 41:51; see

Genesis 48). Also refers to the tribe descended from Manasseh. 2. Son of Hezekiah. Manasseh succeeded Hezekiah as fourteenth king of Judah (2 Kings 20:21). Manasseh was an evil and cruel king. See **KING CHART** on pages 152–155.

MANDRAKES. Wild plants with edible berries and roots that were supposed to help women bear children (Genesis 30:14–16).

MANGER. Feeding trough for animals but used as the first crib of the baby Jesus (Luke 2:7).

An old stone **manger** from the Italian town of Matera.

MANIFEST. Reveal, uncover, openly show, make visible (John 1:31).

MANIFOLD. Many, abundant (Nehemiah 9:19; Ephesians 3:10).

MANNA. A type of bread during the forty years of the Exodus. God provided a whitish substance of nourishment that tasted like wafers with honey (Exodus 16:15–31; Numbers 11:9). It remained after the morning dew evap-orated from the ground, and spoiled—bred worms and stank—if any remained overnight (Exodus 16:19–20). God instructed the Israel-ites to gather enough for a single day but to gather enough for two days on the day before that Sabbath—and the extra manna would stay fresh until the people could gather more. Though the Israelites became tired of the manna and complained, God continued to provide it for forty years. The daily provision helped the Israelites learn dependence on God and obedience to Him.

MANTLE. Covering, robe (2 Kings 2:8–15).

▲ *The mantle could also signify authority. When Elijah was taken up in a whirlwind, Elisha took Elijah's mantle that fell back to earth. Elisha succeeded Elijah and led the people for roughly forty years of ministry.*

MARK (MAHRK). John Mark, of Jerusalem, was an early Christian follower and relative of Barnabas (either his nephew or cousin; compare Colossians 4:10 of KJV and modern translations). John was his Hebrew name; Mark (Marcus) his Roman name (see Acts 12–15; 1 Peter 5:13). Mark authored the Gospel of Mark and perhaps had the apostle Peter as his primary source (1 Peter 5:13).

Mark is noted more for having deserted Paul and Barnabas at Pamphylia on the first missionary trip than for significant positive contributions. When Paul was preparing for his second missionary journey, he refused to take John Mark though Barnabas insisted on taking Mark. The two leaders split over the matter and formed separate missionary teams. Barnabas took John Mark with him, while Paul took Silas. Later, though, Paul strongly commended John Mark as profitable to him for the gospel ministry. And Peter mentioned John Mark as a "son" in the ministry (1 Peter 5:13).

● *What might Mark's life teach us about dealing with our fears and mistakes? What can we learn from Paul's refusal to give a failure a second chance? What can we learn from Barnabas's attitude toward Mark?*

MARK, GOSPEL OF. Though Mark was likely the first Gospel written, it appears second in the New Testament. John Mark wrote this Gospel, in a clear and fast-moving style that focuses on Jesus' ministry and miracles. Some scholars criticize the quality of the Greek writing, while others prefer to point out that Mark is short, quick to read, and includes details that complement the other Gospels.

■ **MARRIAGE**. Commitment of a man and woman to join their lives lovingly in a divinely designed spiritual, mental, and physical relationship (Matthew 19:5–6; Mark 10:7–9; 2 Corinthians 6:14–15; Ephesians 5:21–25). God created marriage, encourages it, and commands unity in it as a lifelong relationship—until death parts the mates (Genesis 2:24–25). Marriage was the first institution, and in it God ordained sexual relations for union and procreation.

● *Why is marriage best between two Christians? (See 2 Corinthians 6:14–15.) Besides obedience to God, what values promote a lifelong marriage between two mates?*

MARTHA (MAHR thuh). Older sister of Mary and Lazarus (Luke 10:38–42). Jesus enjoyed visiting in their Bethany home. Lazarus was their brother.

▲ *Someone has observed that Martha loved service and Mary loved worship. Jesus provided the balance in what He told these sisters in Luke 10:42.*

MARVEL. Wonder, admire, be amazed (Matthew 8:10). May be in a good sense or bad, depending on the context.

MARY (MAY rih). 1. Mother of Jesus (Luke 2:16). Mary was a young Jewish maiden engaged to the carpenter Joseph when God revealed to her that she was to be the mother of the

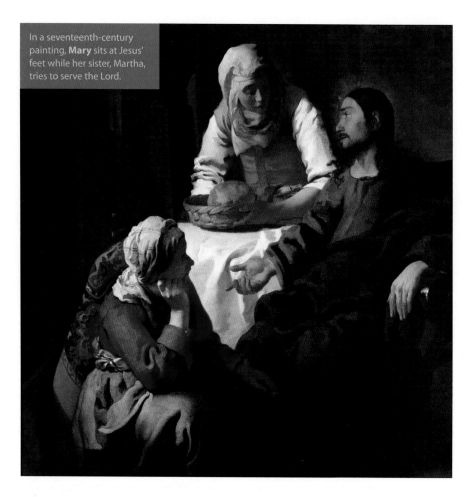

In a seventeenth-century painting, **Mary** sits at Jesus' feet while her sister, Martha, tries to serve the Lord.

Messiah. Joseph learned of these events from an angel in a dream (Matthew 1:18–25). He was obedient in staying betrothed to Mary, then taking her to be his wife. Toward the end of Mary's pregnancy, the couple had to travel from Nazareth to Bethlehem for a taxation census; Jesus was born in the latter town. Mary was present at Jesus' crucifixion and became one of His followers after His resurrection. 2. Mary Magdalene, healed by Jesus, became one of His close followers (Luke 8:1–2). She was present at Jesus' crucifixion and a witness of His resurrection. 3. Mary, sister of Martha and Lazarus (John 11:1). Mary and her family were close to Jesus. Mary seemed spiritually aware of Jesus' destiny as she demonstrated in her act of anointing Jesus with oil (John 12:3–8). 4. Mary, the mother of James and Joses (Matthew 27:56). 5. Mother of John Mark (Acts 12:12). 6. Wife of Cleophas (John 19:25). 7. A female believer who helped Paul (Romans 16:6).

MASTER. Lord, ruler, sir, teacher (Genesis 24:12; Matthew 8:19). Used for many teachers and often used for Jesus. When applied to Jesus, the term had the same sense as "rabbi."

MATTHEW (MATH yoo). A tax collector who responded to Jesus' call to become one of the original twelve disciples (Matthew 9:9; 10:3). He was also known as Levi, and wrote the Gospel of Matthew, which appears first in our New Testament. For many years, Matthew was thought to be the first Gospel written; now, more scholars believe Mark was the earlier.

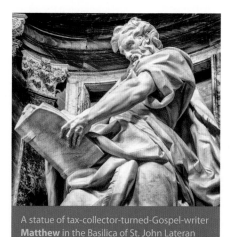

A statue of tax-collector-turned-Gospel-writer **Matthew** in the Basilica of St. John Lateran in Rome.

MATTHEW, GOSPEL OF. First book of the New Testament; written by Matthew. The book focuses on Jesus as teacher and the promised Messiah. This Gospel includes more Old Testament verses than any other New Testament account. Of the four Gospels, only Matthew tells about the wise men and gives perhaps the fullest and most orderly account of the Beatitudes and the Sermon on the Mount. Matthew climaxes with Christ's Great Commission (28:18–20).

MATTHIAS (muh THIGH uhs). A disciple of Jesus chosen over Justus to replace Judas as the twelfth apostle (Acts 1:21–26).

▲ *Acts 1:21–26 identifies both the prophetic need to fulfill Judas Iscariot's place and also the criteria used for the selection. Matthias was chosen over Justus after prayer and casting of lots.*

MEASURE. As a noun in the Old Testament, can refer to various dry or liquid weights such as ephah (Deuteronomy 25:14), cor (1 Kings 4:22), or seah (Genesis 18:6). In the New Testament it can refer to this type of measure or to length or capacity (Matthew 7:2). See **WEIGHTS AND MEASURES**.

MEAT OFFERING. (KJV; "grain offering" in NASB, NIV, and NRSV) An offering presented to God in response to His command (Leviticus 2). Consisted of flour, baked cakes, or raw grain combined with oil and frankincense. It could accompany burnt offerings and peace offerings (Numbers 15:1–9). Also used without the frankincense as a substitute for an animal sacrifice by those who could not afford an animal (Leviticus 5:11–13). Giving one's best grain during worship was part of a ceremony that represented removal of past sins.

MEDE (MEED). Inhabitant of the land of Media, which was located west and south of the Caspian Sea (Isaiah 13:17). The Medes were a strong power. They were known as a rude and uncultivated race. Joined with Babylon to destroy Assyrian kingdom about 612 BC.

MEDIATOR. One who reconciles or brings people back into a right relationship (Hebrews 12:24). A go-between. Jesus is the Mediator between God and humans.

▲ *Philippians 4:1–3 indicates how a Christian might perform the ministry of helping other believers who are at odds to reconcile.*

MEDITATE. Consider, study thoughtfully (Psalm 1:2; 1 Timothy 4:15).

■ **MEEK**. Humble, having a gentle and disciplined spirit (Psalm 25:9; Matthew 5:5). Meek does not mean weak. See **HUMILITY**.

MEET. Besides the common meaning, *meet* can also mean right or proper (Exodus 8:26); necessary or for a good reason (Luke 15:32); qualified or sufficient (Colossians 1:12).

MEGIDDO (mih GID oh). A city west of Jordan in the plain of Jezreel. An important city and the scene of several Old Testament battles. Kings Ahaziah and Josiah died here (2 Kings 9:27; 23:29).

MELCHISEDEC (mel KIZ uh dek). Priest and king of Salem. (*Salem* is an abbreviated term for Jerusalem; see Genesis 14:18; Psalm 76:2; Hebrews 7:1–2). He blessed Abraham (Genesis 14:18–19). The writer of Hebrews referred to Christ as being like Melchizedec—a high priest (Hebrews 5:6–10).

▲ *Read these Bible references to note similarities between Melchisedec (also spelled Melchize-*

Abraham makes an offering to **Melchisedec**, who was likened to Christ who was to come.

dek) and Christ: Genesis 14:18–20; Psalm 110:4; Hebrews 5:6–20; 7:1–21.

MELODY. To make melody meant to play on a harp or other stringed instrument (Isaiah 23:16; Ephesians 5:19).

MEMORIAL. A reminder or token of remembrance (Exodus 3:15; Matthew 26:13).

MENE (MEE nih) **MENE, TEKEL** (TEE k'l), **UPHARSIN** (yoo FAR sin). Aramaic words that appeared on the wall of Belshazzar's banquet hall (Daniel 5:25). Daniel interpreted the words to mean Belshazzar's kingdom was judged by God, found lacking, and would be divided and given to his enemies, the Medes and Persians (Daniel 5:26–27). It happened that night (Daniel 5:30).

MEPHIBOSHETH (me FIB oh sheth). A crippled son of Jonathan (2 Samuel 4:4; 9; 16; 21:7).

■ **MERCY**. Compassion, love, sympathy, deep caring, forgiveness (Psalm 145:9; Ephesians 2:4–5). Giving or receiving care when it isn't deserved. Mercy may withhold or ease expected punishment.

▲ *The Old Testament usage especially links mercy to God's covenant grace that treats man kindly.*

MERCY SEAT. Gold covering on the ark of the covenant. God commanded His people to build the mercy seat and met with them there (Exodus 25:17–22; Leviticus 16:2). Blood was sprinkled on it to symbolize forgiveness of sins (Leviticus 16:15). It was made from gold and bordered by statues of cherubim (angelic beings). See **ARK OF THE COVENANT**.

King Belshazzar sees the "handwriting on the wall"—**mene, mene, tekel, upharsin**—God's message that he would lose his kingdom that night.

MESHACH (MEE shak). New name given to Mishael, friend of Daniel. Ate healthy food with Daniel and entered fiery furnace with the latter two friends because he obeyed God rather than the king (Daniel 1:6, 15; 3:16–30). All were spared from harm in the fiery furnace.

MESOPOTAMIA (MESS uh puh TAY mih uh). Area between the Tigris and Euphrates rivers (Genesis 24:10; Acts 2:9). Babylonia, Assyria, and Sumeria were located there.

MESSAGE, MESSENGER. Word, promise (Judges 3:20; 1 John 1:5). One who brings a word. *Angel* is the Greek word for messenger; and angels were often messengers. In Galatians 3:19, angels almost appear as intermediaries of the Law.

▲ Gospel *translates the word for "good message" or "good news." The Greek letters* eu *before a word usually refer to good; for example, eulogy means "good words." We see angel in the middle of the Greek word for gospel:* euangelion.

MESSIAH. Hebrew term meaning, literally, "anointed one" (Daniel 9:25; John 1:41; Matthew 16:16). *Messiah* translates the Hebrew word that refers to the ruling King or coming Savior. *Christ* transliterates (spells out in English) the Greek word for the Anointed One or Messiah. See **ANOINT, CHRIST**.

METHUSELAH (mih THYOO zuh luh). Son of Enoch and grandfather of Noah (Genesis 5:21). Best known for living 969 years—the longest of all lives on record.

MICAH (MIGH kuh). 1. An Old Testament prophet who prophesied during the reigns of Jotham, Ahaz, and Hezekiah (Micah 1:1). 2. An Ephraimite who hired a Levite to be priest to his idol (Judges 17:7–13). 3. Several other Micahs are mentioned in the Bible.

MICAH, BOOK OF. Old Testament book of minor prophets. Micah preached about 735 to 715 BC to Samaria and Judah but primarily to the latter. He denounced the rich who mistreated the poor, businessmen who were dishonest, and rulers who were unjust. Micah prophesied God's judgment on Israel, and the suffering and restoration of Jerusalem. He called for justice and righteousness (6:8). Micah included both God's denunciation for sin and also consolation for a faithful remnant.

▲ *Micah was inspired to write a classic passage that shows God cannot be satisfied with sacrifices or offerings when the heart attitude is wrong. Micah 6:8 says, "What doth the* LORD *require of thee, but to do justly, and to love mercy, and to walk humbly with thy God?"*

MICAIAH (migh CAY yuh). Prophet in Samaria. Ahab disliked Micaiah because Micaiah told the truth: He predicted the death of King Ahab (1 Kings 22:8).

MICHAEL (MIGH kuhl). 1. A messenger of God (Daniel 10:13; Revelation 12:7). Referred to in Jude 9 as the archangel. 2. There were also several other Michaels.

MICHAL (MIGH kuhl). Youngest daughter of Saul who became David's wife (1 Samuel 14:49).

MIDIAN, MIDIANITES (MID ih uhn, MID ih uhn ight). Abraham's son; Midian's land and descendants (Genesis 25:2; 37:28; Exodus 2:15).

MIDWIFE. A person who helps with the birth of a baby (Genesis 35:17).

A fifteenth-century image by the Flemish painter Rogier van der Weyden shows Jesus with the archangel **Michael**.

Grain on a **millstone**.

■ **MILLENNIUM**. A thousand years. Though not in the Bible, the word *millennium* is used to refer to a thousand-year period in relation to Christ's return (see Revelation 20:2–7). Scholars differ on whether the number is literal or symbolic and on other matters in reference to the return of Christ, but they uniformly believe the Bible teaches the return of Christ.

MILLSTONE. Stones used to grind grain into flour (Deuteronomy 24:6). Smaller ones were used by individuals while larger ones were pulled by animals (Matthew 18:6).

■ **MINISTER, MINISTRY**. Serve, service (Exodus 28:35; Mark 10:45; Ephesians 4:12). A primary goal of Jesus and Christians is to minister to people in need. Ministry is every Christian's calling in "the ministry of reconciliation" (2 Corinthians 5:18). So ministry is both service and witness of all Christians—not just those called to the "vocational ministry."

MIRACLE. God's intervention in humanity, nature, and history (Numbers 14:22; John 2:11). Sometimes translated as "signs," "wonders," or "mighty acts." Miracles carry out God's purpose or reveal God. In the book of John, Jesus performed a series of seven miracles to reveal Himself as the Messiah to those who would see, hear, understand, repent, and be born again.

▲ *Some people believe that the age of miracles concluded with the end of the New Testament era. But, as other theologians have said, miracles and gifts of the Spirit are God's to give whenever He chooses.*

MIRACLES OF JESUS

MIRACLE	BIBLE PASSAGES			
Water turned to wine				John 2:1
Many healings	Matthew 4:23	Mark 1:23		
Healing of a leper	Matthew 8:1	Mark 1:40	Luke 5:12	
Healing of a Roman centurion's servant	Matthew 8:5		Luke 7:1	
Healing of Peter's mother-in-law	Matthew 8:14	Mark 1:29	Luke 4:38	
Calming of storm at sea	Matthew 8:23	Mark 4:35	Luke 8:22	
Healing of the wild men of Gadara	Matthew 8:28	Mark 5:1	Luke 8:26	
Healing of the lame man	Matthew 9:1	Mark 2:1	Luke 5:18	

MIRACLE	BIBLE PASSAGES			
Healing of a woman with a hemorrhage	Matthew 9:20	Mark 5:25	Luke 8:43	
Raising of Jairus's daughter	Matthew 9:23	Mark 5:22	Luke 8:41	
Healing of two blind men	Matthew 9:27			
Healing of a demon-possessed man	Matthew 9:32			
Healing of a man with a withered hand	Matthew 12:10	Mark 3:1	Luke 6:6	
Feeding of 5,000 people	Matthew 14:15	Mark 6:35	Luke 9:12	John 6:1
Walking on the sea	Matthew 14:22	Mark 6:47		John 6:16
Healing of the Syrophoenician's daughter	Matthew 15:21	Mark 7:24		
Feeding of 4,000 people	Matthew 15:32	Mark 8:1		
Healing of an epileptic boy	Matthew 17:14	Mark 9:14	Luke 9:37	
Healing of two blind men at Jericho	Matthew 20:30			
Healing of a man with an unclean spirit		Mark 1:23	Luke 4:33	
Healing of a deaf, speechless man		Mark 7:31		
Healing of a blind man at Bethesda		Mark 8:22		
Healing of blind Bartimaeus		Mark 10:46	Luke 18:35	
A miraculous catch of fish			Luke 5:4	John 21:1
Raising of a widow's son			Luke 7:11	
Healing of a stooped woman			Luke 13:11	
Healing of a man with the dropsy			Luke 14:1	
Healing of ten lepers			Luke 17:11	
Healing of Malchus's ear			Luke 22:50	
Healing of a royal official's son				John 4:46
Healing of a lame man at Bethesda				John 5:1
Healing of a blind man				John 9:1
Raising of Lazarus				John 11:38

MIRE. Thick mud, filth (Jeremiah 38:22; 2 Peter 2:22).

MIRIAM (MIR ih uhm). Older sister of Moses and Aaron (Exodus 15:20). She helped save Moses' life when he was an infant (Exodus 2:4–9) and celebrated the victory at the Red Sea (Exodus 15:20–21). She and her brother Aaron, as adults, criticized Moses' marriage to an Ethiopian woman (Numbers 12:1–15).

MIRTH. Joy, rejoicing, gladness (Isaiah 24:8).

MISCHIEF. Wickedness, injury, evil thought (Psalm 36:4; Acts 13:10).

MISHAEL (MISH ih uhl). Daniel's friend who was renamed Meshach. Ate healthy food with Daniel and entered the fiery furnace but was saved from harm (Daniel 1:6, 15; 3:16–30).

MISTRESS. Woman in charge of household; owner (1 Kings 17:17).

MIZPAH (MIZ pah). The name of various biblical sites and towns. In one Mizpah, east of the Jordan River, Jacob and Laban made a covenant of peace. Jacob set up a stone altar there (Genesis 31:44–50).

▲ *Have you ever seen a sign or piece of jewelry that says, "The Lord watch between me and thee, when we are absent one from another?" It is based on Jacob and Laban's covenant and is referred to as the "Mizpah Benediction" (Genesis 31:49). Today, the words are used as a symbol of love. Originally, though, the statement meant something like this: "Since you and I can't keep an eye on each other when we're out of sight, may God keep you accountable." It was a word of caution between the two as they separated.*

MOAB, **MOABITE** (MOH ab, MOH uh bight). Grandson of Lot. The land east of the Dead Sea that Moab's descendants occupied. Resident of Moab (Genesis 19:37; 36:35). The Moabites were usually enemies of the Israelites. Ruth was a Moabitess.

MOCK. Scorn, insult, laugh at (Job 11:3; Galatians 6:7).

MOLECH (MOH lek), **MOLOCH** (MOH lahk). A god worshiped by the Ammonites (Leviticus 18:21). The rituals included sacrificing children by fire.

MOLTEN. **MELTED** (Ezekiel 24:11). A molten image is metal poured into a form or mold (Exodus 32:4).

MONEY. Early on, Israelites did not have coined money and so used a system of weights in transactions (Genesis 23:16; 1 Chronicles 21:25). Early, a shekel and a talent were weights rather than monetary values. By New Testament times, coins were in use. Because the value of money changes over time, it is difficult to give present-day equivalents. Perhaps it is better to note what each could buy. A denarius (same as a drachma) equaled a day's pay for a Roman soldier or an ordinary laborer. The KJV translates it "penny." A talent was about 6000 denarii. Other money values:

Lepton = Widow's mite = Fraction of a cent
Denarius = One day's pay (translated *penny* in KJV)
Drachma (Greek) = Denarius (Roman)
Stater = 4 Denarii (plural of denarius)
Aureus = 25 Denarii (plural of denarius)
Talent = 6000 Denarii (plural of denarius)

A statue of **Molech**, with an oven in its stomach.

▲ *A modern English dictionary notes that the word* shekel *came into English about the fifteenth century. The shekel was a Hebrew unit of about 252 grains troy weight and could be a coin or other material of that weight.*

MONOGAMY. Marriage with one mate. The Bible reveals God's ideal plan for marriage as one husband and one wife for all of life—until death parts the couple. God designed people to be happiest in such a relationship.

● *Can you think of reasons that make God's ideal plan of monogamy the best one for marriage? Legalizing anything other than God's design of a man and a woman marrying for life does not trump God's plan, nor does it nullify God's Word.*

▲ *Marriage and divorce are common in our society, as in most of the world. But the commonplace nature of divorce does not change God's divine design nor the specific teachings about marriage in the New Testament. "Serial monogamy" is a term some apply to those who marry, divorce, and repeat the cycle. God is both the designer and judge of marriages— but also the forgiver of those who turn to Him in repentance.*

MONEYCHANGER. A person who exchanged foreign currency at a profit. Temple moneychangers made exchanges from Roman coins to the half shekel required for the temple offering (Matthew 21:12).

▲ *Jesus cleansed the temple by turning over moneychangers' tables and driving out very things that made a mockery of God's house. He was angry that the moneychangers had made the Temple a market and "den of thieves" (Matthew 21:12–13).*

MONTH. Hebrew months began with the new moon. See the **CALENDAR CHART** on pages 265–266.

Some of these and their approximate modern equivalents are:
1. Nisan (Abib) = March/April
2. Iyyar (Ziv) = April/May
3. Sivan = May/June
4. Thammuz = June/July
5. Ab = July/August
6. Elul = August/September
7. Tishri (Ethanim) = September/October
8. Marchesvan (Buf) = October/November
9. Chislev = November/December
10. Tebeth = December/January
11. Shebat = January/February
12. Adar = February/March

MORDECAI (MAWR dih kigh). Means "little man." Cousin and guardian of Esther (Esther 2:5). He was a Jewish exile who became an official in the Persian palace. Mordecai worked with Esther to save the Jewish people from slaughter.

MORTAL. Human, subject to death, perishable (Job 4:17; Romans 6:12).

MOSES (MOH ziss). A Hebrew born into Egyptian slavery (Exodus 2:1–2). Spared from death as an infant and raised in the palace by Pharaoh's daughter, Moses fled Egypt at about age forty, after murdering an Egyptian overseer who was mistreating a Hebrew slave. After Moses had been a shepherd and raised a family for about forty years, God called him to return to Egypt to lead the Hebrew people from captivity. During the forty years of Exodus, God gave Moses the Law by which the people were to live and worship.

Moses was able to view the promised land but not enter it because of sin he'd committed (Numbers 20:1–12). Deuteronomy 34 reports the death of Moses, but God was with him. Moses is traditionally held to be the author

Moses, sitting, gets an assist from Aaron and Hur. As long as Moses held up his arms over a battle, the Israelites prevailed (see Exodus 17).

On the **Mount of Olives,** Jesus weeps over Jerusalem.

of the "Book of Law," the first five books of the Bible, with an unknown contributor recording Moses' death.

MOST HIGH. Name to describe God or used for God (Genesis 14:18–22; Acts 7:48). See **GOD**.

MOST HOLY PLACE. The innermost part of the tabernacle or temple. Only the high priest could enter the most holy place, and he could enter only once a year on the Day of Atonement (Leviticus 16). There he made a sacrifice for the sins of the people (Exodus 26:34). The only items in the holy of holies were the ark of the covenant, a small wooden structure covered with gold and containing the Ten Commandments, a pot of manna, and Aaron's rod (Exodus 25). Same as the **HOLY OF HOLIES** and **ORACLE**.

MOUNT, MOUNTAIN. The land in and around Palestine is made up of many hills and moun-

tains, the highest of which is about 9,100 feet above sea level in Syria. Mountains had great significance as places of defense, refuge, and worship. They are symbols of endurance, stability, obstacles, and difficulty, and perhaps point toward eternity itself.

MOUNT OF OLIVES. A mile-long ridge of hills east of Jerusalem (Matthew 21:1). Also called Olivet (Acts 1:12). Jesus went there often.

MOURN. To show pain, grief, sorrow (2 Samuel 13:37; Matthew 5:4). In the Bible death was often associated with weeping, tearing of clothing, and putting on sackcloth and ashes. A period of mourning could last up to seven days, and sometimes professional mourners were hired to help. Mourning was also an expression of grief over sin and of repentance.

MULTIPLY. To heap up, make abundant, increase (Genesis 1:22; Acts 6:7).

MULTITUDE. Great crowd (Judges 4:7; Matthew 4:25).

MURMUR. Grumble, speak with discontent (Exodus 15:24; John 6:41).

MUSTARD SEED. An annual plant that grew quite fast and was popularly thought to have been the smallest of all seeds. However, positive identification cannot be made of the plant Jesus made reference to in His parable of the mustard seed (Matthew 13:31–32). Christ used the parable to illustrate something that starts small and grows rapidly, such as the kingdom of God.

MUSTER. Cause to assemble, gather (2 Kings 25:19).

MUTE. Silent, voiceless, unable to talk (Mark 7:37 NIV).
▲ *Dumb in KJV does not mean stupid or unable to learn; rather, it means speech-impaired.*

MUZZLE. Stop, gag (Deuteronomy 25:4; 1 Corinthians 9:9).

MYRRH. Gum extracted from a shrub used for anointing oil, women's purification, and burial (Genesis 37:25; Matthew 2:11). Known for its pleasing odor, it was one of the gifts of the magi to Jesus.

A Jewish man chooses a **myrtle** branch on the eve Sukkot (the Feast of Tabernacles) in 2010.

MYRTLE. A shrub with good-smelling leaves and white flowers. The Hebrews often used this shrub for shelter in the fields at the Feast of Tabernacles (Leviticus 23:40; Nehemiah 8:15).

MYSTERY. A special revelation of God that was once hidden but now revealed to His followers (Matthew 13:11; Ephesians 3:3–5; 1 Corinthians 2:7–8).

NAAMAN (NAY uh muhn). Commander under Ben-Hadad II, king of Syria. God healed Naaman of leprosy when he obeyed Elisha's command to immerse himself seven times in the Jordan River (2 Kings 5:1–27).

● *If you read Naaman's whole story, you'll see he was offended when told to do the seemingly mundane thing of washing in the Jordan River. Servants, though, suggested Naaman should be willing to do a simple thing in obedience, instead of some great thing of his own choosing. What seemingly small things are you willing to do to obey God?*

NABOTH (NAY bahth). An Israelite vineyard owner (1 Kings 21:1). Jezebel plotted to have Naboth killed so her greedy husband, Ahab, could have Naboth's vineyard.

NADAB (NAY dab). 1. Aaron's oldest son (Exodus 6:23). Together with his father, brother, and uncle, he saw the glory of God (Exodus 24:1, 9–10). Later ordained into the Aaronic priesthood (Exodus 29). Nadab and his brother offered a strange or unholy fire to God, which resulted in their deaths (Leviticus 10:1–2). 2. King of Israel briefly about 900 BC. See **KING CHART** on pages 152–155. 3. Two other Old Testament personalities.

NAHUM (NAY huhm). Old Testament prophet of Judah who preached against Nineveh and Assyria about 620 BC.

NAHUM, BOOK OF. Old Testament book containing sermons by Nahum, a prophet of Elkosh (Nahum 1:1). The book tells of God's judgment on wickedness, especially on the city of Nineveh. Years earlier, Jonah had prophesied judgment; Nineveh had repented, and God had spared the city. But Nahum preached many years after Jonah prophesied; by then Nineveh had returned to sin and faced judgment again.

NAMES FOR CHRIST AND FOR GOD. See **NAMES FOR JESUS** on page 139 and **NAMES FOR GOD** on page 109.

Jesus explains His death and resurrection to two disciples in Emmaus, using the title *Christ* for Himself: "Ought not Christ to have suffered these things, and to enter into his glory?" (Luke 24:26).

NAOMI (nay OH mih). Wife of Elimelech (Ruth 1:2). During a famine the family left its home of Bethlehem to live in Moab. After Naomi became a widow and her two sons died, she returned to her homeland along with her insistent Moabite daughter-in-law, Ruth.

● *Read the four-chapter book of Ruth. Naomi's life went from pleasantness to bitterness, but joy returned to her in the form of a baby in the lineage of the Messiah (Ruth 4:13–17). What does this part of Naomi's journey say to you about keeping faith and hope in God?*

NAPHTALI (NAF tuh ligh). Sixth son of Jacob (Genesis 30:8); Name of Naphtali's descendants and their territory.

NATHAN (NAY thuhn). 1. A prophet who revealed to King David that he would not be allowed to build a temple for God; but David's son Solomon would build the temple. Nathan revealed that David could, however, collect materials and gifts for the project (see 2 Samuel 7; 1 Chronicles 17). Nathan also boldly confronted David with his sins of adultery and murder by use of a parable, which led David to face up to his own sins and confess them in repentance (2 Samuel 12:1–13). 2. Several other Bible men, including a son of David, also bore the popular name Nathan.
● *Where did Nathan get the courage to confront David about his sins? Why might Nathan's parable work better than a direct accusation might have?*

NATHANAEL (nuh THAN ay uhl). A disciple of Jesus, seemingly the same as Bartholomew in lists of the twelve original disciples (see John 1:43–49; 21:2). Nathanael, Peter, and Thomas all referred to Jesus face-to-face as the Son of God or Lord and God (see John 1:49; Matthew 16:16; John 20:28). All three are together in John 21:2, shortly after John described his purpose for writing the Gospel in 20:31: that readers might believe that Jesus is the Christ, the Son of God. John records that as soon as Philip was called as a disciple, he immediately invited Nathanael to meet Jesus (John 1:43–49).

▲ *Matthew, Mark, and Luke all use the name Bartholomew after Philip in listing the twelve disciples (Matthew 10:3; Mark 3:18; Luke 6:14; Acts 1:13), but do not refer to Nathanael. The Gospel of John alone mentions Nathanael, so most scholars feel the names Bartholomew and Nathanael are used interchangeably for the same apostle.*

NAVE. Ring or hub of a wheel (1 Kings 7:33).

NAZARENE (naz uh REEN). A person from the city of Nazareth; used to describe Jesus (Matthew 2:23). In Acts 24:5, which describes a legal proceeding against the apostle Paul, *Nazarenes* refers to Christian believers, described by angry Jews as a troublemaking sect. In this context, the term apparently is one of scorn and ridicule.

NAZARETH (NAZ uh reth). A town in Galilee located seventy miles north of Jerusalem (Matthew 2:23; Mark 1:9). Nazareth is where Jesus grew up.

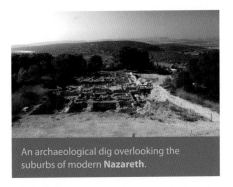
An archaeological dig overlooking the suburbs of modern **Nazareth**.

NAZARITE (NAZ uh right). A person dedicated to God for some special purpose who showed that commitment by taking certain vows for a time. The vows included abstaining from drinking wine, cutting one's hair, and avoiding contact with dead bodies. The time frame for these vows could vary from thirty days to a lifetime (see Numbers 6:2–8; Judges 6:1–21; 16:5–7; Amos 2:11–12). Among the most famous of Nazarites was Samson (Judges 16:17).

● *What might a vow to avoid drinking alcoholic beverages accomplish today? Or committing to some new personal discipline? Read Romans 14.*

NEBO (NEE boh). 1. Name of one or more cities within the territories of Reuben and Judah (Numbers 32:38; Ezra 2:29). 2. Mountain east of the Jordan River where Moses viewed the promised land and died (Deuteronomy 34:1). He was forbidden to enter the promised land because of his disobedience to God.

NEBUCHADNEZZAR (neb yoo kad NEZZ ur). King of Babylon who conquered Judah (the Southern Kingdom) and carried many of its inhabitants into captivity (2 Kings 24–25). Judah included Jerusalem, which Nebuchadnezzar destroyed in 587 BC. He was the king who ordered Daniel's three young friends into the fiery furnace (Daniel 3:19–20). See **KING CHART** on pages 152–155.

NECROMANCER. A person who tries to contact the dead. God's law forbids this practice (Deuteronomy 18:10–12).

NEEDLE, EYE OF. Expression Jesus used to point out the difficulty of a rich person entering the kingdom of God (Matthew 19:24). Often a rich person's priority is riches, not God. It is a myth that "eye of a needle" refers to a narrow gate or opening in Jerusalem.

● *Identify your top three priorities or goals in life. If you had a lot of money, what place might God have in how you would spend those riches?*

NEEDS. Used as a phrase, "must needs" (Luke 14:18) means to be necessary.

NEGLECT. Disregard, overlook (Acts 6:1).

NEHEMIAH (nee huh MIGH uh). Jew who served Persian King Artaxerxes I as cupbearer or personal taster and server of royal food. He received permission to lead Jewish teams to Jerusalem to rebuild the city's fallen walls about 445 BC and to purify temple practices around 432 BC. He exemplified godly servant leadership. He brought revival and covenant renewal to a dispirited people. Nehemiah was a man of action who believed that prayer and action go together (Nehemiah 1:4; 6:3).

NEHEMIAH, BOOK OF. Old Testament Bible book that tells of Nehemiah's return to Jerusalem, his leadership in the rebuilding of the city walls, dedication of the walls, and other reforms he carried out. Nehemiah was both a model organizer and leader in carrying out God's call to him and the people he led.

NEPHILIM (NEF uh lim). Used in some contemporary Bible translations to refer to a variety of

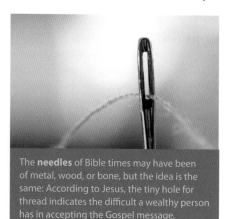

The **needles** of Bible times may have been of metal, wood, or bone, but the idea is the same: According to Jesus, the tiny hole for thread indicates the difficult a wealthy person has in accepting the Gospel message.

unusual people of great size and renown (NIV: Genesis 6:4; Numbers 13:32–33).

NETHER. Lower, under (Exodus 19:17).

NETTLES. Thorns, shrubs (Job 30:7).

NETWORK. Ornamental grill used on the altar of burnt offering (Exodus 27:4). It possibly served as a vent as well as a decoration.

NEW TESTAMENT. This second part of the Bible contains twenty-seven books: the four Gospels, the book of Acts, twenty-one epistles or letters, and Revelation. The New Testament tells of Jesus' birth, life, death, resurrection, and promised return; the growth of the church; instructions, warnings, and encouragements to the church; and prophecy of the end of time. *Testament* means covenant or agreement. The New Testament tells of God's new covenant through Jesus Christ (Hebrews 8:6–10).
- ● *Check the table of contents in your Bible for the names of the New Testament Bible books. Memorize them.*
- ▲ *Both the Old and New Testaments are revelations of God's grace, but we see the ultimate fulfillment of God's divine design in the completeness of the New Testament. The New Testament indicates we are free and are expected to do more under grace than under the requirements of the Law. For example, Jesus' teachings in the Sermon on the Mount show clearly how the saved people of God are to believe, live, and behave.*

NICODEMUS (nik uh DEE muhs). A Pharisee and member of the Sanhedrin (John 3:1) who came to Jesus at night searching for answers to eternal questions. Jesus told Nicodemus he had to be "born again," a spiritual necessity of trusting in Jesus for eternal life. To fail to

trust Jesus was to be spiritually condemned (see John 3:1–18). It appears that Nicodemus became a secret disciple of Jesus, later showing his faith by (1) speaking up when Jesus was wrongly accused; and (2) joining another Pharisee, named Joseph—who provided Jesus' tomb—to prepare Jesus' body for burial.
- ● *Can you tell a friend how to be born again? If you have been born again (if you have become a Christian), write your experience simply on one or two pages of paper. Share those pages with someone who does not yet know Jesus personally. Then take your Bible and share John 3 and Romans 3:23; 6:23; and 10:9–10 with your friend. Ask him or her if they want to trust Jesus and have eternal life—to be "born again."*

NIGER (NIGH JUR). Also called Simeon (Acts 13:1). Leader of the church at Antioch.

NIGH. Near (Psalm 145:18; Matthew 24:32).

NIMROD (NIM rahd). Son of Cush (Genesis 10:8). Nimrod's name means "strong" or "valiant," and he was known as a mighty hunter.

NINEVEH (NIN uh vuh). The last and most important capital of Assyria, located on the Tigris River. It was founded by Nimrod, a descendant of Noah's son Ham (Genesis 10:11). Centuries later, God sent Jonah to warn the people of Nineveh of coming judgment; when they repented, God spared them. Still later, though, Nineveh became sin-ridden again and prophesied destruction came to pass. Babylon destroyed Nineveh in 612 BC.
- ▲ *God does not change, but the Bible shows that God may change His intentions based on people's repentance, prayers, and response to His word. Nineveh's response to Jonah's preaching is one example. King Hezekiah's prayer is another (see 2 Kings 20).*

Under a rainbow—God's promise never again to flood the entire earth—**Noah** and his family offer sacrifices to the Lord.

NISAN (NIGH san). First month of the Jewish year beginning at the end of March (Nehemiah 2:1). See **MONTH** and **CALENDAR CHART** on pages 265–266.

NOAH (NO uh). A righteous man who lived during a time of evil and corruption. God instructed Noah to build an ark (large boat), which would save Noah, his family, and two of each kind of animal (see Genesis 5:28–9:29). God used the flood to destroy all that was evil and start over with Noah and his family.

▲ *For New Testaments insights and further perspective on Noah and the flood, consider these*

Bible references: Hebrews 11:7; 1 Peter 3:20; 2 Peter 2:5.

NORTHERN KINGDOM. Refers to the northern ten tribes of Israel after the division of the kingdom (about 922–912 BC). This area included all the tribal lands except Judah, which became known as the Southern Kingdom (and included the tribe of Benjamin). Israel was one nation before about 950 BC. After Solomon's death a division occurred (1 Kings 14:19–30). Israel continued until 722 BC. Judah continued until 587 BC. See **KING CHART** on pages 152–155.

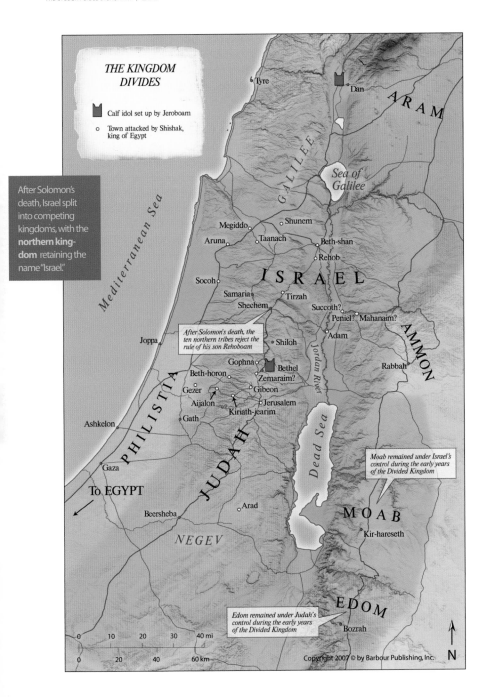

THE KINGDOM DIVIDES

Calf idol set up by Jeroboam

○ Town attacked by Shishak, king of Egypt

After Solomon's death, Israel split into competing kingdoms, with the **northern kingdom** retaining the name "Israel."

Tyre

Dan

A R A M

GALILEE

Sea of Galilee

Mediterranean Sea

Megiddo

Shunem

Aruna

Taanach

Beth-shan

Rehob

Socoh

I S R A E L

Samaria

Tirzah

Shechem

Succoth?

Peniel? Mahanaim?

After Solomon's death, the ten northern tribes reject the rule of his son Rehoboam

Adam

A M M O N

Joppa

Shiloh

Jordan River

Gophna

Bethel

Rabbah

Beth-horon

Zemaraim?

Gezer

Gibeon

Aijalon

Jerusalem

Kiriath-jearim

Ashkelon

Gath

J U D A H

Dead Sea

Moab remained under Israel's control during the early years of the Divided Kingdom

Gaza

To EGYPT

Beersheba

Arad

M O A B

Kir-hareseth

NEGEV

Edom remained under Judah's control during the early years of the Divided Kingdom

Bozrah

E D O M

0   10   20   30   40 mi

0   20   40   60 km

Copyright 2007 © by Barbour Publishing, Inc.

N

NUMBERS. Besides the normal usage of numbers in the Bible, there is also a symbolic usage. Some of these numbers and their meanings are:

   One = unity and uniqueness

   Four, five, seven, ten = completion or perfection

   Six = association with humans

   Twelve = elective purposes of God

   Forty = new developments of God's mighty acts in history.

Three has significance, as in the members of the Trinity, the number of days Jonah was inside a fish, and parts of days Jesus was in the tomb. Ten and twelve with their multiples may be literal or may symbolize completion (for example, one thousand years, Revelation 20:2–7 or 144,000 people, Revelation 14:1).

NUMBERS, BOOK OF. Old Testament book included in the five books of the Law. Its name refers to two censuses (numbering) of Israel's fighting forces (Numbers 1:2–46; 26:2–51). The book details the counting of the tribes, the wilderness wanderings, Levitical and other laws, and preparation for the conquest of the promised land.

● *Numbers describes the wanderings of the Hebrews because of their disobedience. The lesson for us is that God's divine design should always be our first choice. When we say no to God, we necessarily receive discipline, and we wander in our own kind of wilderness until we return to Him.*

NUN (NUN). Father of Joshua (Numbers 14:6).

OATH. Solemn promise of commitment (Genesis 26:28; Matthew 5:33). In the Bible, an oath amounted to a truth reinforced by God or the person or thing sworn by. Consequences were either stated or implied if people didn't keep their commitments. New Testament teaching is basically that oaths shouldn't be needed: a person's word should have integrity in itself (see Matthew 5:33–37; James 5:12).
● *Do people usually take you at your word? Why or why not?*

OBADIAH (oh buh DIGH uh). 1. Governor of Ahab's household (1 Kings 18:3-16). 2. Prophet whose sermons comprise the book of Obadiah. 3. More than ten other Obadiahs appear in the Bible.

OBADIAH, BOOK OF. Shortest Old Testament book; fourth of the minor prophets. Obadiah tells of the judgment of Edom and the restoration of Israel. It emphasizes that God is in charge and faithless pride will be punished.

OBED (OH bed). Son of Ruth and Boaz; father of Jesse; grandfather of King David and ancestor of Jesus (Ruth 4:13–22; Matthew 1:5–6; Luke 3:32). Four other Obeds appear in scripture.

■ **OBEDIENCE**. Believing and doing what God says; living like He wants us to (Romans 6:14–17). Obeying God shows our trust in God and His will. It is also true freedom of choice (Exodus 24:7; 1 John 3:23–24; James 3:3). Jesus' obedience to the Father is a biblical model of obedience for all of us (see Luke 4:43; John 3:34; 5:30; Romans 5:12–21; Hebrews 10:7–10). Throughout the Bible, faith and obedience are linked; obedience is the supreme test of faith.

OBEISANCE. To bow down in deep respect or submission (Genesis 43:28).

OBLATION. Offering, sacrifice (Jeremiah 14:12).

OBSERVE. Besides meaning "to watch," it also means to keep or practice—such as observing the sabbath (Deuteronomy 5:32). *Observe* in the KJV may carry the idea of treating with respect or guarding and protecting (Mark 6:20).
● *How do you observe and respect or keep Sunday? Do you think this is the way God intended? Why or why not?*

OCCASION. Besides the usual meaning, it also means cause or opportunity (Daniel 6:4; Romans 14:13; 2 Corinthians 5:12).

OCCUPY. Do business (Luke 19:13); trade (Ezekiel 27:9); use (Judges 16:11).

ODIOUS. Hated, detestable (Proverbs 30:23; 1 Chronicles 19:6).

ODOR, ODOUR. Smell, incense, perfume (Daniel 2:46; Revelation 5:8).

OFFENCE, OFFEND. Besides its usual meaning, a trap or a stumbling block (Isaiah 8:14; Matthew 16:23). The verb form means to cause to stumble (Mark 9:42).

Frankincense—one of the gifts given the young Jesus—was prized for its **odor** and used in perfumes (Exodus 30:34–35).

OFFER, OFFERING. Verb: To give freely as a gift or a sacrifice, as in worship (Genesis 31:54; Hebrews 9:14). Noun: Gift or present. Biblical offerings include animals, birds, produce, or incense. The nation or individuals made offerings that symbolized the repentance and faith required to have a right relationship with God.

● *God receives offerings from pure hearts and right motives. Especially during the time of the prophets, many people offered sacrifices that God did not accept as worship because of the unrepentant hearts of those making the offerings. Consider whether your offerings of money, time, or effort come from a heart that God accepts.*

OFFICE. Position of service or calling (1 Chronicles 6:32; Romans 11:13; 12:4; 1 Timothy 3:1).

OFFSPRING. Children (Job 5:25; Acts 17:28).

OG (AHG). Amorite king of Bashan (Numbers 21:33–35; Deuteronomy 1:4; 3:1–13). He was of the giant race of Rephaim and was defeated and killed by the Israelites during the conquest of Palestine.

OIL. Usually the product of olive trees, oil was an essential part of everyday life in biblical times (2 Kings 18:32; Matthew 25:3). It was used in trade, religious ceremonies, food preparation, cosmetically, as medicine, and for lamp light. Oil was used in the consecration of priests and kings and also, along with prayer, as a medicine (James 5:14). Among other things, oil symbolized joy (Isaiah 61:3; Psalm 45:7).

OINTMENT. Usually a perfumed oil (Psalm 109:18; Luke 7:37, 46). Ointments were often kept in alabaster containers and were used as cosmetics, in religious ceremonies, and for anointing the dead. Aging and the use of certain ingredients made some ointments very valuable.

OLD TESTAMENT. The Old Testament is made up of thirty-nine books: five books of Law; twelve of history; five of poetry; five major prophets; and twelve minor prophets. Major and minor prophets are named that because of the length of the books, not their importance.

The Old Testament is God's inspired revelation expressed through numerous human writers. In the first book of Genesis, the Old Testament describes God's creation of everything. From there on, the Old Testament records God's ongoing revelation of Himself to humanity—including God's covenant relationship with mankind—through the final book of Malachi. After approximately four hundred years of biblical silence (the "intertestament period"), God inspired the twenty-seven books of the New Testament, which record the fulfillment of the Old Testament revelations of God in Christ and prophesy what is to come eternally.

Fuel for lamps was just one use of **oil** in Bible times.

COMPARISON LISTS OF THE OLD TESTAMENT BOOKS

RABBINIC CANON: 24 BOOKS	SEPTUAGINT: 53 BOOKS	ROMAN CATHOLIC OLD TESTAMENT: 46 BOOKS
THE LAW	**LAW**	**LAW**
Genesis	Genesis	Genesis
Exodus	Exodus	Exodus
Leviticus	Leviticus	Leviticus
Numbers	Numbers	Numbers
Deuteronomy	Deuteronomy	Deuteronomy
THE PROPHETS	**HISTORY**	**HISTORY**
The former prophets	Joshua	Joshua
Joshua	Judges	Judges
Judges	Ruth	Ruth
1–2 Samuel	1 Kingdoms (1 Samuel)	1 Samuel (1 Kingdoms)
1–2 Kings	2 Kingdoms (2 Samuel)	2 Samuel (2 Kingdoms)
The latter prophets	3 Kingdoms (1 Kings)	1 Kings (3 Kingdoms)
Isaiah	4 Kingdoms (2 Kings)	2 Kings (4 Kingdoms)
Jeremiah	1 Paralipomena (1 Chronicles)	1 Chronicles (1 Paralipomena)
Ezekiel	2 Paralipomena (2 Chronicles)	2 Chronicles (2 Paralipomena)
The Twelve	1 Esdras (Apocryphal Ezra)	Ezra (1 Esdras)
Hosea	2 Esdras (Ezra-Nehemiah)	Nehemiah (2 Esdras)
Joel	Esther (with apocryphal additions)	Tobit
Amos	Judith	Judith
Obadiah	Tobit	Esther
Jonah	1 Maccabees	1 Maccabees
Micah	2 Maccabees	2 Maccabees
Nahum	3 Maccabees	**POETRY**
Habakkuk	4 Maccabees	Job
Zephaniah	**POETRY**	Psalms
Haggai	Psalms	Proverbs
Zechariah	*Odes (including the Prayer of Manasseh)*	Ecclesiastes
Malachi	Proverbs	Song of Songs
THE WRITINGS	Ecclesiastes	Wisdom of Solomon
Poetry	Song of Songs	Ecclesiasticus (The Wisdom of Jesus the son of Sirach)
Psalms	Job	**PROPHECY**
Proverbs	Wisdom (of Solomon)	Isaiah
Job	Sirach (Ecclesiasticus or The Wisdom of Jesus the son of Sirach)	Jeremiah
Rolls—"the Festival Scrolls"	Psalms of Solomon	Lamentations
Song of Songs	**PROPHECY**	Baruch (including the Letter of Jeremiah)

RABBINIC CANON: 24 BOOKS	SEPTUAGINT: 53 BOOKS	ROMAN CATHOLIC OLD TESTAMENT: 46 BOOKS
Ruth	*The Twelve Prophets*	Ezekiel
Lamentations	Hosea	Daniel
Ecclesiastes	Amos	Hosea
Esther	Micah	Joel
Others (History)	Joel	Amos
Daniel	Obadiah	Obadiah
Ezra-Nehemiah	Jonah	Jonah
1–2 Chronicles	Nahum	Micah
	Habakkuk	Nahum
	Zephaniah	Habakkuk
	Haggai	Zephaniah
	Zechariah	Haggai
	Malachi	Zechariah
APPENDIX	Isaiah	Malachi
THE CANONICAL BOOKS OF THE OLD TESTAMENT*	Jeremiah	**APPENDIX**
	Baruch	The Prayer of Manasseh
▮ Books of Law	Lamentations	The two apocryphal books of Esdras
▮ Books of History	Letter of Jeremiah	
▮ Books of Poetry and Wisdom	Ezekiel	
▮ Books of the Major Prophets	Daniel (with apocryphal additions, including the Prayer of Azariah and the Song of the Three Children, Susanna, and Bel and the Dragon)	
▮ Books of the Minor Prophets		
*Grouped according to the Christian canon		

OLIVET. Same as the Mount of Olives (see 2 Samuel 15:30; Acts 1:12). The Mount of Olives is a ridge on the eastern side of Jerusalem. Gethsemane, Bethphage, and Bethany are on its slopes.

OLIVE TREE. A slow-growing, crooked tree of immense value in biblical times (Deuteronomy 6:11; Romans 11:17). A cultivated tree grows to about twenty feet in height and can live several hundred years. Oil made from the tree fruit has many uses (see **OIL**). The olive tree is a symbol of fruitfulness and the branch of the olive tree is a symbol of peace.

OMEGA (oh MEE guh). Last letter of the Greek alphabet. *Alpha* is the first letter. Together, the two letters are used symbolically to refer to Christ as the beginning and the end (Revelation 1:8). See **ALPHA AND OMEGA, OMICRON**.

▲ *Greek has two letters for O: omicron (O) and omega (Ω). Omicron is always short in pronunciation; omega has the sound of a long O.*

OMER. A dry measure equal to one-tenth of an ephah, four pints, or about two liters (Exodus 16:16). See **WEIGHTS AND MEASURES CHART** on pages 284–286.

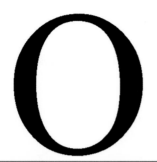

Omicron.

OMICRON. One of two Greek letters that bear the sound O; the sound is short. See **ALPHA AND OMEGA, OMEGA**.

OMNIPOTENCE, OMNIPOTENT. All-powerful (Revelation 19:6). A word that expresses God's essential personhood of being able to do all things through His eternal power (see Genesis 1–2; Job 42:2; Jeremiah 32:17–17; Matthew 19:26; Philippians 4:13).

OMNISPRESENCE. All-presence. A word expressing how God fills the universe in all its parts. He is present eternally everywhere at all times (see Genesis 1–2; Psalm 139:7–12; Jeremiah 23:23–24; Acts 17:27–28).

OMNISCIENCE. All-knowing. A word expressing God's knowledge of all things past, present, and future, eternally (Genesis 1–2; Proverbs 15:11; Psalm 147:5; Isaiah 46:10).

OMRI (AHM righ). 1. Powerful and evil king of Israel, the Northern Kingdom, about 885–874 BC (1 Kings 16:8–29). He moved the capital to Samaria. Omri was the father of the wicked Ahab who succeeded him. See **KING CHART** on pages 152–155. 2. Name of three other Bible personalities.

● *Children tend to imitate their parents, and Omri and Ahab are but two examples of evil succeeding itself. According to Proverbs 22:6, when we train up children in the way they should go they will not depart from it—though this verse does not say that children will never veer from the truth they know. Proverbially, though, Proverbs 22:6 is proven true. The opposite is also true: namely, when evil upbringing leads to evil behavior in a child, the child is following the pattern of the parents. Despite the pattern of parents, each child is responsible under God for his own choices and how he responds to God in Christ and to life itself. What kind of influences have you had? How are you choosing to live your life now?*

ONESIMUS (oh NESS ih muhs). A runaway slave of Philemon (Colossians 4:9). Paul converted Onesimus to Christianity and sent him back to his master with a letter that became the New Testament Bible book of Philemon. The letter urged Philemon to receive Onesimus with forgiveness, as a brother instead of a slave.

● *It seems that Paul's preaching had brought both Philemon and Onesimus to salvation in Christ. In this letter, Paul told Philemon he was willing to pay for anything Onesimus had taken. Since we are all indebted for what Christ did for us on the cross, we are called to have a spirit of forgiveness and brotherhood toward others. Can you think of anybody you need to forgive, or someone who hasn't forgiven you? What would the letter to Philemon suggest you do?*

ONYX. Either a green stone or translucent (see-through) agate with layers of black and white (Exodus 25:7).

OPPRESS. Bruise, crush, overpower, put down or burden (Exodus 3:9; Proverbs 14:31).

Magnified detail of onyx. **Onyx** was one of the stones included on the high priest's breastplate.

ORACLE. 1. Holy of holies (1 Kings 6:16, 23). 2. Divine words or utterances (2 Samuel 16:23; Hebrews 5:12). May sometimes be translated *burden* (compare various translations of the following scriptures: Jeremiah 23:33–34; Ezekiel 12:10 in the KJV, NASB, and NRSV). See **HOLY OF HOLIES; PROPHET.**

ORDAIN. To appoint (Daniel 2:24), establish (Psalm 8:3), or set aside to recognize God's special calling to His service (1 Timothy 2:7).

ORDER. Most common use means to put in arrangement or array (Job 10:22; 1 Corinthians 14:40).

ORDINANCE. Decree, law (Exodus 12:24; Luke 1:6). In the Old Testament, God gave many ordinances for the Hebrew people to observe. Some churches today refer to baptism and the Lord's Supper as New Testament ordinances, since Jesus commanded them as ongoing observances. See **BAPTISM; LORD'S SUPPER.**

OTHNIEL (AHTH nih el). First of the judges. He restored authority and order after the death of Joshua and judged for forty years (Joshua 15:13; Judges 1:11–15; 3:8–11).

OUTCAST. Referred to those dispersed as refugees or exiles (Psalm 147:2; Isaiah 16:4). In John 16:2, the NASB says about persecuted Christians, "They will make you outcasts from the synagogue."
▲ *The KJV does not use the word* outcast *as we do, as one rejected from society in a general way; rather, the KJV uses it in the sense of those driven down or away.*

OVERCOME. Prevail or gain victory (Numbers 13:30; Revelation 2:7).

OVERFLOW. To flood or spill over (Psalm 69:2).

In the Bible, the term *overflow* often indicates a flood of waters.

OVERLAID. Covered (Exodus 26:32; Hebrews 9:4).

OVERSEER. Inspector, administrator (Genesis 39:4; Acts. 20:28). The Greek word for "overseer" is also translated *bishop* (Philippians 1:1; Titus 1:7).
▲ *The Greek word* episkopos *meant "overseer," but was seemingly used interchangeably with "pastor" and "elder." The name of the Episcopalian church is related to this Greek term.*

OVERSIGHT. 1. Error (Genesis 43:12). 2. Responsibility for; be in charge of (2 Kings 12:11; 1 Peter 5:2).

OVERWHELM. Cover, overflow (Psalm 55:5).

OX, OXEN. Cow, cattle (Genesis 12:16). Important in agriculture and sacrificial worship. The "stalled ox" was a symbol of luxury (Proverbs 15:17).

PAIN. Hurt that may be physical or mental and emotional (Psalm 48:6; 55:4; 116:3; Isaiah 13:8; Jeremiah 4:19; Revelation 16:10; 21:4). Pain may be a consequence of sin; however, as the book of Job plainly reveals, not *all* suffering is because of sin.

● *Compare and contrast these references to pain beyond this life: Psalm 116:3 and Revelation 21:4. Pain will be eternally present in hell, but totally absent from heaven.*

PALACE. Residence of the royal family (2 Chronicles 9:11) or the high priest (Matthew 26:3). It could also refer to a fortress or the most prominent or important building in a city.

PALESTINE (PAL uhs tighn). Area east and west of the Jordan River to the Mediterranean Sea. Palestine was also called the promised land, Canaan, Israel, Judea, and today the Holy Land (or perhaps "occupied Palestine"). In New Testament times Palestine was divided into Galilee, Samaria, and Judea (west of the Jordan) and the Decapolis and Perea (east of the Jordan). Palestine was about 70 miles wide and 150 miles long. It has a variety of landscape from seacoast to desert to mountains.

▲ *The violent history and ongoing upheaval of the Middle East have made it difficult to precisely define the geographical boundaries of Palestine and Israel.*

PALM TREE. The date palm grows in the Jordan Valley (1 Kings 6:29). The palm symbolized grace and elegance. Palm branches were used as Jesus entered Jerusalem to symbolize praise (John 12:13).

PALSY. Paralysis (Mark 2:4; Luke 5:18).

▲ *The biblical reference differs from the modern usage of palsy, which describes an uncontrollable shaking as well as other symptoms of the disease.*

PAMPHYLIA (pam FIL ih uh). A Roman province Paul visited on his missionary journeys (Acts 2:10; 13:13; 14:24; 15:38; 27:5). It was a Mediterranean coastal area in south Asia Minor.

PANGS. Pain, distress; used to describe the difficulty of childbirth or as a comparison to that kind of pain (Isaiah 26:17).

PAPHOS (PAY fahs). A city located on the western side of the island of Cyprus, which Paul visited on his first missionary journey. It was then the Roman capital of Cyprus (Acts 13:6).

PAPYRUS. A tall plant that grows in water. When processed, the plant also lent its name to a writing paper. Egyptians invented this *papyrus*, and scribes used it from about 2500 BC through the writing of the New Testament.

Date **palms** in a Jordan Valley plantation.

Much of the original biblical text was recorded on papyrus, as well as other materials.

▲ *To make paper, thin strips of the papyrus stem were laid side by side and overlapped on a hard surface. Then another layer was added crossways. These strips were molded together by beating with a hard instrument. Individual sheets could then be pasted together to form long rolls or scrolls.*

PARABLE. Literally, a story laid alongside of or parallel to a truth or lesson (Numbers 23:7; Mark 4:2). Biblically, a parable is an earthly story that has a heavenly meaning (Luke 15). In story form, parables contained everyday truths that had spiritual applications. Jesus used parables as a major teaching method. See **PARABLES CHART** on pages 198–201.

PARABLES OF JESUS

PARABLE	OCCASION	LESSON TAUGHT	REFERENCES
1. The speck and the log	When reproving the Pharisees	Do not presume to judge others	Matthew 7:1–6; Luke 6:37–43
2. The two houses	Sermon on the Mount, at the close	The strength conferred by duty	Matthew 7:24–27; Luke 6:47–49
3. Children in the marketplace	Rejection by the Pharisees of John's baptism	Evil of a fault-finding disposition	Matthew 11:16; Luke 7:32
4. The two debtors	A Pharisee's self-righteous reflections	Love to Christ proportioned to grace received	Luke 7:41
5. The unclean spirit	The scribes demand a miracle in the heavens	Hardening power of unbelief	Matthew 12:43–45; Luke 11:24–26
6. The rich man's meditation	Dispute of two brothers	Folly of reliance upon wealth	Luke 12:16
7. The barren fig tree	Tidings of the execution of certain Galileans	Danger in the unbelief of the Jewish people	Luke 13:6–9
8. The sower	Sermon on the seashore	Effects of preaching religious truth	Matthew 13: 3–8; Mark 4:3–8; Luke 8:5–8
9. The tares	The same	The severance of good and evil	Matthew 13: 24–30
10. The seed	The same	Power of truth	Mark 4:20
11. The grain of mustard seed	The same	Small beginnings and growth of Christ's kingdom	Matthew 13:31–32; Mark 4:31–32; Luke 13:19
12. The leaven	The same	Dissemination of the knowledge of Christ	Matthew 13:33; Luke 13:2
13. The lamp	To the disciples alone	Effect of good example	Matthew 5:15; Mark 4:21; Luke 8:16, 11:33
14. The dragnet	The same	Mixed character of the church	Matthew 13:47–48
15. The hidden treasure	The same	Value of religion	Matthew 13:44
16. The pearl of great value	The same	The same	Matthew 13:45–46
17. The householder	The same	Varied methods of teaching truth	Matthew 13:52

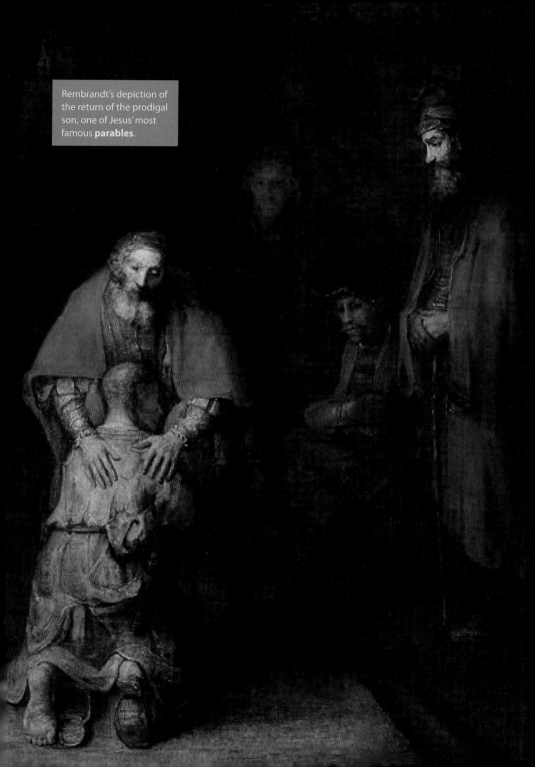

Rembrandt's depiction of the return of the prodigal son, one of Jesus' most famous **parables**.

18. The marriage	To the Pharisees, who censured the disciples	Joy in Christ's companionship	Matthew 9:15; Mark 2:19–20; Luke 5:34–35
19. The patched garment	The same	The propriety of adapting actions to circumstances	Matthew 9:16; Mark 2:21; Luke 5:36
20. The wine bottles	The same	The same	Matthew 9:17; Mark 2:22; Luke 5:37
21. The harvest	Spiritual wants of the Jewish people	Need of labor and prayer	Matthew 9:37; Luke 10:2
22. The opponent	Slowness of the people to believe	Need of prompt repentance	Matthew 5:25; Luke 12:58
23. Two insolvent debtors	Peter's question	Duty of forgiveness	Matthew 18:23–35
24. The good Samaritan	The lawyer's question	The golden rule for all	Luke 10:30–37
25. The three loaves	Disciples request lesson in prayer	Effort of importunity in prayer	Luke 11:5–8
26. The good shepherd	Pharisees reject testimony of miracle	Christ the only way to God	John 10:1–16
27. The narrow gate	The question, "Are there few who can be saved?"	Difficulty of repentance	Matthew 7:14; Luke 13:24
28. The guests	Eagerness to take high places	Chief places not to be usurped	Luke 14:7–11
29. The marriage supper	Self-righteous remark of a guest	Rejection of unbelievers	Matthew 22:2–9; Luke 14:16–23
30. The wedding clothes	Continuation of same discourse	Necessity of purity	Matthew 22:10–14
31. The tower	Multitudes surrounding Christ	Need of deliberation	Luke 14:28–30
32. The king going to war	The same	The same	Luke 14:31
33. The lost sheep	Pharisees object to Jesus' receiving the wicked	Christ's love for sinners	Matthew 18:12–13; Luke 15:4–7
34. The lost coin	The same	The same	Luke 15:8–9
35. The prodigal son	The same	The same	Luke 15:11–32
36. The unjust steward	To the disciples	Prudence in using property	Luke 16:1–9
37. The rich man and Lazarus	Derision of the Pharisees	Salvation not connected to wealth	Luke 16:19–31
38. The importunate widow	Teaching the disciples	Perseverance in prayer	Luke 18:2–5
39. The Pharisee and the tax-gatherer	Teaching the self-righteous	Humility in prayer	Luke 18:10–14
40. The slave's duty	The same	Man's obedience	Luke 17:7–10
41. Laborers in the vineyard	The same	The same further illustrated	Matthew 20:1–16
42. The talents	At the house of Zacchaeus	Doom of unfaithful followers	Matthew 25:14–30; Luke 19:11–27
43. The two sons	Chief priests demand Jesus' authority	Obedience better than words	Matthew 21:28

44. The wicked vine-growers	The same	Rejection of the Jewish people	Matthew 21:33–43; Mark 12:1–9; Luke 20:9–15
45. The fig tree	In prophesying the destruction of Jerusalem	Duty of watching for Christ's appearance	Matthew 24:32; Mark 13;28; Luke 21:29–30
46. The watching slave	The same	The same	Matthew 24:43; Luke 12:39
47. The man on a journey	The same	The same	Mark 13:34
48. Character of two slaves	The same	Danger of unfaithfulness	Matthew 24:45–51; Luke 12:42–46
49. The ten virgins	The same	Necessity of watchfulness	Matthew 25:1–12
50. The watching slaves	The same	The same	Luke 12:36–38
51. The vine and branches	At the Last Supper	Loss and gain	John 15:1–6

PARACLETE. An advocate, helper, or comforter; someone who stands alongside you or acts on your behalf. The apostle John used this Greek word when calling the Holy Spirit the "Comforter" (John 14:16, 26; 15:26; 16:7). In 1 John 2:1, the translation of the word is "advocate," referring to Jesus. The verb form of the word in the KJV is often translated *beseech*; the meaning is, "I call you alongside me." See **HOLY SPIRIT**.

▲ *You will find the word* paraclete *in an unabridged English dictionary.*

PARADISE. A park or garden ground; sometimes used to refer to the Garden of Eden. The New Testament term indicates an eternal dwelling place for those who trust in God (Luke 23:43). In 2 Corinthians 12:4, the apostle Paul described the experience of a man (probably Paul himself) "caught up into paradise."

PARAMOUR. Illicit lover. In Ezekiel 23:20, this sexual terminology refers to the political and spiritual involvement of God's people with pagan Babylon and Egypt.

PARAN (PAY ruhn). Wilderness area in the Sinai Peninsula (between Egypt and Edom); sometimes referred to as Mount Paran (Genesis 21:21). It is part of the area the Israelites wandered through for many years.

PARCHED. Burnt (Jeremiah 17:6). Roasted, as in cooking (Ruth 2:14).

PARCHMENT. Writing material. In 2 Timothy 4:13, the apostle Paul mentions books and parchments, which may have referred to papyrus or leather skins. Whatever the exact medium, Paul wanted his treasured writings with him.

A visitor views **parchment** rolls of the Dead Sea scrolls on display at Qumran.

PARDON. Cover, pass over, forgive the guilty (Nehemiah 9:17; Psalm 25:11).

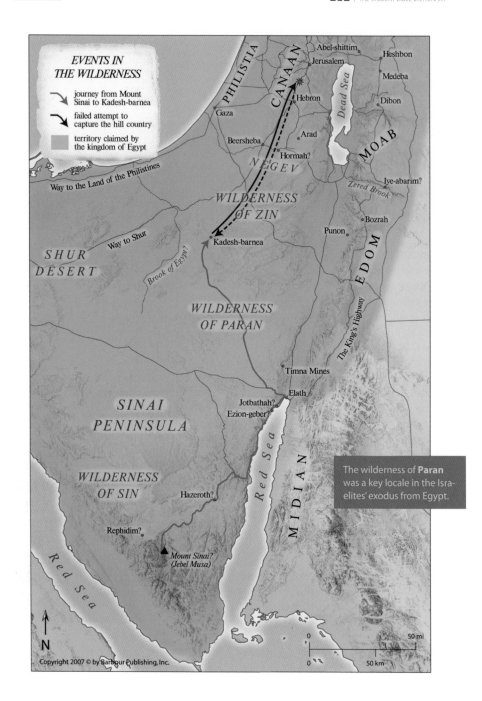

EVENTS IN
THE WILDERNESS

journey from Mount
Sinai to Kadesh-barnea

failed attempt to
capture the hill country

territory claimed by
the kingdom of Egypt

PHILISTIA

CANAAN

Abel-shittim

Heshbon

Jerusalem

Medeba

Gaza

Hebron

Dibon

Dead Sea

MOAB

Beersheba

Arad

Hormah?

NEGEV

Iye-abarim?

Zered Brook

Way to the Land of the Philistines

WILDERNESS
OF ZIN

Bozrah

Punon

EDOM

Way to Shur

Kadesh-barnea

SHUR
DESERT

Brook of Egypt?

WILDERNESS
OF PARAN

The King's Highway

Timna Mines

Elath

Jotbathah?

SINAI
PENINSULA

Ezion-geber?

Red Sea

MIDIAN

WILDERNESS
OF SIN

Hazeroth?

The wilderness of **Paran**
was a key locale in the Israelites' exodus from Egypt.

Rephidim?

Mount Sinai?
(Jebel Musa)

Red Sea

N

0   50 mi

0   50 km

Copyright 2007 © by Barbour Publishing, Inc.

PARTAKE. To join in or have in common, share (Psalm 50:18; Hebrews 3:1, 14).

PARTIALITY. Bias; using the wrong basis for judgment or showing favoritism (1 Timothy 5:21; James 3:17; see also Ephesians 6:9).
● *What's wrong with partiality? Modern Bible translations sometimes use the phrase "respect of persons" in rendering the Greek word that literally means "face-receiver." Does the thought of judging people by their face or outer appearance help clarify what is wrong with partiality?*

PASCHAL. Passover. Paul referred to Christ as our paschal or sacrificial lamb (1 Corinthians 5:7 NRSV). See **PASSOVER**.

PASSAGE. 1. A crossing place (Judges 12:5). 2. Also used today to refer to a section of scripture, one or more verses.

PASSION. Suffering; often used to refer to Christ's crucifixion and death on the cross (Acts 1:3).
▲ *"Passion plays" depict the suffering and crucifixion of Christ. The term's usage to refer to intense desire or longing came into use much later.*

PASSOVER. Feast was instituted the night before God delivered His people from Egyptian slavery (Exodus 12). God instructed the Israelites to mark their doorposts with the blood of a lamb so the death angel would pass over their home and spare their oldest child. Also called the Feast of Unleavened Bread, this feast is still used to celebrate and remember God's deliverance and provision. It is a reminder of God delivering the Hebrews from Egyptian slavery. And ideally in Jesus' time Jews tried to observe the Passover in Jerusalem.

In the New Testament Christ became our sacrificial or passover lamb (1 Corinthians 5:7).

His shed blood and death on the cross delivers us from the stranglehold of sin. See **FEAST CHART** on page 96 and **CALENDAR CHART** on pages 265–266.

PASTOR. Shepherd; one who feeds, leads, and oversees (Jeremiah 2:8; Ephesians 4:11).
▲ *Ephesians 4:11 is the only New Testament reference in the KJV that uses "pastor" in translation instead of "shepherd." The terms* pastor *(shepherd),* bishop, *and* elder *are seemingly used interchangeably to refer to the pastoral role.*

PATIENCE. Longsuffering or enduring; continuing even in the face of difficulties; waiting with confidence and serenity (Romans 5:3; 2 Thessalonians 3:5; James 5:10–11). In James 5:10–11, Job is identified as one who had patience and endurance, and "the patience of Job" is a commonly heard phrase. But Job was not waiting with peace and serenity; rather, his

Lambs were the sacrifice God commanded at the first **Passover**. Jesus became the ultimate Passover lamb with His death on the cross.

patience was a waiting with faithful endurance, showing a commitment to God "though he slay me" (see Job 13:15).

PATMOS (PAT muhs). Small island off the coast of Asia Minor in the Aegean Sea. John was exiled on this island when he received his vision from God and wrote the book of Revelation (Revelation 1:9).

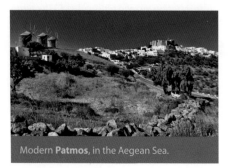

Modern **Patmos**, in the Aegean Sea.

PATRIARCH. Literally, "chief father" or "ruling father." Name given to the founding fathers of the Hebrew race (Abraham, Isaac, Jacob, and Jacob's twelve sons (Acts 2:29; 7:8–9).

PAUL. Greek name of the New Testament apostle and missionary whose Jewish name was Saul. Saul arrived on the biblical scene as a Pharisee who persecuted the Christian church with a religious zeal. But on the road to Damascus, God called Saul to salvation by grace through faith in Jesus Christ. Paul answered the calling, was baptized, and became an apostle of Jesus Christ. He wrote thirteen biblical books that account for almost half of the New Testament. Paul became a strong leader of the early church and defended salvation by grace through faith alone—without works or circumcision or any other Jewish regulations. Paul had been a dedicated Pharisee but became an even more dedicated apostle (see Acts 8:1–3; 9:1–30; 22:1–21; 26:10–11; 23:6; as

well as Paul's own writings). He established and strengthened New Testament churches. Paul was a bridge between Jesus' original apostles and new churches, underlining the fact that the gospel was for Gentiles as well as for Jews.

▲ *Paul's inspired letters to churches and individual Christians became books of the New Testament: Romans, Galatians, Ephesians, Philippians, Colossians, and more (Galatians 1:11–12). Imprisoned for his preaching, Paul wrote a number of his letters from jail (Ephesians 4:1; Colossians 4:18).*

● *God used Paul's strong will and convicted stubbornness in positive ways. How might God use your characteristics for His good?*

PAULINE EPISTLES. Paul's letters to churches or individuals, which have become books of the Bible. They are: Romans, 1 and 2 Corinthians, Galatians, Ephesians, Philippians, Colossians, 1 and 2 Thessalonians, 1 and 2 Timothy, Titus, Philemon. Each was named for the church or individual to whom it was written. The Ephesian letter was probably intended to be circulated among other churches, too.

▲ *Paul typically began each letter by identifying himself and the receiver of the letter; gave a greeting, usually "grace to you and peace" (Romans 1:7); then a thanksgiving for the recipient. See* **PAUL**.

▲ *Some commentators believe Paul authored Hebrews, too. Most scholars, however, have the opinion that someone other than Paul wrote the book.*

PAVILION. 1. Hiding or sheltering place; cover. Movable tent, booth, or canopy (1 Kings 20:12). Figuratively used to mean a protective hiding place that God provided (Psalm 18:11; Psalm 27:5; Psalm 31:20). 2. Nebuchadnezzar spread a royal canopy (translated "pavilion" in KJV) as a sign of God's sovereignty (Jeremiah 43:10). See **CANOPY**.

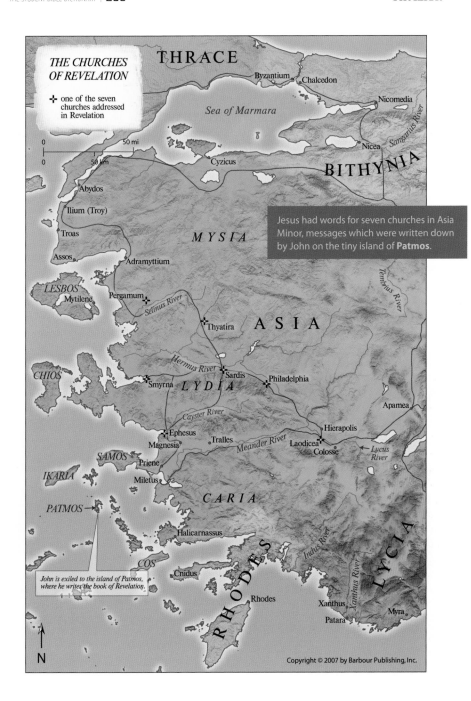

THE CHURCHES
OF REVELATION

✦ one of the seven
churches addressed
in Revelation

0   50 mi
0   50 km

THRACE

Byzantium   Chalcedon

Nicomedia

Sea of Marmara

Nicea

Cyzicus

BITHYNIA

Sangarius River

Abydos

Ilium (Troy)

Troas

Assos

Adramyttium

MYSIA

Jesus had words for seven churches in Asia
Minor, messages which were written down
by John on the tiny island of **Patmos**.

Tembris River

LESBOS
Mytilene

Pergamum

Selinus River

Thyatira

ASIA

CHIOS

Hermus River

Smyrna

Sardis   Philadelphia

LYDIA

Apamea

Cayster River

Ephesus

Magnesia   Tralles

Meander River

Hierapolis

Laodicea
Colosse

Lycus
River

SAMOS   Priene

IKARIA

Miletus

CARIA

PATMOS →

Halicarnassus

Indus River

Xanthus River

LYCIA

John is exiled to the island of Patmos,
where he writes the book of Revelation.

COS

Cnidus

RHODES

Rhodes

Xanthus

Patara

Myra

N

■ **PEACE**. Absence of inner or outer conflict, unity, wholeness (Leviticus 26:6; Luke 1:79). "Peace" (Hebrew *shalom*) was a common biblical greeting that wished both the absence of conflict and God's highest blessing (2 Kings 9:18). Peace with God comes through a right relationship with God in Christ (Ephesians 2:14–17).

PEACE OFFERING. An animal sacrifice to thank or express love to God (Exodus 20:24; Leviticus 3; 7:11–36). The peace offering regularly occurred during the feast of weeks as a token of gratitude to God (Leviticus 23:19–20). The offerers and the observance were all to reflect purity.

PEARL. In the Old Testament probably some type of precious stone (Job 28:18). In the New Testament, *pearl* refers to the product of the clam. Pearl was used for jewelry and decoration (1 Timothy 2:9). In a parable about the incom-parable value of the kingdom of God, Jesus described a "pearl of great price" to symbolize this spiritual truth that the kingdom of God is more valuable than anything else (Matthew 13:45–46).

PENTATEUCH. The first five books of the Bible, the books of Law. These are Genesis, Exodus, Leviticus, Numbers, Deuteronomy. The Pentateuch covered the period from creation through the time of Moses. The Sadducees accepted only these books as Holy Scripture. Other Jews accepted all of the Old Testament as Holy Scripture.

■ **PENTECOST**. Fifty days. Pentecost occurred on the fiftieth day after the feast of the Pass-over. Originally a yearly Jewish celebration of harvest; also called the Feast of Weeks (Deuter-onomy 16:9–10; Acts 20:16; 1 Corinthians 16:8). On the first Pentecost after Christ's resurrection,

At **Pentecost**, tongues of fire appear above the heads of Jesus' followers in this fourteenth-century painting by Duccio de Buoninsegna.

the Holy Spirit uniquely and forevermore came upon believers (Acts 2:1–16). For that reason, Christians connect Pentecost with the coming of the Holy Spirit. See **FEAST CHART** on page 96 and **CALENDAR CHART** on pages 265–266.

● *Imagine yourself observing the Holy Spirit's arrival on Pentecost (see Acts 2:1–11). How might you have reacted? Did you know that the Holy Spirit comes into every Christian's life as a gift and the seal of salvation at the moment they believe? (See Ephesians 1:13; 4:30.) See* **HOLY SPIRIT.**

PERCEIVE. To know, see, understand (1 Samuel 3:8; John 4:19).

PERDITION. Death, destruction, loss (1 Timothy 6:9).

PEREZ (PEE rez). Son of Judah, who was conceived through the trickery of Tamar, Judah's daughter-in-law (Genesis 38).

PERFECT. Whole, complete, mature (Genesis 6:9; Matthew 19:21; Philippians 3:12).

▲ *In Matthew 5:48, Jesus commands His followers to be perfect "even as your Father which is in heaven is perfect." In this context, perfect means more than the definition of whole, complete, or mature. Leviticus 19:2 similarly tells us to be holy, for our God is holy. Only God is completely perfect and holy, but He wants perfection and holiness to be our goal.*

PERFORM. Besides the usual meaning of "to do," it also means to confirm (Deuteronomy 9:5) and to complete (Romans 15:28).

PERGA (PUR guh). Important city in Pamphylia (Acts 13:13). It was here John Mark left Paul and Barnabas on their first missionary trip and returned home.

PERGAMOS (PUR guh mahs). A wealthy city in Asia Minor (Revelation 2:12). In His message to the church at Pergamos, the Lord condemned heretical teachings. Also spelled Pergamum.

PERISH. Be lost or destroyed (Psalm 1:6; John 3:16). The opposite of saved.

PERIZZITES (PER ih zightz). A tribe that opposed Israel and was driven out of Canaan (Genesis 13:7; Joshua 9:1–2).

PERPETUAL. Unending, continuing, of indefinite time (Genesis 9:12).

PERPLEXED. Confused, puzzled (Esther 3:15; Luke 9:7).

PERSECUTE. Treat badly, harass, cause to suffer (Jeremiah 29:18; Matthew 5:10).

PERSEVERANCE. Keeping on, not giving up, lasting consistency, endurance (Ephesians 6:18).

PERSIA (PUR zhuh). A large empire that had great effect on ancient history. Located in what is now mostly Iran, Persia's boundaries changed and expanded through the centuries. In 559 BC

Ruins of ancient **Perga**, a stop on the apostle Paul's first missionary journey.

Cyrus became the King of Persia, and in 539 BC he conquered Babylon. He inherited the Jewish captives and allowed them to return to begin rebuilding the temple destroyed by the Babylonians (Ezra 1:1–4).

PERTAIN. Besides the usual meaning, can also mean "belong" (1 Samuel 27:6 NRSV).

PERVERSE. Twisted out of proper shape, evil, deceitful, devious, rebellious, obstinate, misguided (Proverbs 14:2; Matthew 17:17).

PERVERT. Twist, distort, turn aside (Exodus 23:8; Acts 13:10).

PESTILENCE. Plague, devastating epidemic (Exodus 5:3; Luke 21:11).

PETER (PEE tur). Greek for "rock" (Aramaic for rock is *Cephas,* John 1:42.). Disciple of Jesus whose name was Simon until Jesus gave him the name *Peter,* which means "rock" in Greek (Mark 3:16; Matthew 4:18). His brother Andrew introduced him to Jesus, who called both brothers to be disciples.

Peter is always first in the listing of the disciples and was one of the three closest to Jesus during His ministry. Peter often acted impulsively; after promising he would never desert Jesus, Peter openly denied the Lord during His arrest and trial. Peter was inconsistent, certainly not a "rock" until *after* the crucifixion and resurrection of Christ. But after Jesus' restoration of Peter (see John 21), Peter became a bold and dynamic leader of the early church. He preached the Pentecost sermon (Acts 2) and suffered persecution and imprisonment. Tradition says Peter was put to death during the time of Nero's persecution of Christians.

PETER, 1, 2, BOOKS OF. New Testament books (letters) written by Peter to the Christians in Asia Minor. First Peter sets forth the purpose and privileges of God's people, relationships to others, and encouragement in the time of suffering. The first letter also sets forth standards for an elder or pastor's job and behavior (1 Peter 5:1–4). Second Peter includes guidelines for the Christian life, warnings against false prophets, and thoughts on the second coming of Christ. This letter also shares the heart of God in wanting all to be saved and none to perish (2 Peter 3:9).

PHARAOH (FAY roh). Egyptian ruler or king (Genesis 12:15). A pharaoh invited the family of Jacob (Israel) to Egypt during a famine (Genesis 47:1–6). Later generations of the Israelites were enslaved by a succeeding pharaoh.

■ **PHARISEE** (FER uh see). An influential group of Jewish religious leaders whose name means "separated ones" (Matthew 23; Luke 5:30–32; 14:1–6). Sincere but misled, they believed religious ritual and separation from common sinners was the way to please God and prepare for His coming. As a rule, they did not accept Jesus as the Messiah (Mark 3:6).

▲ *Pharisees followed the traditions of the prophets and believed in a resurrection; Sadducees, on the other hand, followed the traditions of the priests and did not believe in a resurrection.*

● *Some Pharisees stand out for caring about and following Jesus: Nicodemus, Joseph of Arimathea, and Paul. It takes courage to arrive at personal convictions that differ from our social group—and if we publicly share those convictions, they may lead to persecution.*

PHEBE (FEE bih). Spelled Phoebe in modern translations. A ministering servant of the church at Cenchrea. Paul commended her to the church at Rome as one who had helped many people including Paul himself (Romans 16:1–2).

In the home of a **Pharisee** named Simon, a sinful woman anoints Jesus' feet with her tears and wipes them with her hair. When Simon expressed criticism, Jesus told a parable of sin and forgiveness (see Luke 7).

▲ *Modern translations refer to Phebe as a servant, a deacon, a helper, or a minister. The Greek word describing Phebe is the same one used for the English word* deacon. *Whatever her official position, she was clearly a ministering person.*

PHILADELPHIA (fil uh DEL fih uh). City in Asia Minor (Revelation 1:11), the name of which means "brotherly love." Philadelphia was home to one of seven regional churches the Lord commended and/or condemned through His inspired word to John (Revelation 2–3). Only Philadelphia and Smyrna received no condemnation among these seven churches (see Revelation 2:8–11; 3:7–13). Philadelphia was a wealthy commercial city known for its temples and religious festivals.

PHILEMON (figh LEE muhn). Owner of the slave Onesimus, a Christian and fellow worker with Paul. Receiver of Paul's letter to Philemon. Paul challenged Philemon to receive the runaway Onesimus back as a brother rather than a slave.

PHILEMON, BOOK OF. Short New Testament book; a letter written by Paul from prison. Paul encouraged Philemon to receive and forgive his runaway slave, Onesimus, as a new believer in Christ.

PHILIP (FILL ip). 1. One of Jesus' disciples (Matthew 10:3). Philip was from Bethsaida. He brought Nathanael to Jesus, helped with the feeding of the multitudes, and brought Gentiles (non-Jews) to Jesus. 2. One of seven set aside for deacon-like service (Acts 6:5). 3. Two of the Herods (Matthew 14:3; Luke 3:1).

PHILIPPI (FILL ih pigh). A city founded in 358 BC by Alexander the Great's father, Philip II, who named it for himself. By New Testament times, Philippi had become a Roman colony in the province of Macedonia (Acts 16:12). The apostle Paul extended his missionary journey to Philippi after responding to his vision of a Macedonian man's call for help (Acts 16:9–10). Outside Philippi, Paul found a group of women praying at the riverside on the Sabbath. One of them, Lydia (a seller of purple cloth) became a convert, was baptized, and offered hospitality to Paul (Acts 16:9–15). It seems that a church grew out of this encounter. Also in Philippi, Paul was jailed after casting a fortune-telling demon from a young woman in the name of Jesus Christ. Paul and Silas led the jailer and his family to faith in Christ (Acts 16:16–33).

The ancient amphitheater at **Philippi**.

PHILIPPIANS, BOOK OF (fih LIP ih uhns). New Testament book written by Paul while he was in prison. Paul wrote to the church at Philippi to express joy and gratitude for its help and to encourage the people in their faith and witness. "Joy" is the keynote of this brief book with a form of the word mentioned nineteen times.

● *Read the book of Philippians through many times over, and you will never be the same. Philippians is a gold mine of who Christ is, what His people are to be like, and how God will enable and empower Christians to fulfill their lifelong "yes" to God's calling.*

PHILISTIA (fih LIST ih uh). Territory along the Mediterranean seacoast extending from Joppa to Gaza (Psalm 60:8). The area is sometimes referred to as Palestina or Palestine (Exodus 15:14; Isaiah 14:29–31; Joel 3:4). *Philistia* was the name given a small area along the coast where the Philistines lived. At times, the whole land of Canaan was called the "land of the Philistines" (see Zephaniah 2:5).

PHILISTINES (fih LISS teens). Inhabitants of the territory of Philistia (Genesis 21:32). They originated around the Aegean Sea, bringing skills of metal-working and weaponry to the region of Israel. Though the Philistines are mentioned in the time of the patriarchs, they became prominent as enemies of Israel during the time of the judges and the reigns of Saul and David. The Philistines were able to dominate the Hebrews for a time, as part of God's judgment for His people's sin (see Judges 13:1). After other nations had fought the Philistines, David defeated them decisively, and they never regained their former strength.

PHILOSOPHY. Literally, love or study of wisdom, but also, a way of thought. Systems of philosophy were abundant during the New Testament era, and Paul came upon many of them in his travels (see Acts 17:18–21). Though the word *philosophers* appears in Acts 17:18, the term *philosophy* appears in the KJV New Testament only in Colossians 2:8. But in Colossians 2:8 of the NIV, Paul warned Colossian Christians to beware of "hollow and deceptive philosophy" that contradicted the gospel.

PHINEAS (FIN ih uhs). 1. Grandson of Aaron (Exodus 6:25). 2. Sinful son of Eli (1 Samuel 1:3). 3. Father of Eleazar. He returned from exile with Ezra (Ezra 8:33).

PHOENICIA (fuh NISH ih uh). Also called Phenice (KJV; Acts 11:19; 27:12). A narrow strip of land between the Mediterranean Sea and the Lebanon Mountains. The Phoenicians were known for their colorful dyes, seamanship, ship building, and carpentry. Their cedar forests provided material for Solomon's temple (1 Kings 5:8–10). Phoenicia's two principal cities were Tyre and Sidon.

PHRYGIA (FRIG ih uh). An area of land that was a large part of Asia Minor (Acts 2:10). Paul began churches in several cities of this area on his second missionary journey (Acts 16:5–6).

Zeno of Citium (third century BC), founder of the Stoic school of **philosophy** that Paul referenced in Acts 17:18.

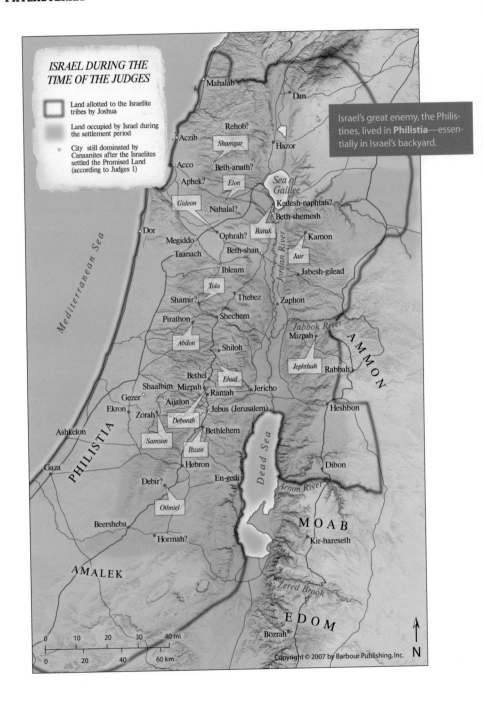

ISRAEL DURING THE
TIME OF THE JUDGES

Land allotted to the Israelite
tribes by Joshua

Land occupied by Israel during
the settlement period

City still dominated by
Canaanites after the Israelites
settled the Promised Land
(according to Judges 1)

Israel's great enemy, the Philistines, lived in **Philistia**—essentially in Israel's backyard.

Copyright © 2007 by Barbour Publishing, Inc.

PHYLACTERIES. Small leather cases worn on the foreheads of Jewish men during prayer times. The following scriptures were written on parchment and placed inside the phylacteries: Exodus 13:1–10, 11–16; Deuteronomy 6:4–9; 11:13–21. Jesus condemned men who wore large phylacteries for show (Matthew 23:5). In Old Testament called "frontlets" (Exodus 13:16).

● *Do you have any personal practices or display symbols that hint of religious show rather than true worship? Pure motives and heart expressions are more important than outward appearances or what people think of us.*

PIETY. Reverence, religious worship (1 Timothy 5:4).

PILATE, PONTIUS (PIGH luht, PAHN shuhs). Roman governor of Judea (Matthew 27:2). Even though Pilate did not find Jesus guilty of any crime, Pilate yielded to pressure and allowed Jesus to be put to death (Luke 23:4,14, 22; John 18:38; 19:4, 6).

PILLAR. 1. Stone monuments set up for memorials or as places of worship for God or idols (Genesis 35:20; Genesis 28:18; Deuteronomy 12:3). 2. Structural supports (1 Kings 10:12). 3. Pillars of cloud and fire were the visual expressions of God as He led the children of Israel through the wilderness (Exodus 13:21).

PINE. Adjective: Type of tree (Isaiah 41:19). Verb: Be sick of heart or waste away (Ezekiel 24:23).

PINNACLE. Highest point of a building (Matthew 4:5).

PIPE. Musical instrument, flute (1 Samuel 10:5).

PISGAH (PIZ guh). Mountain or mountain ridge (Numbers 21:20). Pisgah was the top of Mount Nebo. Place where Moses went to view the Promised Land (Deuteronomy 32:49; 34:1).

PISIDIA (pih SID ih uh). Province in Asia Minor (Acts 13:14). The main city of the province was Antioch.

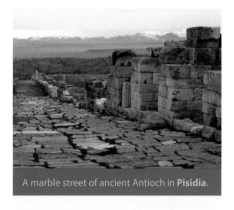

A marble street of ancient Antioch in **Pisidia**.

PIT. Hole or well (Genesis 37:20); grave, death, or Sheol (Job 33:18).

▲ *Sheol was the place of the dead in the mind of Old Testament Hebrews.*

PITCH. Verb: Make a camp, set up a tent (Exodus 17:1; Hebrews 8:2); Noun: Black tar or asphalt-like material (Exodus 2:3).

PITY. Loving-kindness, concern, compassion, mercy (Job 19:20; Matthew 18:33).

PLAGUE. Deadly disease or destruction (Exodus 9:14; Revelation 9:20). God sent the ten plagues upon Egypt to show His power and to persuade Pharaoh to free His people from slavery. The plagues were water turned to blood, frogs, lice, flies, cattle disease, boils, hail, locusts, darkness, and death of the firstborn.

THE TEN PLAGUES OF EGYPT

PLAGUE	SCRIPTURE
1. *Water to blood*—The waters of the Nile turn to blood.	Exodus 7:14–25
2. *Frogs*—Frogs infest the land of Egypt.	Exodus 8:1–15
3. *Gnats* (mosquitoes)—Small stinging insects infest the land of Egypt.	Exodus 8:16–19
4. *Flies*—Swarms of flies, possibly a biting variety, infest the land of Egypt.	Exodus 8:20–32
5. *Plague on cattle*—A serious disease, possibly anthrax, infects the cattle belonging to the Egyptians.	Exodus 9:1–7
6. *Boils*—A skin disease infects the Egyptians.	Exodus 9:8–12
7. *Hail*—A storm destroys the grain fields of Egypt but spares the land of Goshen inhabited by the Israelites.	Exodus 9:13–35
8. *Locusts*—An infestation of locusts strips the land of Egypt of plant life.	Exodus 10:1–20
9. *Darkness*—A deep darkness covers the land of Egypt for three days.	Exodus 10:21–29
10. *Death of the firstborn*—The firstborn of every Egyptian family dies.	Exodus 11:1–12:30

A composite image of the **Pleiades** grouping from the Digitized Sky Survey.

PLASTER, PLAISTER. 1. A wall covering usually made of clay (Deuteronomy 27:2). 2. A mixture made from plant products used medically for warmth, relieving pain, and as an antiseptic (Isaiah 38:21).

PLEDGE. Item of personal property given as a down payment or guarantee for payment of a debt (Ezekiel 18:12). The Old Testament strictly regulated this practice so that the one pledging would not be abused by a lender withholding what had been pledged.

PLEIADES (PLIGH uh deez). A grouping of several stars in the constellation Taurus (Job 9:9).

PLENTY. Abundance, fullness (Genesis 27:28).

PLOWSHARE. Cutting edge of a plow (Isaiah 2:4). Beating swords into plowshares symbolizes a time of peace.

The **plowshare**, in this image, is the metal wedge beneath the horizontal bar.

PLUCK. Snatch, take away (2 Samuel 23:21; John 10:28).

PLUMBLINE, PLUMMET. A measuring device to test the up-and-down straightness of a wall (2 Kings 21:13). It was usually a cord with a stone or metal weight at the end. The term is used symbolically for God's testing of His people: are they straight and true, or out of line with God's design and will? (See Amos 7:7–8.)

POLLUTE. Profane, defile, make unclean (Malachi 1:7; Acts 21:28).

POLYGAMY. The practice of having more than one spouse at a time. (The word is not used in the KJV, though the practice itself is clearly indicated, especially in the Old Testament.
▲ *God's divine design for marriage is a union between one husband and one wife—till death parts them.*

POLYTHEISM. The belief or worship of more than one god. The word is not used in the KJV, but the practice was widespread.

POMEGRANATE. Small tree or fruit of the tree (Exodus 28:33). The fruit has many seeds and red pulp.

Ripe **pomegranates** on the tree branch.

POMP. Pride, show (Isaiah 14:11; Acts 25:23).

POSSESSED. Besides the usual meaning of acquired or taken over, to be possessed also means under the control of the devil or a demon (Matthew 4:24).
● *A Christian is possessed by God in Christ Himself and has the Holy Spirit within him, so no power can take over possession of the true Christian (see Romans 8:6–9, 37–39).*

POSTERITY. Descendants, sons (Daniel 11:4).

POTIPHAR (POT ih fur). Egyptian official under Pharaoh (Genesis 37:36). After Joseph's brothers sold him into slavery to the Midianites, the Midianites sold Joseph to Potiphar. Potiphar's wife tried to seduce Joseph, but he resisted, remained pure, and endured false accusations that led to his imprisonment (Genesis 39:7–20).
● *How might you have reacted in Joseph's situation? Why? Read through all of Joseph's life story (Genesis 30–50) to see how he acted with integrity in each challenge he faced.*

POTSHERD. Piece of broken pottery (Job 2:8).

POTTAGE. A thick vegetable soup (Genesis 25:29).

POTTER'S FIELD. Piece of land in the Hinnom Valley used as a burial ground for strangers (Matthew 27:3–10; Acts 1:18). The money Judas returned for the betrayal of Jesus was used to buy the field.

POUND. A pound weight varied from about twelve ounces in the Roman system (John 12:3) to about twenty ounces in the Hebrew-Greek system (Ezra 2:69). In terms of money, a pound was about one hundred days' wages (Luke

19:13). See **WEIGHTS AND MEASURES CHART** on pages 284–286.

POWER. Strength, authority (Psalm 111:6; Matthew 9:6; Matthew 6:13). God revealed His power through history, acts of nature, individual lives, and the Holy Spirit. Jesus revealed God's power through His miracles, forgiveness, and unfailing obedience even unto death on the cross.
▲ *The Greek word* dunamis *means "power," and compares with our English word* dynamite.
● *How do you see God's power at work today? What impact does a careful reading of Philippians 4:13 have on your view?*

PRAETORIUM (prih TAWR ih uhm). Barracks or building that housed Roman soldiers (Mark 15:16).

■ **PRAISE**. Express honor and gratitude to God through worship, words, attitudes, actions (Psalm 69:30; Luke 19:37).
● *Psalm 103 says repeatedly, "Bless the LORD, O my soul." How can we bless the Lord? Basically, we bless the Lord when we praise Him.*

■ **PRAYER**. Talking and listening to God; an intimate fellowship with God (1 Kings 8:28; Matthew 21:22). Calls for faith and a right relationship with God (Psalm 66:18; James 5:16). May include praising, thanking, confessing, asking, interceding (praying for others), and receiving. When we pause in stillness and realize that God is God, He is speaking to us in prayer.
● *Try each type of prayer. What do you like about each?*

BIBLICAL PRAYERS

TYPE OF PRAYER	MEANING	OLD TESTAMENT EXAMPLE	NEW TESTAMENT EXAMPLE	JESUS' TEACHING
Confession	Acknowledging sin and helplessness and seeking God's mercy	Psalm 51	Luke 18:13	Luke 15:11–24; Luke 18:10–24
Praise	Adoring God for who He is	1 Chronicles 29:10–13	Luke 1:46–55	Matthew 6:9
Thanksgiving	Expressing gratitude to God for what He has done	Psalm 105:1–7	1 Thessalonians 5:16–18	Luke 17:11–19
Petition	Making personal request of God	Genesis 24:12–14	Acts 1:24–26	Matthew 7:7–12
Intercession	Making request of God on behalf of another	Exodus 32:11–13; 31–32	Philippians 1:9–11	John 17:9, 20–21
Commitment	Expressing loyalty to God and His work	1 Kings 8:56–61	Acts 4:24–30	Matthew 6:10; Luke 6:46–49
Forgiveness	Seeking mercy for personal sin or the sin of others	Daniel 9:4–19	Acts 7:60	Matthew 6:12; Luke 6:27–36
Confidence	Affirming God's all-sufficiency and the believer's security in His love	Psalm 23	Luke 2:29–32	Matthew 6:5–15; 7:11
Benediction	A request for God's blessing	Numbers 6:24–26	Jude 24	Luke 11:27–28

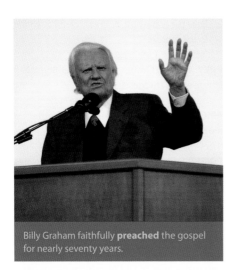

Billy Graham faithfully **preached** the gospel for nearly seventy years.

PREACH. To proclaim, to tell or announce good news about the kingdom of God (Isaiah 61:1; Luke 4:43; Acts 5:42).
▲ *Preaching varies in kind and quality, but the gospel—the good news—never varies: It is always the sharing of the eternal-life-changing message of God in Christ.*

PREACHER. One who proclaims or shares the good news (Ecclesiastes 1:1; Romans 10:14).

PRECEPT. Teaching, command (Psalm 119:4; Mark 10:5).

■ **PREDESTINATION**. Choice or selection beforehand (Romans 8:29–30). God, in His supreme authority and wisdom, chooses those who will trust in Him and be saved. God's predestination occurs in Christ and one's response to Him (Ephesians 1:4–5, 11). Predestination does not remove each person's responsibility for accepting Jesus Christ as Lord and Savior (Romans 10:9–10).
● *Some people are uncomfortable with terms like* predestination, election, *and* foreknowl-

edge. *Whatever our interpretation of these words, the totality of the Bible teaches the vital importance of salvation through faith, by trusting Christ as Lord and Savior.*

PREEMINENCE. First place, supremacy (Colossians 1:18).

PREPARATION, DAY OF. This was the day set aside for getting ready for the sabbath (Matthew 27:62). Since no work was permitted on the sabbath, completion of work and food preparation was done the day before. The day of preparation began at 6 p.m. on Thursday and ended at 6 p.m. on Friday, which was the beginning of the sabbath. See **SABBATH**.

PRESCRIBE. Write (Isaiah 10:1).

PRESENCE OF GOD. God making Himself known and coming face-to-face with people. In the Old Testament, some examples of God's presence are the burning bush (Exodus 3:2–5) and the cloud and pillar of fire (Exodus 40:34–38). In the New Testament God was visible in Jesus Christ (John 1:1–14; Philippians 2:5–11). Throughout the Bible the Holy Spirit revealed the presence of God. His Spirit performs that same work today. See **GOD, HOLY SPIRIT**.
● *How do you experience God's presence day by day? Consider reading at least one chapter of the Bible each day in a quiet and meditative place; then answer this question again.*
See **OMNISCIENCE**.

PRESERVE. Keep, save (Psalm 12:7; Luke 17:33).

PRESS. Noun: An instrument for collecting juice from grapes or olives (Proverbs 3:10). Also, a crowd of people (Mark 2:4). Verb: Strain (Philippians 3:14). Also, devoted entirely (Acts 18:5).

An ancient olive **press** in Israel.

PRESUMPTUOUS. Filled with pride, bold, daring (Exodus 21:14; 2 Peter 2:10).

PRETENCE. Act as a hypocrite or show off (Matthew 23:13–14).
▲ *The Greek word for "hypocrite" is used in Matthew 23 and means to pretend or act under a mask. Jesus condemned actions and attitudes that were outward only, not matching the heart. In common speech, we are to "walk the walk" of what we say we believe in Christ.*

PREVAIL. Become mighty or strong, conquer (Genesis 7:18; Matthew 16:18).

PREVENT. Anticipate (Psalm 119:147); precede (Matthew 17:25; 1 Thessalonians 4:15).
▲ *In the KJV, prevent usually does not mean "to keep from happening." But see Psalm 18:5, 18 for the possible meaning of oppose or hinder.*

Each use of prevent deserves careful attention to the context.

PREY. Victim (Numbers 14:3); something taken in war, spoils (Judges 5:30).

PRIDE. Arrogance, self-trust; opposite of humility (Proverbs 29:23; Mark 7:22).

PRIEST. Someone who speaks to God or relates to God in behalf of others or for oneself. In the Old Testament and early New Testament priests presented sacrifices to God for the people, taught them the law, entered the holiest places of the tabernacle or temple, and met with God (Leviticus 4:26; Ezekiel 42:13–14; Luke 1:8–11). Two major lines of Old Testament priests were the Aaronic (Exodus 28:1) and the Levitical (Hebrews 7:11; Leviticus 6:2–5).

Jesus became our once-and-for-all sacrifice and is now our High Priest (Hebrews 4:14–16); therefore, we no longer need ceremonial sacrifices or priests to represent us or symbolize our worship to God. Every Christian is a priest (1 Peter 2:5, 9), needing only Jesus as Mediator before God. See **MEDIATOR**, **PRIESTHOOD OF THE BELIEVER**.
▲ *Though Old Testament sacrifices symbolized expressions of worship, repentance, thanks-*

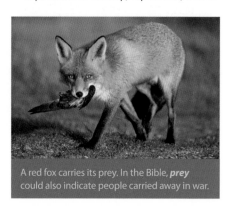

A red fox carries its prey. In the Bible, *prey* could also indicate people carried away in war.

giving, and praise from the hearts of people, no sacrifice saved anyone. God's plan of salvation has never changed: the blood atonement of Jesus Christ provides the actual atoning power—past, present, and future. All are saved by grace through faith, not by works (Ephesians 2:8–10).

PRIEST, HIGH. Leader of worship in the temple or tabernacle (2 Kings 12:10; Matthew 26:3). Also called chief priest (2 Chronicles 26:20; Matthew 2:4). The high priest participated in and supervised the priests offering sacrifices and other priestly functions. He alone had the privilege of going into the holy of holies (innermost part of the temple or tabernacle) on the Day of Atonement (Leviticus 16). Aaron was the first high priest (Exodus 28; 29). See **HOLY OF HOLIES, LEVITES.**

■ **PRIESTHOOD OF BELIEVERS.** All Christians can come directly into the presence of God without a mediator or priest (Ephesians 2:18; 1 Peter 2:5, 9). Jesus provided for us to have this priesthood, and we work under His guidance (Revelation 1:6; 5:10).

▲ *Christians can interpret the Bible for themselves and speak to God themselves. They do not need to go through another believer to contact God, but they can certainly learn about God from other Christians such as pastors and teachers (Ephesians 4:11–12).*

PRINCIPALITIES. Rulers, authorities (Titus 3:1). Also, angelic and demonic powers that could be good or evil (Romans 8:38; 1 Corinthians 15:24; Ephesians 1:21; 6:10–20).

PRISCILLA (prih SIL uh). Also called Prisca. Wife of Aquila. Together they worked beside and ministered with Paul (Acts 18:2–3, 18; Romans 16:3). They also helped a preacher named Apollos understand the way of God more perfectly. They had a church in their house (Acts 18:26; 1 Corinthians 16:19). See **AQUILA.**

PRISON, PRISONER. In the Old Testament, prisons were often small houses or rooms close to the palace (Judges 16:21). Sometimes underground dungeons or cisterns (wells) were used. Most of the confinement was due to political offenses. In the New Testament, political

The dungeon of the Mamertine **Prison** in Rome, which some claim once housed the apostle Peter.

offenses, unpaid debts, criminal acts, and some religious practices were causes for imprisonment (Acts 5:18). Famous biblical prisoners—unjustly held—include Joseph, Samson, John the Baptist, Peter, Paul, and Silas.

PRIZE. A crown or garland awarded in athletic games (1 Corinthians 9:24). Paul used the term to symbolize a spiritual award (Philippians 3:14).
▲ *God's gift of salvation is always by grace—never won or earned. But spiritual prizes may symbolically represent the answering of God's call and staying faithful until the finish line. Paul himself testified that the prize would be "a crown of righteousness" (2 Timothy 4:6–8).*

PROCLAIM. To announce or make known, to preach as a herald (Exodus 33:19; Luke 12:3).

PROCLAMATION. Public announcement (Daniel 5:29).

PROCONSUL. Roman government official responsible for civil and military matters in a province (Acts 13:7 NIV; "deputy" in KJV).

PROFANE. Opposite of holy (Ezekiel 44:23). Critical of God, destructive to God's purposes, having nothing to do with God, godless. Can be an action (Matthew 12:5), a person (Hebrews 12:16), or a descriptive term (1 Timothy 6:20).

PROMISE. Agreement, pledge, contract (Acts 1:4). Obedient and faithful people receive the fulfillment of God's promises (Romans 4:13–14).
▲ *A covenant is an agreed-upon promise. God is always faithful to His promises. And even when humans default on their part of a covenant with God, God is faithful to forgive those who repent and return to Him in faithfulness.*

PRONOUNCE. Speak (Jeremiah 11:17).

■**PROPHECY** (noun), **PROPHESY** (verb). Speak for God, tell God's truth (Mark 7:6; 2 Peter 1:19–21; 1 Corinthians 13:2). Prophets spoke God's Word to a present generation but with truths that often revealed the future (see Revelation 1:17–19).
▲ *Today, many think of prophecy as referring only to the future. In the Bible, though, a prophet first and foremost spoke the word He received from God. That word often did foretell the future.*

PROPHET, PROPHETESS. One who speaks for God (Micah 1:1; Judges 4:4; Acts 21:9). A true prophet said exactly what God said. Both men and women served as prophets; among them were Nathan, Deborah, Daniel, and Anna. Prophets were sometimes well-liked; others, like Jeremiah (known as the "weeping prophet"), suffered rejection for the hard truths God called them to share. False prophets were not called by God and were not to be heeded (1 Kings 18:25–40).

Michelangelo's Sistine Chapel portrait of the **prophet** Isaiah.

THE PROPHETS IN HISTORY (9TH–5TH CENTURY BC)

PROPHET	APPROXI- MATE DATES	LOCATION/HOME	BASIC BIBLE PASSAGE	CENTRAL TEACHING	KEY VERSE
Elijah	875–850	Tishbe	1 Kings 17:1–2; 2 Kings 2:18	Yahweh, not Baal, is God	1 Kings 18:21
Micaiah	856	Samaria	1 Kings 22; 2 Chronicles 18	Proof of prophecy	1 Kings 22:28
Elisha	855–800	Abel Meholah	1 Kings 19:15–21; 2 Kings 2–9; 13	God's miraculous power	2 Kings 5:15
Jonah	775	Gath Hepher	2 Kings 14:25; Jonah	God's universal concern	Jonah 4:11
Amos	765	Tekoa	Amos	God's call for justice and righteousness	Amos 5:24
Hosea	750	Israel	Hosea	God's unquenchable love	Hosea 11:8–9
Isaiah	740–698	Jerusalem	2 Kings 19–20; Isaiah	Hope through repentance and suffering	Isaiah 1:18; 53:4–6
Micah	735–710	Moresheth; Gath; Jerusalem	Jeremiah 27:18; Micah	Call for humble mercy and justice	Micah 6:8
Oded	733	Samaria	2 Chronicles 28:9–11	Do not go beyond God's command	2 Chronicles 28:9
Zephaniah	630	?	Zephaniah	Hope for the humble righteous	Zephaniah 2:3
Nahum	625	Elkosh	Nahum	God's jealousy protects His people	Nahum 1:2–3
Habakkuk	625	?	Habakkuk	God calls for faithfulness	Habakkuk 2:4
Jeremiah	626–584	Anathoth/Jerusalem	2 Chronicles 36:12; Jeremiah	Faithful prophet points to new covenant	Jeremiah 31:33–34
Huldah (prophetess)	621	Jerusalem	2 Kings 22; 2 Chronicles 34	God's Book is accurate	2 Kings 22:16
Ezekiel	593–571	Babylon	Ezekiel	Future hope for new community of worship	Ezekiel 37:12–13
Joel	588 (?)	Jerusalem	Joel	Call to repent and experience God's Spirit	Joel 2:28–29
Obadiah	580	Jerusalem	Obadiah	Doom on Edom to bring God's kingdom	Obadiah 21
Haggai	520	Jerusalem	Ezra 5:1; 6:14; Haggai	The priority of God's house	Haggai 2:8–9
Zechariah	520–514	Jerusalem	Ezra 5:1; 6:14; Zechariah	Faithfulness will lead to God's universal rule	Zechariah 14:9
Malachi	433	Jerusalem	Malachi	Honor God and wait for His righteousness	Malachi 4:2

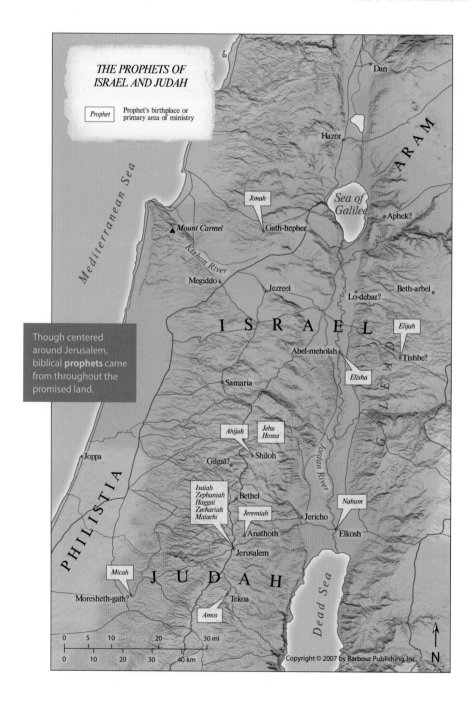

THE PROPHETS OF
ISRAEL AND JUDAH

Prophet | Prophet's birthplace or primary area of ministry

Dan

Hazor

ARAM

Mediterranean Sea

Jonah

Sea of Galilee

Aphek?

Mount Carmel

Gath-hepher

Kishon River

Megiddo

Jezreel

Lo-debar?

Beth-arbel

I S R A E L

Elijah

Abel-meholah

Tishbe?

Though centered around Jerusalem, biblical **prophets** came from throughout the promised land.

Samaria

Elisha

G I L E A D

Ahijah | Jehu Hosea

Gilgal?

Shiloh

Jordan River

Joppa

PHILISTIA

Isaiah Zephaniah Haggai Zechariah Malachi

Bethel

Jeremiah

Nahum

Jericho

Anathoth

Elkosh

Jerusalem

Micah

J U D A H

Dead Sea

Moresheth-gath?

Tekoa

Amos

| 0 | 5 | 10 | 20 | 30 mi |
| 0 | 10 | 20 | 30 | 40 km |

Copyright © 2007 by Barbour Publishing, Inc.

N

■ **PROPITIATION** (pro PISH ee ay shun). Covering, atonement (1 John 2:2). In general, sacrifice that appeases a god. In Christianity, propitiation is Christ's sacrificial death on the cross that makes divine forgiveness possible (1 John 4:10). Propitiation is God's mercy and grace in action to put us in a right relationship with Him.

▲ *Some newer translations, such as the NIV and NRSV, have replaced the term propitiation with the phrase "atoning sacrifice."*

PROSELYTE. A person converted from one religion to another religion (Matthew 23:15).

PROSTITUTE. Verb: Defile or profane (verb; Leviticus 19:29). Noun: Person who performed sexual acts for personal reward. Some religions used acts with prostitutes in their worship. Hosea's wife, Gomer, was a prostitute (Hosea 1); God told Hosea to marry an adulterous woman to symbolize Israel's unfaithfulness to the Lord. Prostitution is forbidden in God's law; it has no place in the worship of the Lord; and the act itself is personally defiling.

PROVE. To try or test (Psalm 17:3; Luke 14:19).

PROVENDER. Animal food made from grains and grasses (Judges 19:21).

Cattle enjoying **provender**.

PROVERB. A short, pithy statement of truth (Proverbs 1:1). Sometimes means an obscure saying or a parable.

▲ *"Proverbial truth" is the rule; any exceptions that occur do not nullify the truth of the rule. Though the Bible says, "Train up a child in the way he should go: and when he is old, he will not depart from it" (Proverbs 22:6), honest observers admit that some children will take a furlough from their good upbringing—and some may not return. Still, the teaching is proverbially true—God's way is the best way to rear a child.*

PROVERBS, BOOK OF. Old Testament book that is a collection of practical truths about wisdom, moral values, and relationships.

▲ *The book of Proverbs is full of useful information on such topics as friendship, family, temptations, and anger. Proverbs 31:10–31 describes a godly woman.*

PROVIDENCE. Provision (Acts 24:2). The theme of God's providence runs throughout the Bible. God is seen not only as the Creator but as the one who plans for, cares for, and guides His creation. He knows the needs of His creation and provides for those needs.

● *When God's providence doesn't seem to match our reality, we are to follow Job's example and press on with a faith that trusts God "though he slay me" (Job 13:15).*

PROVINCE. A political area or district (1 Kings 20:14; Acts 23:34). These areas were ruled by kings, emperors, senators, or procurators.

PROVOCATION. A reason that moves someone to anger (1 Kings 15:30; Hebrews 3:8).

PRUDENT. Intelligent, wise (Proverbs 18:15; Matthew 11:25).

King David the **psalm** writer, in a
stained glass window from England.

PSALM. Generally, a song of praise (1 Chronicles 16:9; Colossians 3:16). But not every psalm in the book of Psalms is a praise song. Among other kinds of psalms, some are called "imprecatory" and contain curses. See **PSALMS, BOOK OF**.

PSALMS, BOOK OF. Old Testament book of poems that were sung. Psalms is the longest book in the Bible and is located approximately in the middle of the Bible. Psalms includes shortest chapter (Psalm 117) and the longest chapter (Psalm 119) in the Bible. David and others are credited with writing the psalms. The 150 psalms were and still are used in Hebrew and Christian worship.

▲ *Not every psalm is a song of praise. The style of poems varies considerably and includes what are known as "imprecatory" psalms—in which the psalm writer calls on God to curse his enemies. Other psalms are confessional in nature, such as David's plea for forgiveness in Psalm 51.*

PUBLICAN. A tax collector who worked for the Roman government (Matthew 9:10). A publican usually collected more taxes than he had to so he could use the extra money for himself. Publicans were despised for their cheating and for serving the Roman government.

● *Can you recall a time in Jesus' ministry when He went to eat with a tax collector? What happened? (See Luke 19:1–10 if you need a reminder.) This event speaks to our own witness.*

PUBLISH. Say, tell, cause to hear, proclaim (Nehemiah 8:15; Mark 1:45).

PUFFED UP. Proud, arrogant, boastful (1 Corinthians 4:6).

PULPIT. Raised platform for a speaker to stand on (Nehemiah 8:4).

PURE. Clean, undefiled (Psalm 24:4; Matthew 5:8).

PURGE. Cleanse, purify (Ezekiel 20:38; Hebrews 9:14).

PURIFICATION. Cleansing (2 Chronicles 30:19; Luke 2:22). In the Bible, ceremonial purification was an important element in worship. The Levites had to purify themselves for service. Individuals had to go through the ritual of purification after contact with a corpse, after menstruation or any other bloody discharge, after childbirth, and after the cure for leprosy. The ritual required a cleansing agent (water, blood, or fire) and a sacrifice (Numbers 31:23). Though Jesus once cleansed ten lepers and instructed them to observe the Law's ceremonial cleansing, the New Testament puts more emphasis on personal purity than on ceremonial purity (1 Peter 1:22).

PURIFY. Make clean (Numbers 19:12; James 4:8).

PURIM (PYOO rim). Feast or festival commemorating the efforts of Queen Esther to bring about the deliverance of the Jewish people from death (see the book of Esther). It's a happy celebration held in the month of March, and is also called the Feast of Lots since *purim* is the Hebrew word for lots. The word *purim* itself does not appear in the KJV. See **FEAST CHART** on page 96 and **DATE CHART** on pages 265–266.

PURPLE. A color that signified wealth or royalty (Judges 8:26; Act 16:14).

QUAIL. A spotted, brown migratory bird (Exodus 16:13). God provided quail for the Israelites to eat in the wilderness.

QUAKE. Tremble (Exodus 19:18; Matthew 27:51); shake with fear (Hebrews 12:21).

QUARRIES. Generally, places where stones for building were gotten, but in the KJV the term also refers to idols or carved stones (Judges 3:19, 26).

QUARTER. A fourth part; a corner, side, extreme end or place (Jeremiah 49:36; Acts 28:7).

QUARTERNION. A company of four soldiers to keep guard (see John 19:23). Acts 12:4 says Herod assigned four quarternions—a total of sixteen soldiers—to guard Peter.

QUENCH. Extinguish, put out (2 Samuel 21:17; Matthew 12:20). The apostle Paul, in 1 Thessalonians 5:19, tells believers not to quench the Holy Spirit. When the Spirit acts, it is wrong to suppress, subdue, or quench His spiritual fire; rather, the response should be, "Yes!"

QUICK, QUICKEN. In the KJV, *quick* means "alive" (Numbers 16:30; Acts 10:42). To "quicken" is to make alive (Psalm 71:20; John 5:21; Ephe-sians 2:1–10). Ephesians 2:1, 5 refers to those who were spiritually dead being quickened—made alive in Christ eternally.

QUIRINIUS (kwi RIN ih uhs). Governor of Syria (Luke 2:2 NIV). In the KJV, the name is spelled Cyrenius (sigh REE nih uhs, KJV).

QUIT. In KJV usage, *quit* often has meanings different from today's meanings. It can be a verb meaning "acquit," as in 1 Samuel 4:9 and 1 Corinthians 16:13, where the reflexive form of the word (acting upon oneself) urges readers to "act like men." In other cases, *quit* may carry the meaning of released from penalty (Exodus 21:28). In yet another context, it carries the meaning of being absolved (Joshua 2:20).

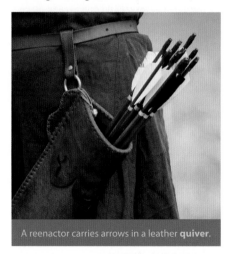

A reenactor carries arrows in a leather **quiver**.

QUIVER. Verb: Tremble (Habakkuk 3:16). Noun: A case for carrying arrows (Lamentations 3:13). The noun is used figuratively in Psalm 127:4–5: "As arrows are in the hand of a mighty man; so are children of the youth. Happy is the man that hath his quiver full of them."

RAAMSES (ray-AM-seeze). Alternate form of Rameses (RAM-uh-seez) (Exodus 1:11). Alternate spellings within the KJV itself. An Egyptian store city built by the Hebrews. See **RAMESES**.

RABBI, RABBONI (RAB igh; ra BOH nigh). Teacher, master (John 1:38; 20:16).
▲ *Rabbi is a shortened form of Rabboni— both of which were Aramaic for "teacher" or "master."*

RACA. Empty, worthless, ignorant, fool (Matthew 5:22).
▲ *"Raca" is an Aramaic term of contempt or abuse.*

RACHEL (RAY chuhl). Younger daughter of Laban, favorite wife of Jacob (Genesis 29:6). Jacob was tricked into marrying Rachel's older sister, Leah, before he could marry Rachel. Rachel remained childless for many years but finally gave birth to Joseph and Benjamin. She died at Benjamin's birth.

RAHAB (RAY hab). 1. Prostitute of Jericho who hid two Hebrew spies and provided escape for them (Joshua 2:1–7). Later she and her family were spared when the city was destroyed. She is cited as an example of faith, courage, and hospitality in Hebrews 11:31 and James

2:25. Rahab was the mother of Boaz and great-grandmother of King David, and is cited in the lineage of Jesus (Matthew 1:5). 2. Poetic name for Egypt (Psalm 87:4; Isaiah 30:7; 51:9 NRSV). 3. Poetic name for primeval sea monster representing forces God overcame in creation (Job 9:13; 26:12; Psalm 89:10).

Rahab delays the king's soldiers, allowing two Jewish spies to escape to her roof and hide under stalks of flax.

RAIL. Insult, mock, jeer, deride, verbally abuse (Mark 15:29).

RAIMENT. Clothing (Genesis 24:53; Matthew 3:4).

RAINBOW. Symbol of God's covenant with Noah to never again destroy the earth with a flood (Genesis 9:8–17). The rainbow is mentioned in John's vision (Revelation 4:3; 10:1).

RAM. 1. Male goat; used frequently in animal sacrifices (Genesis 15:9). 2. A battering ram was a weapon made of a wooden shaft with metal ends. It was rolled on wheels and used to break down gates or walls (Ezekiel 4:2).

RAMA, RAMAH (RAY mah). 1. City of Benjamin on the frontier between Israel and Judah (Joshua 18:25; Matthew 2:18). 2. City in Ephraim that was the birthplace of Samuel (1 Samuel 1:19). 3. Same as Ramoth-Gilead, important city east of the Jordan River. King Ahab received his fatal wound here (2 Chronicles 22:6).

RAMESES (RAM uh seez). Prosperous Egyptian seaport city (Genesis 47:11). Also, the name of a line of Pharaohs but not mentioned in the Bible. Ramses II may have been the pharaoh of the Exodus. See **RAAMSES**.

Statue of **Rameses** the Great at the Great Temple of Abu Simbel, near the border of Egypt and the Sudan.

RAMPART. Fortification wall, usually made of earth (Lamentations 2:8).

RANK. 1. Healthy and full (Genesis 41:5, 7). 2. Line, arrangement, row (Joel 2:7; Mark 6:40).

RANSOM. Covering, the price paid for recovery of a person or thing (Exodus 21:30; 30:12; Matthew 20:28).

● *Jesus gave His life as a ransom for our sins (Matthew 20:28; Mark 10:45; 1 Timothy 2:5–6; Titus 2:14). His sacrifice on our behalf provides the gift of saving grace but calls for our sacrifice in return (Luke 9:23).*

■ **RAPTURE**. May mean either ecstasy or to snatch (be caught up) from one place and put in another. The Christian rapture refers to the second of these meanings. Jesus will come again with those who have died in Christ and join them in the air with those Christians who are still alive (see 1 Thessalonians 4:17). The word *rapture* does not appear in the KJV Bible, but the concept does (Mark 13:26–27; 1 Thessalonians 4:15–17).

● Rapture *came from the Latin for "caught up." Scholars' views differ widely on the rapture and the interpretation of the Bible passages related to it. But the Bible's assurance of Christ's return is enough even if we are uncertain about details of how and when it will all happen. It is not within the scope of this dictionary to try to identify and explain the various views of premillennialism and dispensationalism involved in the varying views of the rapture.*

RASH. Impulsive, reckless, acting hastily (Ecclesiastes 5:2; Acts 19:36).

RAVENING, RAVENOUS. Devouring with greed (Isaiah 35:9; Matthew 7:15).

RAVISH. Rape (Lamentations 5:11; Isaiah 13:16). May also be used to refer to passion (Proverbs 5:19–20; Song of Solomon 4:9).

REALM. Kingdom (2 Chronicles 20:30; Daniel 9:1).

REAP. To gather in a harvest (Leviticus 19:9). Figuratively, the consequence of what one sows—whether good or bad (Galatians 6:7–9).

Asian farmers **reap** rice by hand, not unlike biblical farmers would have reaped their crops.

REAR. In Bible usage, to raise or lift (Exodus 26:30; John 2:20).

REBEKAH, **REBECCA** (ruh BEK uh). Sister of Laban, beautiful wife of Isaac, and mother of Jacob and Esau (Genesis 24:29; Romans 9:10). Rebekah significantly affected historical events by favoring Jacob over his twin brother, Esau. She helped Jacob deceive Isaac so that Esau missed the elder son's special blessing from his father. Then Rebekah helped Jacob escape Esau's wrath.

▲ *Jacob obtained Esau's "birthright" on his own by trading the hungry Esau a bowl of soup for his inheritance (see Genesis 25:29–34). But the theft of Esau's blessing (that was supposed to be bestowed upon the eldest son) was a joint project between Jacob and Rebekah (see Genesis 27).*

REBUKE. Noun: Correction, reproof, strong disapproval (2 Samuel 22:16; Isaiah 25:8). In Philippians 2:15, blameless ("without rebuke"). Verb: to correct, reprove, convince, convict, chide, or bring weight to bear upon (Matthew 8:26; 2 Timothy 4:2).

RECHAB (REE kab), **RECHABITE** (REE kab ight). 1. A Benjaminite who, with his brother, murdered Ishbosheth, Saul's son (2 Samuel 4:2–12). 2. Father of Jehonadab (Jonadab). His descendants became the Rechabites, who lived a nomadic life (2 Kings 10:15). 3. Two other persons had the same name (1 Chronicles 2:55; Nehemiah 3:14).

RECKON. Count, take into account, number, credit, consider, settle accounts with (Leviticus 25:50; Luke 22:37; Romans 4:4, 9–10; Matthew 25:19 NASB, NIV, NRSV).

RECOMPENSE. Give or pay back, give in return, reward (Ruth 2:12; Luke 14:14; Hebrews 10:30).

■ **RECONCILE**, **RECONCILIATION**. Cover or make atonement (Leviticus 6:30; 16:20); restore relationship (2 Corinthians 5:18–20). Christ's death provided for the removal of the barrier of sin to bring people back into a right relationship with God. Renew friendship (Acts 12:22; 1 Corinthians 7:11). Form a unity (Colossians 1:20).

● *In addition to reconciling us to Himself, God has given us the ministry of reconciliation. How can you fulfill this ministry? Note that reconciliation in the New Testament always refers to the restoration of a broken or interrupted relationship.*

RECORD. Testimony or witness (Job 16:19; John 1:19).

▲ *The Greek word for witness is "martyr."*

RECOUNT. Call, summon (Nahum 2:5).

RED SEA. Body of water between Arabia and northeastern Africa (Exodus 10:19; Acts 7:36). The Red Sea has two arms at its northern end: the Gulf of Suez and the Gulf of Aqaba. Although the exact location of the crossing is not known, God miraculously created an escape route across the Red Sea for the Israelites when they were pursued by the Egyptians (Exodus 14).

▲ *"Reed Sea" is often given as a literal rendering of the Hebrew term the KJV translates "Red Sea."*

A view of Egypt over waters of the **Red Sea**.

■ **REDEEM**. To buy back; to free or pay a price for (1 Chronicles 17:21; Galatians 3:13). Christ's death paid for our sins and frees us from the bondage of sin upon our commitment to Him as Lord and Savior. He is our Redeemer.

Reeds at the water's edge.

■ **REDEMPTION**. Release that occurs when a price is paid (Leviticus 25:51–52; Numbers 3:49; Hebrews 9:12). Jesus paid the price for our release from sin (Romans 3:24; Ephesians 1:7).

▲ *In referring to salvation, redemption includes both the deliverance from and the price paid for our sins—namely, Jesus' death on the cross in exchange for our freedom. But the redemption of the cross is not automatic; each person must receive God's grace by owning up to his or her sin, repenting of it, and making a faith commitment to Jesus Christ as Lord and Savior.*

REDOUND. Increase, abound, overflow, be supremely great (2 Corinthians 4:15).

REED. Several different types of stalk or cane plants that grow in shallow water (Isaiah 19:6; Matthew 27:30). The stems of the plants were used in basket-making and in making paper.

REEL. Stagger like a drunk (Psalm 107:27; Isaiah 24:20).

REFINE. Purify (Isaiah 48:10; Malachi 3:2–3).

REFRAIN. 1. Shun, give up, abstain from, restrain, hold back, check, curb (Job 29:9); 2. Restrain, bridle, check, or keep back (Job 7:11; 1 Peter 3:10). 3. Keep away from (Acts 5:38).

▲ *Contemporary translations use* refrain *in the sense of abstaining or keeping oneself from doing something.*

REFUGE. Shelter or place of protection, safety zone (Psalm 46:1).

REFUGE, CITY OF. City designated by Hebrew law that provided safety for a person who had accidentally killed someone. This protected zone kept the victim's family from seeking revenge (Exodus 21:13; Numbers 35:9–34). There were six cities of refuge, three on each side of the Jordan River (Numbers 35:14).

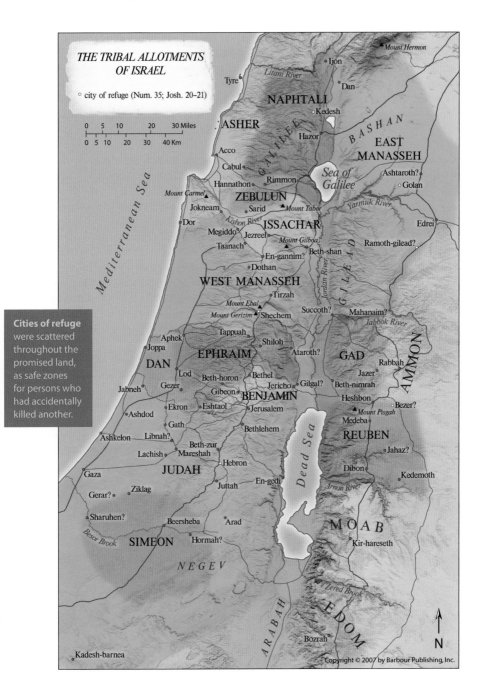

THE TRIBAL ALLOTMENTS OF ISRAEL

○ city of refuge (Num. 35; Josh. 20–21)

0   5   10   20   30 Miles
0 5 10   20   30   40 Km

Cities of refuge were scattered throughout the promised land, as safe zones for persons who had accidentally killed another.

Mount Hermon

Ijon

Tyre
Litani River
Dan

NAPHTALI
Kedesh

ASHER
Hazor

BASHAN

Acco

EAST MANASSEH

Cabul
Hannathon
Rimmon
Sea of Galilee
Ashtaroth?
Golan

GALILEE

Mount Carmel
ZEBULUN
Jokneam   Sarid   Mount Tabor
Dor
Kishon River
ISSACHAR
Megiddo   Jezreel
Taanach
Mount Gilboa
En-gannim?   Beth-shan
Dothan

Yarmuk River

Edrei

GILEAD
Ramoth-gilead?

WEST MANASSEH
Tirzah
Mount Ebal
Mount Gerizim   Shechem
Succoth?   Mahanaim?

Jabbok River

Jordan River

Tappuah
Shiloh
Aphek
Joppa
EPHRAIM
Ataroth?
GAD

AMMON

DAN
Lod
Beth-horon   Bethel
Jabneh
Gezer
Gibeon
Jericho   Gilgal?
Rabbah
Jazer
Beth-nimrah

Ekron   Eshtaol
BENJAMIN
Jerusalem
Heshbon
Bezer?
Ashdod
Gath
Bethlehem
Mount Pisgah
Medeba

Ashkelon
Libnah?
Beth-zur
Mareshah
Lachish
Hebron
REUBEN
Jahaz?

Dead Sea

Gaza
JUDAH
Juttah
En-gedi
Dibon
Kedemoth

Gerar?
Ziklag
Arnon River

Sharuhen?

Beersheba   Arad
SIMEON   Hormah?

MOAB
Kir-hareseth

Besor Brook

NEGEV

Zered Brook

ARABAH

EDOM

Bozrah

N↑

Kadesh-barnea

REGENERATION. To be born again, a new creation (Matthew 19:28; Titus 3:5).

▲ Spiritually speaking, this term describes what happens when a person becomes a Christian (John 1:13; 3:3; 1 Peter 1:23; 2 Corinthians 5:17). Everyone has a first, physical birth, then chooses to sin and becomes spiritually dead. But each person also has the opportunity to be made spiritually alive—to be regenerated, or born again—by turning from sin and to Jesus in trust (Ephesians 2:1–10).

● Evaluate your spiritual condition: Born? Dead? Born again? The Bible teaches that the answer to the first two questions is yes for everyone (Romans 3:23). But you have to own up to your sin, turn from it, and turn to Christ in repentance and faith to be able to answer yes to the last question. What is your answer? If it is anything besides yes, read the scriptures listed, accept Christ, and change the no, maybe, or "I hope so" to yes!

REGISTER. Written record (Ezra 2:62).

REHOBOAM (ree hoh BOH uhm). Son of King Solomon and successor to the throne (1 Kings 11:43; Matthew 1:7 NIV). Because of the heavy tax burden under Rehoboam, the ten northern tribes revolted, dividing the kingdom. Rehoboam was left with the two southern tribes of Judah and Benjamin. The divided kingdom became Israel (ten northern tribes) and Judah (two southern tribes). See **KING CHART** on pages 152–155.

REIGN. Rule, act as a king (Genesis 36:31; Matthew 2:22).

REJOICE. Be glad or happy, exult, sing, leap, enjoy (1 Chronicles 16:31; Psalm 2:11; Isaiah 61:10; John 14:28; Philippians 3:1; Revelation 19:7).

▲ The Bible contains hundreds of references to "rejoicing," "joy," or their equivalents. The book of Philippians by itself, in only four chapters, has nineteen references to joy or rejoicing.

RELIEF. Provision, aid, contribution, support (Acts 11:29).

RELIGION, RELIGIOUS. Belief in and worship of God or gods (James 1:26–27). A person whose religion is genuine will show through attitude and actions his depth of commitment to the one worshiped.

▲ "Religion" for true Christians is a saving relationship with God and the living out of His will. No other religion—no other worship of anyone or anything besides God in Christ—provides salvation. The risen Christ shows the uniqueness of Christianity and the promise of our own resurrection.

REMISSION. Pardon, forgiveness, canceling, release, liberation from (Matthew 26:28; Acts 2:38; 10:43; Hebrews 9:22).

▲ Though Christians may sin again and need to repent and be forgiven for that sin, there is only one remission of salvation from sin to eternal life. This saving remission from sin forever protects the Christian from eternal spiritual death (see 1 John 1:8–9; 3:6–9).

REMNANT. That which is left or remaining (Leviticus 2:3; Matthew 22:6). In the Bible, remnant especially refers to those who survived a political or military situation (2 Kings 25:11). Spiritually, remnant also means those who repent and survive God's judgment. This usage is interpreted in different ways: Some feel it applies to those who returned from the physical Babylonian captivity, while others believe the remnant refers to future generations. Some feel the remnant will be made up of Jewish people, while others interpret it to be a new community of people who trust in Christ, the Messiah (Romans 9–11).

REND, **RENT**. Tear, rip, split (Genesis 37:29; Mark 15:38). The rending of garments was often a symbol for mourning or repentance.

RENDER. Repay or give back (Job 33:26; Matthew 22:21).

RENOWN. Fame (Ezekiel 16:14).

■ **REPENT**. 1. To feel sorrow or regret, or to change one's mind about something. This kind of repentance is even ascribed to God on occasion (Genesis 6:6–9). Some theologians or Bible students struggle to explain how the omniscient God eternally knows everything ahead of time and yet is sometimes spoken of as "repenting" of some intent, plan, or occurrence. Two things stand out in any repentance ascribed to God: (1) Man has chosen to do something other than what God has desired and designed him to do; and (2) God's grace

Caiaphas is shown **rending** his clothing—an ancient sign of horror or grief—at Jesus' supposed blasphemy, identifying Himself with God.

never ends. So, for example, during the Flood the wicked world perished, but Noah found grace. When King Saul, however, moved too far from God's will, there was a reckoning: 1 Samuel 15:29 NRSV reads, "Moreover the Glory of Israel will not recant or change his mind; for he is not a mortal, that he should change his mind" (1 Samuel 15:29). However these references are understood, God's repentance is different from man's. While God's nature and being don't change, He may be grieved.

2. Man's repentance may refer either to mere regret and sorrow or to a godly reaction leading to a changed mind and heart (see Exodus 13:17; Matthew 3:2; 27:3–5; Acts 2:38; 3:19). Judas Iscariot repented in the sense that he was bitterly sorrowful for betraying Jesus, but his repentance lacked the mind- and heart-change from sin to the trust of Christ as Lord and Savior. (Judas ended up killing himself.) Godly repentance, on the other hand, leads to a changed life here and eternal life in heaven. It is the first step to becoming a Christian, the way by which we recognize that life without God is wrong, we feel sorrow for the pain caused by our godless life, and we repent—literally change our minds—to God's way of living. See **BORN AGAIN, REGENERATION.**

REPENTANCE. A godly grief that changes mind, heart, and life through trust in Christ (Jeremiah 26:3; 2 Corinthians 7:8–10). *Repent* sometimes indicates only regret or change of mind (Matthew 27:3); when God is spoken of as repenting, it indicates either regret over mankind's sin or a change of intent when mankind himself has repented and turned to God (as the city of Nineveh did in being spared after Jonah prophesied). See also 1 Samuel 15:11, 29, 35. See **REGENERATION.**

REPHIDIM (REF ih dim). Location where the Hebrews camped during their wilderness wanderings (Exodus 17:1). When the people complained to Moses about their thirst, God instructed Moses to strike a rock to produce water (Exodus 17:1–7).

▲ *An interesting parallel to this story appears in Numbers 20:1–12, where Moses was told to speak to a rock to bring forth water. Moses, however, struck the rock as before. This act of disobedience to God, though it still produced water for the people, led God to state that Moses and Aaron would not enter the promised land.*

REPORT. A record of something seen, heard, or done. Besides these usual meanings, *report* may means testimony, witness, or reputation (Isaiah 53:1; Acts 6:3; 22:12).

REPROACH. Insult, disgrace (Genesis 30:23; Romans 15:3).

REPROBATE. Disapproved; rejected because of lack of worth or being impure; not meeting the standard (Jeremiah 6:30; 2 Corinthians 13:5).

REPROOF. Rebuke, correction (Proverbs 1:23; 2 Timothy 3:16).

REPROVE. Rebuke, convict (Proverbs 9:8; John 16:8).

REQUITE. Repay (1 Samuel 25:21; 1 Timothy 5:4).

RESIDUE. The rest; what's left over (Exodus 10:15; Act 15:17).

RESIST. Oppose, stand against (Zechariah 3:1; Matthew 5:39).

RESOLVED. Have come to know (Luke 16:4).

RESORT. Come to, come together (Psalm 71:3; Mark 10:1).

RESPECT. Accept people by their appearance (2 Chronicles 19:7; Romans 2:11).

▲ *"Face-receiver" is a literal translation of a Greek word for respect. God looks on the heart of man rather than the outward appearance, and He wants us to do the same (1 Samuel 16:7).*

RESPITE. Relief, rest (Exodus 8:15).

RESTITUTION. Restoration; something given back (Job 20:18; Acts 3:21).

RESTORE. Return (Genesis 20:7; Luke 19:8).

■ **RESURRECTION**. Raising to life after death (Matthew 22:23). God's raising of the dead in Christ to eternal life (Romans 6:4–9). Because God raised Jesus from death, He will also raise Christians to eternal life (John 11:25; Romans 6:5). Christ's resurrection is a foundation of the Christian faith and the first fruits of it (1 Corinthians 15:12–21).

▲ *All people will experience a resurrection: Christians to life, non-Christians to condemnation (John 5:29; Acts 24:15). The resurrection gives Christians power and hope (Philippians 3:10). The nature and existence of the resurrection life should encourage believers (2 Corinthians 4:14–5:10).*

REUBEN (RHOO ben), **REUBENITES** (RHOO ben ight). Oldest son of Jacob and Leah (Genesis 29:32). Reuben talked his brothers out of murdering their younger brother, Joseph (Genesis 37:21–22). Reubenites were descendants of Reuben, one of the twelve tribes. They lived east of the Jordan.

■ **REVELATION**. Uncovering, revealing that which is hidden (Romans 16:25). The Bible tells how God revealed Himself to people through

On **resurrection** morning, an angel tells women looking for Jesus' body, "He is not here: for he is risen" (Matthew 28:6).

nature, history, His actions, and supremely through His Son, Jesus (Galatians 1:12; Revelation 1:1).

REVELATION, BOOK OF. Last book in the New Testament. Traditionally, the apostle John is credited with writing this book of prophecy. John recorded his vision from God while he was a prisoner exiled to the island of Patmos. The book includes two chapters of commendation, condemnation, and commands to seven churches in Asia Minor that John knew well. Revelation then contains much vivid

A fifteenth-century depiction of John on Patmos, receiving the **Revelation** of Jesus Christ.

symbolism as God encourages the faithfulness of Christians and warns of the destruction of evil and the unfaithful.

▲ *Revelation is spoken of as "apocalyptic" writing. The word* apocalypse *means "revealing" or "unveiling." Though much of the language and imagery may be difficult for us to interpret, the truth of the book itself is certain: God is supreme and eternally victorious, and will overcome Satan and all evil to deliver His own (see Revelation 21–22).*

REVERENCE. Fear, bow down, respect, honor, hold in awe (Leviticus 19:30; Matthew 21:37).

REVILE. Speak with insult or despising (Exodus 22:28; John 9:28).

REVIVE. Come to life, live again (Nehemiah 4:2; Romans 14:9).

REVOLT. Rebel (2 Kings 8:20).

REWARD. Something given for good (Numbers 18:31; Matthew 5:12) or bad actions (2 Peter 2:13).

● *Standing up for right has both hardships and rewards. How does focusing on the good reward help? Consider Matthew 25:14–30 for both stewardship of life and results from it.*

REZIN (REE zin). King of Syria who fought against Judean king Ahaz (2 Kings 15:37). He was killed by Tiglath-pileser.

RHODA (ROH duh). A young girl at the home of John Mark's mother (Acts 12:13–17). Rhoda, either a servant or guest in the home, was sent to answer the door. She was so overcome with joy at seeing the previously imprisoned Peter outside that she left the door closed and went to tell the others.

RHODES (ROHDZ). An island in the Mediterranean Sea where Paul stopped on a missionary journey (Acts 21:1).

St. Paul's Bay, on the island of **Rhodes**.

■ **RIGHTEOUS**. Right or just, right with God (Malachi 3:18). A person is made right only through God in Christ (2 Corinthians 5:21). See **JUSTIFICATION.**

■ **RIGHTEOUSNESS**. Rightness by God's standards (Isaiah 41:10; 2 Corinthians 5:21). Justice, fairness. Matching life with God's commandments, love, and purposes. Action based on love for God and a relationship with God.

RIMMON (RIM UHN). 1. City in Simeon, also En-Rimmon (Joshua 15:32; Nehemiah 11:39). 2. A rock in Benjamin (Judges 20:45). 3. Father of Baanah and Rechab, the men who killed Saul's son Ishbosheth (2 Samuel 4:2). 4. A Syrian god (2 Kings 5:18).

RITE. Statute, rule (Numbers 9:3).

RIZPAH (RIZ pah). A secondary wife (concubine) of King Saul (2 Samuel 3:7).

● *From the creation of Adam and Eve, God's ideal plan for marriage has been monogamy, a lifelong relationship between one husband and one wife. Scripture often shows that departure from monogamy caused many problems (see the stories of Abraham, Sarah, and Hagar, as well as Jacob, Rachel, and Leah in Genesis 16, 21; 29–30).*

ROBE. An outer cloak or mantle (Jonah 3:6; John 19:2). The robe or mantle was often used for a covering at night.

ROD. A straight stick, also called a staff. Used for punishment (Exodus 21:20), measurement (Revelation 11:1), and defense (Psalm 23:4). God used a rod in a miraculous way to call Moses into service (Exodus 4:2–20) and to deliver the Israelites from the Egyptians (Exodus 14:16).

ROE, ROEBUCK. A small deer (Deuteronomy 12:15).

ROMANS, BOOK OF. New Testament book written by Paul to the Christians at Rome (Acts 20:2–3; Romans 1:1; 15:25–28). Paul wrote the letter to tell of the world's need for salvation and God's provision of this salvation (Romans 3:23; 6:23). It is as close to a summary of Paul's teaching as we have. Salvation comes by God's grace through faith and is not something humans can accomplish or earn (Romans 10:9–10; see also Ephesians 2:8–10). Paul also wrote the letter to tell of his planned visit to Rome, to give guidance with some church problems, and to tell how Christians are supposed to live.

ROME. Capital of the Roman Empire and modern-day capital city of Italy (Romans 1:7). Rome was founded about 753 BC and served the Roman Empire as a powerful city. Located on seven hills beside the Tiber River, Rome was the place of two imprisonments for Paul (Acts 28; 2 Timothy 4).

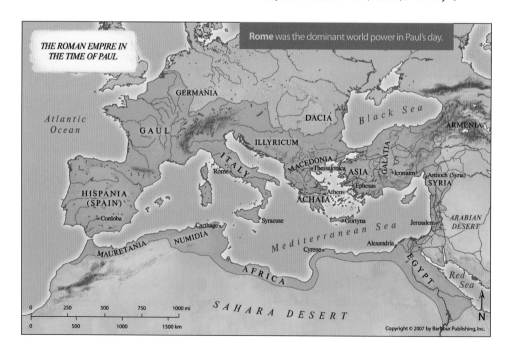

THE ROMAN EMPIRE IN THE TIME OF PAUL

Rome was the dominant world power in Paul's day.

Copyright © 2007 by Barbour Publishing, Inc.

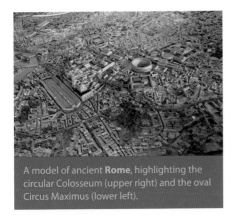

A model of ancient **Rome**, highlighting the circular Colosseum (upper right) and the oval Circus Maximus (lower left).

ROOT. Besides the usual meaning, it also symbolically means the source of a situation (1 Timothy 6:10); stability (Proverbs 12:3); prosperity (Proverbs 12:12). The Root of Jesse and the Root of David are terms used for the Messiah (Isaiah 11:10; Revelation 5:5).

RUDDY. Reddish complexion (1 Samuel 16:12).

RUSH. A tall, slender plant that grows in water; reed (Isaiah 9:14).

RUTH (ROOTH). Woman of Moab who married an Israelite (Ruth 1:4). Ruth's husband came with his family to Moab because of famine in their homeland. At his death, Ruth returned to Bethlehem with Naomi, her mother-in-law. Ruth is the great-grandmother of David and an ancestor of Jesus (Matthew 1:5).

RUTH, BOOK OF. Old Testament book that tells the story of Naomi and Elimelech, who left their homeland in Bethlehem because of famine. They settled in the land of Moab. Elimelech died, and later his two sons died. Naomi was left with her two daughters-in-law, women of Moab. When Naomi decided to return to her homeland, she released the women of any obligation to her and urged them to remain in Moab. Ruth, full of devotion for Naomi, returned with her to Bethlehem. Ruth married Boaz, a kinsman, and became an ancestor of David and Jesus. The book shows the important role a foreigner played in God's plan of salvation.

▲ *Ruth 1:16–17 poignantly shows Ruth's heartfelt commitment and love for her mother-in-law, Naomi. Though the magnificent vow of Ruth's commitment was one between a daughter-in-law and her mother-in-law, many couples today choose to incorporate these verses into their wedding ceremonies.*

SABBATH (SAB buhth). Ceasing. God finished His work of creation in six days (Genesis 2:1), then established the Sabbath by ceasing the work of creation and commanding a special day of rest (Genesis 2:1–3). To keep, observe, or remember the Sabbath means to do no work and to focus on worshiping God on the Sabbath day. God commanded the Sabbath observance (Exodus 20:8–11). Jesus practiced it and taught others about it (Luke 4:16; Mark 2:23–28). Joy and blessings come from observing the Sabbath (Isaiah 58:13–14).

In the Jewish calendar, the Sabbath is the seventh day of the week (Saturday). However, under Mosaic Law, other days might also be set aside and referred to as a Sabbath of rest and worship (see Leviticus 16:30–31).

Christians observe this special day of rest on Sunday because of the resurrection of Jesus on that day and because early Christians worshiped and gathered offerings on Sunday (Matthew 28:1, 6; 1 Corinthians 16:1–2). Nowadays, Christians generally speak of Sunday and the Sabbath interchangeably.

▲ The Pharisees interpreted "no work" too strictly, adding burdens that God never intended (Matthew 12:2; Luke 6:7). They missed the intention of the Sabbath (John 9:16), believing that following rules was more important than caring about people. Jesus emphasized that the Sabbath was made for people, not people for the Sabbath (Mark 2:27).

● While the Pharisees were too strict about the Sabbath, are we sometimes too lenient? Identify ways in which we fail to observe the Sabbath as God intended, setting aside one day a week for rest and worship. Without being legalistic, consider ways to improve your observance of the Sabbath to honor and please God.

SACKCLOTH. Rough clothing worn as a sign of grief for the dead, repentance over personal sin, or sorrow over disaster or trouble (Genesis 37:34; Matthew 11:21). Sackcloth was made of goat or camel hair. It covered the middle of the body or the whole body.

■ **SACRIFICE**. Something offered to God in worship (Genesis 31:54; Mark 12:33). In the Old Testament, sacrifices expressed repentance from sin and obedience to God. There were also other offerings such as a thank offering or sacrifice. No sacrifice ever saved anyone; rather, sacrifices were symbols of repentant hearts and of thanksgiving and worship to God. Jesus Christ became our perfect, once-for-all-time sacrificial Lamb that we might receive God's gift of grace, which takes away our sin (John 1:29; 1 John 1:5–10).

Modern-day Samaritans still conduct animal **sacrifices**. This photo is from Passover 2012 on Mount Gerizim

"Sacrifice" can also indicate an individual commitment to God (Romans 12:1–2). And Luke 9:23 describes "taking up our cross" daily to follow Jesus. This kind of followship is a living sacrifice.

SACRIFICIAL SYSTEM

NAME	REFERENCE	ELEMENTS	SIGNIFICANCE
Burnt Offering	Leviticus 1; 6:8–13	Bull, ram, goat, dove, or young pigeon without blemish. (Always male animals, but species of animal varied according to individual's economic status.)	Voluntary. Signifies propitiation for sin and complete surrender, devotion, and commitment to God.
Grain Offering, also called Meal, or Tribute, Offering	Leviticus 2; 6:14–23	Flour, bread, or grain made with olive oil and salt (always unleavened); or incense.	Voluntary. Signifies thanksgiving for firstfruits.
Fellowship Offering, also called Peace Offering; includes (1) Thank Offering, (2) Vow Offering, and (3) Freewill Offering	Leviticus 3; 7:11–36	Any animal without blemish. (Species of animal varied according to individual's economic status.)	Voluntary. Symbolizes friendship with God. (1) Signifies thankfulness for a specific blessing; (2) Offers a ritual expression of a vow; and (3) Symbolizes general thankfulness (to be brought to one of three required religious services).
Sin Offering	Leviticus 4:1–5:13; 6:24–30; 12: 6–8	Male or female animal without blemish—as follows: bull for high priest and congregation; male goat for king; female goat or lamb for common person; dove or pigeon for slightly poor; tenth of an ephah of flour for the very poor.	Mandatory. Made by one who had sinned unintentionally or was unclean in order to attain purification.
Guilt Offering	Leviticus 5:14–6:7; 7: 1–6; 14:12 18	Ram or lamb without blemish.	Mandatory. Made by a person who had either deprived another of his rights or had desecrated something holy.

■ **SADDUCEES** (SAD joo see). A group of Jewish people who believed only in the books of Law, but not the Prophets and Writings. Contrary to the Pharisees, the Sadducees did not believe in angels or spirits or in a resurrection life after death (Matthew 22:23; Mark 12:18; Luke 20:27; Acts 23:8). Sadducees generally held the high priesthood as well as other ruling roles. Like the Pharisees, they opposed Jesus and His ministry.
▲ *John the Baptist denounced both the Pharisees and the Sadducees (Matthew 3:7–8). Jesus warned His disciples about both the Pharisees and the Sadducees and their teachings (Matthew 16:1–12).*

■ **SAINTS**. Holy ones—set apart (Romans 1:7; 1 Samuel 2:9). All true Christians are saints in the biblical sense of the word (Ephesians 1:12–14; 1 Peter 2:5, 9). They are not perfect people but those who have received Jesus as Lord and Savior and, therefore, have the Holy Spirit within them—which means they're saints, holy ones (Philippians 1:1; 4:21).
● *Are you a saint? Remember: The Holy Spirit lives within each Christian.*

SALEM [SAY luhm]. Abbreviated form for Jerusalem (Genesis 14:18; Psalm 76:2; Hebrews 7:1–2).

Samson defeats a lion with his bare hands—and "the Spirit of the Lord" (Judges 14:6).

■ **SALVATION**. Safety, rescue, deliverance from evil, eternal life (Isaiah 12:2; Luke 19:9–10). Salvation comes only by God's grace when a person receives Jesus Christ as Lord and Savior through faith (Acts 4:12; Titus 2:11). Salvation—with its gift of eternal life—occurs at the moment of trusting in Christ and finds completion upon the believer's death or Christ's return. See **REGENERATION**.

▲ *The word* salvation *contains within its essential meanings "rescue" and "deliverance."*

● *Do you know for sure you are saved? The Gospel of John was written that we might know Christ and believe in Him for eternal life. The Epistles of 1, 2, and 3 John were written so we might know we are saved. When you're asked if you know you are saved, there is no room for answering what you think or hope. It is essential that you know you can answer yes!*

SAMARIA (suh MER ih uh). Important ridgetop city about forty-two miles north of Jerusalem and about twenty miles east of the Mediterranean Sea (2 Kings 3:1; John 4:4). Founded as the capital city of the Northern Kingdom of Israel, it was later controlled by many nations and partly destroyed many times.

Samaria came to refer also to the region around the city of Samaria and finally came to mean the entire Northern Kingdom of Israel (1 Kings 13:32; Jeremiah 31:5). In the New Testament, Samaria was a region in central Palestine avoided by Jews (John 4:9).

SAMARITAN (suh MER ih tuhn). Originally, anyone living in Samaria. Later came to mean a race of persons formed when Jews married non-Jews. Jews intensely hated Samaritans and often refused to set foot in Samaritan territory (Luke 9:52–54; 10:25–37; 17:11–19; John 8:48). Jesus demonstrated that God loved Samaritans, just as God loved Jews (John 4:4–30).

SAMSON (SAM sun). One of the last judges of Israel. Samson was born to a barren couple of the tribe of Dan, who were Israelites under the Philistines at that time (Judges 13–16). The forthcoming birth was announced by an angel because God had plans for Samson. He became a giant of a man known both for his strength and weaknesses. The strength had come with his birth and life as a Nazirite before God; the weakness showed as he intermarried, yielded to sin after slaying Philistines, and indulged himself with Delilah (Judges 16:20–21). Not realizing that sin had caused God to depart from him and that he was now weak, Samson was defeated, blinded, and put to labor by the Philistines. In captivity, he regained his strength and spiritual perspective, praying for God to empower him one more time to judge the Philistines (Judges 16:26–31). The story is a tragedy, but God mentioned even Samson in His great line of faith heroes (Hebrews 11:32).

SAMUEL (SAM yoo el). Prophet and the last judge of Israel. His birth was an answered prayer of his parents, Elkanah and Hannah (1 Samuel 1:20). Before Samuel's birth, his mother promised to give Samuel to God. She sent two-year-old Samuel to serve under Eli the priest. While Samuel was there, the Lord called him to become a prophet/judge and lead Israel back to serve God.

Samuel warned the Israelite people not to worship other gods or to ask for a king. They asked for a king anyway, and Saul became that king. Samuel anointed Saul, and later David, as the first two kings of Israel. Samuel's life was characterized by honesty and fairness.

SAMUEL, 1, 2, BOOKS OF. Two Old Testament books of history named after Samuel the prophet. First Samuel tells about Samuel's life and death and about Saul's life and death. It documents

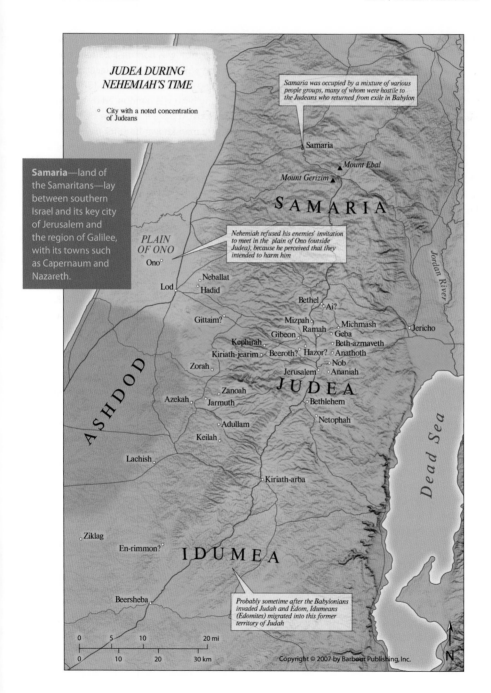

JUDEA DURING
NEHEMIAH'S TIME

○ City with a noted concentration
of Judeans

Samaria was occupied by a mixture of various
people groups, many of whom were hostile to
the Judeans who returned from exile in Babylon

Samaria—land of
the Samaritans—lay
between southern
Israel and its key city
of Jerusalem and
the region of Galilee,
with its towns such
as Capernaum and
Nazareth.

Samaria

Mount Ebal

Mount Gerizim

S A M A R I A

Jordan River

PLAIN
OF ONO
Ono

Nehemiah refused his enemies' invitation
to meet in the plain of Ono (outside
Judea), because he perceived that they
intended to harm him

Neballat
Lod   Hadid

Bethel
Ai?

Gittaim?   Mizpah   Michmash
        Ramah Geba   Jericho
Gibeon
Kephirah   Beth-azmaveth
Kiriath-jearim Beeroth? Hazor? Anathoth
Zorah   Nob
           Jerusalem Ananiah

J U D E A

Zanoah
Azekah   Jarmuth   Bethlehem

Adullam   Netophah

Keilah

Lachish

Dead Sea

Kiriath-arba

Ziklag

En-rimmon?   I D U M E A

Beersheba

Probably sometime after the Babylonians
invaded Judah and Edom, Idumeans
(Edomites) migrated into this former
territory of Judah

A S H D O D

0   5   10   20 mi
0   10   20   30 km

Copyright © 2007 by Barbour Publishing, Inc.

N

the change in Israel from rule by judges to rule by kings. It emphasizes faithfulness to God, no matter who rules. Second Samuel begins with David's anointing as king and includes most of his reign over Israel (2 Samuel 2:4; 5:3–4). The theme of both books is that faithfulness to God brings success and disobedience brings disaster (see 1 Samuel 2:30).

■ **SANCTIFICATION**. God's cleansing process to make a person whole and like Jesus (1 Corinthians 1:30). It affects both character and conduct (Colossians 3:1–17). Sanctification is part of God's will and plan that comes through His Spirit and truth (1 Thessalonians 4:3; 2 Thessalonians 2:13).

■ **SANCTIFY**. Set apart (Genesis 2:3). Dedicate as holy and for God's use (Exodus 13:2). Sanctification is a process that begins when one becomes a Christian and concludes when Jesus returns or we go to be with Him (1 Thessalonians 5:23). All Christians are sanctified at salvation, being sealed by the Holy Spirit (Ephesians 1:13; 5:26). See **SAINT**.

▲ *Though we are sanctified in the sense of having the Holy Spirit guarantee our salvation, we are never perfect or completely pure on earth. Perfection is God's command and our goal, but we will not arrive at that goal short of leaving this life or Christ returning for us (see Ephesians 4:11–16, 30; Philippians 3:12–15; 1 John 1:6–9; 3:6–9).*

SANHEDRIN. Literally, sit together (in council). The 71–member Jewish political and religious supreme court that condemned Jesus (Matthew 26:56–67 NIV; HCSB). The KJV, NASB, and NRSV translate the Greek word for Sanhedrin as *council*.

▲ *Made up of both Sadducees and Pharisees; presided over by the high priest and seemingly dominated by Sadducees. A court to uphold Jewish customs and provide justice—but which almost never gave justice in the New Testament record. Final Jewish authority in all matters of religion, legal, and government affairs so long as it didn't get into the domain of the Roman rule that dominated Palestine in the first century.*

SAPPHIRA (suh FIGH ruh). A believer who died after lying to the Holy Spirit and Peter about the selling price received for a possession. She deceptively kept back part of the actual price, with the knowledge of her husband, Ananias, who died also (Acts 5:1–11). See **ANANIAS**.

■ **SATAN** (SAY tuhn). The devil, the evil one, the enemy (Matthew 4:10). Satan directly opposes God and hinders God's purposes (Zechariah 3:1; Acts 26:18). He slanders God and His people (Job 1:6–12). He wants to control people and destroy them and their devotion to God (John 10:10). Satan works through temptation, deception, and other subtle devices to take away the good God has given (Mark 4:15; 2 Corinthians 11:14; 2 Thessalonians 2:9; Revelation 12:9). His power will one day be taken away, and he will be thrown in hell, where he will be forever (Revelation 20:2). According to Revelation 20:2, the devil and Satan are the same.

● *Which of Satan's temptations are most difficult for you to overcome? How might you avoid those circumstances?*

SAUL (SAWL). Name meaning "asked for." 1. The first king of Israel (1 Samuel 9:15–17). Samuel anointed Saul as king as God had instructed him to. It was not God's original plan for Israel, but He gave the people what they wanted (see 1 Samuel 8). Saul was tall, handsome, and initially a good leader. He won several victories over Israel's enemies but later disobeyed God's commands (1 Samuel 15:11). Saul showed

Israel's first king, **Saul**, is soothed by the harp music of young David, who in time will become Israel's second and greatest king.

himself unworthy to be a leader, displayed jealousy toward David and anger toward his son Jonathan. He and his sons died in a battle against the Philistines (1 Samuel 31). David then became king (2 Samuel 2:4). 2. The Jewish name of the great Christian leader Paul (Acts 13:9). See **PAUL**.

SAVE, SAVED. To rescue, bring to safety, deliver, preserve—both in a general sense and specifically from the judgment of sin (Psalm 18:3; Matthew 18:11; Luke 19:10; Acts 2:21). In a totally different sense, save in the KJV Bible can mean "except." For example, Matthew 11:27 says, "neither knoweth any man the Father, save the Son."

▲ *Ephesians 2:8, which reads "For by grace are ye saved through faith" (KJV), might be translated, "For by grace have you been saved through faith." In Greek, the perfect tense is used. The point is this great truth: We are saved at a point in the past; the salvation continues into the present; and it will continue eternally.*

■ **SAVIOR** (SAY vihawr). Deliverer, one who saves (2 Samuel 22:3; John 4:42). In the Old Testament the word primarily refers to God but is also used of people (Nehemiah 9:27). In the New Testament the word primarily refers to Jesus Christ as God the Son, but also at times to God the Father (Luke 1:47).

▲ *The verb* save *is used much more often than the noun* Savior. *Jesus Christ is both Lord and Savior, but the term* Savior *appears relatively few times in the New Testament compared to the word* Lord. *See Romans 10:9–10 for the apostle Paul's perspective on the two terms: confession of Jesus' lordship leads to salvation.*

SCAPEGOAT. A goat that symbolically bore the sins of God's people (Leviticus 16:20–28). On the Day of Atonement, the priest symbolically transferred the sins of the people to the goat and drove it into the wilderness. A second goat was killed, its blood shed on the Day of Atonement. The two goats represented both blood shed for sin and removal of sin.

▲ Literally, scapegoat *meant the goat that escaped. The term came into English in 1530. In William Tyndale's Bible translation, he chose to express what he believed to be the literal meaning of Hebrew* azazel *(Leviticus 16:8, 10, 26). The Hebrew word is actually a proper name whose meaning is uncertain. The NRSV and some other modern translations use* Azazel *in the text instead of* scapegoat.

▲ Jesus fulfilled the role of both goats of Leviticus, in having His blood shed and removing our sins from us.

Two Nubian ibexes in the Israeli desert, reminiscent of the sacrificial goat and the **scapegoat** described in Leviticus 16.

SCROLL. A book made of flattened papyrus plant or animal skins rolled around sticks at both ends (Revelation 6:14). Also called a roll or book (Luke 4:17).

■ **SECURITY OF THE BELIEVER**. Biblical teaching that those who are saved will continue to be saved. Though the phrase does not occur in the Bible, the concept appears in such references as Romans 8:38–39 and Philippians 1:6. Security of the believer is based on God's effort, not human effort.

● *The Bible consistently teaches that those who are saved and secure are those who persevere in God's grace through faith. Security of the believer is not an excuse for disobeying God. Rather, the doctrine reflects on the new creation in Christ that lives and abides in His grace and seeks to please Him (see Romans 6:1–4).*

SEER. Literally, one who can see; a synonym for a prophet (see 1 Samuel 9:9; 1 Chronicles 29:29). God's prophets were able to see the present and future as God revealed it.

■ **SELAH** (SEE luh). A musical notation or cue for a pause or some other action (Psalm 3:2; Habakkuk 3:13).

▲ Selah *is a Hebrew term that may come from a word meaning "to lift up." But no one knows the meaning for sure. It could indicate a musical pause or a shift from a lower to a higher key.*

SEMITES (SEM ights). People of Assyria and other groups of people believed to be descendants of Noah's son Shem (sometimes spelled Sem; Genesis 5:32; Luke 3:36). Though diverse as peoples, they spoke similar languages including Hebrew, Aramaic, Arabic, Canaanite, and Moabite.

A portion of a psalms **scroll** from the famous Dead Sea Scrolls discovery.

SEPTUAGINT (SEP too uh JENT). A Greek translation of the Hebrew Old Testament made before the time of Jesus Christ. The Roman numeral LXX (seventy) refers to the Septuagint; many scholars believe there were originally seventy translators (or possibly seventy-two) of the version. In English, the term *Septuagint* appeared to refer to the translators as early as 1577 and to the Old Testament Greek translation itself in 1633.

▲ *Some scholars comment that Ptolemy II of Egypt brought scholars to Alexandria, and they completed the translation in seventy-two days, but this time frame is questionable.*

SEPULCHRE. Grave, tomb, burial place (Genesis 23:6; Matthew 27:61). Sepulchres were cut out of rock, often carved in the walls of existing caves (Mark 15:46). Many bodies were buried together. After a body decayed to the bones, these remains were often moved to a hole in the back of the cave to make room for the next body. *Sepulchre* is also used to describe empty religion and inner wickedness (Matthew 23:27; Romans 3:13).

The "garden tomb" in Jerusalem, claimed by some to be the burial place of Jesus.

SERAPHIM (SER uh fim). Literally "the burning ones." Winged angels who served as messengers for God. No one knows exactly what they look like, but they have six wings (Isaiah 6:2). See **CHERUBIM**.

SERPENT. Snake, especially a poisonous one (Psalm 58:4). A symbol for Satan or evil (Genesis 3:1; Matthew 23:33), though God changed a rod into a snake and then back into a rod as confirmation of His call to Moses (Exodus 4:1–5).

■ **SERVANT**. One who serves another either by enslavement or for wages (Genesis 19:19; Romans 1:1). In the Bible, a variety of words are used for "servant." They almost always indicate a degree of inferiority, ranging from slavery to domestic help—but more often than not the former. Occasionally, "servant" was a polite form of reply, such as Samuel's "speak, LORD, for thy servant heareth" (1 Samuel 3:9).

▲ *Everyone serves someone or something—and may be enslaved to a person or habit. Choosing to be a servant or slave of Jesus, however, sets one free (Romans 6:6–7; 8:2; John 8:34). The apostle Paul referred to himself as slave and Jesus as Lord. The HCSB translates, "If I were still trying to please people, I would not be a slave of Christ" (Galatians 1:10; see also Philippians 1:1).*

■ **SEXUALITY**. Maleness or femaleness. Sexual intercourse is a good gift from God intended for marriage (Genesis 1:27–28; 2:19–25). Sexuality is more than just physical; it is also an intimate means of expressing love through the sharing of mind and heart. Sexuality, expressed through the union of marriage, honors God and is blessed by Him.

SHADRACH (SHAD rak). New name given to Hananiah, friend of Daniel. Ate healthy food with Daniel, Meshach, and Abednego, and entered the Babylonian king's fiery furnace with the latter two (Daniel 1:6, 15; 3:16–29).

Shadrach, Meshach, and Abednego are unharmed by the flames of King Nebuchadnezzar's furnace—heated seven times hotter than usual (Daniel 3:19).

SHEKEL. Unit of measure equaling about 11.5 grams or 0.4 ounce (Exodus 30:23–24).

SHEMA (SHEE mah). English writing of the first Hebrew word of Deuteronomy 6:4, meaning "hear." The Shema came to include all of Deuteronomy 6:4–9, a confession of faith in the one true God and commitment to His commandments. Jesus quoted from the Shema (Deuteronomy 6:4–9) in Mark 12:29.

THE SHEMA (DEUTERONOMY 6:4–9)

4 Hear, O Israel: The Lord our God is one Lord:
5 And thou shalt love the Lord thy God with all thine heart, and with all thy soul, and with all thy might.
6 And these words, which I command thee this day, shall be in thine heart:
7 And thou shalt teach them diligently unto thy children, and shalt talk of them when thou sittest in thine house, and when thou walkest by the way, and when thou liest down, and when thou risest up.
8 And thou shalt bind them for a sign upon thine hand, and they shall be as frontlets between thine eyes.
9 And thou shalt write them upon the posts of thy house, and on thy gates.

The **Shema** (Deuteronomy 6:4) is inside the *mezuzah* attached to doorposts of Jewish homes.

SHEOL. Old Testament name for place of the dead. See **HADES, HELL.**

SHEPHERD. While the words *shepherd* and *sheep* are familiar in general usage, their biblical symbolism is too important to dismiss without comment. A shepherd is a person who cares for sheep by feeding, protecting, pasturing, and nurturing them in every way—to the point of guarding them with his life.

Genesis 49:24 refers to God as "the Shepherd, the Rock of Israel" (NRSV). Psalm 23:1 says, "The Lord is my shepherd, I shall not want" (NRSV). In the New Testament, Jesus is described repeatedly as the unique shepherd: "I am the good shepherd" (John 10:11, 14); "There shall be one fold, and one shepherd" (John 10:16). Hebrews 13:20 refers to "Our Lord Jesus, that great shepherd." First Peter 2:25 describes believers as sheep who had gone astray "but are now returned unto the Shepherd and Bishop of your souls." First Peter 5:4 refers to elders (the same as pastors and bishops) receiving a reward "when the chief Shepherd shall appear."

Shepherd appears many times in a general sense in scripture, but also in the special sense of one who spiritually feeds, pastures, nurtures, guards, and protects believers. John 10 records Jesus' wonderful picture of His pastoral role and stewardship. The term *pastor* appears in the New Testament only once, in Ephesians 4:11; it indicates a shepherd of souls. In the Old Testament, *pastor* appears eight times— all in Jeremiah—to translate a Hebrew word elsewhere translated "shepherd."

▲ *Shepherd, pastor, bishop, overseer, and* elder *are used interchangeably in the New Testament to refer to the role of feeding, tending, and caring for spiritual sheep and lambs (see John 21:15–17). The high calling of pastor requires a great sense of the calling of the role. Pastors are accountable to God for their stewardship of the flock.*

■ **SIN**. Missing the mark of God's will by choice and because of human weakness (James 1:14–15; Romans 7:24–25). Actions or attitudes that disobey God, betray Him, or fail to do good (Romans 3:23; James 4:17. All have sinned and continue to come short of the glory of God—even Christians (Romans 3:23). Sin always brings pain.

▲ *The only unforgivable sin is unwillingness to accept God in Christ (Matthew 12:31).*

● *How can we keep from sinning? (See 1 Corinthians 10:13; Philippians 4:13.)*

SIN OFFERING. Any offering given after sin to reflect a repentant heart. Often, an offering given when someone sinned unintentionally (Leviticus 4:2–35).

SOLEMN ASSEMBLY. A day to give full attention to God and to humble one's soul (Leviticus 23:36). Solemn assemblies were religious events such as the one that occurred as part of the Day of Atonement. See **DATE CHART** on pages 265–266.

SOLOMON (SAHL uh muhn). A son of David and the third king of Israel. Solomon was born to Bathsheba and David after their first son died. Solomon is best known for his wives, his wisdom, and for building the temple (1 Kings 3:12–28; 6:1). He also helped organize the nation, maintained peace most of the time, and built magnificent structures. Although Solomon was known for wisdom, he did not always act wisely, obey God, or lead well

Solomon awes his countrymen by solving a dispute between two prostitutes who both claimed a live baby was hers, while a dead baby belonged to the other. The new king suggested cutting the baby in half and giving each woman an equal share. The true mother immediately gave up her claim to the child—and Solomon promptly handed the boy over to her.

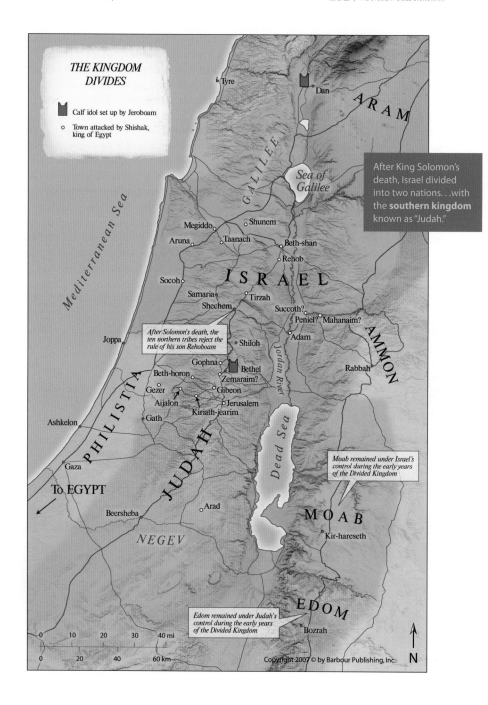

THE KINGDOM DIVIDES

Calf idol set up by Jeroboam

o Town attacked by Shishak, king of Egypt

After King Solomon's death, Israel divided into two nations. . .with the **southern kingdom** known as "Judah."

Tyre

Dan

ARAM

Sea of Galilee

GALILEE

Mediterranean Sea

Megiddo
Shunem
Aruna
Taanach
Beth-shan
Rehob

Socoh

ISRAEL

Samaria
Tirzah
Shechem
Succoth?
Peniel? Mahanaim?

After Solomon's death, the ten northern tribes reject the rule of his son Rehoboam

Joppa

Adam

Shiloh

AMMON

Gophna
Bethel
Beth-horon
Zemaraim?
Rabbah

Gezer
Gibeon
Aijalon
Jerusalem
Kiriath-jearim

Jordan River

Ashkelon

PHILISTIA

Gath

JUDAH

Dead Sea

Gaza

To EGYPT

Beersheba
Arad

Moab remained under Israel's control during the early years of the Divided Kingdom

MOAB

NEGEV

Kir-hareseth

Edom remained under Judah's control during the early years of the Divided Kingdom

EDOM

Bozrah

0   10   20   30   40 mi

0   20   40   60 km

Copyright 2007 © by Barbour Publishing, Inc.

N

(1 Kings 11:9–10). Read about him in 1 Kings and 2 Chronicles.

SONG OF SOLOMON, BOOK OF. Old Testament book composed of six love songs from a husband to his wife and a wife to her husband. The book celebrates love between a married couple—a tender, honest, delightful, and appreciative love. Many Jews and Christians also see the book as representing the strength of the relationship between God and His people and the closeness between Christ and His church. Also called Song of Songs, the literal Hebrew name.

▲ *Christians over the centuries have interpreted the Song of Solomon both literally and symbolically (or as an allegory). As the inspired Word of God, the Song has a message for all of us; and that message has to do with love.*

● *Read Song of Solomon to pinpoint the parts you consider most representative of true love.*

SOUTHERN KINGDOM. Same as Judah (but also contained the tribe of Benjamin). When Solomon died, rebellion divided the nation of Israel (1 Kings 14:19–30). The Northern Kingdom was made up of ten tribes that withdrew from King Rehoboam's rule about 922–912 BC and continued to be known as Israel. Judah was left as the Southern Kingdom. The Southern Kingdom continued until 587 BC when Babylonia conquered it. See **KING CHART** on pages 152–155.

■ **SOVEREIGNTY OF GOD**. Absolute authority and rule of God (Isaiah 45:5–6; Romans 9:20–21). God alone has sovereignty.

SPAN. Linear measure equaling about nine inches (Exodus 28:16). Measured by the distance between the outstretched thumb and little finger or with three palms of a hand. A

cubit is two spans. See **WEIGHTS AND MEASURES CHART** on pages 284–286.

■ **SPIRIT**. Wind, breath, essence of being (Genesis 1:2; Luke 1:80). Often means the Holy Spirit (John 1:32). Sometimes refers to demons as unclean spirits or evil spirits (Matthew 8:16). See **HOLY SPIRIT**.

God's Holy **Spirit** is often described in scripture as appearing like a dove.

SPIRITUAL. Usually of God, like God (1 Corinthians 2:15–16; Ephesians 5:19). Occasionally refers to spirits against God (Ephesians 6:12). True spirituality is obeying God in everyday life.

■ **SPIRITUAL GIFTS**. Abilities given to believers by the Holy Spirit (1 Corinthians 12:7). Every Christian has at least one spiritual gift. We are to use spiritual gifts to build up other believers, build up the church, create unity, express love, and reach new Christians (Ephesians 4:13–16). For sample lists of these gifts see 1 Corinthians 12–14; Romans 12:4–8; Ephesians 4:11–13.

● *What are your spiritual gifts? Consider asking a pastor or friend to suggest what your gift might be.*

STATUTE. Law or command (Ezekiel 18:21).

■ **STEWARD, STEWARDSHIP**. One who manages money or possessions for another. In the

Old Testament, a manager of a house (Genesis 43:19). In the New Testament, a guardian (Galatians 4:2) or foreman (Matthew 20:8). Christians are stewards for God (1 Peter 4:10). Stewardship is accountability for deciding how best to spend time, talents, and possessions God has given to us (Luke 12:42). Failure to risk being a good steward—burying your talent instead of investing it—is wickedness (Matthew 25:14–30).

● *Are you God's steward? How does this affect your actions and attitudes? As you answer these questions, consider your total life: convictions, behavior, work, time, goals, and unfolding life.*

SUBJECT. Obedient to (Luke 2:51). Under the control of, liable to (Hebrews 2:15).

■ **SUBMISSION, SUBMIT**. Yielding, to yield. Christian submission is to voluntarily yield in love and consider another's needs more important than one's own (Ephesians 5:21; James 4:7).

SUFFER. 1. Allow, let, permit (Mark 10:14). 2. Be in pain, go through troubles (Matthew 16:21). In the KJV, context sometimes determines whether "let" has the meaning of permit or prevent.

■ **SUPPLICATION**. Plea or prayer (Job 8:5). Sincere and humble asking (2 Chronicles 6:19; Esther 4:8; Ephesians 6:18).

SWADDLING CLOTHES. A long piece of linen used to wrap babies (Job 38:9; Luke 2:7). Swaddling clothes were wrapped tightly to prevent movement. Perhaps, this tightness made babies feel secure.

SYCAMORE. Tree with wide-spreading branches that were good for climbing (Luke 19:4). A cross between a fig and a mulberry tree, Bible sycamores were different from today's sycamore trees. Poor people ate their figs and used the wood (1 Kings 10:27). Sometimes spelled "sycomore" (KJV).

Sycamore trees in modern Tel Aviv, Israel.

SYNAGOGUE. Jewish place of worship, study, and meeting (Psalm 74:8; Matthew 4:23) that arose after the destruction of the temple in 587 BC. Like the word *church* today, *synagogue* means both a community of believers and the place in which they meet. Men and women sat separately. The most important people sat in the front. There were several worship leaders. Competent members of the congregation were invited to read and explain the scripture. When Jesus did this, people were amazed (Luke 4:16–22).

▲ *Synagogue services typically consisted of reciting the Shema (Deuteronomy 6:4–9), prayers, scripture readings from the Old Testament, a sermon, and a benediction.*

TABERNACLES, FEAST OF. Annual Hebrew feast for the purpose of thanking God for the harvest (Leviticus 23:34–36). Also called the Feast of the Booths or the Ingathering. The people lived in booths during the feast as a reminder of their ancestors' nomadic life in the wilderness. The feast took place from the fifteenth to the twenty-second day of Tishri, a month approximately equivalent to our October. See **FEAST CHART** on page 96 and **CALENDAR CHART** on pages 265–266.

■ **TABERNACLE**. A tent or temporary dwelling place, especially for worship (Exodus 25:8–9; Matthew 17:4). Specifically, the meeting place whose measurements and materials God gave in detail to Moses (Exodus 25–27; 33:7–10). This tabernacle was a portable worship center where the Israelites met with God during their wilderness wanderings. It served as a place of worship until Solomon built the permanent temple in Jerusalem. In the New Testament, Jesus Himself became the place of meeting (Hebrews 9–10). Symbolically, the term *tabernacle* may refer to the physical body (2 Corinthians 5:1–4).

● *While God has never been restricted to a tabernacle, tent, temple, or church building, He has called His people to set aside special times and places to gather to worship Him. While this worship does not require a building, gathering together is part of God's divine design and will for us (see Hebrews 10:19–25).*

TABITHA (TAB ih thuh). Name meaning "gazelle"; another name for Dorcas, a follower of Jesus who did many good works in His name. When she died, widows of Joppa grieved over her and God brought Tabitha back to life following Peter's prayer (Acts 9:36–42).

▲ *Peter's words of "Tabitha, arise." (Acts 9:40) echo the tender Aramaic words Jesus spoke in raising a twelve-year-old girl from death: "Talitha cumi"—the equivalent of, "Daughter, arise!" (Mark 5:41).*

TABLE, TABLET. Besides the usual meanings, can mean a writing surface or writing pad (Luke 1:63). The Ten Commandments were written on tables (Exodus 32:15–16).

TACHE. Hook or clasp (Exodus 26:6; Exodus 36:13, 18).

TALENT. A unit of weight and money. As a weight, about seventy-five pounds (Exodus 25:39; Revelation 16:21). As money, it was equal to three thousand shekels in Palestine (but thirty-six hundred shekels in Babylon). Talents could be in gold or silver, with silver being worth about one-fifteenth of the gold. Whatever the exact comparison with our money, a talent was a huge sum of money that would require years of common labor to earn

A modern re-creation of the ancient **tabernacle**, in the Israeli desert at Timna.

TAMAR

A clay **tablet** from around 2300 BC, on display in the Louvre Museum.

(Matthew 18:24; 25:14–30). See **MONEY CHART** on pages 284–286.

● *Whether talent refers to money or ability—as it does today—the Bible teaches that the possessor has both an opportunity and a responsibility. How are you investing your talents? (See Matthew 25:14–30.)*

TAMAR (TAY mahr). Means "palm." 1. Wife of Er, the eldest son of Judah (Genesis 38:6). 2. Virgin daughter of David. Her half brother Amnon lusted for her, raped her, then despised her (2 Samuel 13:1–15). This sinful act led to Amnon's own death at the hands of his half brother (and Tamar's full brother) Absalom (2 Samuel 13:20–29).

TANNER. Dresser of animal hides (Acts 9:43). A tanner converts animal skin into leather by removing the hair and soaking it in a solution.

TARRY. Wait, stay behind, prolong, delay (Habakkuk 2:3; Hebrews 10:37).

TARSHISH (TAHR shish). 1. Personal name given to a great grandson of Noah, a Benjamite warrior, an official of King Ahaseurus of Persia, and others (Genesis 10:4, 1 Chronicles 7:10, Esther 1:14). 2. A wealthy Mediterranean trading port (Isaiah 23:1; Jeremiah 10:9; Ezekiel 27:12). Jonah sailed for Tarshish in an attempt to escape God (Jonah 1:3).

A Roman-built road in modern **Tarsus**.

TARSUS (TAHR suhs). Birthplace of Paul the apostle and capital of Cilicia in Asia Minor (Acts 9:11, 30; 11:25; 21:39; 22:3). It was a learning center known for philosophy and literature and was about ten miles from the Mediterranean Sea.

TASKMASTER. Oppressive overseer (Exodus 1:3; 3:7; 2 Samuel 20:24). Taskmasters supervised forced labor projects. In the book of Exodus, taskmasters forced Hebrew slaves to complete public works projects for Pharaoh.

TASSEL. Twisted cord fastened to the four corners of the outer garment worn by Jews to remind them of their covenant with God (NIV: Numbers 15:38–39; Matthew 23:5; "fringe" or "border" in KJV).

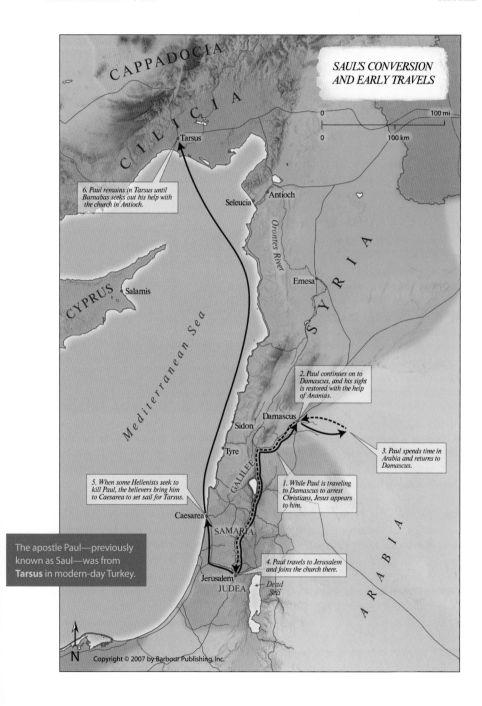

SAUL'S CONVERSION AND EARLY TRAVELS

0   100 mi
0   100 km

CAPPADOCIA

CILICIA

Tarsus

6. Paul remains in Tarsus until Barnabas seeks out his help with the church in Antioch.

Antioch

Seleucia

Orontes River

SYRIA

Emesa

CYPRUS

Salamis

Mediterranean Sea

2. Paul continues on to Damascus, and his sight is restored with the help of Ananias.

Damascus

Sidon

3. Paul spends time in Arabia and returns to Damascus.

Tyre

GALILEE

5. When some Hellenists seek to kill Paul, the believers bring him to Caesarea to set sail for Tarsus.

1. While Paul is traveling to Damascus to arrest Christians, Jesus appears to him.

Caesarea

SAMARIA

ARABIA

The apostle Paul—previously known as Saul—was from **Tarsus** in modern-day Turkey.

4. Paul travels to Jerusalem and joins the church there.

Jerusalem

JUDEA

Dead Sea

N

▲ *The word translated "tassel" also means edge, border, hem; and it is the same word used when the woman touched the hem of Jesus' garment and was healed (Matthew 9:20; Luke 8:44).*

TAX. Verb: Register people or possessions (Luke 2:1,5; Acts 5:37); also set a value on something to determine what portion to charge for support of government or religion (2 Kings 23:35). Noun: Charges imposed by government or religious group (Exodus 30:13; Matthew 17:24). For example, all Israelites paid half a shekel to support tabernacle worship (Exodus 30:13).

▲ *Jews were overtaxed in both the Old Testament and the New Testament (1 Kings 12; Luke 19:2–8). In the New Testament, tax collectors commonly collected more than was necessary and pocketed the excess. This unfair practice was a reason tax collectors were called "sinners" (Matthew 9:11 NIV). Some felt it was wrong to pay even fair taxes to Rome, but Jesus urged citizens to pay what was due to Caesar (Mark 12:14–17).*

TEACH. Cause to understand. Jesus was called "Teacher" (John 3:2). Teaching is a spiritual gift (1 Corinthians 12:28; Ephesians 4:11). The teacher must also be a learner (2 Timothy 2:15).

TEKOA, TEKOAH (tih KOH uh). Town about six miles southeast of Bethlehem, best remembered as the home of Amos and a wise woman who sought help from David (2 Samuel 14:2).

TEMPERANCE. Self-control; use of a level head and sound mind (1 Corinthians 9:25; Galatians 5:23; 2 Peter 1:3–8).

TEMPEST. Violent storm, whirlwind, hurricane, flood (Job 27:20; Matthew 8:24).

■ **TEMPLE.** House or place of worship (Psalm 11:4; Matthew 21:12). King Solomon built the first temple, completed about 950 BC. It was destroyed in 587 BC. A second temple and later Herod's Temple were situated on the original site. More important than these historical buildings, Christians—as a group or as individual believers—are the temple of God (1 Corinthians 3:16; 6:19). As God's temple, Christians are set apart to be holy, pure, and the dwelling place of His Spirit. The Bible says God will destroy those who defile this temple (1 Corinthians 3:17).

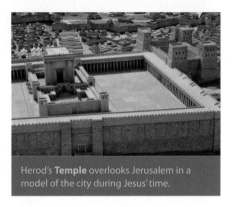

Herod's **Temple** overlooks Jerusalem in a model of the city during Jesus' time.

■ **TEMPTATION.** Enticement to do wrong, testing (Galatians 6:1 James 1:13–14; James 1:12). Temptation is a desire to yield to sin, to do a wrong thing that appeals to you. It comes from Satan and is deceptive (Luke 4:1–13). God can help you avoid temptation and prevent you from giving in to it (Luke 11:4; 1 Corinthians 10:13). Temptation itself is not sin, but yielding is. Successfully enduring temptation brings blessing and spiritual growth (James 1:12).

It is against God's nature to tempt anyone to sin. But He does allow testing and proving, providing both grace to endure and power to overcome these trials (see Genesis 22 and the book of Job). Temptation is to do wrong; testing is to prove faithfulness and endurance.

● *What wrong actions or attitudes are most tempting to you? How might yielding to temptation bring bad consequences? How do you win victory over temptation? A standard of value is essential for recognizing temptation. The Bible identifies God's standards of values. But Christians can detect temptations disguised in modern clothing with the help of both the Bible and God's Spirit.*

TEMPTATION OF JESUS. A forty-day period during which the devil tempted Jesus (Mark 1:12–13; Matthew 4:1–11; Luke 4:1–13). This time of temptation occurred at the beginning of Jesus'

ministry, as Satan attempted to divert Jesus from God's plan. Satan's temptation was accompanied by scripture quotations; Jesus rejected each of Satan's temptations with scriptures of His own. Jesus felt temptations as strongly as we do, but He did not give in (Hebrews 2:18; 4:15).

● *Examine the Bible passages listed earlier in this entry to discover Satan's tempting strategies and Jesus' resisting strategies. Some temptations are so strong that the Bible commands us to flee from them (see 1 Corinthians 6:18; 10:14; 1 Timothy 6:10–11; 2 Timothy 2:22). When we resist the devil, the Bibles says he will flee from us (James 4:7).*

Satan **tempts** Jesus, who's been fasting for weeks, to turn a stone into bread. Jesus quotes scripture to deflect the temptation.

TEN COMMANDMENTS. Basic rules for life that God gave the Israelites (Exodus 20:1–17; Deuteronomy 5:6–21). The commandments reveal God's will for our relationship with Him and with others. The first rules deal with mankind and our relationship to God. The second set covers our relationship to other people. The commandment to honor one's father and mother is said to be the first commandment with a promise (Ephesians 6:2).

●*To understand the purpose of each commandment, read it until you feel you understand its meaning. Then restate each commandment in your own words, and try to make your statement positive. For example, "Thou shalt have no other gods" could become "worship only the One true God."*

THE TEN COMMANDMENTS

COMMANDMENT	PASSAGE	RELATED OLD TESTAMENT PASSAGES	RELATED NEW TESTAMENT PASSAGES	JESUS' TEACHINGS
You shall have no other gods before me	Exodus 20:3; Deuteronomy 5:7	Exodus 20:23; 34:14; Deuteronomy 6:4, 13–14; 2 Kings 17:35; Psalm 81:9; Jeremiah 25:6; 35:15	Acts 5:29	Matthew 4:10; 6:33; 22:37–40
You shall not make for yourself an idol	Exodus 20:4–6; Deuteronomy 5:8–10	Exodus 32:8; 34:17; Leviticus 19:4; 26:1; Deuteronomy 4:15–20; 7:25; 32:21; Psalm 115:4–7; Isaiah 44:12–20	Acts 17:29–31; 1 Corinthians 8:4–6, 10–14; Colossians 3:5; 1 John 5:21	Matthew 6:24; Luke 16:13
You shall not misuse the name of the Lord	Exodus 20:7; Deuteronomy 5:11	Exodus 22:28; Leviticus 18:21; 19:12; 22:2; 24:16; Ezekiel 39:7	John 5:12	Matthew 5:33–37; 6:9; 23:16–22
Remember the Sabbath day by keeping it holy	Exodus 20:8–11; Deuteronomy 5:12–15	Genesis 2:3; Exodus 16:23–30; 31:13–16; 35:2–3; Leviticus 19:30; Isaiah 56:2; Jer. 17:21–27	Hebrews 10:25	Matthew 12:1–13; Mark 2:23–27; 3:1–6; Luke 6: 1–11
Honor your father and your mother	Exodus 20:12; Deuteronomy 5:16	Exodus 21:17; Leviticus 19:3; Deuteronomy 21:18–21; 27:16; Proverbs 6:20	Ephesians 6:1–3; Col. 3:20	Matthew 15:4–6; 19:19; Mark 7:9–13; Luke 18:20
You shall not murder	Exodus 20:13; Deuteronomy 5:17	Genesis 9:6; Leviticus 24:17; Numbers 35:33	Romans 13:9–10; James 5:21	Matthew 5:21–24; 19:18; Mark 10:19; Luke 18:20
You shall not commit adultery	Exodus 20:14; Deuteronomy 5:18	Leviticus 18:20; 20:10; Deuteronomy 22:22; Numbers 5:12–31; Proverbs 6:29, 32	Rom. 13:9–10; 1 Cor. 6:9; Heb. 13:4; James 2:11	Matthew 5:27–30; 19:18; Mark 10:19; Luke 18:20
You shall not steal	Exodus 20:15; Deuteronomy 5:19	Leviticus 19:11, 13; Ezekiel 18:7	Romans 13:9–10; Ephesians 4:28	Matthew 19:18; Mark 10:19; Luke 18:20
You shall not give false testimony	Exodus 20:16; Deuteronomy 5:20	Exodus 23:1, 7; Leviticus 19:11; Psalm 15:2; 101:5; Proverbs 10:18; Jeremiah 9:3–5; Zechariah 8:16	Ephesians 4:25, 31; Colossians 3:9; Titus 3:2	Matthew 5:37; 19:18; Mark 10:19; Luke 18:20
You shall not covet	Exodus 20:17; Deuteronomy 5:21	Deuteronomy 7:25; Job 31:24–28; Psalm 62:10	Romans 7:7; 13:9; Ephesians 5:3–5; Hebrews 13:5; James 4:1–2	Luke 12:15–34

Moses displays the tablets of the **Ten Commandments** to the Israelites. The rays of light emanating from his head are an artistic representation of the biblical phrase "his face shone" (Exodus 34:29).

TENDER EYED. Soft, timid; possibly indicating eye weakness or disease (Genesis 29:17).

▲ *Translators vary in their interpretation of the meaning of "tender eyes": The NRSV reads, "Leah's eyes were lovely." The NLT reads, "There was no sparkle in Leah's eyes." And the HCSB says Leah's eyes were "ordinary." Whatever "tender eyed" means exactly, Jacob's choice for a wife was Rachel over Leah.*

TENT. A portable living space. Tents in biblical days were usually woven of black goats' hair and stretched over poles (Genesis 9:27; 13:3). Floors varied in material: goats' hair, straw, or other matter as families could afford. The word *tent* was sometimes used figuratively (Isaiah 54:2; Habakkuk 3:7; Zechariah 12:7).

TERAH (TEE ruh). Personal name meaning "turning," "duration," or "wandering." Father of Abraham (Genesis 11:26–32). He lived to the age of 205 (Genesis 11:32).

TERAPHIM (TER uh fim). Idols used as household gods or for magic to try to tell the future (Judges 18:14). They were kept in the house and possibly used as proof of inheritance rights. God condemned worship or use of teraphim (Genesis 35:2; Exodus 20:4).

TERRESTRIAL. On or belonging to earth (1 Corinthians 15:40).

TERRIBLE. Eliciting terror, awe, dread, fear, respect, or reverence (Daniel 7:7; Hebrews 12:21).

TESTAMENT. Will (Hebrews 9:16). Covenant, agreement between God and people (Matthew 26:28; Hebrews 7:22). The Bible is divided into two divinely inspired Testaments that document covenants between God and people. The Old Testament was a covenant of promise, and the New Testament was a covenant of fulfillment (Galatians 3:8–29). Both covenants came as gracious gifts of God.

● *To see how the two Testaments relate to each other, read Galatians and Hebrews.*

▲ *Note that the word* Testament *in the KJV appears only in the New Testament, but the word* covenant *is used in both the Old Testament and the New Testament for the same purpose. Therefore, see* **COVENANT**.

TESTIFY. To tell about as an eyewitness, to state as true, to prove (Deuteronomy 8:19; Acts 2:40).

■ **TESTIMONY**. Witness (Ruth 4:7; John 3:32). Sharing of experience. In the Old Testament, the word often referred to the Law or Ten Commandments (Exodus 25:21). In the New Testament, *testimony* usually refers to teaching, preaching, or revelation about Jesus (Revelation 1:9).

TETRARCH. Small-time ruler of a small Roman territory in the early Roman Empire (Luke 3:1). Literally, "fourth part."

THADDAEUS (THAD ih uhs). One of Jesus' twelve apostles (Mark 3:18). Same as Lebbaeus (Matthew 10:3). Possibly the same as Jude (short for Judas) who wrote the book of Jude. See **JUDE**.

THANK. Bless, declare blessed, profess, confess, praise, give thanks for food or actions or people (2 Samuel 14:22; Matthew 11:25; Acts 27:35).

▲ *Several Hebrew and Greek words are used in the Bible to indicate blessing, praise, or thanksgiving. In New Testament Greek,* eucharisteo *is used most often. We can see this word in English when we refer to the Eucharist and we give thanks to God in communion.*

THANK OFFERING. Offering to show thanks to God for a gift or for His help (2 Chronicles 29:31; 33:16; see also 1 Timothy 2:1).

THANKSGIVING. Gratitude, especially toward God, for a gift or action (Jonah 2:9; 2 Corinthians 4:15). Thanksgiving is an important element of Christian worship expressed in everyday life as well as during worship services. Many psalms express thanksgiving.

● *How do you show thanksgiving in word? Action? Attitude? In thanking God for the gift of our salvation regularly we join the apostle Paul (2 Corinthians 9:15). We know that God wants our thanksgiving for His blessings and in all things (see Luke 17:16–17; 1 Thessalonians 5:18).*

THENCE. From there (Genesis 11:8; Mark 1:19).

THEOPHILUS (thih AHF uh luhs). Apparently an early Christian convert. Luke addressed the Bible books of Luke and Acts to this person (Luke 1:3; Acts 1:1). The name means "friend of God."

THESSALONIANS, 1, 2 BOOKS OF (thess uh LOH nih uhns). New Testament letters from Paul to believers at Thessalonica. Paul had visited a synagogue and begun a church in Thessalonica. Others who did not believe Paul's message became jealous and enlisted an unruly mob that caused an uproar. Christian brothers helped Paul leave and go on to Berea (Acts 17:1–11).

In response to Timothy's good report about the Thessalonians, Paul wrote 1 Thessalonians. In this first letter Paul encouraged and reassured the Thessalonian Christians, gave thanks for their expressed faithfulness and love, defended his motives, and answered questions about the return of Jesus Christ.

In 2 Thessalonians, Paul used a more serious tone to address continuing confusion about the return of Christ, correct the mistaken belief that Christ had already returned, urge lazy Christians to go back to work, and emphasize the need for steady faith in the midst of suffering and trouble. Paul seemed to have a special affection for the Thessalonians.

THESSALONICA (THESS uh loh NIGH kuh). Both the largest city and Roman capital of Macedonia (Acts 17:11; 1 Thessalonians 1:1). It is now Thessaloniki, the second largest city in Greece. Thessalonica served as an important harbor and commercial center. Paul visited Thessalonica, began a church there, and later wrote two letters, which became the Bible books 1 and 2 Thessalonians. Thessalonica was named for the daughter of Philip II and half sister of Alexander the Great.

Ruins of a Roman palace in the midst of modern **Thessalonica**, called Thessaloniki in Greece.

THICKET. A thick growth of trees, shrubbery, or thorns (Genesis 22:13; Isaiah 9:18; Jeremiah 4:7).

THISTLE. A prickly plant that existed in several varieties in Bible times (Genesis 3:18; Matthew 7:16). Used also as a symbol for trouble, judgment, or wickedness (2 Kings 14:9).

THITHER. There, to that place (1 Samuel 10:22; Matthew 2:22).

THOMAS (TAHM uhs). One of Jesus' twelve apostles; also called Didymus, which means "twin" (Mark 3:1). He was eager and teachable. He went with Jesus to Judea at the risk of death (John 11:16). Thomas asked for evidence that Jesus had really arisen from being dead. Jesus gave that evidence, which drew from Thomas awed belief and reverence (John 20:24–28).

▲*Thomas is known as "Doubting Thomas" for questioning Jesus' resurrection. However, he is also known for dedication, conviction, and bravery.*

THONGS. Straps (Acts. 22:25).

THORN IN THE FLESH. An affliction of the apostle Paul. He did not identify the problem except to say that it was a messenger from Satan to buffet him and keep him humble (2 Corinthians 12:7–10). Guesses are plentiful, including poor eyesight (see Galatians 4:13–15). More important than knowing the nature of the affliction is that Paul accepted it as an opportunity to show God's grace over weakness (2 Corinthians 12:9).

THRESH. To separate grain from husks (Isaiah 28:27; 1 Corinthians 9:10). Threshing could be accomplished by beating sheaves of grain with

A farmer **threshes** grain in early 1900s Israel.

a rod, by walking oxen or other animals over the sheaves, or by using a threshing sledge. The process took place on a piece of ground, a large flat rock, or a threshing floor. Threshing floors were located where the wind could blow away the small pieces of husk called chaff.

THRONG. Squeeze, press, crowd together (Mark 5:31).

THUMMIM (THUHM im). Objects used at times, along with **URIM**, to help a seeker try to find the will of God (Exodus 28:30; Leviticus 8:8). The objects of unknown shape and size were carried in the high priest's clothing. Urim and thummim may have been stones, serving as a type of sacred lots. Perhaps users drew them from a bag and whichever came out first was the answer.

THYATIRA (thigh uh TIGH ruh). Hometown of Lydia, one of the first missionary converts to Christianity (Acts 16:14). A church grew there. The Lord praised the church at Thyatira for its works, love, service, faith, and patience. However, He condemned it for allowing Jezebel's followers to prosper (Revelation 2:18–24). Thyatira served as the center of several trade guilds.

TIBERIAS, SEA OF (tigh BIR ih uhs). A sea also known as Chinnereth and the Sea of Galilee (Numbers 34:11; John 6:1). See **GALILEE, SEA OF**.

▲ *Tiberias was also the name of a city on the southwestern shore of Galilee.*

TIDINGS. News (2 Samuel 4:10; Luke 2:10; Romans 10:15).

TIGLATH-PILESER (TIG lath-puh LEE zur) or **TILGATH-PILNESER** (TIL gath-pill NEE zur). King of Assyria from 745 to 727 BC (2 Kings 15:29). He conquered much of the Northern

Kingdom of Israel and carried off its inhabitants to Assyria.

TIGRIS (TIGH griss). One of two rivers of Mesopotamia, first cited in a description of the Garden of Eden (NIV : Genesis 2:14; Daniel 10:4). *Hiddekel* is the Hebrew name of the Tigris (KJV). Today the Tigris runs past Baghdad. See **EUPHRATES**.

TILL. Plow, plant, cultivate (Genesis 2:5).

TIMBREL. Percussion instrument, like a tambourine (Psalm 81:2).

TIME. Jews divided months into weeks of seven days ending with the sabbath (our Saturday; Exodus 20:11). The Hebrew day began at sunset. Hebrew months began with the new moon. See **CALENDAR CHART** on pages 265–266.
▲ *God created an island of time within eternity, which is without beginning or end. Eternity continues; time will not always. Within time, we choose either to receive God's light and salvation in Jesus Christ or to ignore this most important decision of life. Each person must make a timely decision about eternity within his or her lifetime.*

THE JEWISH CALENDAR

YEAR		MONTH	ENGLISH MONTHS (APPROXIMATE)	FESTIVALS	SEASONS AND PRODUCTIONS
SACRED	CIVIL				
1	7	Nisan/Abib (30 days)	April	1 New Moon 14 The Passover 15 – 21 Unleavened Bread	Spring rains (Deuteronomy 11:14) Floods (Joshua 3:15) Barley ripe
2	8	Iyyar/Ziv (29 days)	May	1 New Moon 14 Second Passover (for those unable to keep first)	**Harvest** Barley harvest (Ruth 1:22) Wheat harvest Summer begins No rain from Apr. to Sep. (1 Samuel 12:17)
3	9	Sivan (30 days)	June	1 New Moon 6 Pentecost	
4	10	Tammuz (29 days)	July	1 New Moon 17 Fast for the taking of Jerusalem	**Hot season** Heat increases
5	11	Ab (30 days)	August	1 New Moon 9 Fast for the destruction of temple	The streams dry up Heat intense Vintage (Leviticus 26:5)
6	12	Elul (29 days)	September	1 New Moon	Heat intense (2 Kings 4:19) Grape harvest (Numbers 13:23)
7	1	Tishri/Ethanim (30 days)	October	1 New Year, Day of Blowing of Trumpet; Day of Judgment and Memorial (Numbers 29:1) 10 Day of Atonement (Leviticus 16) 15 – 21 Booths (Leviticus 23:24) 22 Solemn assembly	**Seed time** Former or early rains begin (Joel 2:23) Plowing and sowing begin

YEAR		MONTH	ENGLISH MONTHS (APPROXIMATE)	FESTIVALS	SEASONS AND PRODUCTIONS
8	2	Marchesran/ Bul (29 days)	November	1 New Moon	Rain continues Wheat and barley sown
9	3	Chislev (30 days)	December	1 New Moon 25 Dedication (John 10:22, 29)	**Winter** Winter begins Snow on mountains
10	4	Tebeth (29 days)	January	1 New Moon 10 Fast for the siege of Jerusalem	Coldest month Hail and snow (Joshua 10:11)
11	5	Shebat (30 days)	February	1 New Moon	Weather gradually warmer
12	6	Adar (29 days)	March	1 New Moon 13 Fast of Esther 14–15 Purim	Thunder and hail frequent Almond tree blossoms
13	Leap year	Veadar/Adar Sheni	March/April	1 New Moon 13 Fast of Esther 14–15 Purim	Intercalary month

Note 1: The Jewish year is strictly lunar, being twelve lunations with an average 29.5 days making 354 days in the year.

The Jewish sacred year begins with the new moon of spring, which comes between our March 22 and April 25 in cycles of nineteen years.

We can understand it best if we imagine our New Year's Day, which now comes on January 1 without regard to the moon, varying each year with Easter, the time of the Passover, or the time of the full moon which, as a new moon, had introduced the New Year two weeks before.

Note 2: Hence the Jewish calendar contains a thirteenth month, Veadar or Adar Sheni, introduced seven times in every nineteen years, to render the average length of the year nearly correct and to keep the seasons in the proper months.

Note 3: The Jewish day begins at sunset.

TIMOTHY. A native of Lystra who learned the scriptures from his Jewish mother, Eunice, and grandmother, Lois (Acts 16:1). His father was a Greek. *Timothy* means "honoring God," and that he did as he served alongside the apostle Paul, who was his father in the faith (1 Timothy 1:2). Timothy accompanied Paul on missionary journeys and was listed along with Paul in the sending of six letters: 2 Corinthians, Philippians, Colossians, 1–2 Thessalonians, and Philemon.

TIMOTHY, 1, 2, BOOKS OF (TIM uh thih). Books Paul wrote to young "Timothy, my own son in the faith" (1 Timothy 1:2). First Timothy warns against false teaching. It also gives instructions for church worship, presents characteristics of church leaders, and encourages Christian service. Second Timothy, apparently written near the end of Paul's life, gives encouraging advice to Timothy including how to endure and to serve Christ faithfully.

▲*One commentator has said the difference between 1 and 2 Timothy is this: 1 Timothy describes an ideal church every pastor ought to have, while 2 Timothy describes the ideal pastor every church should have.*

●*Read these scriptures to see which verses most strongly apply to your life right now: 1 Timothy 4:12–16; 6:6–10; 2 Timothy 1:7; 1:12; 2:15; 3:16–17; 4:18. Why? How?*

TISHBITE (TISH bight). Used to identify Elijah (1 Kings 17:1). It appears to refer to a tribe or a location such as a village name.

■**TITHE**. One tenth, a tenth of money or possessions (2 Chronicles 31:5–6). To tithe is to give a tenth of one's money to God (Malachi 3:10). Tithing is a way to obey and worship God (Deuteronomy 14:22–29; Malachi 3:10). To fail to tithe is to rob God (Malachi 3:8).
▲*Three instances of the word* tithe *appear in the Gospels when Jesus commended what was done but condemned what was left undone. The other seven instances of "tithe" in the NT appear in the book of Hebrews. The nature of the New Testament is not to focus on the minimum requirements of the Old Testament law; rather, the focus is on grace that goes beyond law and on being a cheerful giver, who gives proportionately to one's income (1 Corinthians 16:1–2; 2 Corinthians 9:7).*
● *Consider Jesus' praise for the widow who gave her only two mites, which he considered greater than the gifts of others who gave out of their prosperity (Mark 12:41-44). Tithing is an Old Testament doctrine with new meaning under giving under grace and giving cheerfully. Malachi 3:8–10 still deals with a question we Christians need to answer in our giving.*

TITTLE. Could refer to any small mark—such as a dot or an accent mark—on a Hebrew or Greek letter or word (Luke 16:17). See **JOT**.
▲*We might compare the jot and tittle to our saying, "Cross your T's and dot your I's," indicating the smallest marks that complete or fulfill our writing.*

TITUS (TIGH tuhs). A Greek Christian coworker with the apostle Paul, who may have converted Titus to Christ (Titus 1:4). Titus traveled on missionary journeys with Paul and took Paul's first letter to the Corinthians with the assignment of helping the church correct its problems (see 2 Corinthians 7:13–15).

TITUS, BOOK OF. New Testament book Paul wrote as a letter to a Christian coworker named Titus. Paul wrote to encourage Titus in the face of opposition, to remind him to hold on to sound faith and sound doctrine, to urge him to seek Christian leaders with good character, and to show him how to teach.
● *God's ways call for sound beliefs lived out in godly behavior (Titus 3:8). Identify at least one example of a spiritual teaching that results in a God-pleasing behavior.*

TOIL. Labor, hard work (Genesis 5:29; Matthew 6:28).

TOKEN. Sign, proof, signal (Genesis 9:12; 2 Thessalonians 1:5).

TOLERABLE, TOLERATE. Bear, able to stand a hardship (Matthew 10:15).

TOLL. Tax, a measured amount (Ezra 4:13).

TOMB. Burial place (Job 21:32; Matthew 27:60). In New Testament times, tombs were often caves or cut-out areas in stone because of the difficulty of digging in the rocky ground. Many tombs had shelves on which to lay the bodies. They also had heavy stone doors to seal the tomb. Jesus was buried in a tomb large enough for someone to sit inside (Mark 16:5). See **BURIED, SEPULCHRE**.

■ **TONGUES**. Besides the usual literal meaning of tongues, a reference to languages (Genesis

A **tomb** near Nazareth, dating to around the time of Christ.

10:5; Acts 2:4). The gift of tongues is a spiritual gift that comes with cautions and restrictions about its use (1 Corinthians 12–14). Speaking in tongues may refer to a foreign language or a unique utterance understood only by God or with His help. (See Acts 2:4–11; 1 Corinthians 14:1–33.)

▲ *Though some look down upon Christians who claim to have the gift of tongues, all the gifts of the Spirit are God's to bestow on anyone at any time He chooses.*

TORAH. Hebrew word meaning "law" or "teaching" and used to refer to God's teachings. *Torah* came to mean the first five books of the Old Testament (Genesis, Exodus, Leviticus, Numbers, Deuteronomy). The word does not appear in the KJV.

TORMENT. Torture, inflict pain (Hebrews 11:37). Evil causes torment.

TOW. Short fibers of flax, easily broken and, therefore, used as a symbol for what is weak or temporary (Judges 16:9).

TOWER. Tall structure that gave watchmen a vantage point for guarding cities, vineyards, pastures, and more. Towers ranged in size from a single room to a huge fortress. Used figuratively for God's salvation (2 Samuel 22:51).

● *Identify the specific towers in: Genesis 35:21; Judges 9:46; Song of Solomon 4:4; Nehemiah 3:1.*

TO WIT. Namely, that is (Esther 2:12; Romans 8:23).

▲ *KJV translators inserted "to wit" nearly twenty times to facilitate clarity in the English. One exception is the "to wit" of 2 Corinthians 5:18–19, which is part of the original Greek.*

TRADITION. Beliefs, teachings, practices, or rules handed down from the past (Matthew 15:2–3; 2 Thessalonians 2:15).

● *Ideally, traditions are accurate, good, and helpful; but some traditions are inaccurate, bad, and destructive. Try to think of an example of each. Evaluate traditions against God's Word.*

TRAIN. Noun: Part of a long robe that trails behind the wearer (Isaiah 6:1). Also, a procession of attendants (1 Kings 10:2). Verb: Teach (Proverbs 22:6).

■ **TRANSFIGURATION**. Transformation, change of appearance (Matthew 17:2). This term described Jesus' appearance when He was glorified and shone with a heavenly brightness as He stood with Peter, James, and John. Moses and Elijah appeared with Jesus (Matthew 17:1–8; Mark 9:2–8).

▲ *The Greek term is used for our English word metamorphosis.*

TRANSFIGURED. Changed, transformed (Mark 9:2). During the Transfiguration the disciples saw Jesus' glory, the brightness, splendor, and radiance of God's presence (Matthew 17:1–8; Mark 9:2–8; Luke 9:28–36).

● *What thoughts and emotions do you think you might have experienced had you been at Jesus' transfiguration?*

Jesus, glowing brightly, speaks with Moses and Elijah as Peter, James, and John fall to the ground in fear during the **transfiguration**.

■ **TRANSFORMED**. Changed: outwardly or inwardly (Mark 9:2; Romans 12:2; 2 Corinthians 3:18 NIV). In the Bible, transformation often results from an encounter with God in Christ. See **REGENERATION**.

TRANSGRESS. Cross the line, step over from right to wrong, rebel, disobey God (1 Kings 8:50; Luke 15:29). To transgress is to be a trespasser against God and His will.

■ **TRANSGRESSION**. Lawlessness, sin, rebellion against God (Proverbs 12:13; 1 John 3:4).

TRANSLATE. Transfer, such as the transfer of a kingdom from one person to another (2 Samuel 3:10) or the transfer of believers into God's kingdom (Colossians 1:13) Also, change from life on earth to life in heaven without dying (Hebrews 11:5).

▲ *Translate also means "to put into another language." The Bible was originally written in Hebrew and Greek. Bible scholars and skilled linguists have translated the Bible into English and many other languages. English translations of the Bible include the King James Version, New International Version, New American Standard Version, New Revised Standard Version, and Holman Christian Standard Bible. Living languages are ever-changing, so it is necessary for translators to put the faith of the fathers into the language of their children. That largely explains the newer translations and the continuing work on translation; however, better understanding of original languages and new manuscripts help, too.*

TRAVAIL. Labor, very hard or painful work (Job 15:20; Isaiah 53:11). Childbirth is a specific kind of travail (Isaiah 23:4; John 16:21).

TREACHEROUS. Disloyal. Unreliable, tricky, deceitful (Hosea 6:7).

TREAD. Trample. The past tense is *trodden* (Lamentations 1:15).

TREASON. Betrayal, conspiracy (1 Kings 16:20).

TREASURE. What is valued (Matthew 6:20–21). Not limited to what you can see or touch.

● *Our value system shows up in how we make priorities and use time, effort, and money. Identify the five highest priorities in your life, and consider those you treasure most.*

TREE OF KNOWLEDGE OF GOOD AND EVIL. A tree in the Garden of Eden (Genesis 2:9). God prohibited Adam and Eve from eating from the tree, demanding their obedience and loyalty. Satan tempted Eve by saying the tree would help her to be like God. Both Adam and Eve disobeyed God by eating from the tree. Rather than making them like God, their actions brought shame, guilt, separation, and exclusion from God. Sin brought death into mankind's existence (Genesis 2:16–17; 3:1–24).

▲ *Each person is responsible for his or her own sin (Isaiah 53:6; Romans 3:23; 6:23). Though Adam and Eve introduced and contaminated mankind with sin, everyone makes their own choice both about sin and choosing or rejecting Jesus Christ as Lord and Savior.*

● *What leads people to sin? Wanting to be like God? Disobedience? Rebellion? Or something else?*

● *The phrase "forbidden fruit" comes from this experience. Why do we want what we can't have? How can we keep from yielding to temptation and sin?*

TREE OF LIFE. Tree in the Garden of Eden that symbolized eternal life. Adam and Eve had access to this tree until they chose to disobey God (Genesis 2:9, 16–17; 3:22–24).

TRESPASS. False step, sin, violation of God's rights or the rights of a fellow human (Leviticus

Adam and Eve leave the perfect Garden of Eden for a now-fallen world full of death and danger—their punishment for disobeying God by eating from the **tree** of the knowledge of good and evil.

6:2; Matthew 6:14). The act of going beyond one's right and injuring another.

TRIAL. Event to try, prove, or test (Ezekiel 21:13; Hebrews 11:36). Being brought before a court to confirm or acquit a charge of wrongdoing (Mark 13:11 NIV).

TRIBES OF ISRAEL. Jacob, later called Israel, had twelve sons. The descendants of those twelve sons became the twelve tribes of Israel (Numbers 13:4–15; Matthew 19:28). During the period of the Judges, each tribe had its own leaders and laws. The tribes became a unified nation when Saul became the first king of the Israelites—with interruptions of the unity from time to time. Next, King David enhanced Israel's unity, as did David's son Solomon. After Solomon's death, however, Israel divided into the Northern Kingdom of ten tribes (called Israel); and a Southern Kingdom (called Judah) comprised of the tribes of Judah and Benjamin.

The twelve sons of Israel (Jacob) were:

1. Reuben
2. Simeon
3. Levi
4. Judah
5. Issachar
6. Zebulun
7. Joseph (from whom came the tribes of Ephraim and Manasseh)
8. Benjamin
9. Dan
10. Naphtali
11. Gad
12. Asher

This mosaic in Jerusalem depicts the twelve sons of Jacob—heads of the twelve **tribes of Israel**—as described by Jacob in Genesis 49.

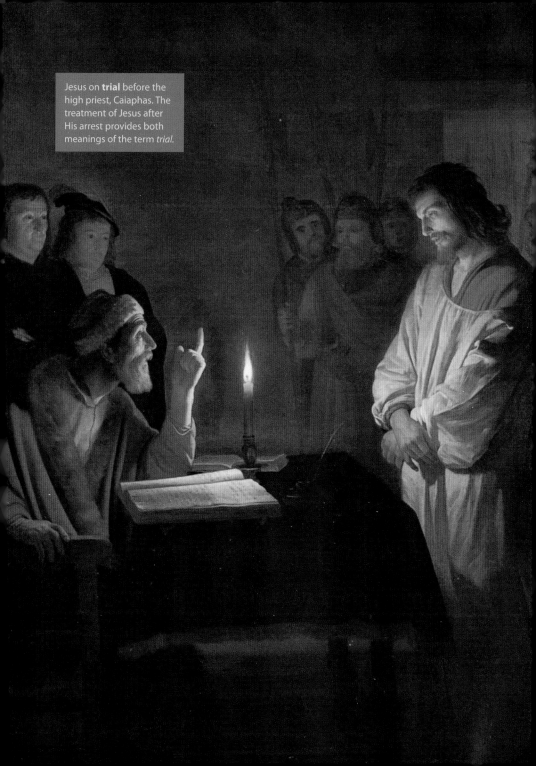

Jesus on **trial** before the high priest, Caiaphas. The treatment of Jesus after His arrest provides both meanings of the term *trial*.

■**TRIBULATION**. 1. Troubles caused by an outside source (Acts 14:22; 1 Thessalonians 3:4; Revelation 2:10). Oppression. Can be physical, mental, or spiritual. Tribulation cannot separate Christians from God or destroy them (Romans 8:33–39; John 16:33). God will comfort Christians through tribulation and deliver them from it (2 Corinthians 1:3–4; Deuteronomy 4:30–31; 1 Samuel 26:24; the book of Revelation). 2. The eventual result for persons who do evil (Romans 2:9). 3. A period of excessive troubles near the end of the world or before the Lord's return (Mark 13:24; Daniel 12:1; Revelation 7:14).

●*Why do you think God allows Christians to go through tribulation? What scriptures give comfort and strength regardless of current or future tribulation?*

TRIBUTE. Tax forced upon a conquered people, a payment required by a superior (Ezra 4:20). Tributes required of conquered nations sometimes undermined the nation's economy.

■**TRINITY**. Threefold. People's way of referring to the Godhead: God the Father, God the Son, God the Spirit (Matthew 28:19). The word *trinity* does not appear in the Bible, but references to the Godhead do (1 Corinthians 12:4–6; 1 Peter 1:2; Matthew 3:16–17). In human language, we necessarily speak of the Personhood of God expressed as one-in-three and three-in-one; *Trinity* is the term used in Christian theology.

●*The Trinity is God's mystery. Every attempt to illustrate the Trinity is inadequate. Some people think of the Trinity in this way: God is like water. The chemical compound (H_2O) comes in solid (ice), liquid (water), and gas (steam). Each has specific functions: Ice cools, water quenches thirst, steam cooks and cleanses. Others picture three separate matches brought together as one flame and suggest that this illustrates God the Father, God the Son, and God the Holy Spirit. The Bible teaches that only one God works with His creation in the three persons of Father/Creator, Son/Savior, and Spirit/Comforter. The Trinity shows God has personal relationships and expresses love within His own Being. How do you evaluate these pictures? What picture helps you understand the Trinity? See* **GOD, HOLY SPIRIT, JESUS**.

TRIUMPH. Rise above, cry aloud, sing, shout, be victorious over (Exodus 15:1; Psalm 47:1; 2 Corinthians 2:14; Colossians 2:15).

TRIUMPHAL ENTRY. Jesus' entrance into Jerusalem on the Sunday before His crucifixion (Matthew 21:1–9; Mark 11:1–10; Luke 19:29–38; John 12:12–16). It is called Palm Sunday because palm branches were laid in Jesus' path. The triumphal entry is important because during that event Jesus as the Messiah was publicly recognized. Until then Jesus refused public recognition of Himself as Messiah and ministered outside Jerusalem. Riding into Jerusalem on a colt fulfilled Messianic prophecy (Zechariah 9:9).

▲*When Jesus rode into Jerusalem, people cried, "Hosanna!" which means, "Save us!" They would shortly cry, "Crucify Him!"*

TROAS (TROH az). An important city and seaport on the Roman province of Asia a few miles south of ancient Troy (Acts 20:5). Paul visited Troas on two missionary journeys.

TROPHIMUS (TRAHF ih muhs). Gentile (non-Jew) who became a Christian in Ephesus and later accompanied Paul (Acts 21:29).

TROUGH. Structure that holds animal feed or water (Exodus 2:16). Can also hold bread dough (Deuteronomy 28:17 NIV).

TROW. Think (Luke 17:9).

TRUE, TRUTH. Genuine, honest, sincere, actual, reliable, able to be trusted (Psalm 33:4; Matthew 22:16). Actual fact rather than pretense, appearance, or claim. God is the one source of truth and Jesus is called the Truth (John 14:6).

TRUMPETS, FEAST OF. An annual Hebrew feast that celebrated the new civil year with a blast of trumpets (Leviticus 23:23–25; Numbers 29:1). It occurred on the first day of the seventh month, Tishri, which is approximately our month of October. See **FEAST CHART** on page 96 and **DATE CHART** on pages 265–266.
▲This feast is now Rosh Hashanah, the second most holy day in the Jewish calendar.

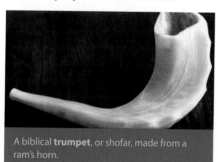

A biblical **trumpet**, or shofar, made from a ram's horn.

■**TRUST**. Depend on, put one's confidence in (Proverbs 3:5; 2 Corinthians 1:9). A confident hope (2 Corinthians 1:10). Belief (1 Thessalonians 2:4).
▲The verb trust is active; in the New Testament, faith in Christ is an action. That means belief is more than intellectual; it is a conscious commitment of head, heart, attitude, and action in serving God in Christ as Lord and Savior.

TUMULT. Uproar, confusion, rowdy assembly (Psalm 83:2; Matthew 27:24).

TUNIC. Loose-fitting, knee-length, shirt-like garment worn by men and women under their outer clothes (Mark 6:9 NIV).

TURBAN (NIV). Brimless headdress formed by winding cloth around the head (Job 29:14). The high priest wore a special one (Leviticus 8:9). Removing one's turban symbolized mourning (Ezekiel 24:17).

TURTLEDOVE. Dove. Bird used by poor people for sacrifice (Leviticus 12:6–8; Luke 2:24).

TWAIN. Two, both (Isaiah 6:2; Mark 5:41).

TWILIGHT. A specific boundary between sunset and complete darkness (1 Samuel 30:17; 2 Kings 7:5). Also, some usages appear to refer to darkness (Job. 3:9; 24:15; Ezekiel 12:6).

TWINED. Two or more strands twisted together; interlaced (Exodus 26:1).

TWO-EDGED. Sharp on both edges (Hebrews 4:12).

TYCHICUS (TIK ih kuhs). Christian and fellow minister with Paul. Tychicus accompanied Paul to Jerusalem and was later sent by Paul to Ephesus and Colosse (Acts 20:4).

TYRE (TIRE). Ancient Phoenician seaport city famous for wealth, wickedness, independence, and boldness (2 Samuel 5:11; Luke 6:17). It was north of Carmel and south of Sidon. Enemies found it difficult to capture Tyre because it was well protected by breakwaters and stood on a rocky island half a mile off the coast.

In the Old Testament David and Solomon had friendly alliances with Tyre. Jezebel, a daughter of the king of Tyre, promoted Baal worship. Old Testament prophets denounced Tyre. In the New Testament Jesus preached in Tyre, and Paul spent a week there. See **PHOE-NICIA, SIDON**.

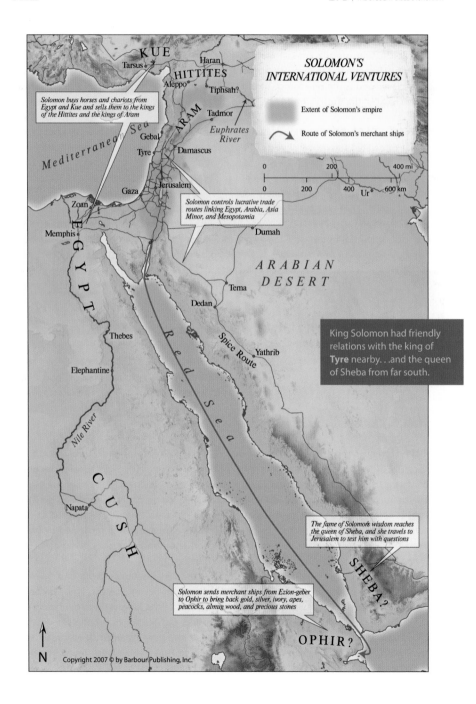

KUE

Tarsus

Haran

HITTITES

Aleppo Tiphsah?

Solomon buys horses and chariots from Egypt and Kue and sells them to the kings of the Hittites and the kings of Aram

ARAM

Tadmor

Euphrates River

Gebal

Tyre Damascus

Mediterranean Sea

Jerusalem

Gaza

Solomon controls lucrative trade routes linking Egypt, Arabia, Asia Minor, and Mesopotamia

Zoan

Memphis

EGYPT

Dumah

ARABIAN DESERT

Tema

Dedan

Thebes

Red Sea

Spice Route

Yathrib

Elephantine

Nile River

CUSH

Napata

SOLOMON'S INTERNATIONAL VENTURES

Extent of Solomon's empire

Route of Solomon's merchant ships

| 0 | | 200 | | 400 mi |

| 0 | 200 | 400 | 600 km |

Ur

King Solomon had friendly relations with the king of **Tyre** nearby. . .and the queen of Sheba from far south.

The fame of Solomon's wisdom reaches the queen of Sheba, and she travels to Jerusalem to test him with questions

Solomon sends merchant ships from Ezion-geber to Ophir to bring back gold, silver, ivory, apes, peacocks, almug wood, and precious stones

SHEBA?

OPHIR?

N

Copyright 2007 © by Barbour Publishing, Inc.

UNAWARES. Without knowing or realizing; unforeseen, sudden, unexpected (Deuteronomy 4:42; Joshua 20:3; Luke 21:34; Hebrews 13:2).

UNBELIEF. Literally, not believing. No faith or trust or lacking of faith (Matthew 13:58). The term often indicates disobedience to God or disbelief in Him (Romans 11:30; Hebrews 4:6, 11).
▲ *John 3:18 indicates that those who do not believe are the unsaved who already stand condemned and without eternal life.*

UNCIRCUMCISED. As an adjective, a term meaning "not circumcised"; it describes males who have not had a small circle of skin removed from around the front of the penis. In referring

A Jewish baby is circumcised in Jerusalem. In the Bible, *uncircumcision* was a term originally used to describe non-Jews.

to the "uncircumcised," the Bible indicates those who are not Jewish in faith, as well as the physically uncircumcised.

For biblical Jews, circumcision was more than a simple medical procedure. It was a ceremonial rite that began with Abraham, a symbol of the sealing of a covenant commitment with God (Genesis 17). In the New Testament, the "Uncircumcision" was a Jewish reference to Gentiles, who were non-Jews or unbelievers (Ephesians 2:11).

Even in the Old Testament, circumcision had a spiritual component described as a circumcision of the heart (Deuteronomy 10:16; 30:6; Jeremiah 4:4). Abraham's righteousness by faith was declared years before the seal of circumcision came into being (see Romans 4:11; compare Genesis 15:6; 17:10–27). Like other ceremonial matters of the Old Covenant, circumcision was not carried over into the New Testament church because of the New Covenant of grace. The apostle Paul and others refuted the insistence of some Jews that Gentiles be circumcised (see Acts 15:1–29). The New Testament clearly shows salvation is by grace through faith, without any works—such as circumcision—added on (Ephesians 2:8–10). Gentiles do not have to "become Jewish" to become Christians.

UNCLEAN. Defiled, impure, polluted (Leviticus 5:2; Romans 14:14). In the Bible, there were two kinds of uncleanness: ceremonial and moral. Under Jewish law a person became ceremonially unclean by eating certain food, having contact with the dead, having leprosy, having a bodily discharge, or having undergone childbirth. The unclean person had to go through a ceremony of purification. (See Leviticus 11–12; 26–28.) God's moral laws were spelled out in the Ten Commandments and other portions of the Old Testament. In the New Testament, uncleanness for Christians was primarily spiritual impurity in one form or another (Matthew 5–7; Ephesians 5:1–10).

Jesus heals ten lepers. Leprosy made Israelites **"unclean,"** separating them from their fellow citizens.

UNDEFILED. Clean, pure; any person or thing not tainted with evil (Psalm 119:1–3; Hebrews 7:22–28; James 1:27).

UNFAITHFUL. Deceitful, in the KJV (Psalm 78:56–57; Proverbs 25:19).

UNGODLY. Godless, wicked, irreverent (Psalm 1:6; Romans 5:6).

UNHOLY. Opposition to God or to what is sacred. Not set apart for God, unclean, profaned (Leviticus 10:10; Hebrews 10:29); wicked, godless (1 Timothy 1:9; 2 Timothy 3:2).

UNLEAVENED. Food prepared without yeast (Genesis 19:3; Exodus 12:8, 39; Mark 14:1).

UNLEAVENED BREAD, FEAST OF. The Feast of Unleavened Bread, also called the Passover, was celebrated to help the Israelites remember God's deliverance from the hands of the Egyptians (Exodus 12). God instructed the Israelites to omit leaven (yeast) from their bread because of the need for a hasty departure from Egypt. Leavened bread requires time to rise. See **PASS-OVER** and **FEAST CHART** on page 96.

■ **UNPARDONABLE SIN**. Sin that is beyond forgiveness, identified as blasphemy against the Holy Spirit or hardness of heart that goes beyond responding to and repenting before God (Exodus 8:32; Matthew 12:31–32; Mark 3:28–29; Luke 12:10). To blaspheme the Holy Spirit is to persistently ignore or discredit His work in one's life.

The person who blasphemes the Holy Spirit chooses to reject Christ. That person's heart becomes so hard that it is dead to God. Obviously, the person who has a concern about his relation to God has a heart that is still alive and not beyond repentance and God's forgiveness.

● *Many think they have done something so bad that God could never forgive them. If you are concerned about God's forgiveness, that is one indication you have not committed the unpardonable sin. Upon a person's true repentance, God is always willing to forgive and save. Consider the apostle Paul's conversion in Acts as proof: God forgave Paul in spite of his former persecution of the church—which was a direct attack on Jesus Himself (see Acts 9:4). Understanding this truth is critically important to Christians in witnessing to others.*

UNRIGHTEOUS. Opposite of being righteous and acceptable to God; unjust (Isaiah 55:7; 1 John 1:9; Hebrews 6:10). See **JUSTIFICATION**.

UNSEARCHABLE. Cannot be understood or traced; unfathomable (Job 5:9; Psalm 145:3; Romans 11:33; Ephesians 3:8).

UNSPEAKABLE. Indescribable, inexpressible (2 Corinthians 9:15; 1 Peter 1:8).

UNTIMELY. Not the natural or proper time— early or late (Job 3:16; Revelation 6:13).

UNWITTINGLY. Without knowledge or knowing, unintentional, by mistake (Leviticus 22:14; Joshua 20:3).

UPHOLD. Support, sustain (Psalm 51:12; Hebrews 1:3).

UPPER ROOM. Second-floor room where Jesus met with His disciples shortly before His arrest, trial, and crucifixion (Mark 14:15; Luke 22:12; John 13–17). Scene of our Lord's last supper. It was here Jesus prepared His disciples for His death, the Holy Spirit's coming, and their ministry of reconciliation (see John 13–17).

UPRIGHT. Having strong moral character and integrity (1 Samuel 29:6); to stand straight or erect (Leviticus 26:13; Acts 14:10).

UPROAR. Loud noise, riot, tumult (1 Kings 1:41; Matthew 26:5; Acts 19:35–20:1).

UR. Ancient city of Mesopotamia, located southeast of Babylon (Genesis 11:31). It was a prosperous city and the hometown of Abraham.

URIAH (yoo RIGH uh). 1. Husband of Bathsheba (2 Samuel 11:3). Because of King David's adulterous affair with Bathsheba and her resulting pregnancy, David sent Uriah to the frontlines of battle so he would be killed. 2. Priest in Jerusalem (2 Kings 16:10). 3. A prophet and another priest by this name.

URIM (YOO rim) and **THUMMIM** (THUHM im). Objects used by the high priest to try to find the will of God (Exodus 28:30; 1 Samuel 28:6–25). The objects of unknown shape and size were carried in the high priest's clothing. Urim and thummim may have been stones, serving as a type of sacred lots. Perhaps users drew them from a bag and whichever came out first was the answer. See **THUMMIM**.

USURY. Interest charged for a loan (Exodus 22:25; Matthew 25:27). Jews were not allowed to charge other Jews interest, but it was all right to charge a non-Jew (Deuteronomy 23:19–20).

▲ *In the KJV, usury is not used in the modern sense of charging excessive or illegal interest. In contemporary translations the word* interest *is usually used (see Matthew 25:27 in KJV vs. NASB).*

UTTER. Verb: Speak (Proverbs 23:33; Matthew 13:35). Adjective: Complete, total (1 Kings 20:42).

UTTERANCE. Speech (Acts 2:4).

UZZA, **UZZAH** (UHZ zuh). Son of Abinadab who died while touching the ark of the covenant (2 Samuel 6:3–8; 1 Chronicles 13:7–11). Several other Old Testament men bore this name also.

UZZIAH (uz ZIGH uh). Also known as Azariah (see 2 Chronicles 26:1; 2 Kings 15:1,13). King of Judah, the Southern Kingdom (2 Kings 15:1–13). He was a strong and successful king who reigned for fifty-two years. However, he came to a sad end. He was afflicted with leprosy after he tried to assume the priestly duty of offering incense in the temple (2 Chronicles 26:16–20). Uzziah is also the name of other Old Testament men. See **KING CHART** on pages 152–155.

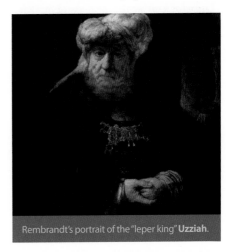

Rembrandt's portrait of the "leper king" **Uzziah**.

● *Read the book of Esther to see the providential hand of God at work in history.*

VEIL. (Also spelled **VAIL** in some KJV Bibles.) Covering (Genesis 24:65; 2 Corinthians 3:13). Curtain (Exodus 26:31; Matthew 27:51). The temple veil or curtain separated the holy place from the holy of holies. Only the high priest was allowed to pass through this veil and only on the Day of Atonement. When Christ was crucified, the temple veil tore in two. This symbolized that Christ's death provided personal, individual access to God.

VAIN, **VANITY**. In the KJV, usually means "empty" or "futile" (Psalm 73:13; Ecclesiastes 1:2; 1 Corinthians 15:14). But the word is used to translate a number of Hebrew words that have different meanings. "Falsehood" can be a meaning of *vain* in the KJV (Exodus 20:7). In the KJV the word *vain* never means conceited.

▲ *The book of Ecclesiastes uses the word* vain *(or* vanity*) more than thirty times to reflect life's meaningless or emptiness. Ecclesiastes reflects humanity's search for success and meaning apart from God; without God, all is vain or empty. The New Testament commentary might be stated as Jesus' words in Matthew 16:26: "What is a man profited, if he shall gain the whole world, and lose his own soul? Or what shall a man give in exchange for his soul?" The focus of the Lord's instruction was the kingdom of God.*

VENGEANCE. Justice, revenge, repayment (Psalm 94:1; Hebrews 10:30). The term may describe legitimate punishment for a wrong (Genesis 4:15). The Bible often notes that vengeance belongs to God (Romans 12:19). Though justice and punishment have their place in society, only God can judge completely and fairly—so revenge is a motive humans must guard against.

VENTURE. At random, innocently, without specific aim (1 Kings 22:34; 2 Chronicles 18:33).

VERILY, VERILY. "This is the truth" or "This is really important" (John 14:12). Jesus and others used this phrase often to introduce or accent a truth. The NASB translates the phrase as "Truly, truly"; the NIV, "I tell you the truth"; the HSCB and certain others, "I assure you."

VALIANT. Brave, strong (Jeremiah 46:15; Hebrews 11:34).

VARIANCE. Separate (Matthew 10:35). Dispute, strife (Galatians 5:20).

VASHTI (VASH tigh). Wife of Ahasuerus, king of Persia (Esther 1:9). When Vashti refused to parade her beauty in front of the king's guests, Ahasuerus removed Vashti as queen and replaced her with Esther.

Queen **Vashti** contemplates the loss of her royal position.

VESSEL. Instrument, container, utensil (Genesis 43:11; Exodus 25:39; Matthew 25:4); symbolically, a person chosen as an instrument (Acts 9:15).

VESTMENT, VESTURE. Clothing, garment (2 Kings 10:22; Matthew 27:35).

VEXATION. Sadness, wrong (Ecclesiastes 1:14); trouble (2 Chronicles 15:5); destruction, anguish (Deuteronomy 28:20; Isaiah 65:14).

VILE. Despised, filthy, dishonored (Psalm 12:8; James 2:2).

VINE, VINEDRESSER. A creeping or climbing plant that produces, melons, cucumbers, or grapes. Usually in the Bible the word refers to a grapevine (Genesis 40:10; Matthew 26:29). Grapes were a staple food in Bible times, eaten either fresh, dried as raisins, or used in winemaking. Those who took care of the vines were called vinedressers. Symbolically, *vine* could refer to Israel (Hosea 10:1). Jesus referred to Himself as the "true vine" and His disciples as branches (John 15:1, 5).

VINEGAR. Sour liquid produced from fermentation of grain or fruit (Numbers 6:3; Matthew 27:34). Nazarites were not to drink vinegar (Numbers 6:3). Jesus refused a vinegar mixture offered to ease His pain at the crucifixion (Mark 15:36; John 19:29).

VINEYARD. A field where grapes are grown, usually enclosed by a wall for protection against animals and thieves (Genesis 9:20; Matthew 20:1). Vineyards also had watchtowers for lookouts to give added protection. During harvesttime some grapes were left in the vineyard for gleaning (or collection) by the poor and strangers (Leviticus 19:10). See **GLEAN**.

VINTAGE. Harvest or yield of grapes (Leviticus 26:5).

VIOLATE. Do violence to (Ezekiel 22:26).

VIPER. Poisonous snake (Job 20:16; Acts 28:3). John the Baptist and Jesus used the term to refer to the wickedness of the religious leaders (Matthew 3:7; 12:34).

VIRGIN. A person who has not had sexual intercourse (Genesis 24:16; Matthew 25:1).
● *What standards of sexuality do you have? How do they reflect God's standards revealed in the Bible?*

VIRGIN BIRTH. The birth of Jesus produced through the miraculous intervention of God's Spirit and without human intercourse (Matthew 1:18–25).

VISAGE. Face, form, or appearance (Isaiah 53:14; Daniel 3:19; Lamentations 4:8).

VISION. A special message or revelation from God (Daniel 2:19; Acts 9:10). A vision could contain instructions or interpretations of present-day or future occurrences. God often gave visions to Old Testament prophets.
● *In a modern-day sense, God plants His will in the lives of those who look for it. What do you feel God's will is for you? How can you find that will? (See Matthew 6:33.)*

A large **vineyard** in Galilee, northern Israel.

VOID. Empty, lacking (Genesis 1:2; Proverbs 7:7; Romans 4:14).

VOW. A personal, voluntary promise. In the Bible, the vow is almost always to God (Genesis 28:20; Acts 18:18). Sometimes the vow was conditional on God's action or response; sometimes it was simply a dedication of devotion to God.

● *Vows are serious business—especially vows made to God (see Ecclesiastes 5:4).*

Today, the term **vow** is most often used in relation to wedding ceremonies. In the Bible, vows were generally made to God.

VULGATE. A term indicating common, ordinary language as opposed to a literary or classic style. The phrase "Latin Vulgate" refers to a translation of the Bible that St. Jerome is credited with completing about AD 400. The Latin Vulgate ultimately became the official Bible of the Roman Catholic Church for about a thousand years.

To understand the Latin Vulgate, it may be helpful to trace the history of God's Word from its original writing through early translation efforts. The Old Testament was written in Hebrew and some Aramaic, the New Testament in Greek. About 250 BC, scholars translated the Old Testament into Greek, and this translation became known as the Septuagint (see **SEPTUAGINT**). As the gospel spread, translators made the Bible, in whole or in part, available in Latin, Syriac, Coptic, Ethiopic, Armenian, and Georgian. But in the AD 300s, Pope Damasus I authorized Jerome to produce one standard Latin Bible from existing manuscripts and versions. Just as the New Testament was written in "Koine Greek" (the everyday language of the people), Jerome worked in the Vulgate Latin, the common language of the people.

The story of the Vulgate sheds light on the purpose and value of Bible translation. When the New Testament books were written, Greek was the universal language even though Greece no longer controlled the Bible lands. As Rome took the place of Greece, Latin gradually replaced Greek, so the people needed a Latin translation of the Bible as earlier generations had needed the Septuagint in Greek. The language of a culture tends to endure beyond changing rulers and governments. But people always need the Bible in the common, everyday language of each era.

was demolished. But the Old Testament sacrificial system and the Levitical high priesthood gave way to the New Covenant in Jesus Christ (Matthew 26:26–29) also. Jesus' atoning death on the cross demolished the wall of hostility that had divided mankind; Jesus provided for the unity and peace of all mankind in God in Christ Himself (see Ephesians 2:14–22; Colossians 3:11). The Law and other divisions would no longer divide mankind from coming to God together.

WAGES. Payment for labor or services, reward (Genesis 29:15; 30:28–34). Also used as the payment of judgment for sin (Romans 6:23).

WAIL. Cry or beat the chest as a sign of grief or repentance (Esther 4:3; Revelation 1:7).

WALK. Used literally (Exodus 2:5; Matthew 4:18). Also used to refer to a person's complete lifestyle and behavior (Genesis 5:24; Romans 8:4; Ephesians 2:2, 10; 4:1).
● In Ephesians 4:1, the KJV uses a form of the word calling three times, focusing on "walking" worthily of God's calling. How might God evaluate your lifestyle?

WALL. Literally, a wall of any kind (Proverbs 24:31). Walls of sun-baked clay surrounded and protected houses and cities in biblical times (Ezra 5:8; Nehemiah 2:17; Acts 9:25). Symbolically, wall was used to indicate salvation (Isaiah 26:1), truth and strength (Jeremiah 15:20), and protection (Zechariah 2:5).
▲The "wall of partition" in Ephesians 2:14 referred to both a literal wall separating Jews and Gentiles in the temple's worship area and a wall of cultural and religious hostility between the two groups. When Jesus died, "the veil of the temple was rent in twain from the top to the bottom" (Matthew 27:51). A literal wall

WANTONNESS. Looking with lustful eyes, lewdness, sexual immorality (Romans 13:13; 2 Peter 2:18).

WARD. A prison or guarded place (Genesis 42:16–19; 2 Samuel 20:3).

WARE. Utensils, things for sale (Nehemiah 13:16).

WASTE. Noun: place of desolation or drought (Leviticus 26:31); loss (Matthew 26:8). Verb: to destroy or try to destroy (Galatians 1:13).

WATCH. A time of guard duty (Nehemiah 4:9; Matthew 14:25).
▲Hebrews divided watches of the night into three; the Romans four (see Judges 7:19; Mark 6:48).

WATCHER, WATCHMAN. A person who keeps guard, a lookout (2 Kings 9:17). Watchmen were stationed on the walls of a city to warn of approaching enemies. They were also placed in the fields and vineyards during the time of harvest to watch for thieves.

WATCHTOWER. A high structure where a lookout could watch for approaching danger (Isaiah 21:8).

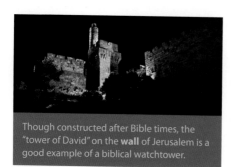

Though constructed after Bible times, the "tower of David" on the **wall** of Jerusalem is a good example of a biblical watchtower.

WAX. As a noun, the solid but easily melted substance secreted by bees and used in candles (Psalm 68:2). As a verb, to become or grow (1 Chronicles 11:9; Luke 1:80).

WEAN. Cause a child to become independent of his mother's nourishment (1 Samuel 1:23).

● Babies require milk, but are expected to grow and ultimately be able to eat meat. This truth has a spiritual parallel (see 1 Corinthians 3:2; Hebrews 5:12–13). Spiritual growth requires weaning from spiritual milk to spiritual meat.

WEDDING. A festive occasion of marriage. The wedding included singing, dancing, and feasting that lasted one or two weeks (Matthew 22:31).

WEEKS, FEAST OF. Celebrated a successful barley harvest and came seven weeks after the Passover (Leviticus 23:15–21). Second of three annual festivals (Deuteronomy 16:16). No work was to be done, and every male went to the sanctuary (Leviticus 23:21). Sin and peace offerings were made. See **PENTECOST** and **FEAST CHART** on page 96.

WEIGHTS AND MEASURES. See chart on pages 284–286.

TABLE OF WEIGHTS AND MEASURES

WEIGHT

BIBLICAL UNIT	LANGUAGE	BIBLICAL MEASURE	U. S. EQUIVALENT	METRIC EQUIVALENT	VARIOUS TRANSLATIONS
gerah	Hebrew	1/20 shekel	1/50 ounce	0.6 gram	gerah; oboli
bekah	Hebrew	½ shekel or 10 gerahs	1/5 ounce	5.7 grams	bekah; half a shekel; quarter ounce; fifty cents
pim	Hebrew	2/3 shekel	1/3 ounce	7.6 grams	2/3 of a shekel; quarter
shekel	Hebrew	2 bekahs	2/5 ounce	11.5 grams	shekel; piece; dollar; fifty dollars
litra (pound)	Greco-Roman	30 shekels	12 ounces	0.4 kilogram	pound; pounds
mina	Hebrew/Greek	50 shekels	1 ¼ pounds	0.6 kilogram	Mina; pound
talent	Hebrew/Greek	3,000 shekels or 60 minas	75 pounds–88 pounds	34 kilograms–40 kilograms	Talents/talent; 100 pounds

LENGTH					
BIBLICAL UNIT	**LANGUAGE**	**BIBLICAL MEASURE**	**U.S. EQUIVALENT**	**METRIC EQUIVALENT**	**VARIOUS TRANSLATIONS**
handbreadth	Hebrew	1/6 cubit of 1/3 span	3 inches	8 centimeters	handbreadth; three inches; four inches
span	Hebrew	½ cubit or 3 handbreadths	9 inches	23 centimeters	span
cubit/pechys	Hebrew/Greek	2 spans	18 inches	0.5 meter	cubit(s); yard; half a yard; foot
fathom	Greco-Roman	4 cubits	2 yards	2 meters	fathom; six feet
kalamos	Greco-Roman	6 cubits	3 yards	3 meters	rod; reed; measuring rod
stadion	Greco-Roman	1/8 milion or 400 cubits	1/8 mile	185 meters	miles; furlongs; race
milion	Greco-Roman	8 stadia	1,620 yards	1.5 kilometer	Mile

DRY MEASURE					
BIBLICAL UNIT	**LANGUAGE**	**BIBLICAL MEASURE**	**U.S. EQUIVALENT**	**METRIC EQUIVALENT**	**VARIOUS TRANSLATIONS**
xestēs	Greco-Roman	½ cab	1 1/6 pints	0.5 liter	Pots; pitches; kettles; copper pots; copper bowls; vessels of bronze
cab	Hebrew	1/18 ephah	1 quart	1 liter	cab; kab
choinix	Greco-Roman	1/18 ephah	1 quart	1 liter	measure; quart
omer	Hebrew	1/10 ephah	2 quarts	2 liters	omer; tenth of a deal; tenth of an ephah; six pints
seah/saton	Hebrew/Greek	1/3 ephah	7 quarts	7.3 liters	measures; pecks; large amounts
modios	Greco-Roman	4 omers	1 Peck or ¼ bushel	9 liters	bushel; bowl; peck-measure; corn-measure; meal-tub
ephah (bath)	Hebrew	10 omers	3/5 bushel	22 liters	bushel; peck; deal; part; measure; six pints; seven pints
lethek	Hebrew	5 ephahs	3 bushels	110 liters	half homer; half sack
cor (homer)/koros	Hebrew/Greek	10 ephahs	6 bushels or 200 quarts/14.9 bushels or 500 quarts	220 liters/525 liters	cor; homer; sack; measures; bushels/sacks; measures; bushels; containers

		LIQUID MEASURE			
BIBLICAL UNIT	LANGUAGE	BIBLICAL MEASURE	U.S. EQUIVALENT	METRIC EQUIVALENT	VARIOUS TRANSLATIONS
log	Hebrew	1/72 bath	1/3 quart	0.3 liter	log; pint; cotulus
xestēs	Greco-Roman	1/8 hin	1 1/6 pints	0.5 liter	pots; pitchers; kettles; copper pots; copper bowls; vessels of bronze
hin	Hebrew	1/6 bath	1 gallon or 4 quarts	4 liters	hin; pints
bath/batos (ephah)	Hebrew/Greek	6 hins	6 gallons	22 liters	gallon(s); barrels; liquid measure/gallons; barrels; measures
metretes	Greco-Roman	10 hins	10 gallons	39 liters	firkins; gallons
cor (homer)/koros	Hebrew/Greek	10 baths	60 gallons	220 liters	cor; homer; sack; measures; bushels/sacks; measures; bushels; containers

WELFARE. Peace, completeness, prosperity (Genesis 43:27; Nehemiah 2:10).

▲ *Asking others about their welfare was the equivalent of our greeting, "How are you?" (see Genesis 43:27; Exodus 18:7).*

WELL. A hole or pit dug in the ground to get water (Genesis 16:14; John 4:11). In the arid Bible lands wells were very important. Dispute over the ownership of a well was a frequent source of strife (Genesis 26:15 and following).

▲ *Though most wells were dug, the term might also refer to a fountain or spring (John 4:6).*

WHEAT. The basic grain of the ancient Near East (Ezra 7:22; John 12:24). Wheat was ground between stones to make flour. Many varieties of wheat existed, but it is difficult to identify the specific grain referred to in scripture. The KJV often refers to wheat or grain as *corn* (Mark 4:28). Wheat is sometimes used as a symbol of true commitment to God (Matthew 3:12, 13:24–31; Luke 3:17). Wheat harvest was celebrated

with the Feast of Weeks, later called Pentecost. See **FEAST OF WEEKS** and **PENTECOST**. Also see **FEAST CHART** on page 96.

WHELP. Lion's cub, dog's pup, or other young animal (Nahum 2:11–12). Used figuratively of Judah and Dan (Genesis 49:9; Deuteronomy 33:22).

WHENCE. From where (Genesis 16:8; Philippians 3:20).

WHEREAS. Because, since (Isaiah 60:15; James 4:14).

WHIRLWIND. Hurricane, tempest, violent wind (Isaiah 66:15; 2 Kings 2:1, 11).

▲ *Some of the Hebrew words translated whirlwind could refer to any kind of strong wind—not just one that whirled.*

WHITEWASHED. Covered with a thin coat of white paint. Looks white or fine on the outside but is unclean and corrupt on the inside (Matthew 23:27 NIV). Translated "whited" or "untempered mortar" in KJV (Ezekiel 13:11).

▲ *Jesus referred to scribes and Pharisees as being like whitewashed sepulchers that looked beautiful on the outside but contained dead men's bones and uncleanness inside (Matthew 23:27). His condemnation was against hypocrisy.*

WHITHER. Wherever, where (Genesis 28:15; Ruth 1:16–17).

WHOLE, **WHOLESOME**. Complete, perfect, entire, healthy, well, or restored to health (Proverbs 15:4; John 5:6).

WHORE, **WHOREDOM**. Prostitute, one who had sexual intercourse with someone besides a marriage partner for money or in some pagan religious practice (Leviticus 21:9). The prostitution of worship—from God to idols—seemed to break God's heart and bring judgment upon the idolaters (Ezekiel 6:8–10). Used symbolically in Revelation 17:1. Whoredom was considered a crime punishable by death (Genesis 38:24). Used figuratively for idolatry (Hosea 1:2). See **PROSTITUTE**.

WICKED. Sinful, evil, bad, worthless, without value, wrong, cruel, malignant (Psalm 9:16; Matthew 25:24–30; 2 Thessalonians 3:2).

●*Many have referred to "sins of commission" and "sins of omission." Some sins are obvious— immorality, violence, lying, etc. If these sins are not part of our lives, we might feel "holier than thou"—like the Pharisee thanking God that he was not like the publican begging God's forgiveness (Luke 18:10–14). But Jesus identified a different kind of wickedness—that of doing nothing with what God has given us (see Matthew 25:24–32). In light of this aspect of "wickedness," consider your life before God.*

WIDOW. Woman whose husband has died (Exodus 22:24; Luke 2:37). Widows were protected by law and given help (Deuteronomy 27:19; Acts 6:1). Because they did not inherit their husband's property, they were poor and helpless.

▲*James 1:27 notes that pure religion is to take care of widows and orphans in their distress and to keep oneself unstained from the world. Regardless of other deacon qualifications (1 Timothy 3:8–13), the seed role of deacon service began when the early church dealt with a group of Grecian widows who were being neglected in the distribution of daily food. The church took immediate action to meet this ministry need (see Acts 6:1–6).*

●*Considering our aging population, what can you do to help a widow (or widower)?*

WILDERNESS. Barren and rocky desert or uncultivated land suitable for nomads and grazing (Deuteronomy 1:19; Matthew 15:33). Wilderness areas were often rocky deserts with little rainfall—not necessarily sandy areas. Other wilderness areas had considerable growth.

▲*Because the Hebrews rebelled against God after He freed them from Egypt, they wandered in the wilderness for forty years. The New Testament warns present Christians not to make the same mistake (1 Corinthians 10:1–12).*

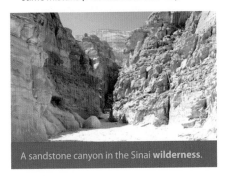

A sandstone canyon in the Sinai **wilderness**.

WILT. Second person singular of *will*; be willing, want to (Judges 1:14; John 5:6).

WIMPLE. A covering, cloak, shawl, mantle (Isaiah 3:22).

WIND. Besides its usual meaning, the term in the original Bible languages has been translated "breath," "spirit," or "Holy Spirit" (see Genesis 6:17; Psalm 51:10–17; John 3:5–8; Galatians 5:16–23). In the KJV, Psalm 55:8 and James 1:6 use other separate words for *wind*. In 2 Timothy 3:16, the Greek verb literally is "God-breathed," translated in the KJV as "given by inspiration of God."

WINE. Juice pressed out of grapes and then fermented (Numbers 6:3; Matthew 9:17). Wine was part of meals, a disinfectant, and a medicine (Matthew 26:29; Luke 10:34; 1 Timothy 5:23). The Bible warns against drinking strong, mixed wine or too much wine (Proverbs 23:29–32). Part of the Nazirite vow included abstaining from drinking wine (Numbers 6:1–4; see also Luke 1:15).
- ▲ *Wine could refer to juice, wine diluted with water, or undiluted wine. The vivid passage in Proverbs 23:29–32 is referring to the danger of strong wine that results in drunkenness—and what can happen when one is in that condition. It is worth noting that in the climate of Israel, juice without refrigeration likely would soon become alcoholic to some extent.*
- ● *What is involved in deciding whether to drink wine or alcoholic beverages? See Romans 14:13–23; 1 Corinthians 10:31; 1 Timothy 3:3; Titus 1:7; 1 Peter 4:3 for important considerations. Consider, too, that excessive drinking can become a medical as well as a moral or spiritual problem.*

WINEBIBBERS. Persons given to drinking wine (Proverbs 23:30; Matthew 11:19).

WINE PRESS. A device used to make wine from grapes (Nehemiah 13:15). Winemakers often walked on grapes in large stone vats to squeeze out the juice. The juice left the wine press through a small drain at one end, was collected in large jars or wineskins, then allowed to ferment (become alcoholic). The wine press is used in images of God's judgment (Revelation 14:19–20).

A **wineskin**.

WINESKIN. Container for wine, made from a whole animal skin (Mark 2:22). The skins stretched as the wine fermented, so old, brittle skins would not do.
- ▲ *Bottle translates the Greek word for wineskin in Matthew 9:17; Luke 5:37–38.*

WINNOW. Process of removing threshed grain from its uneatable parts (Ruth 3:2; Matthew 3:12). A person would pick up wheat stalks with a winnowing fork and shake or toss them

People around the world still **winnow** grain as biblical farmers did. These women are winnowing in Shigatse, China.

into the breeze. The heavy grain would fall to the ground, and the chaff would blow away. Winnowing could also occur before a fan.

■ **WISDOM**. Understanding, knowledge gained by experience (2 Chronicles 9:23; 1 Corinthians 1:17); a gift of God (James 1:5). Wisdom is a characteristic of God. The books of Job, Proverbs, and Ecclesiastes are called Wisdom Literature. Sometimes people include James in the New Testament as Wisdom Literature.
● *Knowledge and wisdom are not the same thing. Wisdom is a gift of God that lets people make right choices and live lives decisively for God. Ultimate wisdom comes only from God.*

WISE. One who applies knowledge to real life, understands, decides skillfully (Proverbs 10:5; Ephesians 5:15). Not all who are called wise are truly wise (Genesis 41:8; Romans 11:25). The truly wise obey God.

Though the Bible never says how many **wise men** visited young Jesus, tradition says three—perhaps because of the number of gifts they brought.

WISE MEN. 1. An educated class of persons responsible for preserving and transmitting learning (1 Chronicles 27:32). 2. Men who came from the East to see Jesus (Matthew 2:1). They appear to be astrologers. Though

tradition has said there were three and even assigned them names, the Bible does not specify either.

WIT, WIST, WOT. Old English for "know" (Genesis 24:21; Luke 2:49).

WIT, TO. Namely, that is (Esther 2:12; Romans 8:23).

WITHER. Dry up, fade, wear away, weaken (Psalm 102:4; 1 Peter 1:24).

WITHSTAND. Resist, strengthen self, stand up against an opponent, endure (2 Chronicles 13:7; Ephesians 6:13).

■**WITNESS, WITNESSING**. Testify, tell what you have seen or experienced (Genesis 31:44; John 1:7). The New Testament usage is from the Greek root word *martyr*. A Christian is to be a witness by sharing personal experience of what Jesus has done in him and for him or her (Acts 1:8; Mark 5:19). In the New Testament era and since then, countless witnesses have faced death, persecution, and hardship because of their witness.

WIZARD. Knowing one, magician or sorcerer, one who speaks to the dead (Isaiah 8:19). Wizards were readily available but unreliable (1 Samuel 28:3–19). The Bible strictly forbids seeking advice from wizards, also called mediums (Leviticus 19:31).
●*Why does God forbid seeking advice from wizards? (Note that the source of wisdom must be God-given; biblically, that excludes wizards or magicians.)*

WOE. Deep sorrow, grief, misery, or trouble (Numbers 21:29; Proverbs 23:29; Ezekiel 2:10; 1 Corinthians 9:16; Revelation 9:12). Also used in denouncing (Isaiah 5:8–22; Matthew 23:16).

WOMAN. Human being created in the image of God and to be the counterpart of man (Genesis 1:26–27). See **MAN**.

▲ *God created man and woman to reflect His image in creation and to complete each other (1 Corinthians 11:11–12). Man is not superior to woman as a created being. However, God has a divine design for orderliness in marriage and the yielding of one's will to the other at times. Functionally, in marriage, the husband is to be the spiritual leader. Genesis 5:2 says, "Male and female created he them; and blessed them, and called their name Adam, in the day when they were created." Man and woman together are "mankind."*

WOMB. Uterus, site of an unborn baby's growth until birth (Genesis 25:24; Luke 1:15). "Fruit of the womb" means children (Deuteronomy 7:13).

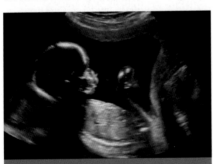

Ultrasound technology allows us to "see" into a woman's **womb**, something God has always done, according to Psalm 139:13.

WONDER. Miracle, astonishing or amazing event (Exodus 4:21; Matthew 24:24). Also a feeling of amazement (Acts 3:10) or the act of marveling or being amazed (Luke 2:18). Wonders and signs often appear together to refer to miracles from God and their meaning (Acts 15:12).

● *What do you find wonderful about God?*

WONT. As accustomed to, in the habit of (Numbers 22:30; Luke 22:39).

WORD. Expression, statement, communication, speech (Deuteronomy 32:1; Matthew 8:8). May be a single word or an entire message. In addition to the usual meanings, *word* often refers to God's revelation to people (Matthew 4:4). God's Word includes His directions, purpose, will, and plan. God's Word comes through the person Jesus Christ (who is the Word; John 1:1–5, 14), through prophets and teachers (Micah 1:1), and through personal revelation (2 Samuel 23:2; Revelation 1:1–2). The Bible is God's Word (2 Timothy 2:15; 3:16–17).

▲ *Words have great power for good or evil. In the Bible, one's spoken word was frequently seen as something that could not be canceled (Genesis 27:33). However, only God's Word has absolute power (Genesis 1:3, 6, 9, 11, 14, 20, 24, 26; Isaiah 55:11).*

● *What power does God's Word have in your life? Regular study of God's Word pleases Him and equips us with truth for living and witnessing (see 2 Timothy 2:15).*

WORK. Action that leads to results (Job 34:25). God works to create, save, guide, care for, and sustain (Psalm 8:6; Philippians 1:6). Human works as an attempt to earn salvation are vain and futile; we are saved by God's gift of grace through faith, never by works (Ephesians 2:8–9). However, we are God's own "workmanship," created to do His good works (Ephesians 2:10). Spiritual works are to be motivated by love for God and others, not by self-interest. While works do not save, they do provide evidence of our spiritual condition, revealing whether we are truly children of God (1 John 3:1–10). According to the book of James, the kind of faith that saves is reflected in godly works (James 2:14–26).

● *What kind of works is your faith producing?*

WORLD. Earth, universe, era or age (Isaiah 64:4; Matthew 12:32; Acts 17:24). Can also mean the present life on earth (Galatians 1:4) or life in heaven (Luke 18:30).

WORM. Creeping, spineless creature used as an image of lowliness or weakness (Job 17:14; Psalm 22:6; Isaiah 41:14).

WORMWOOD. Bitter, nonpoisonous plant that symbolized bitter, sad experience (Lamentations 3:19).

▲ The Old Testament pictures wormwood as the opposite of justice and righteousness (Jeremiah 23:15). In Revelation 8:11, a destructive star is called by this name.

■ **WORSHIP**. Verb: to adore, obey, reverence, focus positive attention on (Exodus 34:14; John 4:23). Noun: any action or attitude that expresses praise, love, obedience, and appreciation for God (see Micah 6:8). We can express worship through obedience: when our motives are godly, our actions are right and we treat God the Father and people the way Jesus did (Matthew 5–7; 25:37–40). Worship can be private or public (Matthew 6:6; Hebrews 10:24–25).

● Think of at least three ways you express worship to God. What are your motives?

■ **WRATH**. Anger, God's consistent attitude and response to sin (Romans 1:18). God's wrath is grief that expresses itself in correcting us and

Wormwood stalk.

motivating us to do right (1 Thessalonians 5:9; Romans 13:4; Revelation 16:1).

● How do you feel about God's wrath? What about human wrath or anger (Ephesians 4:26)?

WREST. To turn aside or distort (Exodus 23:6; 2 Peter 3:16).

WROTH. Angry (Genesis 4:5; Revelation 12:17).

WROUGHT. Done, worked (Psalm 45:13; 2 Corinthians 12:12).

XERXES (ZURK seez). King of Persia from 486–464 BC (NIV: Ezra 4:6; Esther 1:1; Daniel 9:1; KJV: Ahasuerus). He was the son of Darius and grandson of Cyrus the Great. He battled against the Greeks in revenge over a previous loss.

XMAS (EKS-muhs or KRIS-mus). "Xmas" does not appear in the Bible, but is worthy of an entry both because of its meaning and the misunderstanding over this abbreviation. Xmas was recorded in English as early as 1551 as an abbreviation for Christmas. The Greek spelling for Christ is *Xristos*, with the "X" being the Greek letter *chi*, pronounced much like our English letter "k." The *mas* in Xmas stood for worship or mass—or, in earlier English, "Christ festival" or "Christmas Day." In earliest usage, "Xmas" was simply an abbreviation that was well understood.

● *Some Christians have mistakenly felt that the Xmas abbreviation was an effort to remove Christ from Christmas. But the abbreviation of "Christ" with the Greek "X" goes back at least a thousand years. We do well when we don't accuse abbreviators of trying to remove Christ from Christmas. On the other hand, spelling out Christmas avoids the misunderstanding of "Xmas."*

A relief of the Persian king **Xerxes**. Servants carry a parasol and whisk for shooing away flies.

XP (CHI-RHO). An abbreviation for the name Christ that often appears in symbols and art. This abbreviation contains the first two Greek letters of the name for "Christ," with the Greek "P" really being pronounced as the English "R."

YAHWEH (YAH weh). Personal name for God. English pronunciation of the Hebrew consonants **YHWH**. Usually translated "the Lord" (Exodus 3:15). Communicates that God both exists and is present with His people as a personal God. See **GOD**.

The Hebrew tetragrammaton (four-letter depiction) of the personal name of God, **Yahweh.**

▲ The Hebrew name YHWH for God appears over six thousand times in the Old Testament. The original Hebrew did not have vowels; hundreds of years later, Masoretic scholars added vowels from Adonai—a name for "Lord"—to the places where YHWH appeared and, consequently, the word Jehovah came into being. The KJV usually translated YHWH with Lord, but there are seven exceptions that use the term Jehovah: Exodus 6:3; Psalm 83:18; Isaiah 12:2; 26:4; and in place names in Genesis 22:14; Exodus 17:15; and Judges 6:24.

● The Jewish people held God's name in great reverence, but modern society tends to use "God" lightly. Why is that? How can you honor God's name?

YEA. "Yes" is the basic meaning (Deuteronomy 33:3; Matthew 9:28). However, the word sometimes has one of the following meanings: also, even if, truly, but. Sometimes used to emphasize that the answer to a question is yes: translated "truly" or "indeed" (Genesis 3:1).

YEAR OF JUBILEE. The fiftieth year after seven cycles of seven years (forty-nine years). In the year of Jubilee, servants were freed; and possessions were returned to the original owners (Leviticus 25:9–14). The year of Jubilee gave a new start to those who had had to sell themselves or their land to escape poverty.

YEARN. Feel deeply for (Genesis 43:30; 1 Kings 3:26).

YOKE. A wooden frame that joins and enables two animals to work together (Deuteronomy 21:3). Often used in the Bible as a symbol of oppression, slavery, or burden (2 Chronicles 10:4; Galatians 5:1). However, Jesus described His yoke as easy, meaning well-fitting (Matthew 11:28–30).

▲ In the Bible as a whole, the term yoke appears more than fifty times—mostly in a context of hardship, burden, slavery, or bondage. Jesus' "yoke" of teaching fit well and lifted people, and was a great contrast to the burdensome yoke of the Pharisees. Jesus said the Pharisees would not lift a finger to lighten the yoke of man-made rules and regulations they had added to God's laws (see Matthew 23:2–4).

● Second Corinthians 6:14 warns against being "yoked together" with an unbeliever. Why? Whether in the partnership of marriage or business or anything else, what is the value of being equally yoked?

YONDER. Beyond, there (Numbers 16:37; Matthew 26:36).

ZACCHAEUS (za KEE uhs). Greek form of a Hebrew name meaning "innocent." This meaning was far from the truth of Zacchaeus until he met Jesus (Luke 19:2–9). Zacchaeus was a chief tax collector, a very short man who climbed a sycamore tree to see Jesus. Jesus called Zacchaeus down and went to his house for dinner. That day, Zacchaeus repented of his dishonest practices and was saved. His changed life led him to return whatever he had taken illegally—and to add interest to it.

● *After meeting Jesus, Zacchaeus was a changed man who went above and beyond in making restitution to people he'd cheated. What has been your response to your own salvation experience? Is there any wrong that you should correct now?*

Jesus calls to the diminutive tax collector **Zacchaeus**, who had climbed a tree for a better view of the Lord's passing through Jericho.

ZACHARIAS (zak uh RIGH uhs). Greek form of Hebrew name Zechariah. Priest who was the father of John the Baptist (Luke 1:5). Another Zacharias was the son of Barachias who was stoned to death by the Jews (Matthew 23:35).

ZADOK (ZAY dahk). Name means "righteous." A priest in the days of David (2 Samuel 8:17). Other Zadoks were the father of Jerusha (2 Kings 15:33) and a person who sealed the covenant with Nehemiah (Nehemiah 10:21).

ZEAL. Enthusiasm, eagerness (Isaiah 59:17). The word can mean eagerness to make the desires of God become reality (Numbers 25:10–13; Acts 22:3). Zeal can be inaccurate or misdirected (Romans 10:2). A person with zeal is described as "zealous."

ZEALOT (ZEHL uht). One who acts with great zeal or enthusiasm for a cause, often militantly (Matthew 10:4 NIV). *Zealot* came to designate a member of a Jewish political group who tried to overthrow Roman oppression.

▲ *Jesus called a zealot named Simon to be one of His disciples (see Luke 6:15).*

ZEBEDEE (ZEB uh dee). Father of James and John, who were disciples of Jesus, and husband of Salome (Mark 1:19; Matthew 27:56; Mark 15:40). Zebedee was a fisherman by trade.

ZEBULUN (ZEB yoo luhn). Jacob's tenth son; also, the tribe named for Zebulun (Genesis 30:20; Judges 4:6). This tribe of Israel lived between the Sea of Galilee and Mount Carmel.

ZECHARIAH (zek uh RIGH uh). Means "Yahweh remembered." Can be spelled Zachariah. Among the many Zechariahs are these: 1. A king of Israel who reigned for six months in 746 BC and then was assassinated. He was the son

A statue of the disciple called Simon the **Zealot**. Simon is sometimes shown with a saw, since legend says he was put to death with a saw.

of Jeroboam II (2 Kings 15:8). See **KING CHART** on pages 152–155. 2. The prophet Zechariah, active from 520–518 BC, who urged the Israelites to rebuild the temple after the Exile (Zechariah 1:1). His prophecies are recorded in the book of Zechariah. 3. Grandfather of Hezekiah (2 Kings 18:2). 4. A gatekeeper in the temple (1 Chronicles 9:21). 5. One of Josiah's overseers in repairing the temple (2 Chronicles 34:12). 6. Musician who helped Nehemiah (Nehemiah 12:35). 7. Godly advisor of King Uzziah (2 Chronicles 26:5). 8. Son of Jehoshaphat the king; his brother Jehoram killed Zechariah when Jehoram became king (2 Chronicles 21:2–4).

ZECHARIAH, BOOK OF. Old Testament book in the minor prophets section. It records the rebuilding of the temple after the Babylonian

captivity (sometime after 538 BC). Even more than the rebuilding, the prophet Zechariah emphasized the relationship to God that the building represented (Zechariah 10:6). Zechariah 1–8 prophesies the restoration of Jerusalem, rebuilding of the temple, and purification of God's people. Zechariah 9–14 focuses on the awaited Messiah and the final judgment. Zechariah contained more messianic prophecies than any of the other minor prophets.

ZEDEKIAH (zed uh KIGH uh). Means "Yahweh is my righteousness" (or "Yahweh is my salvation"). Zedekiahs in the Bible included: 1. A false prophet who wrongly encouraged Ahab to attack the Syrians at Ramoth-Gilead (1 Kings 22:11–12). 2. The last king of Judah who reigned from 596–587 BC (1 Kings 24:17–18). Nebuchadnezzar, king of Babylon, made Zedekiah king of Judah. When Zedekiah rebelled, the Babylonians destroyed Jerusalem and removed Zedekiah from power. Four other Zedekiahs appear in scripture.

ZEPHANIAH (zef uh NIGH uh). Bible Zephaniahs include: 1. Prophet and author of the book of Zephaniah (Zephaniah 1:1). 2. The priest who requested prayer for Israel, reported false prophecy from Babylon to Jeremiah, and was later executed by Nebuchadnezzar (Jeremiah 29:24).

ZEPHANIAH, BOOK OF. Old Testament book in the minor prophets, written before the Babylonian captivity. The book contains a prophecy of doom for Judah's worship of other gods, a promise of punishment for other nations, and a picture of the restoration of Jerusalem with a faithful remnant of God-honoring citizens. Though the book of Zephaniah contains much about God's judgment with woe, gloom, and sadness, the last part is a song of the Lord. When Israel was fully restored, Zephaniah shared that the Lord would "joy over thee with singing" (Zephaniah 3:17).

ZERAH (ZEE ruh; also, ZARA and ZARAH). Means "sunrise." Zerah was a twin born to Tamar and her father-in-law, Judah. Zara is named in the genealogy of Jesus Christ (Genesis 38:24–30; Matthew 1:3).

ZERUBBABEL (zuh RUHB uh buhl). Means "descendant of Babel." Grandson of King Jehoiachin who, after being held captive in Babylonia, returned to Jerusalem as governor. He led in both the initial failed attempt to rebuild the temple and then the later successful one (Ezra 3:2–4:4; 5:2).

ZEUS (ZOOS). Greek name for the ruler of the gods, corresponding to the Roman name Jupiter (Acts 14:12 NIV; Jupiter in KJV). Followers of Zeus believed Zeus controlled the weather. Much to Barnabas's dismay, he was called Zeus after a man was healed. Paul was called Mercurius (Mercury) because he was the chief speaker. These two missionaries were upset that they had been credited with the miracle and treated like gods, so they tore their clothes and took the opportunity to teach about the true God (Acts 14:8–18).

ZION (ZIGH uhn). Fortress, name for Jerusalem or a part of Jerusalem (Psalm 2:6; Revelation 14:1). Originally, *Zion* referred to the oldest part of Jerusalem, a southeastern hill. Later it also included the northeastern hill on which the temple was built; finally it referred to the entire city. *Zion* can also refer to the whole nation of Israel (Isaiah 1:27), the city of God in the age to come (Isaiah 28:16), or to heaven (Isaiah 59:20).

ZIPPORAH (zip POH ruh). One of the daughters of Reuel (also called Jethro), priest of Midian; first wife of Moses (Exodus 2:16–21; 3:1–2).

A bust of **Zeus** discovered in the twelfth century AD, and assumed to be a Roman copy of a Greek original.

KEY TO PRONUNCIATION

SIGN	EXAMPLE	RESULTS
ay	day, name	DAY, NAYM
a	hat, cat	HAT, CAT
ah	rah, far	RAH, FAHR
e, eh	care, fare	KEHR, FEHR
u, uh	about, around	uh BOWT, uh ROWND
aw	awl, call	AWL, CAWL
u, uh	afraid	uh FRAYD
ee	daemon, demon	DEE muhn
uh	Elijah	ih LIGH juh
ay	mail, hail	MAYL, HAYL
igh	aisle	IGHL
uhm	Adam's apple	A duhms
uhn	Roman	ROH muhn
k	cord, chorus	KAWRD, KOH rus
s, ss	city	SIH tih
ee	mete, Crete	MEET, KREET
e, eh (uh)	met, let	MEHT, LEHT
u, uh	term	TUHRM
i, ih	elastic	ih LASS tihk
g	get	GEHT
gh, j	germ	JUHRM
igh	high, sign	HIGH, SIGHN
ih	him, pin	HIHM, PIHN
ee	machine	muh SHEEN
u, uh	firm	FUHRM
o, oh	note, rode	NOHT, ROHD
ah	not, rot	NAHT, RAHT
uh	amok	uh MUHK

SIGN	EXAMPLE	RESULTS
aw	or, for	AWR, FAWR
f	alpha	AL fuh
z	his, muse	HIHZ, MEWZ
ss	kiss	KISS
yoo, ew	tune, mute	TYOON, MEWT
uh	huh, tub	HUH, TUHB
u, uh	hurl, furl	HUHRL, FUHRL
oo, ew	truth	TREWTH
th	thin	THIHN
t	Thomas	TAHM uhs
sh	attraction	uh TRAK shuhn
i, ih	city	SIH tih
Seldom Used Marks		
uh	Balaam	BAY luhm
ih	Colossae	koh LAHS sih
oh	pharaoh	FAY roh
aw	author	AW thuhr
ee	sea	SEE
eh	zealous	ZEH luhs
ee	gee	JEE
oo, ew	brew	BREW
uh	legion	LEE juhn
yaw	Savior	SAYV yawr
oy	boil	BOYL
uhn	onion	UHN yuhn
uhr	author	AW thuhr
ow	out	OWT
uh	zealous	ZEH luhs

ABOUT THE AUTHORS

JOHNNIE GODWIN majored in Greek and religion at Baylor University and holds a Master of Divinity degree from Southwestern Baptist Theological Seminary. Johnnie lives in Nashville, Tennessee, and has spent many years in publishing, pastoring, and consulting. Now he counts writing among his retirement activities.

PHYLLIS GODWIN is Johnnie Godwin's wife. She earned a diploma of Theology from Southwestern Baptist Theological Seminary. Phyllis is in her fourteenth year of writing for *MISSION MOSAIC*, a magazine of the Women's Missionary Union in Birmingham, Alabama.

KAREN DOCKREY, author of thirty books, earned a Master of Divinity from Southern Baptist Theological Seminary. Her passion is the Bible study experience and then living the truths discovered there. She has designed Bible study curriculum, edited it, written it, and taught with it. She regularly uses Bible study tools, convinced that all of us are smarter than one of us.

ART CREDITS

A: Aaron–Azazel

13 WM; 14 WM (top); FL/yeowatzup (bottom); 15 WM; 17 WM; 18 WM/Ps2613; 19 SS; 20 SS; 22 TBP; 23 SS; 24 WM/Ori229; 29 SS; 30 WM/The Yorck Project

B: Baal–Byword

33 TBP (left); WM/Jastrow (right); 34 WM/Andreas Praefcke; 35 WM/U.S. Navy Builder 2nd Class Jerome Kirkland; 36 WM; 37 SS; 38 WM/Gia.cossa; 39 SS; 40 SS; 44 TBP; 45 WM; 47 SS

C: Caesar–Cummin

48 SS (left); WM (right); 50 WM/Юкатан; 52 SS; 53 WM/Luc Viatour; 54 SS (all); 56 SS (left); Todd Bolen (right); 57 SS; 58 WM; 59 SS; 60 SS; 63 WM; 65 SS

D: Dagon–Dwell

67 WM; 71 SS (left); WM/Effi Schweizer (right); 72 SS; 73 SS; 74 WM/Google Art Project; 75 SS; 76 SS; 78 WM; 79 SS; 80 WM/Reinhardhauke; 81 SS

E: Ear–Ezra, Book of

83 WM (top); SS (bottom); 86 WM; 87 SS; 88 WM; 89 SS; 92 WM

F: Face–Future

93 SS; 94 WM; 97 SS (left); WM/Sheila Thomson (right); 98 WM/Thunderchild5; 100 SS (both); 101 SS

G: Gabriel–Guilty

102 SS; 104 SS; 106 WM/Tango7174 (top); WM (bottom); 110 WM; 111 DPI

H: Habakkuk–Hyssop

114 SS; 118 DPI; 119 SS (both); 120 SS (both); 122 SS; 123 SS; 124 SS; 125 WM; 126 SS

I: I Am–Israelite

127 SS; 128 SS; 129 SS; 130 SS

J: Jacob–Justified

133 WM/The Yorck Project; 134 SS; 135 SS; 137 SS; 138 DPI; 140 SS (both); 141 TBP; 143 WM/James G. Howes; 144 SS; 147 DPI; 148 SS

K: Kadesh–Korah

150 SS; 155 WM/Hanay

L: Laban–Lystra

157 SS; 158 Todd Bolen; 159 SS (both); 160 SS; 161 SS; 163 SS (both); 165 SS; 166 TBP (left); SS (right)

M: Maccabees–Mystery

188 SS; 170 SS; 172 TBP; 173 SS; 174 TBP; 175 WM; 176 TBP; 177 SS; 179 WM; 181 WM; 182 WM; 183 SS

N: Naaman–Nun

184 TBP; 185 SS; 186 SS; 188 WM/The Yorck Project

O: Oath–Ox

192 WM/snotch (left); SS (right); 196 SS (both)

P: Pain–Purple

197 SS; 199 WM; 201 SS; 203 SS; 204 SS; 206 WM/The Yorck Project; 207 SS; 209 WM; 210 SS; 211 WM/Shakko; 213 SS; 214 NASA, ESA, AURA/Caltech, Palomar Observatory (left); SS (right); 215 SS; 217 SS; 218 SS (both); 219 WM/Chris73; 220 WM; 223 SS; 224 SS

Q: Quail–Quiver

226 SS

R: Raamses–Ruth, Book of

227 WM; 228 SS; 229 SS; 230 SS (both); 233 WM; 235 SS; 236 WM; 237 SS; 239 SS

S: Sabbath–Synagogue

240 SS; 242 SS; 246 SS; 247 SS (top); WM/Library of Congress (bottom); 248 SS; 249 SS; 250 SS; 251 TBP; 253 SS; 254 WM/Dr. Avishai Teicher/Pikiwiki Israel

T: Tabernacle–Tyre

255 SS; 256 WM/Jastrow (left); WM/Nedim Ardoğa; 258 SS; 259 DPI; 261 SS; 263 SS; 264 WM/Pikiwiki; 268 SS; 269 SS; 271 WM; 272 SS; 273 TBP; 275 WM/Olve

U: Unawares–Uzziah

277 SS; 278 SS; 279 TBP

V: Vain–Vulgate

280 WM; 281 SS; 292 SS

W: Wages–Wrought

284 SS; 287 SS; 288 SS (both); 289 SS; 290 SS; 291 SS

X: Xerxes–XP

292 WM/Jona Lendering

Y: Yahweh–Yonder

293 SS

Z: Zacchaeus–Zipporah

294 WM; 295 WM/Joseolgon; 296 SS